T0336475

Applied Lean Business Transformation

A Complete Project Management Approach

Dennis P. Hobbs, CPIM

Copyright ©2011 by Dennis P. Hobbs

ISBN: 978-1-932159-79-0

Printed and bound in the U.S.A. Printed on acid-free paper
10 9 8 7 6 5 4 3 2 1

Library of Congress Cataloging-in-Publication Data
Hobbs, Dennis P., 1947-
  Applied lean business transformation : a complete project management
approach / by Dennis P. Hobbs.
      p. cm.
  Includes bibliographical references and index.
  ISBN 978-1-932159-79-0 (hbk. : alk. paper)
  1. Production management. 2. Lean manufacturing. 3. Project management.
I. Title.

TS155.H5747 2011
  658.5--dc22   2011002860

Phone: (954) 727-9333
Fax: (561) 892-0700
Web: www.jrosspub.com

CONTENTS

INTRODUCTION

For years, Lean manufacturing technology has been the subject of a great deal of dialogue among manufacturers. Manufacturing companies are fascinated by Lean. Professional organizations of numerous types of industries and industrial disciplines along with their corresponding industry press regularly extol the fantastic benefits of Lean manufacturing. It's hard to pick up an industry publication without finding an article about the great benefits some company has received as a result of a Lean implementation project. It's no wonder the benefits so highly touted by professional organizations and claimed by numerous companies with Lean factories are too great to be ignored. It's also no surprise the siren song of Lean benefits is extremely hard to resist by conscientious manufacturers continually seeking to improve performance in their manufacturing facilities. Many have embraced Lean manufacturing as the panacea for all of their manufacturing ills.

After all, what company doesn't dream of participating in the claims of 60 to 90% reduction in lead times, 15 to 75% reduction in inventory and working capital, 10 to 50% increase in workmanship quality, 5 to 25% improvement in productivity, and 5 to 40% increase in utilization of shop floor square footage along with a laundry list of other fantastic benefits — and these claims are just the benefits reported from the shop floor! Similar improvement percentages are being claimed by these companies throughout their entire enterprises, including the supply chain and the administrative and back office routines.

The savings in time and money alone could easily be the single best reason why manufacturers should seek the reported benefits of Lean. It's true that saving time and money is a great benefit in its own right and perhaps even worthy enough on its own to merit a Lean transformation, but the real goal of any Lean operating system is to increase a company's share of the market in which it competes. It's one thing to be the producer with the lowest cost, the fastest delivery time, and the best quality, but if those benefits don't increase competitiveness by increasing the company's percentage share of the market pie, what's the point of achieving the benefits? Posting the Lean benefits on a bulletin board next to your company's cafeteria entrance means nothing if those benefits cannot be used to capture market share at the expense of your company's competitors. Unless an increased market share is the result, a Lean transformation is merely an academic exercise. The benefits provided by a Lean manufacturing business transformation must become *differentials* for your company — differentials that provide customers with a reason to buy your company's products rather than your competitor's products — differentials that define what makes your company better than a competing company. Without differentials, how can you distinguish your company from all the other *me too* manufacturers in the marketplace? Differentials are the essence of competition!

One of the first considerations for any company contemplating a transformation to the Lean operating system should be a discussion about how the benefits of Lean would help the company increase its market share in a fiercely competitive world. Struggling to gain market share by offering a new differentiator in a market full of competitors or just trying to maintain an existing differentiation is always a long hard-fought battle for most manufacturers. In a marketplace full of competitors, the battle is worth it! If your company's products could be delivered to customers in the shortest lead time, with the best quality, and the most competitive cost in the market, would your company's customers be more likely to place purchase orders with your company or with a competitor who is unable to provide these differentials? Achieving superior product differentiation over your competitors is the *single best reason* for implementing Lean. Price, delivery time, and quality are the three greatest differentiators for most companies, but they're not the only ones. In the crusade to gain market share, Lean manufacturing methods offer other benefits that provide additional strategies for even greater differentiation over competitors.

A lower pricing strategy. Lean strategies for developing differentials include shorter manufacturing lead times that reduce the need to maintain high levels of work-in-process and finished goods inventories as buffers to satisfy customer demand within the customer-quoted lead time. Typically, the amount of work-in-process and finished goods inventories is equal to the total number of days of manufacturing lead time. If manufacturing response time through the factory is reduced with a Lean transformation, a corresponding reduction occurs in the amount of work-in-process and finished goods inventories maintained to support the lead time goals. Lead time and inventory reductions are significant factors in reducing total costs and creating opportunities for lower pricing strategies. Reduced inventories and faster inventory turns, along with the corresponding reduction of working capital, facilitate a more-competitive pricing differentiation strategy. The resulting working capital reductions are not "pie in the sky."

Portions of the savings in working capital can be reinvested in the form of price reductions to leverage market share away from your company's competitors that have higher prices. Investing the entire amount of the working capital reduction might be unnecessary to secure this differentiation. Investing only the amount needed to keep the price of your products less than your competitors' prices may be all that's necessary. Any working capital funds not invested in a reduced pricing structure can be redirected to any number of other investments for the company, including cash! Over the long term, competing on price alone may not be the single best strategy, but as long as your company is the lowest cost producer in its marketplace, the differential of a pricing strategy will always be available as a weapon for increasing your market share.

A faster delivery strategy. Enhanced quality created by parts-per-million quality levels, improved productivity, better floor space utilization, reduced scrap and rework, increased employee participation, and simplified administrative routines all help to create differentials that can be used to increase market share. The Lean operating system provides manufacturers with tools they can use to eliminate the non-value-adding move, wait, storage, and queue times associated with a traditional operating system. When non-valued-added time is eliminated from the total manufacturing time, products are able to complete the manufacturing cycle much faster than before, resulting in a reduction in the manufacturing response time to customer's orders, providing the company with an important delivery strategy. Having the fastest delivery time because of a shorter response time through the factory is, of course, an important product differentiation. When placing purchase orders, customers for whom speedy delivery or on-time delivery is a critical differentiator will likely choose your company based on its capability to deliver their orders in less time than your competitors.

If the benefits of Lean are so great, why then aren't more manufacturers reporting success with their transformation efforts? The Association for Manufacturing Excellence sought to answer this question by surveying senior leaders in a study of North American manufacturing companies. The results were revealing (see George Koenigaecker, Leadership and the lean transformation, in *Manufacturing Engineering*, November 2005: Vol. 135, No. 5). Of the respondents who reported:

- 41% said they didn't know what Lean was and weren't interested in pursuing it
- 34% indicated they were familiar with the Lean concept, but didn't know how to go about implementing Lean in their companies

- 22% indicated that their firm was on the Lean path, but they weren't getting the results they expected and were unsure if they were doing the things necessary to succeed
- 3% indicated their Lean business transformation was successful and they were achieving great results

The results of the survey are eye-opening. Reengineering, Flow, JIT, and numerous other strategies using a myriad of names as well as the fundamental concepts of Lean have been discussed and debated for at least 25 years. Countless articles have been written about Lean, including its benefits and why companies should embrace its methods. For example, Toyota has been reporting well-documented success since 1945 when the company began working on reducing setups. Toyota has an incredible success story. The results aren't exaggerated. Numerous books have been written about the Toyota Production System. (Anyone interested in understanding the benefits of Lean and wanting to get excited about Lean technology should read about the Toyota Production System. Informative books include *The Machine that Changed the World: the Story of Lean Production*, Womack, Jones, and Roos 1990; *Lean Thinking*, Womack and Jones 2003; *Lean Manufacturing Implementation*, Hobbs 2003; and numerous other widely available publications.) During the past 25 years, an entire generation of manufacturing professionals has been exposed to Lean technologies through innumerable seminars, workshops, and presentations. Surprisingly, after all this exposure to Lean, only 25% of the survey respondents have attempted any type of Lean initiative, with only 3% reporting great success. Why?

Most manufacturers have a natural sense of skepticism as well as an abundance of common sense. Their common-sense antennas are telling them to not believe that all of the companies claiming these successful Lean transformations have accomplished the promised Lean benefits in the magnitude reported. Some of the claims about success with Lean have sounded just too fantastic to be true! Surely the benefits have been exaggerated!

The good news is that Toyota is no longer the sole successful Lean manufacturing story in the world. Much of what is written about Lean today comes from the experiences of many companies from all over the world. These commentaries praise the benefits received from numerous Lean business transformations across many industry types. They tell stories, describe case studies, and document a broad range of benefits that a large number of companies have received as a result of their Lean initiatives. These accounts are exciting to read, but more than just exciting, these stories are true!

Before outright discounting the Lean claims of success as being too outlandish to be believable, skeptics should consider what achieving just 50% of the published range of benefits would mean to their companies. For most manufacturers, even if the results from a Lean business transformation delivered a conservative 50% improvement over the current performance, those results would represent a significant operating improvement for their companies.

The 41% of manufacturers who don't know what Lean is and aren't interested in pursuing Lean technology must be satisfied with their current manufacturing performance and their percentage share of the market. If so, they're fortunate to be in that position. The remaining 34% and 22% of manufacturers, however, know their companies are capable of better performance and are convinced that the benefits of Lean manufacturing can help them achieve it. They just need a chronological, step-by-step project management approach for completing a successful business transformation to Lean.

Some manufacturers may think the Lean transformation process is more complicated than it really is because too often it's made to *sound* complicated. Many Lean proponents, consultants, and practitioners work hard to make a difference for companies in countless enterprises around the globe, but there are others who try to make a Lean transformation sound as complicated as possible. They use esoteric theories, jargon, and proprietary terminology as a technique to make straightforward, common-sense Lean technology sound complicated and convoluted. Some use fear as a tactic to convince manufacturers that transforming their enterprises to Lean using their own internal resources is foolhardy and doomed to failure. These fear tactics are designed to cause manufacturers to doubt their ability to accomplish a Lean transformation project using their own resources. These persons try to convince manufacturers that the only hope for achieving Lean success is obtaining assistance from an outside expert. In most cases this is not true! What is true is that an outside consultant provides previous implementation experience and possesses the project management skills required to move a company through its transformation. Certainly there are many good reasons to use an outside consultant for a Lean transformation project, but fear of utilizing internal resources is not one of them.

Because of the influence of the Toyota Production System on Lean thinking, some manufacturers are convinced that they have to learn an entire glossary of Japanese manufacturing terms as a prerequisite for implementing Lean. A successful Lean business transformation doesn't rely on using a trendy vocabulary. In fact, taking the time and energy to learn a new vocabulary just to transform a facility to Lean is not only a non-value-adding activity, it's the antithesis of Lean! Aside from using a few Japanese terms to describe a specific method, the business transformation techniques of applied Lean use common engineering terminology familiar to serious, well-read manufacturers anywhere in the world. Learning Japanese manufacturing terminology is certainly a nice option, but it's not a requirement for success.

Applied Lean Business Transformation: A Complete Project Management Approach is presented in three parts. The chapters in Part I discuss:

- How traditional planning systems automatically embed waste into the operating system, causing the expenditure of excessive amounts of time and money
- How the Lean manufacturing system works to produce products and services in only the sum of their work content time
- What the advantages are of line balancing, linking processes together, and producing products one at a time at a measured rate of production
- How the Lean operating system matches customer demand to manufacturing resources to offset the seven wastes of manufacturing
- Where the Lean operating and MRP systems are compatible and how they can use the strengths of each to work together
- What the different types of kanban systems are and how they are used for different applications
- How a Lean operating system conflicts with the three paradigms of a traditional planning system and how these paradigms impact the application of a Lean operating system
- How the Lean operating system creates conflicting objectives that challenge traditional performance metrics (whether using a computer-based MRP system or the forecast planning of shop order routines completed on a manual basis)
- How to predict and assess where resistance to the transformation of a Lean operating system may occur and how to manage change resisters
- How to make the business case for implementing the Lean operating system (a Lean transformation must provide differentials and a return on investment for the implementation effort)
- How non-value-added work is minimized during the manufacture of products in a Lean operating system

The four chapters in Part I explain the basic logic of the Lean operating system compared to the operation of the traditional systems in use today — how it works and how it differs from those traditional planning systems. The Lean operating system does not support the same requirements imposed on manufacturing by a planning system (i.e., MRP). Lean is not designed around today's modern planning systems and their day-to-day operating methodology. The Lean operating system is an entirely different way of producing products to meet customer demand. Lean considers a product to be only the combination of its work content and a pile of parts. Both work content and component parts are considered resources. Compared to current planning system logic that uses batch production methodology designed to maximize the utilization of resources, Lean methods simply combine the minimum work content and its pile of parts to produce a product. Any non-value-added move, storage, queue, and wait time is excluded. The two manufacturing methodologies are totally opposite of one another. The Lean operating system has demonstrated over time that products can be produced faster with less lead time, smaller inventories, lower product cost, and better quality than with a traditional planning system. Naturally, manufacturers are attracted to the greater benefits promised by a Lean operating system. Regardless of their success, over half of them have come to the conclusion that Lean is a better methodology for producing their products.

Harvesting the low-hanging fruit available with a handful of separate improvement projects will certainly deliver some benefits to your company, but only a total conversion to a complete Lean operating system can deliver the full range of Lean benefits. At the same time, responding to the lure of the benefits of the Lean operating system and going forward with a total transformation project requires careful consideration. Part I of this book outlines the benefits of the Lean operating system, how these benefits are achieved, how the Lean system differs from modern planning systems, how day-to-day operations will change, how the company culture will be challenged, how to deal with resistance to change (no, not everyone will agree with changing the operating system), and how to determine if the return on the investment required to implement Lean justifies the changes to your company's operating systems. As with any change, it goes without saying that before beginning a Lean business transformation, a manufacturer must be committed to making the changes necessary to existing systems so the full benefits of the Lean operating system can be received. Embracing the benefits of Lean is easy to do, but a sound evaluation cannot be made about the value of implementing a Lean operating system unless your company understands the challenges to be confronted during the change process. Providing an understanding of these challenges is the goal of Part I. It's only prudent to proceed with a business transformation with your eyes open and to be prepared to deal with the changes you will face.

After reading Part I, you will be able to make a better decision about whether a Lean operating system is a good solution for your company and if it will resolve your manufacturing performance issues. You will be able to develop a business case for transforming your company's factory to a Lean operating system with full knowledge of the challenges that will face you when doing so. In the end, if the benefits of transforming your company to a Lean operating system do not provide the expected product differentials and costs savings to offset the risks of implementing Lean, your company should not invest in making a transformation. Ultimately, your decision must be based on the value of the long-term benefits received and the return on investment for your company.

Should a decision be made to transform your company to a Lean operating system, you will find a step-by-step, scientific, mathematical factory modeling, project management methodology for completing your Lean transformation project in Part II. The five chapters in Part II not only review the benefits of a Lean operating system, but they also provide a series of applied methods for transforming your current operating system into a Lean operating system. The techniques discussed in Part II describe:

- The chronological, step-by-step methodology used to convert a traditional operating system into a Lean operating system
- How products, processes, and customer demand are managed from a Lean perspective
- The use of mathematical formulas to determine the number of factory resources needed to meet customer demand and how resources are used to design the Lean shop floor layout
- How process maps and the associated calculations are used to design a factory to determine a future volume as a statement of factory capacity
- How to utilize resource and kanban calculations with a series of process maps to manage both daily and future factory operations
- How to use Takt line design techniques to achieve factory balance even with variable process standard times
- How assigning standard work to workstations, operator flexibility, and quality criteria reduce lead time and working capital requirements, while improving workmanship quality
- How to minimize the finished goods inventory by managing production output to match actual customer demand
- How to design and implement the different applications of kanban and how a material kanban system provides maximum capability to meet unscheduled configured customer demand
- How a supplier certification program reduces raw material costs and facilitates the receipt of consistent quality material

After reading Part II, you will be able to design your shop floor and service and administrative cells into a one-piece-at-a-time, work-in-standard-time only Lean facility.

Part III describes how to operate your Lean operating system on a day-to-day basis and how to expand the Lean methodology to include support organizations. Part III also describes how transactional processes in back offices and administrative areas must change to reflect the changes on the shop floor. Part III discusses:

- Why changes are required from the current performance goals and measurements to performance measurements that reinforce Lean goals across the enterprise to support the Lean operating system
- Why service routines and administrative processes operating as single-function silos must be redesigned to support the goals of the Lean operating system
- Why the development of systems that complement the maximum flexibility of resources on the shop floor and align with customer service goals must be implemented
- What changes are necessary in the manufacturing support organizations to support and improve the Lean operating system across the enterprise
- How specific functional departments must be redesigned to share the common goals of the company
- Why there is an increased need for communication throughout the enterprise

With the results of the AME survey in mind, this book will be of little use to the 41% of senior managers who don't know what Lean is and have no interest in finding out about it. It's not for managers who are familiar with Lean, but are unwilling to evaluate its potential against traditional methods or alternative strategies. With all the evidence currently available describing the benefits of Lean, reading another book will not convince those who are unwilling to be convinced. In fact, this book is not intended to convince anybody to do anything they don't want to do in their manufacturing facility. A Lean implementation without a commitment to its success is doomed to failure.

This book is for the 22% of manufacturers who have taken the initiative to implement a Lean operating system, but have not realized the results they expected. These manufacturers are encouraged to take another look at a Lean transformation and try again using some new techniques. It's also for the 34% who are convinced of the benefits of Lean, but don't know how to go about achieving a successful Lean transformation. This book provides those manufacturers with a chronological, step-by-step project management approach for completing a business transformation to Lean. The steps for identifying required resources and materials are objective, scientifically derived, mathematically modeled, and straightforward. They can be applied to any product or service in any industry. The numerators and denominators in the calculations can be iterated over and over again until an ideal Lean factory design is identified. The Lean factory design work is completed by team members selected from within your company who have specialized knowledge and experience in their respective disciplines. The methodology requires consensus from management to always be obtained before advancing to the next step. This ensures acceptance of decisions made by the implementation teams for the whole organization along each step of the way toward a total transformation. The ideal Lean operating system can then be designed and implemented to produce products in the sum of their work content time with minimum working capital requirements, high quality at the task level, and the lowest cost in their market segment.

The manufacturer who is already on the Lean path, but receiving only modest results is challenged to once again revisit the methodology used to accomplish their Lean transformation. Often the fear of a new system can cause a manufacturer to take a guarded, safe, minimum- to low-risk approach to a Lean business transformation. Taking an approach that was so safe that only a few traditional systems (or none) were challenged may have resulted in few benefits being realized. Using a safe, conservative approach designed for a specific purpose by taking baby steps toward change while expecting to realize the benefits of a full-blown Lean business transformation will lead to disappointment. Fear of a new system combined with a safe, low-risk approach will compromise the benefits received: fear + a conservative approach = disappointing results! A manufacturer can only expect to reap what has been sown. This book will provide a manufacturer who is receiving modest results from their Lean transformation with the information needed to take a closer look at their transformation project.

Lean thinking, the tools, and the practices can significantly help your company and its supply chains to reduce costs and improve productivity and profits, but don't forget that the total value stream has a full array of problems. It's likely no single tool will resolve all the company's problems. Don't discount the value of blending other improvement tools and techniques when working on improvement projects. Kaizen, six sigma, value stream mapping, TPM, SMED, ERP, SCM, CRM, PLM, and other improvement enablers all have a place in improvement activities. Rather than having endless debates about the merits of each, recognize that each one has its place in the total enterprise improvement universe.

When all is said and done, deciding to implement a Lean operation system (or not to) should be determined by the results of a mathematical review of the facts — objective, hard-and-fast, derived results. Gathering all the information needed for the numerators and denominators of mathematical modeling can be a difficult and time-consuming process. More difficult than gathering the information, however, is making the cultural changes required in your organization to achieve a Lean transformation. Changing the operating culture is usually necessary in most companies. Cultural change is rarely easy. No book can possibly predict all the cultural challenges your company will confront, but this one identifies the most common ones and provides recommendations for dealing with them.

The Lean operating system is not for every company, but to dismiss giving it fair consideration because of a common-sense or gut feeling that the benefits are too good to be true would be a huge disservice to your company and its stakeholders. Any manufacturer seeking to improve an operating system must perform due diligence by evaluating the benefits and the return on investment from a Lean transformation compared to the costs of making the transformation. Alternative methodologies must also be evaluated. There's usually more than one way to accomplish almost everything. The approach to achieving a successful Lean business transformation as described in this book is an approach that's worth consideration. If you decide to initiate a Lean transformation project, this book will provide you with all the practical tools necessary for making a decision to transform your company to a Lean operating system and the mathematical formulas, techniques, and methods needed to complete your transformation project.

Some personal observations. Many *how to* books provide a general understanding of some basic Lean techniques and the Lean operating system. The goal of these books is to give readers just enough information to interest them in the subject of Lean. Most of them reveal little about how to actually implement a Lean operating system. The objective for many is to encourage employment of the consulting services of the author! That's not the objective of this book. When requested, I will always consider assisting with a Lean business transformation, but my primary objective for writing this book is to provide manufacturers with a complete *how to* handbook for completing a Lean business transformation using only their internal resources. This book isn't research work. I didn't invent the technology. Others passed their knowledge on to me. I have simply relayed the techniques I have learned from my experiences with dozens of factory conversion projects over the years. I know the methodologies and techniques I've described in this book work. Other transformational methodologies exist. Explore all of them. Another objective is to provide manufacturers considering a Lean transformation with the facts needed to make an informed decision about undertaking a transformation to the Lean operating system in the first place. Only you can determine if the benefits and return on investment for your company from a Lean operating system are worth the effort required to implement the transformation. Being sold the idea of a Lean transformation will not compensate for a lack of commitment. Your commitment to work through the organizational battles presented during a Lean transformation must be strong. Always do what's best for your company. I firmly believe the Lean operating system is the best method to enable the manufacturing and service areas in your company to meet customer demand with the lowest possible cost, highest possible quality, and fastest delivery time possible. My greatest ambition is to make an impact on the number of successful Lean business transformations — to increase the number from the reported 3% to some greater number. I wish you great success with your Lean business transformation!

ACKNOWLEDGMENTS

Reading from a book can teach us about theories, but only by putting those theories to work on the factory floor can we reinforce our knowledge about them. Nothing replaces hands-on experience. I am thankful for the many people who provided me with knowledge, insight, and hands-on experience.

First, thanks to my clients. Your manufacturing processes, great products, and unique spirit have challenged me. I spent many sleepless nights thinking about Lean line designs for each of your factories! You allowed me to work side by side with you in your facilities, applying the skills I learned from 35+ years of experience. Thank you for entrusting me with such a great responsibility. Most of all, thank you for having the courage to make the changes necessary to improve the performance of your manufacturing and administrative systems. May you continue to enjoy all of the benefits promised by the Lean operating system.

Thanks also to students from around the world who attended the seminars and workshops I conducted. For me, education is a two-way street. Teaching workshops to different cultures causes me to do the critical thinking necessary to go beyond theory to embrace the many different viewpoints about the practical applications of Lean technology. Your attention to detail, serious observations, and thoughtful questions make me a better instructor. Continue your education. Strive to learn as much as you can so that your company can be as successful as possible.

Thanks to Edd Freeman, my former partner. Everyone is inexperienced at some point in their career. You spent many late nights in conference rooms, restaurants, bars, and hotel rooms pouring over the nuances of Lean technology with me and developing transformation strategies for our clients. It has been said that two heads are better than one — working with a great mind like yours confirms this truism. Thanks for being a good friend.

Thanks to John Denzel, Steve Taylor-Jones, and Roy Humphrey, consultants at JCIT, who taught me there is another way to operate a manufacturing facility.

JCIT, a consulting firm using a technology known as Demand Flow Technology®
to design flow manufacturing lines, is blessed with many bright consultants who
helped me understand the benefits of line balancing and kanban systems. Thanks
also to JCIT for inspiring many of the illustrations and concepts used in this book.

Finally, thanks to Marion Merrill Dow for the time I spent in the pharmaceu-
tical industry learning about implementing and operating MRP systems.

ABOUT THE AUTHOR

 Dennis P. Hobbs has over 38 years of line and staff experience, including 19 years in materials and operations management in the pharmaceutical and electromechanical manufacturing industries. He has held the positions of manager of systems and materials control, director of program development, director of education, director of technology, vice president, and senior consultant. He has led project teams in the implementation of two different MRP systems and subsequently became responsible for the daily operation of those systems. He has completed Lean manufacturing consulting engagements in the United States, Mid-East, Pacific Rim, and Europe. He has spoken at several APICS annual conferences and at numerous local chapter meetings. He is often invited to speak at company and professional association meetings and public seminars.

During the last half of his career, Dennis has concentrated on Lean consulting and Lean manufacturing education. He actively works with companies that are interested in transforming their manufacturing facilities into a Lean operating system. As a Lean consultant, he has led dozens of implementation teams in the transformation of their manufacturing facilities from batch-based, order-launched systems to one-piece-at-a-time Lean operating systems. He is as comfortable on the shop floor with his sleeves rolled up as he is in a corporate boardroom making a formal presentation.

Since 1994, Dennis has trained over 2500 manufacturing professionals at all organizational levels in Lean manufacturing methodologies. In addition to the United States, he has conducted his *Lean Manufacturing Implementation* workshop in New Zealand, Australia, China, Thailand, Malaysia, Singapore, Indonesia,

The Philippines, Egypt, Jordan, United Arab Emirates, Bahrain, Russia, and the Republic of Belarus. In addition to his workshop, he conducts a Lean startup program that includes classroom training specializing in the client's product combined with startup and mentoring activities to launch the client's Lean transformation project.

Dennis has a bachelor's degree in business administration from the University of Missouri at Kansas City. *Applied Lean Business Transformation: A Complete Project Management Approach* is his second book on the subject of Lean. His first book, *Lean Manufacturing Implementation: A Complete Execution Manual for Any Size Manufacturer*, was published in 2003. He currently serves as Principal Member of Mfg. Matters, LLC, a company specializing in Lean manufacturing transformations, consulting, and education. He may be contacted at dennis.hobbs@mfgmatters.com.

Web
Added
Value™

Free value-added materials available from
the Download Resource Center at www.jrosspub.com

At J. Ross Publishing we are committed to providing today's professional with practical, hands-on tools that enhance the learning experience and give readers an opportunity to apply what they have learned. That is why we offer free ancillary materials available for download on this book and all participating Web Added Value™ publications. These online resources may include interactive versions of material that appears in the book or supplemental templates, worksheets, models, plans, case studies, proposals, spreadsheets, and assessment tools, among other things. Whenever you see the WAV™ symbol in any of our publications it means bonus materials accompany the book and are available from the Web Added Value™ Download Resource Center at www.jrosspub.com.

Downloads available for *Applied Lean Business Transformation: A Complete Project Management Approach* consist of:

- *Standard Work and Operation Definition Templates*: for recording the standard work definition of each process and assigning individual standard work tasks equal to a Takt time to each workstation
- *Line Startup:* a checklist for Lean line startup and a series of tips for effectively managing a Lean line during its first few days of operation
- *Lean Line Control Board*: an Excel® worksheet that models a control board to be used for monitoring the production rate of a manufacturing line
- *Sequencing Board*: for modeling the FIFO sequencing of customer demand into both main and feeder processes
- *Kanban Shortage Procedures:* a review of procedures outlining the responsibilities of material-handling personnel to keep the Lean line operational in the event of a material shortage
- *Operator Flexing Demonstration:* an animated PowerPoint® program that demonstrates operator flexing in response to an in-process kanban (IPK) in multiproduct production using a two-bin material kanban system
- *Pull System Demonstration:* an animated PowerPoint® program that demonstrates how a pull system operates in a printing shop and the use of multiple IPKs to maintain flow between unequal machine resources

PART I
MAKING THE CASE FOR A
LEAN TRANSFORMATION

THE APPLIED LEAN BUSINESS TRANSFORMATION: BEFORE AND AFTER

Applied Lean methods are a series of scientific, objective techniques that cause work tasks in a process to be performed with a minimum of non-value-adding activities, resulting in greatly reduced wait time, queue time, move time, administrative time, and other delays.

Lean operating systems seek to identify and eliminate all non-value-adding activities in design, production, supply chain management, and other activities used to satisfy customer requirements.

A Lean facility is capable of producing a product or service in only the sum of the value-added work content time required to change its form, fit, or function.

The definition of a Lean facility is straightforward. How could any manufacturer disagree with changes in the form, fit, or function that add value to their products? Certainly no manufacturer would argue with the idea of eliminating non-value-adding activities. Once the decision has been made by a company to implement a corporate strategy of making a transformation to a Lean operating system, the process of eliminating non-value-adding activities while simultaneously adding value to a product are much easier talked about than done. Even as great enthusiasm about the upcoming changes builds throughout the organization, *where* and *how* to begin the Lean business transformation soon become a great challenge.

SOME THOUGHTS ABOUT THE LEAN STRATEGY

Lean operating system concepts have been around for a long time. While frequently using different names, the fundamental concepts of Lean have been the subject of many industry and trade publications for many years. Many manufacturers are therefore very well read about the theories of the Lean operating system. They understand the Lean concepts and the potential benefits to their companies. Eliminating waste is also nothing new. Just the idea of eliminating non-value-adding waste makes common sense. Most manufacturers have been trying to eliminate waste and make their operations as efficient as possible since the first day they opened their doors.

If Lean concepts make such common sense, are easy to understand, and the benefits are so great, why then is success using the Lean operating system still illusive for many manufacturers? In an effort to find answers, the Association for Manufacturing Excellence (AME) surveyed senior management in manufacturing companies in North America.[1] Results from respondents to this 2005 survey are revealing:

- Did not really know what Lean was: 41%
- Knew about Lean concepts, but did not know how to achieve them: 34%
- Were on a Lean path, but were not achieving the expected results and were unsure the necessary things were being done: 22%
- Had implemented a Lean enterprise transformation and were achieving great results: 3%

Even though respondents to the AME survey stated that the Lean concepts were well known, their dilemma seemed to be in understanding *how* to achieve Lean benefits and *where* to begin a Lean transformation project. The answer, of course, for a manufacturer as to *where* to begin a Lean transformation is *on the shop floor*. Begin with the area that will yield the greatest return on the investment of time and efforts by managers and the staff assigned to the transformation project. For a manufacturing company, this area is the shop floor. After the shop floor has been successfully transformed and is operational, focus can then shift to administrative and service routines in the company. Once the decision as to *where* to begin the project has been made, deciding *how* to implement the Lean concepts in the factory usually becomes the greatest challenge for any business transformation. (Welcome to the 34% of all manufacturers who do not know how to begin a Lean transformation.[1])

Lean operating system techniques are easy to read about and understand, but putting them into action on your own shop floor is not so easy. Because most manufacturers have long used computer-based MRP or other manual systems modeled after MRP-style planning systems for their entire careers, the application of Lean concepts in the real world of the shop floor may seem totally foreign to them. Although easy to understand when read in a book, Lean techniques are not intuitive for those who have only used an MRP-style planning system during their entire careers. Implementing a Lean operating system will definitely challenge the familiar, comfortable MRP assumptions about utilization of resources and how customer satisfaction is achieved.

The Lean operating system and the planning systems commonly used today seek to accomplish the same goal: use production resources to satisfy customer demand. The Lean operating system, however, takes an entirely different approach to accomplishing that goal. The Lean operating system uses a *minimalist strategy* of matching only the exact number of production resources necessary to meet the actual customer demand.

What Is the Return on Investment?

The reason any manufacturer should consider a transformation to Lean in the first place would, of course, be to receive one or all of the benefits promised by the Lean operating system: reduced lead time and inventory, increased quality and better productivity, optimized shop floor space, and increased market share. As tempting as these benefits are, it does not matter if a company is the largest in the world or the smallest, at the end of the day, any company needs to see a return on investment in real dollars and cents from any efforts to conduct a Lean business transformation. Simply stated, a company implementing a Lean operating system needs to see an increased share of their market resulting from the promised shorter lead times, which in turn yield higher profit margins, with better earnings per share because of smaller working capital requirements and an increased cash flow. Other frequently reported benefits from manufacturers who have installed a Lean operating system to differentiate their companies from their competitors include:

- Manufacturing lead time reductions of 50 to 90%
- Inventory reductions of 15 to 75%
- Productivity increases of 5 to 25%
- Floor space reductions of 5 to 40%
- Yield/quality improvements of 10 to 50%

Use Bold Initiatives or Take Baby Steps as an Implementation Strategy?

When a Lean business transformation begins, the Lean transformation team is usually very excited about participating in the project. They just want to get on with the action! The last thing they want is to go to the next monthly professional association meeting and have nothing to talk about with their peers. They certainly don't want to be perceived as not being current with any new technology. At the same time, deep down, the team members probably worry about the personal risks associated with making such significant changes at the company. (What will the effect be on my career if the transformation initiative doesn't meet expectations?) If the Lean business transformation is sponsored at the corporate level, executive leadership might prefer to dampen project expectations by pursuing a compromise strategy that gives the appearance that executive leadership is supportive of making forward progress, but minimizes their personal risk. (A common practice for executive leaders is positioning themselves to accept accolades for a job well done, while remaining prepared to shift the blame to others if the results are less than expected, e.g., by being able to say, "I told you so.") This type of leadership strategy presents another personal risk for transformation team members. Not unexpectedly, dealing with their natural human "fight or flight" instincts may affect the strategy decisions of the transformation team. Should they pursue leadership's compromise strategy to reduce personal risk, but then incur the risks of receiving reduced benefits? How hard will individual team members drive the project if they have doubts that they will be supported by leadership when the time for the transformation is at hand? If there are doubts about upper management's commitment to the project, the transformation team will constantly be hobbled by the need to take baby steps toward change. A toe will always be in the water to "check the temperature" before moving forward with the initiative. (Dissatisfaction with the benefits received was reported by 22% of the respondents to the Lean survey.[1] Could this dissatisfaction possibly have been the result of everyone not being on board with the transformation project?)

An unfortunate outcome of disappointing results is that subsequent efforts to implement a Lean transformation project will fall on deaf ears in management. Managers who sponsored a past project that only resulted in little to no success will be much less likely to repeat future sponsorship of any new Lean project.

Use Stand-Alone Techniques as an Implementation Strategy?

Because of the natural desire for a rapid payback with minimal risk and investment, many companies opt to implement Lean techniques as stand-alone technologies. Stand-alone technologies are easier to understand and implement than a total Lean transformation. Supporting implementation of Lean techniques one at a time is a fairly safe strategy. By implementing stand-alone technologies, these companies can claim they have implemented a Lean operating system while at the same time minimizing risk should a single-initiative fail. This *safe* approach allows the management at these companies to boast about implementing Lean without revealing that a safer, less-ambitious methodology was actually implemented. A description of their implementation strategy, however, often reveals that the project teams are actually mobilized around implementing one of the popular stand-alone techniques, e.g., kaizen, six sigma, value stream mapping, 5S, or visual management.

Making any type of improvement effort is, of course, always good, but Lean implemented as a stand-alone technique rarely yields the benefits expected when the project begins. It's true that some benefits are usually received as a result of a stand-alone project, but when the expected benefits don't materialize and the expectations of the Lean project aren't met, the result is, of course, disappointment. Implementation of stand-alone techniques is *not* a substitute for a comprehensive Lean business transformation. When used as a Lean transformation, autopsies of these projects revealed that using a stand-alone implementation strategy was the primary reason for disappointment: 22% of manufacturers reported that they failed to achieve the expected returns.[1] (If the transformation project was restricted to the implementation of a few *safe* projects, did a Lean transformation actually take place?) If your strategy is to take a minimalist approach to Lean, then expect to receive a corresponding level of benefits as well.

Value stream mapping, 5S, and kaizen are three popular stand-alone techniques often implemented as substitutes for a true Lean transformation. Although the probability of achieving the level of benefits expected from a true Lean transformation by implementing one of these techniques as a stand-alone project is very remote, understanding each one is important for comparing them with a total Lean business transformation.

Value Stream Mapping

Value stream mapping is an interactive technique used to help identify the elements of business process activities that add value or do not add value to an end product (or service). VSM seeks to define the information and the material flow of a product from a consumer to a producer by documenting a product's production path from door to door (customer order to customer receipt), showing all of the linkages between the information flow and the material flow. Once conversion processes are identified, individual tasks within each process are documented. Tasks are then designated as value-added or non-value-added. Using only value-added tasks, a future-state map (a vision) is then created. Using the future-state map, non-value-added steps are identified as candidates for elimination. VSM helps visualize the waste in a system, which can then form the basis of the implementation plan. VSM produces a tally of non-value-added steps that includes the setup, move, and queue time elements of lead time.

VSM is a very popular technique used by companies claiming to be implementing a Lean business strategy. VSM is an exciting, highly visible process in an organization. For a manager, VSM dovetails nicely with traditional, delegation-style management. Business schools and other institutions frequently teach management skills with less emphasis on leadership. Students are taught that delegation is a skill that must be learned to become successful. (How else can managers do everything and still expect to manage their organizations?) VSM is an excellent tool for *identifying* the current processes, the individual tasks of each process, the value-added and non-value-added tasks, and the time, material, and information flow from customer order to customer receipt. VSM also does an excellent job of *quantifying* the benefits possible with a Lean operating system, but it still does little to define *how* these benefits can be achieved.

How VSM works. VSM is an exciting team activity. Team members enjoy developing a value stream map. Typically, a VSM team is assembled in a conference room to begin documenting the processes necessary to produce a product. Often a facilitator documents process activities by writing them on Post-it® Notes. The Post-its are then stuck on a conference room wall where the activity occurs. As team members get into the spirit, more and more activities are identified, and Post-it Notes are written at near-frenzied speed. When all team members are satisfied that all of the process activities have been identified, the facilitator switches to identifying the non-value-added individual tasks of each process. Post-it Notes once again begin to be written as team members continue to identify more and more non-value-added activities. Eventually, when the team members have exhausted their knowledge of the processes and tasks, the facilitator combines the Post-it Notes into value-added or non-value-added groups. The value-added activities are then used to create a future-state VSM. The non-value-adding activities are earmarked for elimination. Individual team members are then assigned the responsibility for eliminating the tasks and processes that have been identified as adding no value.

Once assignments for eliminating non-value-adding activities have been delegated to VSM team members, the projects are added to the team member's key performance indicators and to the monthly goals and objectives measurement report. The individual team member is now responsible for the progress of the assigned performance improvement. Naturally, this works well to provide cover for managers who are not invested in the success of the Lean business transformation. Blame for any lack of progress can easily be transferred to the team member who is responsible for progress. On the other hand, if the transformation is successful because of the hard work and perseverance of the team member, the manager can proclaim the success of his/her leadership!

VSM is a *single technique* that identifies only the *magnitude* of Lean opportunities (along with present and future-state projections). The opportunities are then managed by delegation to a team member (just like all other projects). If implemented as a Lean initiative, what are the realistic expectations for measurable success from VSM? The company still has the same management tools it has always used to bring about improvement. How successful have those tools been in the past? In the end, the success of using VSM as a Lean business transformation depends on the capabilities of the individual VSM team members. Some will be successful; others will not.

It's no surprise that 22% of Lean initiatives using VSM techniques started with great fanfare and excitement, but ultimately ended in disappointment because the expected results were not received.[1] Where was the return on investment? The team members probably wondered if they did the necessary things to succeed. Why did VSM fail to generate the expected lead time and working capital benefits for your company? Did VSM increase the company's market share?

5S

5S is a methodology that uses five Japanese terms to describe a disciplined, standardized workplace and housekeeping system:

- *Seiri (sort).* Organize all tools and materials in the workplace area. Keep only essential items. The result will be less clutter that could interfere with productive work.
- *Seiton (straighten).* Establish an orderly workplace. Arrange tools, equipment, and materials systematically to facilitate easy access with the least amount of wasted effort. "A place for everything and everything in its place" ensures that tools, equipment, and materials are consistently in an assigned location and eliminates searching for them when they are needed.
- *Seiso (shine).* Keep the workplace clean, neat, and well organized. Shine is designed to support the first two disciplines. Shine includes making time available on a daily basis to clean all work areas and to restore everything to its proper place when not being used.
- *Seiketsu (systemize).* Apply consistent, standardized work practices throughout the facility. Everyone knows their responsibilities. Systemize is designed to facilitate adherence to the first three disciplines.

- *Shitsuke (sustain).* Once established, maintain the four disciplines. Sustain is designed to ensure that focus stays on maintaining the new standards for keeping the workplace clean, neat, orderly, efficient, and safe — day after day, year after year — so no gradual return to old behaviors occurs.

The disciplines of 5S are to become intuitive and part of the daily workday routine. They are designed to be the way business is done every day in the facility. Companies with successful 5S initiatives report the following benefits:

- Better communication and information sharing
- Reduced training cycles for new employees
- Increased levels of product quality
- More available plant and office space
- Reduced machine downtime
- Reduced call time per customer
- Reduced callbacks
- Improved productivity
- Improved morale
- Improved safety (reduced accident rate)

5S benefits are excellent, but can the financial impact of a successful 5S project be quantified? Do the benefits of 5S reduce lead time and working capital requirements and increase market share?

Sponsoring a 5S project as a Lean initiative is very popular. After all, 5S methodology uses Japanese terminology. It was invented in Japan. It sounds so great! Frequently 5S projects are touted as Lean implementations. The manufacturing area has received a new coat of paint, bright lighting has been installed, and new motivational and performance measurement signage has been hung. Silhouette boards have been placed at the workstations. The trash cans have been labeled. The new 5S area is so beautiful! Customers on plant tours are routed through the area to show them the "Lean" manufacturing area (they're, of course, impressed, which makes a really positive statement about the company!). As the individual steps of the 5S project are implemented, proper disposal is made of any materials, tools, or equipment designated as excess or unnecessary for the production of goods or services. Labeling these unnecessary tools, equipment, and materials as excess makes them non-value-added and therefore part of a Lean program. Regardless of whether the methodology is called 5S or Lean, who could argue with objectives that include the disciplines of order and cleanliness in the workplace? Aren't these universally desired attributes of Lean or otherwise?

If ever there were a boilerplate program, 5S is it! To its credit, a 5S project is great for improving workplace organization. The benefits received from 5S initiatives, however, are more likely to be more cosmetic, lifestyle-related, or qualitative improvements that are difficult to quantify in real financial terms. 5S by itself has little to do with lead time and working capital reduction.

As with VSM, the responsibility for implementing 5S project tasks is usually delegated to a manager. The success of a 5S implementation is therefore dependent on the manager's skills. The manager's name is attached to key performance indicators. Progress is monitored by a periodic goals and objectives measurement report. As with VSM team members, some managers will be more successful than others.

A manufacturer substituting 5S for a Lean program is likely to fall into the category of manufacturers who are disappointed with their Lean initiatives because they did not receive the expected results.[1] The manager of the 5S project may have done everything necessary to receive a return on the investment of time and money to ensure the success of the project, but may still not receive the expected benefits from the project. Why was there little return on investment? Why did 5S fail to increase market share? Why did 5S fail to reduce lead time and inventory?

Kaizen

Kaizen is a Japanese term meaning *improvement*. Kaizen strategy aims at eliminating waste through slow, incremental, constant, continuous improvements. A kaizen activity can be a series of small changes over a long period of time or a dramatic one-time, large-scale, radical change. Large-scale improvement is attractive because it can deliver incremental improvements in the shop floor footprint and in lead time reduction, working capital investment, inventory reduction, and quality improvement. The term *kaizen* is often used in the context of *kaizen blitz* or *kaizen event* in which the deployment of team resources focuses on improvement in individual work cells (by reducing setups) or streamlining work tasks.

Kaizen blitz. A kaizen blitz usually focuses on a single process at a time. A kaizen blitz commonly involves a fast, short-term analysis performed by a multidiscipline team studying every activity of the process, system, product, or service to identify the tasks that add costs from non-value-adding activities. The team is empowered to eliminate the non-value-adding activities. Very little training is needed to begin a kaizen blitz. Team participation time is often worked into a team member's normal work schedule. Kaizen blitzes are exciting activities. They're often sponsored as a "Lean" implementation. The Kaizen blitz usually has high visibility throughout an organization. Employees clamor to become team members because kaizen blitzes usually yield measurable benefits. The results from a kaizen blitz are deemed to be *good* because they identify non-value-adding activities that do not change the form, fit, or function of the process, system, product, or service. A kaizen event is also considered to be *cheap* because internal resources do the work and often the solutions identified for elimination are inexpensive.

Kaizen event. A kaizen event is usually completed quickly. A kaizen event is undertaken on a one-team/one-process-at-a-time basis. Once a kaizen event identifies the non-value-added activities in a process, subordinate projects to implement the recommendations of the event must be completed. Depending on the number of processes, the time required for a team to work its way through all the activities can be extensive. Unless more teams can be added to implement the recommendations, starting a new kaizen event must wait until the team members can be reassembled. Kaizen team members have regular jobs. A kaizen event will represent extra work for the team members. Even though some job overlap is possible, kaizen event team members will always be concerned about personal time management.

Many companies claim to have a strategy to *kaizen their way* to Lean. As with VSM and 5S, kaizen is a single stand-alone technology. Kaizen events are frequently limited in scope and are undertaken one process at a time. Kaizen events are effective by generating savings from the elimination of the non-value-added activities in a single process. By the time the last process undergoes a kaizen event, it's time to re-kaizen the first process (which, of course, is a characteristic of continuous improvement). Unless sufficient manpower is dedicated to kaizen blitzes to implement the subordinate project recommendations of the event team, the speed of an individual kaizen event is often too slow to satisfy the benefits expectations of a total Lean transformation. Kaizen as a stand-alone methodology for a Lean business transformation will always be dependent on the amount of manpower dedicated to it. Even with these limitations, kaizen techniques are used in subsequent continuous improvement activities following a successful Lean business transformation.

Beware of a Transformation in Name Only

The benefits of Lean are hard to ignore, but many companies are so risk adverse that championing so-called Lean projects by using stand-alone methods instead of a total Lean transformation is a real temptation. For a manager, could anything be better than receiving great benefits while taking very little risk of causing upheaval in the company? Project leadership of a Lean initiative is a really great showcase for a manager's skills, even if very little real change is realized because the transformation is in name only! Any accomplishments, no matter how small, can be embellished in periodic reports to greatly enhance a personal career. For the risk-adverse company, these limited improvement programs can plow ahead using a *flavor-of-the-month* approach even though the conclusion has been made that just tweaking the existing operating model yet another time will not give the company the leap forward needed to create an operating system that provides the product differentiation needed to capture greater market share and improve operating profits.

Companies taking the safe approach miss having a total improvement strategy — a strategy that identifies the real business challenges and matches the right resources and implementation methodologies to the right opportunities. Playing it safe will never generate the benefits that can be expected from a true Lean initiative. Slow, small, flashy results from safe, low-risk programs can never provide the differentials needed to increase sales revenues and return greater earnings per share and stockholder value, while capturing greater market share.

A Lean business transformation does not stop operation after a one-time harvesting of the low-hanging fruit in manufacturing. Lean thinking must permeate all aspects of an enterprise. Instead of trying to wring out additional enhancements just one more time using standard tools and methods or using safe stand-alone Lean techniques learned at a business school, a serious Lean manufacturing initiative considers making revolutionary changes that provide the benefits needed to beat competitors in the race for market share. Lean manufacturing methodologies that take a more *holistic* approach to maximizing operating systems must be embraced. A company that is serious about improvement knows total Lean success cannot be claimed from individual islands of improvement — it just takes too long.

Beware of Other Organizational Units with Conflicting Agendas

Once the commitment has been made to implement a Lean business strategy, most Lean transformation projects begin on the manufacturing shop floor. Common organizational areas include manufacturing management, engineering, materials management, quality assurance, and operations. Once implemented, the transformation project becomes highly visible throughout the organization. Because of this high visibility and all the fanfare surrounding the Lean transformation project, everyone wants to get in on the action! Other organizational groups with other projects may attempt to incorporate their projects in the Lean transformation project. Diluting the purpose of a Lean transformation by including other projects can create considerable diversion and wasted time for the Lean project team. Separate the Lean project from any "contaminating" projects that could jeopardize its success.

Just as some functional departments in the company are very anxious to get in on the action because of the high visibility of the Lean initiative and to be well-positioned for any success realized, other groups may want to keep their distance until the Lean initiative is significantly successful or attracts very positive attention. The managers of these departments know the potential benefits of Lean, but they fear change. They may actually be relieved when the Lean transformation begins outside their areas of responsibility. This fear of change is misdirected. Address it with education and training because eventually all functions of the organization will be impacted by the successful Lean initiative.

Although a Lean business transformation will eventually require the support of all functions within the company, watch out for any single functional group that begins to hijack the Lean project by using it as a forum to advance the group's own agenda under the auspices of participating in a Lean business transformation. Also watch out for functional groups that are resistant. These groups can "suck the air out" of a Lean transformation project by making it subservient to their own agendas or causing it to be practically invisible in the company.

Team manager commitment is essential. Enthusiastic team members and the Lean project itself can be negatively impacted by a team manager who lacks commitment to the transformation strategy. A noncommitted manager might be willing to sacrifice a naïve transformation team member to an unproven strategy by remaining silent just to see how many hits the team member will take from opponents of the project. Without the manager's guidance, the team member might invest significant time working on a strategy that does not benefit the Lean transformation project and subsequently is detrimental to the team member's regular daily work activities. If the results are disappointing or the strategy fails, the team member's name (and perhaps professional reputation) could become associated with the failure, possibly impacting their career. The uncommitted manager, on the other hand, remains unaffected. Without the team manager's support, other team members may become discouraged by the lack of results and become burned out and less willing to participate in future assignments. A metaphor for this is a bacon and egg breakfast. The chicken is involved, but the pig is committed. The uncommitted manager is happy to only be involved, leaving all risk to the committed team members.

Leadership must be appropriate. Antennas should go up when an outside group seeks to gain leadership of a Lean business transformation. For example, if the Lean transformation project is designated for the manufacturing area, then project leadership usually falls under the manufacturing, engineering, materials management group, or even the controller's office. If the Lean implementation project is being championed by the human resources group, then it's prudent to question the motivation of the human resources for seeking leadership of a manufacturing project. Often an outside group only wants to participate in or gain leadership of a Lean project as a method to promote their pet projects under the umbrella of Lean. If leadership of an implementation designated for a specific area is abdicated to a group that receives no direct benefit from the project, then the Lean business transformation process can easily become hijacked by the hidden agenda of another group.

Watch out for pet projects disguised as Lean projects. Some groups are so concerned about creating the appearance of being busy that they continuously seek out projects to justify their existence. A Lean business transformation is a perfect vehicle for a group trying to solve the dilemma of "a solution looking for their problem." To make their projects more palatable, these groups claim that their projects have the same goals as the Lean transformation project. The names of their projects may even be disguised by friendly sounding nomenclature designed to make the Lean implementation team feel comfortable with the goals of their projects. Although introduced under highly appealing names, many pet projects do little to effect the true, long-term change of a Lean business transformation. Significant damage to Lean implementation strategies may actually be done by the subterfuge. Because the project concepts presented by these outside groups may not match the goals of the Lean project, they're usually forgotten 24 hours after they have been presented. Examples of programs associated with change, but having little to do with a Lean transformation include:

Physical space relationship	Visual management systems	Affinity diagramming
Force field analysis	Project management	Brainstorming
Spaghetti diagramming	DISC	Ladder of inference
Myers-Briggs type indicator	Situational leadership	Conflict resolution
Left-hand column technique	Active listening	Wilderness team building
Productivity and time management	Process consultation	
8D process	Knowledge-based management 3P, 5C, 5Z, 6MS, 6W, 7QC tools	

The time and energy spent on diversionary and pet projects take time away from the time available for concentrating on the real implementation methodologies needed to meet the goals and objectives of the Lean transformation project. The transformation team may find itself struggling to get back on track again and again. If sufficient time is wasted and little or no results are reported, then obtaining sponsorship of ongoing or future Lean business transformation projects will be hard to come by.

Although every functional group with an overall business transformation strategy will eventually have an opportunity to participate in or lead a Lean business transformation project focused on their area of expertise, ensure that a Lean implementation project is sponsored by the functional group that has the appropriate knowledge and expertise crucial for the Lean project's long-term success. Beware of pet projects that have *little to do* with the goals of a Lean transformation project. Beware of diversionary projects that have *nothing to do with Lean*. Like pet projects that receive no direct benefit from a Lean transformation, diversionary projects actually dilute the purpose of a Lean transformation project. Do not mistake training sessions that do not address the goals of the Lean transformation as being part of a Lean business transformation.

Carefully Consider the Lean Methodologies

A company among the 34% of companies that indicate they're familiar with Lean, but don't know how to go about achieving a Lean transformation,[1] must make a decision about which Lean technology to implement to achieve the company's improvement goals. Do not take making this decision lightly. Many technologies are available to a company struggling to get on the right implementation track and start making progress with its Lean initiatives, but which one is best? Which technology will maximize the benefits and realize the maximum return on investment and at the same time incur the least amount of risk, effort, and expense? Making the decision about the *best* Lean methodology for your company will require using your best management decision-making skills.

When considering a Lean methodology, many companies unconsciously enable the familiar *decision triangle* during the decision-making process. According to the rules of the decision triangle, three critical attributes of any project are interrelated: *good, fast,* and *cheap*. Although these attributes are interrelated, only *two* can be optimized at any one time. So, if a project needs to be good and fast, then it cannot be completed cheaply; if a project must be good and cheap, then it cannot be completed quickly; or if a project is to be cheap and fast, then it cannot be good. Even though the decision triangle is not a scientific method, historically, these relationships appear to hold true. A decision triangle, however, merely illustrates *historical observations*. A company that embraces the logic of the decision triangle when making a decision is likely to have the same dynamics in their Lean transformation. Nonetheless, each company must consider these three attributes as they set realistic goals for their Lean business transformation project.

Consider the savings and benefits from Lean. When making a decision about beginning a Lean business transformation, estimate the savings and benefits. These savings estimates then become the financial baseline for making the decision to begin the business transformation. (They can be used later for tracking improvements in key performance indicators when the Lean system becomes operational.) An objective analysis of the savings and benefits will reveal if a Lean transformation will be beneficial or not. Don't be influenced by promotional material about Lean or promises of benefits made from outside your company to convince you otherwise. If the baseline savings are *not sufficient* to justify a business transformation, or if the required Lean system changes *do not offer* the differentials necessary to improve performance and increase market share, then *do not proceed* with a Lean transformation project. There is no point in doing the work required for the Lean project or creating the turmoil associated with redesigning your current operating system unless doing so yields significant benefits for your company. Instead, put existing management resources to work on initiatives that will yield a greater return on investment for the company rather than proceeding with a Lean transformation.

Consider the climate for change in your company. Even if there is financial justification to begin a Lean business transformation, other factors in your company may come into play to prevent the Lean project from moving forward: lack of competitive pressure; satisfaction with the current market share; leadership in the industry that causes complacency; increasing cultural reluctance to changing the status quo; and actual fear of change. Tried-and-true, comfortable manufacturing methods may have been passed on from one generation to the next. Even if these methods weren't the best, they worked. Over the years, these methods were accepted and seldom challenged. Transforming your company to have the capability to meet demand by producing only the actual customer orders in the sum of their value-added work content time, instead of producing batch quantities generated by the planning system, will require you to have curiosity, courage, and vision. A Lean change agent must be curious — there just might be better ways to meet the challenges of satisfying customer demand. A change agent must be willing to give a new method its "day in the court of improvement." A change agent must have the courage to challenge the status quo. A business transformation leader must visualize early on how to leverage the benefits from a Lean operating system across the enterprise, beyond the four walls of manufacturing, to seize market share from competitors. Changes agents must be "ambassadors" of Lean methodologies. When all is said and done, everyone in the company must embrace the Lean methods as the new status quo.

Consider the support for Lean in your company. The transformation of the company to a Lean operating system cannot be championed at only the grass roots level. If the business transformation is unlikely to be supported by executive leadership, then any efforts to implement Lean from the bottom of the organization upward will be like pushing a string. Don't waste your time thinking otherwise. Instead, work diligently to achieve a critical mass of change agents throughout the company to help you make the case for change. Devote time to companywide training and education, even for executive leadership, to demonstrate the benefits of a Lean transformation. Build an advocacy with several departments in the company, especially the sales and marketing group. Most manufacturers benefit significantly from a Lean transformation, but the real benefits are enjoyed by the sales and marketing organization. Working in conjunction with the sales and marketing group, demonstrate that the benefits realized from a Lean transformation can be put to work immediately to capture market share from competitors.

Even when the financial benefits from a Lean implementation are great, change doesn't come easy or free. By definition alone, implementing the Lean operating system will require changing current methodology. It will be an entirely new way of operating the company. When considering transforming your company using a Lean operating system, *always* compare retaining the current operating strategies to implementing the new Lean strategy. Be certain that implementing a Lean operating system is the *best* business decision for your company.

TAKE A HOLISTIC APPROACH TO LEAN TRANSFORMATION

Manufacturers already know there are non-value-adding costs embedded in their manufacturing facilities — that's why they're considering implementing a Lean manufacturing strategy in the first place. They're familiar with the dramatic benefits of Lean and no longer need to be convinced of the benefits of eliminating non-value-adding wastes. They also know that implementing Lean by taking a series of small, safe, baby steps and using stand-alone techniques will not bring the results needed to improve their competitiveness. They know changes must be revolutionary and that if dramatic results are not quickly realized from making these changes that forward inertia will be difficult to maintain. To be successful, they know the Lean business transformation must follow a methodical, disciplined implementation approach across the entire enterprise while at the same time proceeding at a pace that shows benefits quickly but also allows the company's organizational culture enough time to adapt to the changes. After considering all these things, proceeding with the implementation of a Lean business transformation is usually not very hard decision for a company to make. Once a decision has been made to proceed with a Lean business transformation, manufacturers have to decide *where* (what area and why) the transformation is to begin and *how* to complete the transformation so they can begin reaping the maximum benefits of Lean.

Where (what and why)? In manufacturing usually answers the *where should we begin* question because the manufacturing area is usually where the most money is spent in a manufacturing company. Not only is the manufacturing area where the money is spent, but it's also the most logical place to begin improving the entire enterprise. All products are made up of three costs: labor, overhead,

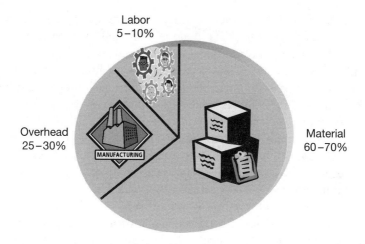

Figure 1.1. Labor, overhead, and material costs: what area yields the best return on management time?

and material. Concentrating on reducing these manufacturing costs will yield the best return on investment from the Lean business transformation (Figure 1.1).The Lean business transformation project seeks to identify and eliminate any labor, overhead, and material activities on the manufacturing shop floor that do not change the form, fit, or function of a product. Any activity that does not change the form, fit, or function of a product is considered waste (overproduction, inventory, extra processing steps, motion, defects, waiting, and transportation) and is a candidate for elimination by the Lean operating system. For most facilities successfully reducing or eliminating non-value-added waste will require the manufacturing facility to be redesigned. A redesign is usually necessary to establish the capability to produce products using only the value-added time required to build them. In order to successfully redesign the facility to reduce or eliminate non-value-added waste requires understanding where and how the waste became embedded in the current manufacturing system in the first place. Beginning the Lean transformation of the manufacturing process will yield the best financial return on the investment of management time spent by teams assigned to the project. The return on investment will be evidenced by the funds liberated from the manufacturing processes as a result of the Lean transformation project.

How? After the start of a business transformation implementation project is the point at which making forward progress becomes difficult. According to the AME survey cited earlier, 22% of manufacturers worked up the courage to begin their Lean implementation.[1] Some of these manufacturers even achieved Lean benefits, but the results were disappointing. Maybe they chose the safe path of a low-risk implementation using a stand-alone technique and the benefits received were too small to justify the additional management time necessary. Maybe the transformation team members had no template or methodology for implementing the Lean operating system and the shotgun approach they used diluted the power of their combined efforts. Maybe the implementation project took too long and team members lost their enthusiasm for the Lean transformation. Whatever the reason, forward momentum for the Lean transformation is now in doubt. New Lean initiatives may be in jeopardy. The biggest challenge now for the transformation team members is *how* to complete the transformation to a Lean operating system so it will deliver the expected benefits for the company. A poor experience with a Lean transformation or having disappointing results is unfortunate. It's discouraging for transformation team members and for other manufacturers who are considering a Lean business transformation of their own, but there's good news. The good news is that there is a systematic, objective, repeatable, mathematically modeled, project management methodology that can be used for transforming a traditional manufacturing operating system into a Lean operating system for any company or product in any industry. Part II will describe these methodologies for implementing a Lean operating system, the *how*, in greater detail and provide business decision-making tools that can be used to model solutions offered by a Lean strategy compared to a current strategy.

Proceed with a holistic Lean implementation, one that incorporates all of the elements of Lean. This is the best way to ensure that maximum benefits are achieved from the initial Lean transformation effort. Having a successful initial Lean implementation project will also help perpetuate a continuous improvement culture throughout the company while maintaining enthusiasm for subsequent implementation efforts and expanding the Lean transformation processes beyond the manufacturing shop floor to the entire company. Even with a holistic approach to the Lean business transformation and a systematic, objective, repeatable, mathematically modeled, project management methodology to transform the manufacturing facility into a Lean operating system, you will have challenges.

The challenge of existing responsibilities. Managers in traditional operating systems usually don't have the luxury of time to investigate the reasons why inventory levels are too high, lead times are too long, material shortages occur too frequently, and why never-ending expediting is the order of the day. They're too busy trying to meet customer demand and get customer orders out the door to invest much management time on eliminating non-value-added work. They understand the impact of ever-present waste in the system. They know there are opportunities to save time, activity, and money on the shop floor, but there's no time left in the day to look for them after completing the day-to-day quest to meet customer demand and achieve utilization goals. The only option is to continue focusing on maintaining goals and objectives that have been handed down to them as a series of interconnected policies and procedures dictating how products are to be produced and how the reward system impacts their success. Often they have functional responsibility for only one component of the entire manufacturing process. They therefore focus only on their single tree, not the whole forest! How waste gets into the operating system throughout the company is a mystery or of little concern. They're too busy meeting their daily responsibilities.

The challenge of change. When observing many organizations, finding a "well-oiled machine" is common. Employees know how to do their jobs and perform them well. Policies and procedures have been developed, proven, and time-tested for getting the prescribed work done. As a result, even the most creative traditional managers cannot visualize using a holistic approach across the entire system as the best way to achieve improvement of individual issues at the functional level. The company may be suffering from the symptoms of wasted activities that cause long lead times, huge inventories, and deteriorating quality. The working capital percentage of investment may be continuing to increase. When the time comes for process improvement, however, their first instinct will be to dust off the old, trusted, time-tested management methods to try to solve these issues, even if they have come to the conclusion that revamping the existing operating system one more time and using the same old solutions will most likely return disappointing results. Why not try something new? Change will be difficult even when some managers are wondering if the old methods have any life left in them or if they will continue to be effective when customers are no longer loyal to the company. What if competition comes from many points on the globe? Even when old methodologies simply don't offer the solutions needed to eliminate waste and make the company more competitive, some managers will prefer to use the same old solutions to solve problems. Addressing diminishing returns by using new solutions is a scary prospect, particularly for more-tenured managers. They have worked for a long time to finely hone policies and procedures, to make life stable and easy, and to achieve a comfortable daily routine that supports the status quo. They would rather rework the old tried and true models that have always ensured a comfortable life. The old models have served them well in the past.

Staying competitive, or even alive, in a new and often global environment requires asking questions. Can using the old, comfortable methodologies actually continue to serve the organization in today's environment? Can using solutions that have served the organization so well in the past deliver the incremental benefits necessary to remain competitive and stay in business? Although many manufacturers have concluded the old tried and true methods are not enough in the new competitive environment, they're still afraid to try anything new.

THREE LONG-STANDING PARADIGMS THAT DRIVE COSTS IN MANUFACTURING

The whole purpose of a business enterprise is pretty simple — to make a profit by selling products or services to those who desire these particular goods or services. For manufacturers, profit is made by purchasing raw materials and then adding value to those raw materials by applying machine or labor resources to convert them into a product that satisfies customer demand. Then, by selling the manufactured product at a price greater than the costs required to produce the product, a profit is made that can be shared with stakeholders. The same is true for service and administrative functions. The business proposition for a manufacturer is also simple — to provide the resources (people, machines, workstations, and inventory) necessary to convert raw materials into finished products that customers are willing to buy while efficiently utilizing those manufacturing resources to maximize profit.

Over the years, manufacturers have created three distinct operating paradigms for meeting the simple business proposition of satisfying customer demand:

- Grouping resources by function
- Routing products through departments in batches
- Using level production schedules

These three paradigms were developed over the last century, beginning with early manufacturing pioneers such as Alfred P. Sloan, Henry Ford, and Fredrick Taylor. Even today, these manufacturing concepts continue to guide how manufacturers meet customer demand and produce products. They rely on self-imposed manufacturing systems that have evolved into standard operating methodologies for facilitating the conversion process for manufacturing products. Over time the concepts became supported by cost accounting systems and performance indicators that measure the efficiency of manufacturing operations. Maintaining an allegiance to these paradigms is the source of much of the non-value-added work generated in factories today and the primary cause of most of the seven wastes created by traditional manufacturing processes.

Ask any manufacturing manager, engineer, scheduler, or factory designer to describe how demand is processed through their manufacturing facility or why the factory is configured the way it is and they will loosely describe how these three paradigms operate without actually referring to them specifically. Don't be surprised if some managers are unable to acknowledge, describe, or even explain why or how these operating paradigms came to be. Many might be hard pressed to even describe how their departments affect the entire system or how all the individual parts from their departments are linked together to make a product. They don't know *why* they do what they do — they're just responsible for the efficiency of their department! If a response is offered, it will be likely be along the lines of *that's how it's always been done* or *that's how I was taught in school* or *that's how the certification exam requires it to be done.* Most often the response will be *that's how my predecessor taught me to do it.* Manufacturing conventions are almost never challenged, they're just perpetuated.

Paradigm 1: Group Resources by Function

The first paradigm is to group like resources together (e.g., people, machines, workstations, and inventory). This paradigm is manifested by the existence of departments (Figure 1.2). Manufacturers prefer grouping resources such as machine tools, welding, electronic assembly, quality control, assembly, painting, etc. into separate departments and then assigning a manager to be responsible for the utilization and efficiency of each department. This *silo* management style of grouping resources into departments was advocated by Alfred P. Sloan. Sloan pioneered the idea of having individual managers and separate accounting for each division at General Motors in the 1930s. On the shop floor, grouping similar resources into separate departments facilitates two major requirements: maximizing efficiency and utilization while maximizing resource output and evaluating managerial effectiveness.

Grouping to maximize utilization. Grouping similar resources enables a manufacturing area to produce maximum output by utilizing the capacity made available by newer, better, and faster machines. Optimizing machine output began at a time when innovations in machine technology replaced labor productivity as the primary focus for competitive advantage. Optimizing machine output is still in widespread use today. By using the technological advantages provided by machine capacity, fewer human resources are required to produce the same amount of products. Soon, the size of production runs in the machine center was based on achieving maximum utilization and whatever made a machine the most productive. This quest for productivity became the catalyst for larger and larger batch sizes — the larger the batch size, the fewer the setups and the better the efficiency against the established standard time. Soon, batch manufacturing became the norm for machining centers. Because the machining center is usually the gateway work center for the rest of the manufacturing processes, whatever batch size was produced became the batch size for all subsequent manufacturing departments. Unfortunately batches sized for what makes a machine productive

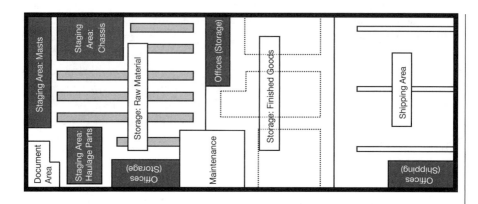

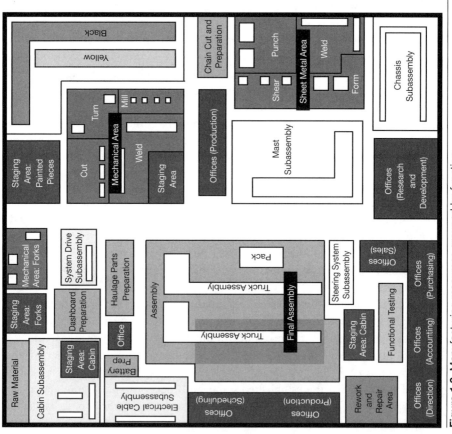

Figure 1.2. Manufacturing resources grouped by function.

rarely have any relationship to actual customer demand. If the batch size in a downstream department is smaller than the batch size in the machine center, any excess inventory produced by the machining center will be sent to a WIP (work-in-process) inventory location as unsold inventory.

Lean considers the overproduction of products and the resulting unsold inventory to be a waste of manufacturing resources. A Lean system controls costs by concentrating on the largest element of product cost: materials and the material costs associated with inventory. Sometimes a planner or scheduler is able to cancel a production order before it reaches a completed state, but any unfinished production units that were created will remain as WIP inventory. The only solution for this WIP inventory is to add additional costs by disassembling the unfinished production into component parts for use in future production runs, cannibalizing the parts to resolve a current part shortage, or waiting until the next production run to make an adjustment in the quantity to build. This WIP inventory must continue to be managed, so additional waste is created by the extra processing steps, the defects resulting from damage during storage, and the cost of carrying unsold inventory. If these costs cannot be passed on to a customer, they must be subtracted from the company's profit margin.

Waste caused by the overproduction of products is generated every day in a traditional manufacturing environment. Most traditional planning systems include a feature in the item master that rounds up the explosion quantities to a *minimum run quantity*. However, what are the odds on any given day that customer demand will exactly match the predetermined batch size established for the convenience of machine utilization or a planning system? This also applies to each stock-keeping unit in the master schedule and the exploded quantities down through the planning levels of the MRP system. If there is no customer demand for manufacturing output, where else can the unsold overproduction quantities go but to in-process WIP storage or the finished goods warehouse?

Grouping to evaluate managerial effectiveness. Grouping resources into departments facilitates the second element of the Albert Sloan revolution: assign a manager to a department and then evaluate the manager's effectiveness in utilizing the assigned resources. This technique is a convenient management tool that facilitates the top-down chain of command in organizations that delegate responsibility. Utilization of resources is measured as:

Total units produced × standard time ÷ time available per period

The manager's performance is reviewed periodically throughout the year. Performance measurements are especially important in annual reviews. Salary adjustments are often made based on the manager's success against a preset utilization target during the annual performance review. Other performance measures are part of an annual performance review, but utilization as a performance measurement for the return on investment is the primary measure for evaluating the total performance of a traditional production manager. Based on the first manufacturing paradigm of grouping resources by function with utilization as the most important performance measurement, what naturally becomes the number one motivator for any department manager? Build as much as possible as fast as possible! When *ideal performance* is 100% utilization of resources and production managers are measured and paid based on the output of those resources, it's no surprise to find that production departments in this type of environment are very, very highly utilized. Inventories and working capital levels are also equally high. What is the more expensive component of product cost, labor or materials (see Figure 1.1)? For this reason, the Lean operating system challenges the concept of utilization of resources as the best measurement of manufacturing performance.

Grouping to evaluate departmental performance. Manufacturing processes in factories are rarely, if ever, equal in capacity. When capacities are unequal and departments are measured against a maximum utilization performance goal, a department with excess capacity can only produce excess inventory in the drive to achieve maximum utilization of its resources. There's no other way to achieve their utilization goals. The pressure to report maximum utilization is intense. Conversely, a department with insufficient capacity cannot keep up with a department having excess capacity. This department is always behind. The only way to keep up is to work on weekends, use persistent overtime, etc. In this department, schedules are usually constructed to minimize changeovers by grouping similar work together to achieve maximum utilization. If due dates are ignored to allow production orders to be campaigned together, meeting on-time customer demand becomes secondary. Often, even by using these techniques, the department may still not be able to catch up. Material costs are the most expensive cost component of manufactured products. With that in mind, what is the non-value-added cost of overproduction by departments with excess capacity? What is the cost of inventory built in excess of customer demand simply to achieve departmental utilization goals? Is achieving maximum utilization with little regard for true customer demand worth the cost of producing unsold inventory? What is the value of constructing schedules and grouping similar work together in departments with insufficient capacity if these departments can never catch up with the departments having excess capacity? What is the cost of failing to meet customer due dates? A traditional non-Lean factory always manifests its capacity imbalances when the departments in the manufacturing process have excess inventories.

On your next visit to the shop floor, look for large amounts of WIP inventory. Rarely is this WIP inventory the *right* inventory in the *right* amount needed to meet future unscheduled customer demand. Everywhere on the shop floor that this type of inventory imbalance occurs, WIP investment and extended lead times are the only mechanisms available in the traditional manufacturing system to absorb the excess capacity of imbalanced manufacturing departments. When first-in/first-out (FIFO) discipline is followed for processing customer orders, capacity imbalances also add to the product lead time. Customer orders must wait their turn in a queue as part of a batch to be processed. Queue time is always non-value-added time. Capacity imbalance impacts a manufacturer in real financial terms. Increased working capital investment is required to support the WIP inventories caused by the production of arbitrary batch sizes and the required queue times. Imbalanced departments with excess capacity can always be identified by the large backlog of production orders waiting in a queue to be scheduled. During your next trip to the shop floor, ask to see the production order backlog. Because WIP materials have been allocated to these production orders, they also represent an additional working capital investment.

Utilization as a key performance measure causes organizational conflict. When utilization is the key performance measure in a manufacturing department, achieving maximum utilization will conflict with the key performance measures of other departments. For example, the inventory turn rate is typically the responsibility of the materials management group while the sales and marketing department provides customer-quoted lead time to the customer. The production and inventory control department relies on WIP inventory levels to properly operate their planning systems. When the customer-quoted lead time for an order is missed or lead time becomes a moving target because of fluctuating WIP levels, the objectives of the other responsible organizational groups cannot be met. These dissimilar objectives create a significant source of conflict between manufacturing, materials management, production and inventory control, and sales and marketing groups. Conflicting objectives cause mistrust and posturing among the different functional groups within the company. They add non-value-adding costs from expediting and daily rescheduling of customer demand in the manufacturing and sales departments. Production managers measured on their utilization of resources will naturally focus primarily on output volume. They have little or no interest in any performance metrics not measured in their department. Other important measurements such as inventory turn rate, customer-quoted lead time, and on-time delivery of customer demand are the responsibility of some other organizational function. It's *every man for himself* when it comes to customer service versus resource utilization! Who suffers most with all this dissention between departments? The customer! Additional pressure for utilization also comes from the controller's office. Utilization of machine and labor resources is reported on a daily basis. Anything short of 100% utilization causes a *negative variance* to be generated. When this occurs, production managers must explain why their department utilization was less than 100%. Successful managers will do everything possible to avoid having to answer for a negative variance. Successful managers use whatever trick is available to make sure their resources run at maximum utilization! They use any scheme or device to be certain their department's resources are fully utilized, including increasing the department's lead time so production orders are released by the planning system sooner. They group production orders together to better amortize the time lost to changeover. They allow work to be completed in advance of MRP-planned start dates with little regard to planned due dates. Unfortunately, inventory produced in advance of a planned due date in an effort to achieve maximum utilization results in unsold WIP inventory being produced.

All this non-value-added activity (and the unsold inventory produced) is the result of grouping resources together just for the sake of managing performance goals with no concern for a balanced capacity. A Lean operating system is not driven by the need to be fully utilized. A Lean operating system seeks balance among the manufacturing resources. A Lean operating system utilizes only the minimum resources necessary to produce customer demand.

Paradigm 2: Route Products in Batches

Once manufacturing resources have been grouped by function and organized into departments, the next paradigm is the requirement to route customer demand through the departments in the form of production orders (shop orders, etc.). These production orders are issued in predetermined batch or minimum run quantities as a result of the output of the planning process. Batch quantities can also be based on a production manager's discretion. Orders start at a gateway department and move sequentially from one department to the next throughout the facility. Work is added to each batch in each department until all the products in the batch are 100% complete.

When a product is scheduled to enter the manufacturing area, a *shop packet* is created by the planning system. The shop packet contains a production order (or shop order) authorizing the utilization of manufacturing resources and a scheduled routing document indicating the sequential order of production by department. A listing of the materials maintained in the planning system (from the bill of materials) is forwarded to the materials warehouse. Components necessary for producing the product are then pulled from the warehouse. These components join the production order to accompany the product as it is routed through the manufacturing area. As the order is completed in each department, the amount of labor used to produce the order is reported on the scheduled routing document and returned to the production control department for database maintenance of the planning system. The production control department uses this information to track the progress of the production order as it moves through the manufacturing area. Material usage in each department is recorded to accumulate the labor and material costs at each stage of the manufacturing process. Labor and material transactions ensure inventory accuracy for future planning system operations. Product status transactions also ensure the location of a customer order in the factory is known. When the production order has been completed, labor and material usage is compared to the standard cost by the cost accounting group. Notification of any variance from the standard is distributed to department managers for explanation.

In a planning system, batch size is commonly referred to as the *minimum run quantity*. When the planning process calculates a negative on-hand inventory quantity, a production order with the quantity rounded up to the minimum batch size will be recommended for release into production. This predetermined batch-size order quantity is then entered into the planning system's parameters as a static number. Because the quantity is static, it rarely, if ever, corresponds to an actual quantity ordered by a customer. When a customer's order quantity does not match the predetermined order quantity, either excess inventory will be produced or an additional production order in the incremental batch quantity will be issued. In either case, when an unsold batch quantity exceeds a customer's order quantity, excess inventory will always be produced. This excess inventory is retained as WIP or as expensive FGI (finished goods inventory) (Figure 1.3).

How is batch size determined? Some companies use scientific methods to establish the minimum run quantity, e.g., the EOQ method (economic order quantity) which calculates ideal batch size by factoring annual usage, setup costs, and inventory carrying costs into the calculation. In many other companies, the logic for establishing batch size is unknown (or long forgotten). The minimum batch size may have been established arbitrarily using some criteria or methodology known only to the person responsible for establishing the minimum run quantity. (Who established the batch size? What criteria did they use? Are they still with the company?) Even if batch sizes were determined using a logical methodology, the determination might have been made when the planning system was first established. Has it been updated to match current planning parameters? Even the most sophisticated methods and computer models currently available have little likelihood of ever matching batch quantities to the actual customer demand. This of course, guarantees continued excess inventory and increased working capital requirements whenever capacity is greater than

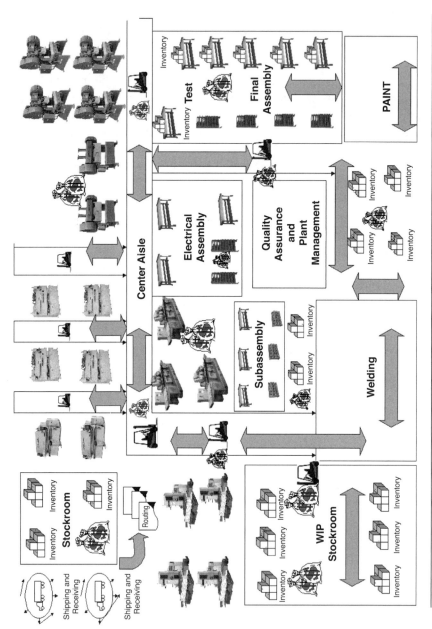

Figure 1.3. Batch routing of products through manufacturing departments.

customer demand. No matter what system is in existence or preferred, a review of your minimum run quantity is probably long overdue.

Large batches facilitate utilization. Machine setups adversely impact utilization. Production units cannot be run when a machine is idled for set up. Managers in manufacturing departments often request increased batch sizes to reduce the total number of machine setups required: fewer setups = more units produced = better utilization. While a large batch size assures longer run times for production orders, the resulting increases in inventory are of no consequence to the performance rating of the department. The department managers aren't measured on inventory turns. They're not responsible for unsold overproduced units. They don't have any responsibility to explain excess inventory; see Figure 1.3.

Accumulating orders facilitates utilization. Astute manufacturing managers learn to accumulate as many production orders as possible to ensure their departments always stay well utilized with plenty of work to do. Besides increasing utilization, having as many production orders *at the ready* as possible provides more opportunities to campaign production orders together to avoid unwanted setups. Accumulating production orders is accomplished by requesting the production control department to release future production orders in advance of their scheduled start date. To accommodate a manufacturing department manager's request for more production orders, the production control department must release planned or firm planned orders early from the planning system by accelerating due dates forward or by increasing the quantities in the planning system.

Accelerating due dates or increasing production order quantities affects material requirements generated by the planning system. Both frequently cause material shortages because materials designated for the requirements of future production orders are consumed by the expedited orders requested by the department managers looking to increase utilization in their departments. Consuming materials allocated for future orders can also negatively impact customer promised due dates. One customer's on-time delivery date may be sacrificed for another customer's early delivery. Either way, department managers achieve their departmental utilization goals while the customer service department tries to explain the missed due date to the customer. A common practice to resolve material shortages is the cannibalization of allocated components in staged or in-process production orders. This practice adds to the clerical maintenance of the stock status database of the planning system. Resolution of material shortages also results in expending additional non-value-added manpower time and energy by planners and schedulers to expedite production materials. They have to handle these changes every day. Expediting materials frequently requires premium transportation costs to be incurred by premature shipments and the early receipt of materials from suppliers. In addition to the non-value-added time required for database maintenance by planners and schedulers trying to keep the planning system as accurate as possible, producing products ahead of schedule always creates unsold WIP inventory. (How many material shortages occur in your manufacturing facility? How much expediting is done on your shop floor to expedite needed materials? How many planners are required to manage these shortages? Is the manufacturing department's performance measurement of maximum utilization with little or no accountability for inventory and materials in opposition to the materials control department's performance measurement of maintaining minimum inventories? Does this opposition create conflicting objectives? Is arguing and posturing over conflicting objectives often a daily ritual in your facility?)

Increasing the number of released production orders can also be accomplished by increasing subassembly lead times at the departmental level on the indented BOM, which subsequently extends the planning horizon. Extending the planning horizon by increasing departmental subassembly lead times also results in a longer lead time at the finished goods level. A longer lead time at the finished goods level affects the customer-quoted lead time. When manufacturing lead time begins to exceed the customer-quoted lead time of your competitors, your company will likely lose sales revenue to those competitors. As customers look for better delivery promises, your company's market share will suffer.

Batch orders and accelerated orders are detrimental to lead time. Besides increasing WIP and finished goods inventories, static production order quantities and accelerated production orders are also detrimental to lead time. When batches of orders with predetermined quantities are released into the manufacturing area, it's impossible to start and run all of them simultaneously. A priority decision must be made as to which order to start first. Usually priority decisions are made by a department manager or a designated planner. To help make the proper prioritizing decision, sequencing criteria have been developed to guide the decision-making process. These priority sequencing criteria might include shortest setup time, shortest unit run time, available operator skills, the opportunity to campaign production orders, or ease of operation. (Is on-time delivery included in your priority sequencing criteria?) Once an order is selected as the first one to be run, all other released production orders in the preassigned batch quantity must wait in a queue: the second order will run next, followed by the third, fourth, fifth, and so on. Using FIFO methodology, all orders must wait their turn in the queue. As a customer, if your order is fifth in the queue, your order must wait for all of the other units in the first, second, third, and fourth orders to be run in the assigned sequence. Although queue time can significantly affect lead time, queue time never adds value to the form, fit, or function of the product! The more production orders waiting, the longer the queue time and therefore the longer the customer lead time. Queue time is a major component of manufacturing lead time. Astute department managers know that longer queue time means more production orders will be issued from the planning system. Having more orders waiting in the queue provides a department manager with many opportunities to *cherry pick* production orders so they can be run in a sequence that maximizes the department's utilization. The additional production orders issued may help the department manager maximize utilization, but they also lengthen product lead time.

The queue time dynamic is more prevalent in departments at the lower levels of the indented BOM. Departments at lower levels of the BOM always have more latitude for lead time management before delivery at the top of the BOM, the SKU level. They also have most of the allocated and uncommitted raw material inventories and partially completed WIP residing on the shop floor. If necessary, departments at lower levels can easily expand their available lead time simply by consuming the downstream department's lead time, thereby delaying an order's start date for as long as possible to facilitate the grouping of production orders into long runs with little time lost to setups. This flexibility affords huge opportunities to improve utilization, but at the cost of the inventory required to support the production orders released to manufacturing. The magnitude of this utilization benefit is diminished by the department's position on the indented BOM and the amount of planning lead time assigned to that department. Meanwhile, at the top of the BOM, at the SKU level, little latitude for compressing lead time remains if all of the standard lead time has been leisurely consumed by lower-level departments. At the highest level in the BOM, meeting the customer order due date often requires increased heroic expediting activities, while the departments at the lower levels of the BOM are unconcerned about the turmoil they've created above them to get the customer order out on time!

Although queue time dynamic is more prevalent in lower-level departments, it's still in play at every other level of an indented BOM. It's repeated each time a production order in a predetermined batch size moves from one department to the next. Imagine multiple production orders for multiple products being routed through multiple departments in predetermined static quantities with multiple priority decisions being made that are driven by different sequencing rules! Predetermined minimum-run quantities routed through manufacturing in batches seldom reflect actual customer demand — often they appear as the proverbial egg passing through a snake. The complexities of production control are the victim of this multiplier effect on the shop floor. With all of this gaming of the traditional planning system going on each day, it is easy to understand why WIP and FGI levels and lead times increase.

Observe your shop floor. How much activity is devoted to expediting orders to match changing customer expectations, resolving material shortages, maintaining planning system information requirements, managing paperwork, de-allocating and reallocating materials, moving materials, planning and shortage meetings, and practicing overall reactive crisis management? Now, consider the definition of Lean operating systems:

> *Lean operating systems seek to identify and eliminate all non-value-adding activities in the design, production, supply chain management, and other activities used to satisfy customer requirements. A Lean facility is capable of producing a product or service in only the sum of the value-added work content time required to change its form, fit, or function.*

Do any of the expediting, de-allocating and reallocating of materials, meetings, system maintenance requirements, and overall reactive crisis management activities make a change to the *form, fit, or function* of the product? What do these activities cost your company? How does achieving high utilization levels decrease the cost of products and make your company more competitive? Are the benefits of achieving maximum utilization really worth all the non-value-adding activities required to achieve them?

Paradigm 3: Seek Level Production Schedules

The third manufacturing paradigm that traditional manufacturers loyally cling to is forcing their facilities to follow level production schedules between planning periods — even though they know their customers rarely purchase products in the same predictable manner as their production schedules. True, some customers may only repeat the interval of their orders twice a year, but they're quite likely to change the product type, volume, or some product feature with every order. Some customers even frequently change the product type or the volume *after* an order has been placed. Looking at aggregate customer order patterns on a day-to-day basis will confirm the saw-tooth appearance of customer demand. The traditional operating system prefers a level production schedule more for ease of managing production activity throughout the manufacturing facility than for meeting actual customer demand.

Customers are no different than manufacturers when managing working capital — because of the cost of carrying inventory and because fast delivery from manufacturers is an expectation, customers order products from their manufacturing suppliers as close as possible to their own actual customer demand in an effort to minimize their own working capital investment. They're not concerned about the problems their fluctuating order patterns might cause the manufacturers or the manufacturers' suppliers. They never communicate with the manufacturers' other customers to discuss order-leveling strategies that would benefit the manufacturers. The manufacturers are left to decide on their own how best to operate their manufacturing facilities.

Using the traditional scheduling and planning systems widely used today, if irregular customer order patterns were introduced directly into the manufacturing area, then chaos would be the result. The variability of the actual demand cascading down to the shop floor would cause violent swings in labor and material requirements, erratic resource utilization, and uneven logistics.

How is disruption caused by uneven customer demand avoided? To avoid the potential for disruption in the manufacturing facility from uneven customer demand patterns, traditional planning systems use an intermediary *smoothing function* that is placed between actual customer demand and the manufacturing shop floor. The most common mechanism for smoothing erratic customer demand is the operation of a "master schedule." The planning/scheduling department is responsible for using this master schedule to "massage" uneven customer demand into a level production schedule. Leveling customer demand into a schedule in which the requirements are the same from day-to-day obviously has benefits: the peaks and valleys are taken out of the daily operation of the production facility and demand for raw materials from suppliers is smoothed out (Figure 1.4).

Level production schedules require estimating customer demand. Naturally, the farther visibility can be projected into the future, the greater the opportunity will be for smoothing customer demand into a level production schedule. All that is necessary to have this greater visibility is to have the longest planning horizon possible, but if the planning horizon is projected too far into the future, actual customer demand may not be known. If actual customer demand is unknown, then demand must be estimated. This estimated customer demand, along with any production order backlog, is then used to round out a production schedule to ensure maximum manufacturing capacity is utilized. Longer planning horizons for projecting customer demand further into the future are reflected in longer customer-quoted lead times just to facilitate the development of level production schedules. These longer customer-quoted lead times usually do not resemble the actual manufacturing response times required to produce a product. Planning horizon lead times are frequently used simply to allow maximum flexibility for shuffling planned and firm planned orders around in the horizon to create the optimum level production schedule.

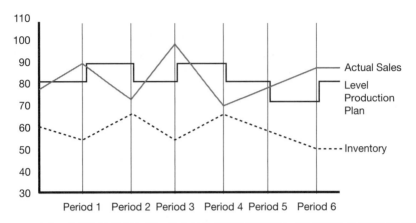

Figure 1.4. A leveled production plan.

Level production schedules require estimating the product mix and quantities. When schedules are developed based on future *and* uncertain demand, the product mix and the quantities of that demand must also be estimated. The estimate of future demand is known as a *forecast.* A forecast of future customer demand is required to satisfy the development of level production schedules when no actual customer demand is in the planning horizon. This estimated demand then appears in the master schedule as planned and firm planned orders. Unfortunately, no forecast is ever 100% accurate, so the risk of having errors in projecting customer demand is inevitable.

Level production schedules can negatively affect inventory levels. Having level production schedules is great for manufacturing department managers, but level production schedules can have a negative effect on WIP and FGI levels. If the stated lead time, including the time needed for leveling the schedule, is longer than the customer-quoted lead time, then production orders will be launched into manufacturing in advance of the receipt of actual customer demand. The production orders are issued into manufacturing in the hope that customers will eventually buy the products in the exact configurations and quantities as produced! Because production orders authorize the consumption of labor, machine, and material resources to manufacture the products, in the quantities (batch sizes) requested, on the orders, launching orders ahead of the receipt of actual customer demand means valuable resources are committed to the production of products based only on estimated demand. At a certain point in the production process, in the absence of customer orders, unsold production will usually complete the manufacturing cycle and be sent to a finished goods warehouse. Committing resources to estimated demand is a gamble. Although the forecast cycle that created the unsold production is soon forgotten, the inventory remains! (How much of the FGI in your warehouse is there because of unfulfilled customer demand?) When customers do not buy a configuration or an exact quantity produced, the unsold products become WIP or FGI. FGI is the most expensive type of inventory on a manufacturer's balance sheet! FGI represents a large investment in working capital. It represents lost opportunity costs from funds and materials being tied up in inventory. If the unsold unit mix consists of popular models, then the units may sell quickly and spend little time in the FGI, but if the finished units are unpopular configurations built as result of a forecast, these units might spend months or even years in the FGI. Slow-moving units are at risk of becoming obsolete. At some point in time, they may require disposition. Although unsold FGI can sometimes be used or disposed of in various ways, disposal options usually mean lower selling prices. Unsold FGI just costs money to own!

Use FGI for a new production order. Sometimes units in FGI can be substituted for the units in a new production order. Even if the FGI is not a perfect match with the customer's specification, modifying an existing configuration to match the customer's demand in *less than* the customer-quoted lead time required for new production may be a viable option.

Use FGI as buffer inventory. Having unsold FGI provides planners with the ability to meet fluctuating customer demand. Most planners secretly like to have buffer inventory on hand in the event that a customer orders a product configuration that is not included in the current production schedule. When this happens, the customer's demand can be met immediately by offering a selling price discount for taking the unsold units being held in the FGI warehouse. The customer's demand is satisfied and the unsold FGI inventory is reduced, but at the cost of a reduced profit margin from the sunk costs associated with the unsold inventory sitting in FGI for a length of time.

The worst-case scenario for FGI. Units sitting in unsold FGI for so long that they are identified as slow moving or obsolete can often be offered at "fire sale" prices to selected customers. Fire sales prices are highly discounted and result in lost sales revenue. It's even possible that some units will require disposal at a loss. If the FGI units cannot be sold, they might be cannibalized for parts and the carcasses scrapped. At worst, whole units might be scrapped outright — neither of these alternatives is value-added.

Level production schedules affect the net requirements for resources. If forecasted products are used to create level production schedules, these forecasted products must be included in the netting formula of the planning system to calculate the net requirements for production schedules. Even if unsold orders are in the manufacturing queue or the planning system, any commitment of resources must be considered as a statement of allocation of manufacturing resources already issued to the shop floor and waiting to be completed. In addition to the machine and labor resources required to produce them, all new and existing production orders are also a statement of inventory. Open production orders and the amount of actual inventories on hand are tangible numbers. They're easily confirmed by accurate record keeping. A forecast, on the other hand, is always an estimate of what the company thinks customers will buy. A forecast has the usual error rate. If customer demand quantities are underestimated or forecasted quantities do not materialize into actual customer demand, then existing production schedules must be recalculated and new schedules issued. These new schedules and the subsequent MRP explosion routines are required to recalculate inventories that were based on a previous inaccurate forecast. Manufacturing resources were committed to production orders and schedules were based on an inaccurate forecast!

Management of level production schedules and any resulting inventory fluctuations is usually the responsibility of the production and inventory control and/or the materials management groups. Inventory turn rate and customer fulfillment are key performance measurements for them, but the two measures can present a dichotomy. On one hand, they are responsible for keeping all inventory classifications at investment levels in line with inventory goals, but on the other, they must ensure that customer demand is satisfied while ensuring utilization targets are met for the departments on the shop floor. So, while striving to ensure utilization and to keep inventory optimized at levels within guidelines, but still needing to keep customers satisfied within the customer-quoted lead time, the production and inventory control/materials management groups will usually tolerate higher FGI levels as a buffer inventory. The logic is that they would much rather explain higher inventory levels than to explain an inventory stock-out that created backorders, lost sales, or a line stoppage to supervisors. In the meantime, the planners and schedulers are chasing an elusive customer demand curve, hoping to outguess customer demand, while trying to meet their on-time delivery goals with a minimum amount of inventory investment. Unfortunately, customer demand can never be accurately predicted, so they usually just wind up managing the resulting inventories.

TRADITIONAL PLANNING SYSTEMS ENABLE THE THREE MANUFACTURING PARADIGMS

During the early 1970s, a few manufacturers began to implement MRP (material requirements planning), a new technology that promised to help balance and satisfy the requirements for introducing and managing customer demand on the manufacturing shop floor; to provide future visibility into material requirements for suppliers; and to track manufacturing performance. Since those early days, both Western as well as global manufacturers have implemented MRP systems to manage customer demand, raw materials, and inventories. MRP systems have improved greatly over the years. Now, with the advent of cheaper computing power, the era of computer-based MRP planning systems has arrived. (Although the net requirements MRP planning model is used in emerging market countries, their use of computerized planning systems is less widespread.) Many branded systems are now available. Each has special differentiating features. The debate about which system a company should choose is considerable. Regardless of the numerous features of competing MRP systems, all use the same basic formula to determine the net requirements to satisfy customer demand:

$$\text{Forecast + open customer orders} - (\text{on-hand inventory} + \text{released production orders}) = \text{net requirements}$$

Non-computer-based planning systems also solve the same basic netting formula for scheduling a manufacturing facility.

Once an MRP system has completed calculation of the formula for every SKU and BOM item, the output is reported as a *suggested* recommendation. If the materials being planned are purchased items, the resulting *order action report* is directed to the attention of a buyer in the purchasing department. If the materials being planned are manufactured items, the order action report is sent to a planner/scheduler in the production and inventory control section. Due and start dates are calculated by the planning system for every level in the indented BOM. At this point, the output of the planning system is only a suggestion based on input information. Although planners and buyers have the responsibility to accept or reject the MRP recommendation for the suggested expenditure of resources to respond to customer demand, suggested order requirements from the planning system are usually accepted and purchase orders for raw materials are placed with suppliers while shop packets containing the suggested production orders and routing files are released to the shop floor and used to construct a production schedule.

MRP systems soon became the new gold standard for operating manufacturing facilities. In the 40+ years since MRP systems were first introduced, they have

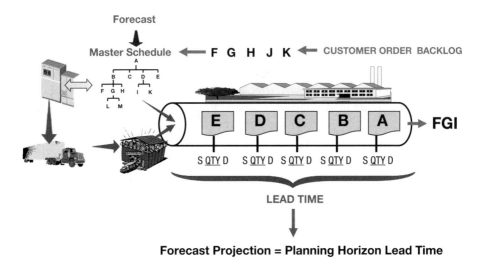

Forecast Projection = Planning Horizon Lead Time

Figure 1.5. A master schedule using the MRP planning and operating model. S, scheduling; D, dipatching.

been warmly embraced by manufacturers around the world. Computer-based MRP systems were revolutionary for schedulers and planners who had increasing needs to convert ever-changing customer demand into schedules complete with start and due dates for all production orders sent to the individual manufacturing departments as well as to prioritize customer demand. Once released, the shop floor control and inventory reporting modules kept track of the released production orders, provided for inventory transactions, and followed customer demand moving through the manufacturing facility. The MRP systems were also revolutionary for managing the requirements of customers, cost accounting, sales, quality control, manufacturing, distribution, purchasing, engineering, and other functional units in the organization needing knowledge about activities on the shop floor. Figure 1.5 illustrates the MRP operating model.

MRP systems embed the three manufacturing paradigms in traditional operating systems. MRP system designers and programmers have no reason to question the *why* of traditional operating systems. They just write code. They follow the specifications given to them by users. This code embeds the three paradigms of manufacturing. (If programmers had stopped to challenge the prevailing wisdom at the time, early MRP products might never have left the design laboratory!) Often, planner/scheduler jobs in many companies are entry-level positions. Planners/schedulers using MRP systems also have little time to consider how the system works. In the drive to do a good job, they're usually very task-oriented. They focus more on doing the job than taking time to ponder the logic of the work itself. Increasingly, planners and schedulers are likely to be recent university graduates or individuals with little historical reference for why most systems work the way they do. Since the introduction of MRP systems 40 years ago, two and sometimes three generations of manufacturing and materials management professionals have used an MRP system for some portion of their careers. When recalling their experiences, most say they never questioned *why* the MRP system required them to do what they did to operate it. When confronted with the learning curve for operating the systems, their first challenge was to just master the technology. They just performed the work as instructed by their predecessors. Without question, the next generations of practitioners continued to institutionalize those same learned methodologies into the long-held, legacy policies and procedures used for operating their manufacturing plants today. Newer planning systems are more efficient. They include many new planning parameters to satisfy the special needs of manufacturing clients, but still very few system users ever question *why* their respective factories are organized into departments, *why* products are routed through the factory in batches, or *why* the schedules don't reflect actual customer demand. They don't challenge the issuance quantity of orders. On and on you hear, generation after generation, *It's just the way the system works. This is the way my predecessor taught me. There's nothing to be done about it. It's the same way I'll teach my successor.*

The next time you hear *the system won't let me do it,* just remember: it's not the computer system that won't permit something. MRP programs are just a series of ones and zeroes that reflect the defined management parameters given to them. The real villains behind the statement *the system won't let me do it* are the operating policies and procedures written to ensure compliance to the three manufacturing paradigms. The three manufacturing paradigms are hard-coded into the MRP operating system. The MRP system simply facilitates these paradigms as part of its operating system.

TRADITIONAL MANUFACTURING SYSTEMS DRIVE THE THREE PARADIGMS

With the considerable knowledge we have about the seven wastes of manufacturing, why is it so difficult for manufacturers to make significant progress toward reducing or eliminating them? The answer: *the three manufacturing paradigms.* The root cause of each of the seven wastes can be traced back to an allegiance to one or all of these paradigms. Understanding *how* the three manufacturing paradigms are embedded into traditional planning systems will provide manufacturers considering implementing a Lean operating system with a view of the challenges that will be encountered when changing the current operating system of their MRP-driven manufacturing facilities. Only by challenging and eventually changing these long-held, almost "sacred" paradigms, can a manufacturer become part of the 3% of manufacturers who claim success with their Lean implementation projects.[1]

Processing customer demand into saleable products uses a series of different manufacturing resources. A review of how the MRP system authorizes the utilization of manufacturing resources to meet customer demand is worth a closer look.

The net requirements. MRP is an order-based system. A calculation is performed at both the master schedule level and the MRP level. The MPS (master production schedule) and the MRP system then determine the start dates, due dates, and quantities by time-phasing the requirements based on the lead times documented in the BOM. This process is performed as a computer routine used by the MRP system and is commonly known as an *explosion of requirements* based on planning guidelines for a fixed snapshot in time. The net requirements determined by the explosion process are recorded as an *order* in the MRP system:

Gross requirements (forecast + customer orders)
− inventory (on-hand inventory + open customer orders) = net requirements

MPS explosion activity is performed for all end item products and for all the parts in the BOMs. Subsequent MRP explosions (time-phasing requirements × quantities on the BOM) are performed on a regularly scheduled basis. The output of an MRP explosion is a series of recommended order actions for materials. Based on information in the item master, these materials can either be purchased from suppliers or manufactured in house. The net requirements output will then be separated into recommendations for materials to be purchased and orders to be manufactured:

$$\text{Net requirements} \begin{cases} \text{purchased – purchasing buyer – PO} \\ \text{manufactured – planner/scheduler – production schedule} \end{cases}$$

Make or buy the net requirements? Make or buy designations are the result of an extensive decision-making process. Purchased items are the responsibility of a buyer. Manufactured items are the responsibility of a planner. Orders are presented on a part-by-part basis to the planner or buyer in the form of a recommended action. The planner or buyer then responds to the recommended action: agreeing with the recommendation suggested by the planning system or changing the order by moving the recommended due date in or out; by increasing or decreasing the quantity; or simply by canceling a requirement.

Process the released production orders. Traditional manufacturers group similar resources together into departments and then route production orders from one department to the next in batch quantities. Each department manager is responsible for determining the priority of all released production orders issued to the department, but which order should be processed first? One of the great strengths of traditional planning systems is their ability to establish due and start dates for the production orders they issue. To accomplish this, the MRP system requires three pieces of critical information:

- *Departmental sequence*: how the products are scheduled to move through manufacturing
- *Lead time*: the lead time required in each department to complete the work
- *Due date*: the due date requested by the customer for the end product or the date required by forecasted demand

A device known as an *indented bill of material* is used to communicate how products are processed in a manufacturing facility to the planning system. A BOM lists the component parts for each SKU product. BOMs also use a technique known as *indenting* (an *indented* BOM) to document the manufacturing sequence and the lead time required in each department where work is required. Each level recorded in an indented BOM mirrors the sequential routing of an end item through the manufacturing departments. The lead time information necessary for establishing due and start dates in each department is also recorded on the indented BOM.

How an indented BOM works. In addition to the parts required to produce a product, an indented BOM begins by identifying the gateway department where work is performed at its lowest level. As the work is completed in the gateway department, the next department where work is required becomes the next level on the BOM. This sequence continues on and on until all departments where work is required have been recorded as an individual level of the BOM. Each product has its own unique indented BOM. Each sequence (or level) in the BOM also has a lead time that records the time required to complete the work in a department. A subassembly part number is assigned to every level in the BOM. Subassembly part numbers are necessary to identify the work that was completed by each department on the BOM. Once issued, subassembly orders are tracked through the individual manufacturing departments to record labor and inventory usage and to monitor progress through manufacturing until the order is closed as it is completed. The sum of the value of incomplete or partially completed products plus the raw material components determines the amount of WIP and the amount of working capital investment required to produce customer demand. Once an indented BOM is available, establishing the due and start dates at all departments throughout the manufacturing facility is straightforward. Only one level of an indented BOM does *not* have its due date established by the planning

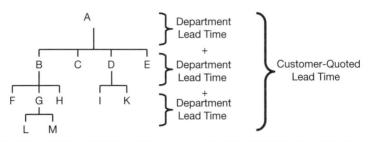

Figure 1.6. The scheduling logic for an indented BOM.

system — the very top level, the end-item level (or SKU). The end-item level is the parent part number — a finished unit that has been assembled or fabricated from one or more components. Typically, the *master schedule* is the function of the master production schedule (MPS) and establishes the due date for the end-item level. Once this date is established and using the lead times recorded on the BOM, start and dues dates for each level in the indented BOM can be established.

Based on the customer's requested delivery date and any requirements in the manufacturing facility for a level schedule, the master scheduler function establishes a due date for each product (SKU) making up the customer demand. Beginning with this due date and the lead times recorded on the indented BOM, due and start dates at each level of the BOM are established for each department by scheduling backward in time, down through each level of the indented BOM, subtracting the lead time for each level from the due date set by the master scheduler, until the due and start dates have been established at each level of the BOM down to the gateway department. Figure 1.6 shows the scheduling logic of the indented BOM.

The sum of the lead times determines the customer-quoted lead time. The sum of the lead times through each level in an indented BOM becomes the customer-quoted lead time for a product. Each parent product in the product catalog has its own customer-quoted lead time. (Even though individual lead times at each level on the BOM may be inflated to accommodate the three paradigms, the resulting customer-quoted lead time will still be the stated minimum amount of time required to produce the product through all of the departments in the manufacturing facility.) Rarely is the manufacturing department ever challenged on a stated lead time established at the departmental level. Usually, a lead time offered by manufacturing is just accepted at face value and recognized as a "sacred" value. If not challenged, the lead time goes straight to the indented BOM and is recorded for posterity. Yet when a customer-quoted lead time is unacceptable to a customer, the first approach to resolving the gap between the customer-quoted lead time and manufacturing's response time is to buffer the amount of WIP and FGI inventories to compensate for the gap. (Rather than challenging the

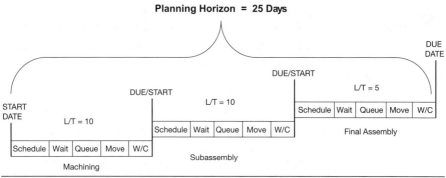

Figure 1.7. A 25-day planning horizon. L/T, lead time; W/C, work content.

lead times, they just get expedited!) Customer-quoted lead time establishes the inventory policy for an entire company, which can have a significant impact on inventory investment. Even though right under their noses, only a few companies see the relationship between customer-quoted lead time, department lead time on the BOM, and inventory investment!

The lead times establish the minimum planning horizon. The lead times on the indented BOM also establish the minimum planning horizon necessary for the master scheduler function to level the production schedule by planning customer demand fulfillment using MRP logic. The planning horizon states how far into the future the master scheduler must establish due dates for production orders released to the manufacturing department to allow sufficient lead time for manufacturing them, beginning with the start date of the first level on the BOM (Figure 1.7). The longer the lead time, the longer the planning horizon must be — and the more production orders that must be issued to the shop floor. Lead times, the length of the planning horizon, the quantity of production orders, and the resulting inventory become parts of a vicious cycle of longer lead times and increased working capital investment feeding on one another.

How many of the seven wastes of manufacturing result because of needing to satisfy the three traditional paradigms of planning systems? Even using the advanced planning systems currently available, as long as resources are grouped by function, products are produced in batches, and level schedules are sought, is it a surprise that manufacturers still have these wastes in their factories?

ARE LEAN AND MRP COMPATIBLE?

Both Lean manufacturing and MRP have the goal of satisfying customer demand while also achieving optimum utilization of resources, but each system has a different approach to achieving optimum utilization. MRP systems institutionalize existing manufacturing paradigms by launching *scheduled production orders in batch quantities* to the shop floor that are sized to achieve *maximum utilization* of resources. The Lean operating system uses only the *minimum* amount of resources needed to meet *actual customer demand*. Achieving full utilization is a *secondary goal* for the Lean system.

Most MRP systems in use today have been designed to support the three traditional planning paradigms driving resources to achieve 100% utilization. Electronic or not, if planning routines continue to embrace these three paradigms, then the questions about Lean compatibility and MRP will never go away. Embracing Lean techniques will challenge manufacturers to reevaluate their existing procedures, paradigms, and operating policies that support full utilization of resources against the simple idea of matching resources with customer demand by using only the resources necessary to meet that demand. This same reevaluation process can be used by manufacturers who do not use computer-based planning systems, but remain loyal to full utilization by following the three paradigms during manual planning routines.

MRP systems are completely flexible. MRP systems can be operated under any set of rules established by the user. If, however, a manufacturer is not willing to challenge the traditional paradigms that drive the current operating system, then simply changing the parameters in the MRP system to reflect a Lean "wish list" will serve no purpose. Change must occur in the way policies and procedures guide the operating system. Change must occur in how demand is managed on the shop floor and how performance is measured. As long as a manufacturer is content to live with the consequences of achieving maximum utilization of resources at all costs rather than receiving the benefits of using the minimum resources needed to meet customer demand, a Lean business transformation will never get beyond philosophical conversations. If, however, a manufacturer is committed to achieving the benefits of a Lean operating system and willing to challenge the concept of full utilization as the ideal factory performance metric, the manufacturer must acknowledge that the seven wastes of manufacturing are embedded in the manufacturing processes by the planning paradigms. It's a good place to start.

The question is not *is MRP compatible with Lean?* Instead, the question is *can an existing operating system be modified from its goal of full utilization to the goal of meeting customer demand using only the minimum number of resources necessary to produce it?*

SEEING THE FOREST THROUGH THE TREES

A manufacturer can easily get so caught up in the maintenance and operation of the computerized planning system that they get to the point where operating the MRP system takes precedence over the primary goal of the organization — *meeting customer demand*! For example, various functional groups may insist that the planning system provide them with information designed to specifically address their unique requirements. Modern planning systems accommodate these requests by offering numerous add-on database parameters to modify the output of the planning system to meet the requirements of these functional groups. Maximizing the information received from a planning system is not a bad thing, but if maintaining the planning system and meeting specialized information requirements becomes more important than optimizing resources, reducing working capital, and meeting customer demand, then the mission of the MRP operating system has been lost.

MRP systems provide a mechanism for managing customer demand by issuing production orders or purchase orders. The purchasing department deals with creating orders to suppliers and maintaining them based on recommendations from the MRP planning system. In manufacturing, a shop floor control (SFC) system (or a PAC, production activity control system) is used to manage and monitor production orders created by the MRP system after the orders have been issued to the factory floor. SFC/PAC systems are common in mature MRP manufacturing facilities. Figure 1.8 illustrates the MRP planning and execution model.

The SFC system requires a routing file to be attached to every production order generated for launch into the manufacturing department by the MRP system. The routing file documents the correct manufacturing sequence, department by department, and is used to track progress of the order as it advances through the different manufacturing processes. Manufacturing must report the progressive status of the production order and record the quantity of product or subassembly produced, the amount of labor used to complete the work, and the materials used (as well as any scrap). To ensure accurate feedback is provided to the planning system, the work required to use and maintain a routing file can mean a significant commitment for manufacturing department staff that includes planners, schedulers, and expediters. Industrial engineering resources needed to create and maintain the routings must also be in place. Based on the level of detail and the structure of a routing file, the number of transactions required to accomplish this tracking of production orders can be significant. Once the SFC system is in place, several organizational functions soon become dependent on its output:

- Cost accounting uses the standard hour reporting features for the labor reporting system and variance management.

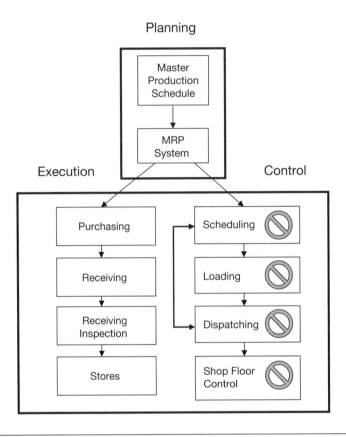

Figure 1.8. The MRP planning, execution, and control model.

- Engineering uses the labor reporting system data to maintain standard hours.
- Materials management uses the tracking status to determine on-hand inventory or scheduled receipts by department for accurate netting of requirements for the next MRP explosion iteration.
- Production management depends on the information to develop future staffing requirements.
- Production control establishes schedules, derives present and future capacity requirements, and creates performance measurements based on the output.

The Lean manufacturing system does not rely on output from the MRP system for execution of its manufacturing plan. Although the part of the MRP process that generates recommended purchasing orders can be used in Lean manufacturing, production order output from the MRP system for management of a Lean line is not. Feedback to the planning system tracking production orders is optional or even unnecessary with a Lean operating system. If production orders generated from an MRP explosion are unnecessary, then routing files are also unnecessary. If routing files are not required, then routing management systems such as individual department scheduling, shop floor control, department planning, and capacity requirements planning that require feedback input from a routing management system (dispatch function) are also no longer necessary. The Lean operating system requires only the *sequencing* of customer demand at the beginning of the line or a subassembly process. The Lean manufacturing methodologies are very straightforward and easy to understand and use. Usually manufacturing management and shop floor employees quickly embrace them.

Support organizations, on the other hand, have systems that are designed around the output of the SFC system and the routing feedback information. It is the lack of dependency of the Lean operating system on MRP output and the feedback mechanisms that creates barriers for support groups during the implementation of a Lean manufacturing system. These groups see little benefit for their departments. They may even see the implementation of a Lean operating system as a threat to their continuing existence. For this reason, convincing support organizations about the benefits of a Lean operating system can be difficult.

Over the years, manufacturers have been asked to understand many new technologies. Lean techniques are among the latest. Often the abundance of buzzwords and terminology associated with the Lean operating system causes more misunderstandings than the technology itself. The same is true for MRP and Lean compatibility. MRP (as well as ERP, enterprise resource planning) and Lean are often represented as being conflicting technologies, when both actually have the capability to be complementary. They are not mutually exclusive of one another! In fact, each has strengths that can enhance the other. The benefits to be gained from combining the two technologies are even more evident today than ever before. Working together, MRP and Lean can make a formidable team. Manufacturers must learn to take advantage of what MRP and Lean do best. Planning systems *plan* and Lean systems *execute*.

No better methodology exists for *projecting* future materials requirements than MRP techniques. Lean techniques, however, are better for *allocating* machine, labor, and material resources and *executing* customer demand requirements on the shop floor. When a manufacturer uses Lean manufacturing methodologies, the new relationship between MRP and Lean should be the basis for collaboration. The key is to exploit the individual strengths of each system and to be willing to modify or discontinue any modules of the MRP system that conflict with the Lean operating system.

REFERENCE

1. George Koenigsaecker, Leadership and the lean transformation, in *Manufacturing Engineering*, November 2005: Vol. 135, No. 5; available at http://findarticles.com/p/articles/mi_qa3618/is_200511/ai_n15847432/.

2

THE LEAN OPERATING SYSTEM: A DIFFERENT WAY OF THINKING

From Chapter 1, we know the benefits of Lean transformations touted by manufacturers are significant. On the surface, the Lean operating system makes sense. Even manufacturers who are just considering a Lean transformation and have only read about the Lean operating system agree that the methods and techniques are easy to understand. Manufacturers who have implemented a Lean operating system confirm that the Lean methods and techniques are actually just the application of common sense.

So, if all of this is true, why do some manufacturers decide to delay implementing a Lean business transformation entirely or opt to only implement safe, stand-alone techniques such as VSM, 5S, kaizen, and visual management in lieu of a complete Lean operating system? Could one reason be that the thoughts of challenging the current planning system are just too intimidating to even consider initiating a Lean transformation? (Could leadership be unwilling to confront the status quo? Could leadership be fearful of change? Could leadership just be too comfortable?)

Regardless of the reason, understanding how the features of the Lean operating system challenge current planning paradigms can provide a new perspective to help manufacturers overcome the fear of initiating a total business transformation. Figure 2.1 illustrates the traditional manufacturing techniques and the benefits of the Lean manufacturing operating system. Perhaps understanding how the features of a Lean system generate benefits will renew the courage of

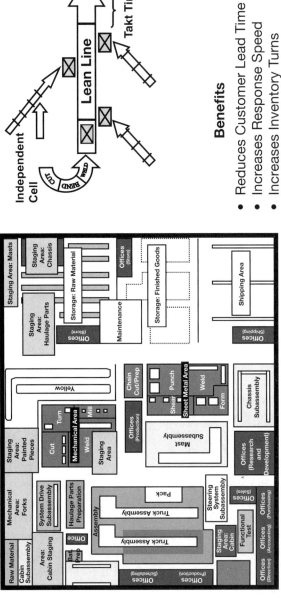

The Lean Manufacturing Model

Backflush

Lean Line

Takt Time

Independent Cell

CUT BEND WELD

Benefits

- Reduces Customer Lead Time
- Increases Response Speed
- Increases Inventory Turns
- Turns Inventory into Cash
- Adds Flexibility
- Improves Customer Satisfaction

Traditional Manufacturing Model

- Resources Grouped by Function
- Batch-Based, Scheduled, Planned, Order-Launched Planning Systems

Figure 2.1. Traditional manufacturing techniques versus the Lean manufacturing system.

manufacturers who want to begin a transformation to Lean as well as those who have already started a transformation, but are dissatisfied with the results and are now unwilling to take the next steps toward a total Lean transformation.

Students of manufacturing methods already know about the promised benefits of the Lean operating system. They have absorbed all they can from reading about the system's features. When they compare the benefits and common-sense features of a Lean operating system side by side with the complexity and costs of their current operating models, making the transformation to a Lean operating system seems to be completely reasonable. Making a transformation makes good business sense!

A Lean business transformation sounds so easy and so simple to do. The Lean operating system makes so much common sense. Resisting the urge to begin the transformation project today can be really difficult! Making hasty, uninformed decisions, however, can be a trap. Sometimes the temptation of achieving the benefits of a Lean operating system can easily lure manufacturers into making decisions that have not been carefully considered. The failure of some Lean business transformation projects can be traced to having a poorly executed implementation strategy. Just ask the 22% of manufacturers who have started implementation projects, but are very unhappy with their results.[1]

As a change agent, it's important to be as informed as possible. You must understand how the mechanisms of a Lean operating system work together to provide benefits. You must understand how the features of the Lean operating system provide greater benefits than the batch-based, scheduled, order-launched system currently in place. You must always be prepared to explain the differences between the Lean operating system and the current operating system. You must thoroughly understand the Lean operating system to make an informed decision about proceeding with a Lean business transformation. As a change agent, you will also need to make a convincing case with management for proceeding with a transformation effort.

OPERATIONAL FEATURES OF THE LEAN OPERATING SYSTEM

Making a successful transformation from a current operating system to the Lean operating system is a straightforward process. It's based on the application of several common-sense principles. What seems most difficult for manufacturers to grasp is *how* to replace a current operating system with the Lean operating system. *Where* should the Lean transformation process begin? What sequence of events must occur to replace one system with another? It's difficult to imagine how the current operating system could be replaced with a new Lean system because the manufacturing methods used by each are so different. These differences in manufacturing methods might make the two systems seem to be complete opposites, but *efficient utilization of resources* to meet customer demand is the goal of both. The Lean operating system just uses a different approach to achieving the goal of efficient utilization of resources.

The Lean operating system and the manufacturing of products. The Lean operating system considers any product to have two separate elements: the material content and the work content. The Lean operating system operates as two separate systems when producing a product. One system addresses the material content and another system addresses the work content of the product. A Lean manufacturing facility is a collection of labor and machine resources working in dissimilar manufacturing processes to produce a product at the lowest possible cost and to change the form, fit, or function of the raw materials into a product that is appealing in the marketplace (and that can be sold at the highest price the marketplace will accept).

Traditional planning systems and the manufacturing of products. Traditional manufacturing systems in use today manufacture products using one system with an indented bill of material (BOM) attached to the stock keeping unit (SKU) to describe the manufacturing process. Current traditional manufacturing systems are designed to promote maximum utilization of resources (machines and/or labor). Maximum utilization of resources is accomplished by establishing minimum run quantities (batches) that have been calculated to maximize labor productivity and machine uptime. As long as a traditional factory's capacity is not exceeded, meeting customer demand is accomplished by a series of scheduling and priority decisions in each department. Beyond producing sufficient products to satisfy customer demand and meeting productivity and maximum uptime goals, the materials used to manufacture a product cannot be separated from the production of an SKU. For this reason, inventory levels must be of *secondary* concern in a traditional manufacturing system.

The Lean operating system and resource utilization. The Lean operating system has a different approach to meeting customer demand. Maximum utilization of labor and machine resources is *not* the primary goal of a Lean operating system. Instead, the goal of the Lean operating system is to meet customer demand by using only the *minimum* amount of resources. In the Lean operating system, customer demand determines the amount of resources required. In a Lean system, the resources required must equal the customer demand: customer demand = the resources needed. Matching resources to customer demand also requires less WIP and FGI inventories. For most manufacturers, the Lean approach to meeting customer demand means some machine and labor resources will at times be underutilized.

The philosophical dichotomy of the two systems concerning utilization of resources requires a fundamental change in thinking for most manufacturers. Manufacturing practitioners who are hard-wired from years of exposure to traditional planning systems and the maximum utilization of factory machines and labor may find embracing this difference in thinking difficult. The success of a Lean transformation, however, is dependent on the ability of these manufacturing practitioners to make a mental paradigm shift in their thinking about utilization. Making this shift in thinking is *mandatory* for the designated change agent leading the Lean business transformation!

The Lean operating system uses completely different operating methods to satisfy customer demand that are clearly visible on the manufacturing shop floor. These operating methods are the basis for achieving the highly desired benefits promised by a Lean operating system:

- One-unit-at-a-time production of products
- Balanced resources
- Linked resources
- Flexible resources for matching resources to customer demand
- Standard work assigned to each workstation
- Quality at the task level
- Kanban management of the materials, production rate, and quality

ONE-UNIT-AT-A-TIME PRODUCTION

Producing products one unit at a time is a key feature of the Lean manufacturing system. One-unit-at-a-time production is in direct conflict with existing thinking about traditional operating methods in which batch production is the norm. Current planning system methods require predetermined batch sizes that reflect a *minimum run quantity* for a production order whereas the Lean operating system uses *one unit* as the ideal manufacturing batch size quantity. The logic in a Lean operating system is that a manufacturing resource (labor or machine) can work on only one unit at a time at a workstation. Because a resource can only work on one unit at a time, the time required for any material waiting in a batch quantity before or after the process is considered *waste* by the Lean model (when waiting, the material's form, fit, or function is not being altered).

From Chapter 1, recall that in addition to the material wastes associated with overproduction, batch sizing creates additional working capital costs. Also recall that department managers in traditional planning systems are motivated to have the largest batch sizes possible to ensure maximum utilization in their departments. This practice contributes to producing inventories that are in excess of what is necessary to meet customer demand. Overproduction increases working capital costs. Delays related to large batch-sized quantities also cause other production orders (which are also in batch-sized quantities and in different states of completion) to wait in other departments and be counted in the cost of WIP inventory. The inventory investment can be significant. Now consider what batch processing and all the wait time associated with it can do to customer lead time! Assuming that production batches are processed through consecutive departments using a FIFO (first-in/first-out) methodology:

- What is the cumulative impact on the production lead time of batches of in-process inventory waiting a turn to have their form, fit, or function changed?
- What is the amount of time required for all units in a predetermined batch size to be completed in the gateway department prior to being routed to the next department?
- How much time in queue will elapse before batch processing begins if multiple production orders are waiting at a department workstation?
- How much time will be required to process all the batches through all the departments listed on the indented BOM?
- How much queue, wait, and move time will be added to the customer-quoted lead time?
- How long will valuable working capital be invested to support batch production?

The advantages of one-unit-at-a-time production. When producing one unit at a time, lead time is the sum of *only* the value-added time expended to change the form, fit, or function of one unit. In the Lean operating model, no units are tied up in predetermined batch sizes waiting in a queue to be produced. Depending on the physical size of a product, flowing products one unit at a time (one-piece flow) can mean less transportation (waste) is incurred from moving product batches from one department to the next. Although inventories are reduced, the Lean manufacturing system is not a zero inventory system. Some WIP and raw material inventories will still remain in a one-unit-at-a-time flow system, but the amounts will be limited to the number of workstations where sequential work is being done on partially completed units. The working capital required to support the shorter lead times will be proportionate to the shorter lead time required for the production of one unit at each workstation. The cost relationship of flowing one unit at a time and the customer-quoted lead time can be measured by the amount of time required to perform only the standard work and the resulting working capital investment: shorter lead time = less working

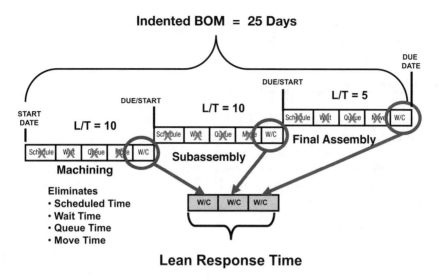

Figure 2.2. Producing products in the sum of their work content time. L/T, lead time; W/C, work content.

capital (Figure 2.2). If a defective unit is discovered at a workstation, only that unit and any units in production upstream from the workstation will be of suspect quality. If a defect is identified during the production of a batch quantity, the quality of the entire batch will be suspect. The benefit of having only one unit (or a few) of suspect quality is possible because one-unit-at-a-time production requires that an operator *never* pass a defect to the next downstream workstation. One-unit-at-a-time production methodology also provides the ability for rapid changeover from manufacturing one product to manufacturing another. Managing unplanned orders and meeting emergency customer demand is therefore simplified. Instead of setting a large batch aside or completing all of the unfinished units, the one-unit-at-a-time product flow can be changed as soon as the first workstation on the Lean line clears the last unit of the previous product running on the line.

The challenges of one-unit-at-a-time production. The one-unit-at-a-time flow system will be in direct conflict with the traditional operating system practice of running minimum quantities, grouping like processes into departments, routing work in batch-size quantities in each department, and launching work orders to achieve level production schedules.

Compare the savings in lead time and inventory investment from the Lean operating system with the lead time and inventory levels of the current operating system model. Continued loyalty to batch production methodologies for the purpose of achieving departmental utilization is an expensive strategy that costs your company money and time.

BALANCED RESOURCES

Balanced resources are a second key feature of the Lean operating system. *Balanced resources* means that departments with capacities in excess of the customer demand are not required to utilize their excessive capacities. The production rate and the throughput from each balanced process are to be identical. Just like the Lean feature of one-unit-at-a-time production, balanced resources are in direct conflict with traditional planning models that strive to achieve 100% utilization of all available resources regardless of the actual customer demand.

The test for traditional planning systems is for demand to *never* exceed the available capacity during a planning period. If the capacity is exceeded, the solutions are to move the batch order causing the capacity to be exceeded to a later period; authorize a one-time reduction of the quantity of the batch order; or cancel the entire order.

Modern MRP planning systems do a great job of providing solutions for reacting to customer demand that is *in excess* of scheduled capacity, but traditional planning systems have no effective solution for responding to customer demand that requires *less than* full capacity. In traditional planning systems, it's 100% utilization all the time! When required capacity is *less than* maximum utilization, unsold customer demand is moved into the current planning period to absorb the excess capacity. The traditional planning system parameters continue to drive the system to achieve maximum utilization while using FGI fluctuations as the principal method to offset the consequences of lower customer demand.

Traditional operating systems group *like* resources into individual departments. Grouping resources in this way and then expecting that they will achieve equal capacity across the factory is unrealistic. Departments in a factory also cannot be established based on dividing the *number of resources* by the *number of departments*. Depending on the work done in each department and the number of resources in each department, some departments will always be likely to have more capacity than others. If full utilization were to be achieved in these departments, and no customer demand is waiting to consume their output, then producing unsold WIP or FGI (i.e., overproduction) will be the only way to absorb the excess capacity.

Underutilization of available capacity creates a negative variance. If resources are underutilized and the actual performance of manufacturing is less than expected when compared to the past performance, a negative variance is created by the cost accounting system. Depending on the corporate structure of the company (and the country in which it operates), avoiding a negative variance can be a very important activity. For example, if a Lean manufacturer has no stockholders and operates as a single site, reporting a negative variance can easily be explained in the context of the Lean operating system — utilization is not the prevalent performance measurement in a Lean operating system. If, however, the company is a single- or multisite organization that has stockholders, explaining the variance and its impact on the annual report may be much more difficult. Sister companies in the same reporting group are required to use consistent reporting and accounting methods. An individual company site operating with a Lean system using performance measures that are not based on traditional resource utilization goals will therefore most certainly stand out from all the other companies in the group (and in the industry)! Corporations in the United States are required to adhere to the guidelines of GAAP, or generally accepted accounting principles, to ensure standard and consistent corporate reporting. (Similar reporting guidelines exist in most other countries.) Explaining negative variances is much easier for companies implementing a Lean operating system if they do not have a mandate to follow GAAP. See Chapter 12 for a discussion of GAAP.

Full utilization of available capacity results in accumulating WIP inventories. Any labor productivity gained by the full utilization of available capacity in a process will be embedded in the WIP inventory. Excess WIP inventory in a process indicates imbalance between the resources and customer demand. When looking for productivity improvement opportunities, look no further than the point where WIP inventory has accumulated. Reducing excess WIP provides a great opportunity for reducing resource costs, thereby saving working capital.

The advantages of balanced resources. Recall from Chapter 1 that materials costs are the most expensive cost component of a product. For most companies, saving material costs will yield a much greater return on working capital investment than any savings in labor productivity for the items consumed by a WIP inventory. The Lean operating system utilizes only the minimum amount of resources necessary to meet changing customer demand each day, without regard for capacity or the full utilization of the existing resources. The Lean operating system establishes a maximum capacity that ensures that the capacity is sufficient to meet customer demand. In the Lean operating system, if customer demand requires less than the available resource capacity available, 100% utilization is not artificially forced by adding demand into a period simply to achieve full utilization. Rather than driving resources toward full utilization, the Lean operating system avoids the wastes caused by overproduction, product movement, inventory, and added transportation by simply having less than full utilization of resources. For example, when a labor resource is not required, the Lean operating system relies on the flexibility of the operator to move to some other area in manufacturing to adjust the headcount of the process to match customer demand. Simply keeping a redundant labor resource busy during a period of low customer demand causes lower productivity. When demand is less than the available capacity, labor resources usually just slow down to fill up the available time or produce unnecessary or unsold inventory just to stay busy (utilized) during a shift.

The challenges of balanced resources. The challenge presented by the Lean operating system to the full resource utilization paradigm of the traditional operating system can create a major roadblock for the long-term success of a Lean transformation. The full-utilization paradigm is a historic performance measurement that has been pounded into the mindset of manufacturing managers, controllers, and C-level managers in traditional operating systems for years. Resource utilization is often a major performance measurement used in their annual review. Department managers in a traditional operating system are responsible for the resources assigned to them. For some of these department managers, this responsibility for resources can take on a form of ownership that evolves into a source of power. When challenged, these department managers will often do anything necessary to maintain the status quo of their resources (their power) in the organization. Safeguarding the status quo of their departments often manifests itself as resistance to the Lean transformation initiative. The challenges from the controller's office resulting from the conflict between the Lean operating system and the full resource utilization paradigm, however, can be even more difficult to handle. The cost accounting system compares the amount of resource hours available to a manager to the actual amount of hours used to make the reported units produced in a reporting period. If the reported unit count and the time are below what could be produced with the existing capacity and time available, the result is a *negative variance*. The controller's office then reports the underutilized resources to the department manager as a negative variance. The manager must explain why his department did not achieve full utilization for the period. Department managers use numerous gimmicks and tricks and expend significant energy to ensure that negative variances do not occur. The methods used to avoid receiving a negative variance report often create an environment of gamesmanship that only adds time and costs. These efforts make no change to the form, fit, or function of the products.

Failing to successfully challenge the full utilization paradigm of a current planning system model can seriously threaten the long-term success of the Lean operating system. It's no exaggeration to say that losing the battle with the full utilization paradigm issue is a common cause of Lean operating system failures.

If the recurring presence of negative variances cannot be replaced with more meaningful performance measures that indicate the true performance of manufacturing improvements — improvements in quality, product cost, and customer satisfaction — managers and other champions of the Lean operating system will soon tire of their continuous need to defend the Lean operating system. Reverting to the old operating model just to silence the constant pressure from critics would make life so much simpler! When this type of thinking begins to cause defections, the Lean operating system will be the loser in the company! In advance of any Lean transformation effort, prepare for the impending explanations that will be needed for negative variances that are generated because of the Lean operating system. As a Lean change agent, be comfortable with explaining the utilization paradigm shift that is required. Be proactive in developing a joint strategy partnership with the controller's office.

LINKED RESOURCES

A process is defined as *a series of sequential work actions performed by either labor or machines to change the form, fit, or function of a product.* Recall from Chapter 1 that in a traditional manufacturing system with a supporting planning system, labor and machine resources performing the work of a process are grouped together into a department. (Recall also that grouping similar resources into departments is paradigm 1 of the traditional manufacturing operating model.) These resources that have been consolidated based on process similarities are located in a centralized location where the standard work of their process is performed. Grouping like resources into a department helps to simplify the management of resources (e.g., measuring the input and output of a department for productivity purposes) and to develop the expertise necessary to complete product processing in the most efficient manner possible, but this form of departmental organization and location has nothing to do with the equal distribution of capacity.

A centralized location for the purpose of grouping similar resources into a department is of no consequence in the manufacturing of a product in the Lean operating system. The Lean operating system requires *only* the resources needed for the manufacture of a predetermined mix and volume of products. Resources are decentralized by placing them adjacent to one another in the sequence in which they are used to produce a product. By placing an individual resource next to its downstream resource, the output of the resource can be immediately consumed by the next resource in the production sequence. In the Lean operating system, resources (labor, machines, and workstations) are no longer members of a department — they're members of a Lean manufacturing line. After physically locating the resources in the sequence in which they are used in production, the resources are *linked* to one another by the signaling of production of the next unit by a kanban signal that authorizes the expenditure of that resource.

Determining production schedules in the traditional production model. For a traditional planning system, four things must be known to develop a schedule for manufacturing a product in a factory:

- What are the *processes* (or the departments) required for manufacturing the product?
- In what *sequence* (or order) does the product advance through manufacturing?
- At what *time* (or when) must work begin in each production department?
- What *component parts* are required to build the product?

In a traditional planning system, an *indented bill of materials* (BOM) is used to communicate this information to the planning system. A manufacturer using a traditional planning system uses a *master schedule* to translate customer demand into production requirements for manufacturing. The individual managing the master schedule must have three additional pieces of information:

- The *due date* (the customer's expectation of delivery)
- The *lead time* for each level in the indented BOM
- The *quantity* of the product to be produced

How an indented BOM works. Indenting a BOM with the steps required to build a product records the sequential steps of production, beginning at the first process and ending at the final process. The final process is the top-most level of the BOM — the finished product level. The finished-product level is also known as the *stock keeping unit* (SKU). Each level in the BOM also records the lead time for each step. During the scheduling exercise, beginning with the highest level of product completion — the finished product or SKU level — each subassembly in the BOM subtracts the lead time from the due date at the highest level of the BOM and works downward through all levels until ending at the first process. Based on the lead time established for each level in the BOM, this backward scheduling technique establishes start and due dates for each level in the BOM. The lead time offset establishes the start date for beginning work at each level. Beginning with the initial due date required for the SKU level, the resulting start date at the first level in the BOM becomes the due date at the next lower level in the BOM. This lead time offset routine is repeated at each level until a start date for the gateway department (the lowest level in the indented BOM) is established. The gateway department is the entry point where raw materials are first introduced into the manufacturing process. The sum of the lead times through each level in the BOM then becomes the statement of the customer-quoted lead time for the product. When reviewing an indented BOM, notice that each level represents a different manufacturing department in the factory. Developing production schedules is simplified by grouping production orders that have the same start date in each respective manufacturing department with the corresponding level in the indented BOM. Having information about the sequential build structure of the product is crucial in a traditional planning operating system to time-phase the start and completion times for the subassemblies in each department. Demand quantities for component parts and production requirements (also known as *load quantities*) are then determined by multiplying the demand quantity times the *quantity per* indicated on the BOM. Demand quantities are calculated at each level in the BOM, resulting in the number of products to be produced in the lead time for each process along with the quantity of purchased material indicated for each process. Demand volumes, component materials, and start and due dates are then communicated to each department on the indented BOM by a production order released by the planning system.

Determining production schedules in the Lean operating model. The master schedule and the indented BOM are also used to communicate customer demand to a Lean factory. As with the traditional planning system model, the Lean operating model also needs to know the processes required for producing the product, the sequence in which the products will advance through manufacturing, and the customer's demand quantities. The Lean operating model, however, approaches *production* of the demand quantities much differently. The Lean operating system still requires work to be completed through a series of dissimilar processes for the production of any value-added product, just as a typical manufacturing method does. The Lean operating system still seeks to achieve the maximum *efficiency* of resources, just as a traditional operating system does. The Lean operating system, however, identifies the processes and the resources necessary to produce a predetermined mix and volume of products in a sequence *one time* (during the design and layout of the factory). The Lean operating system does not use preset batch sizes. The Lean operating system does not route products through a series of departments in preset quantities. In the Lean operating system, demand is established daily based on *actual* customer orders. The resources to be assigned to produce that demand are then identified. Products are produced in only the sum of their work content time to achieve maximum efficiency.

The advantages of linked resources. The Lean system is not driven to maximize the utilization of resources. The Lean system does not require all resources necessary for completing a process to be grouped together into a single functional department. The Lean operating system seeks only to match the number of resources required (labor, machines, workstations, and inventory) to produce a single day's quantity of customer demand. The Lean operating system only needs three pieces of information to produce a product:

- The *manufacturing processes* required for building the product
- The *sequence* in which the processes will be used
- The *number of resources* required to match customer demand that day

The Lean operating system does not require an indented BOM to do this. Once the production processes, the sequence of those processes, and the number of resources have been identified, all that remains to be known to produce customer demand efficiently is the physical placement of the processes so they match the sequence in which their output is consumed. In the Lean operating system, processes are balanced so that work is completed at the same speed. Physically locating processes adjacent to one another encourages products to flow from one labor or machine resource to another with little motion wasted by moving products from one process to the next. The physical linking of resources is a key feature of producing products in only the sum of their work content. By using resources that have been balanced, even dissimilar processes can produce products at the same rate. Special-order products can be manufactured in the customer-quoted lead time plus the sum of any additional value-added time required for completing any additional specialized work content.

The challenges of linked resources. Because the Lean operating system requires balanced and linked resources to be physically arranged so they follow the sequential production of a product on the Lean line, the organizational structure of traditional functional departments requires review and often requires restructuring. Some departments may shrink in size. Others may be completely dissolved. Naturally, both of these situations can create resistance from department managers. A Lean change agent should expect resistance when current departmental structures must be modified and operators are necessarily reassigned to other processes on the Lean line as a result of the Lean transformation. A Lean change agent should also expect utilizing only the minimum labor and machines resources needed to meet customer demand rather than pursuing full utilization of all available resources as a measure of successful performance to cause conflict with the existing full utilization practices of the traditional system.

In the end, each company must make a basic decision. Are the benefits of faster response time, reduced lead time and working capital, improved quality, and growth of market share offered by a Lean transformation greater than the benefits of avoiding conflict and maintaining the status quo of the current planning model operating system?

FLEXIBLE RESOURCES FOR MATCHING DEMAND

In a traditional planning system, resource utilization is king. To achieve maximum utilization of manufacturing resources, traditional planning systems use only one speed — "produce as much as possible as fast as possible." Utilization requirements often dictate a production schedule that has little or no concern for the creation of unsold inventory. As long as the manufacturing departments in a traditional manufacturing system meet their utilization goals, and are not held accountable for excess inventory investment, the penalty for any unsold inventory produced by them becomes a problem for the materials management (inventory control) group. Even though the manufacturing group is left unscathed by the production of excess inventories, the entire company pays the price for unsold inventory.

Recall from the discussion of balanced resources that a traditional planning system is hard-coded to maximize utilization of manufacturing resources and to achieve full utilization of a department's capacity without exceeding the stated capacity of the department (the function of the capacity planning module of a traditional planning system). The traditional planning system has no method to handle demand (sales) that is *less than capacity* during a planning period. So when no customer demand is available, a common practice in traditional planning systems to fill the gap between actual demand and capacity is to allow the production of customer demand *ahead* of the demand's originally requested delivery date. The overriding policy in a traditional planning system is that excess capacity must be utilized. A policy of 100% utilization of excess capacity, of course, can cause unsold products to be produced, but as long as the capacity of a traditional planning system is fully utilized, the resulting changes in demand scheduling are deemed necessary and good.

Departmental manufacturing capacity in the traditional operating model.
With a policy of 100% utilization, capacities that have very little to do with actual daily fluctuating demand are established for manufacturing departments in the traditional operating model. During the next annual budget planning process, the resources for these manufacturing departments are planned using demand forecasts. Based on these forecasts, capital expenditure requests for the acquisition of additional resources (labor, workstations, and machines) are initiated. Once these capital expenditure requests are approved and the manufacturing strategy is implemented, new capacities, including any new capacities needed to meet the forecasted demand for the departments, are established. Once these new capacities are established, little attention is given to them or to fluctuating customer demand until the next budgeting period. Should the forecasted customer demand not be realized, the pressure to utilize the newly acquired capacities still remains.

Because the performance of traditional manufacturing departments is measured by their utilization of resources, subsequent policies and procedures will always be deployed to maximize the output of departmental resources. So, like the one speed of the planning system, departmental policy in traditional manufacturing departments is easy to articulate — "make as much as we can as fast as we can!" If the production of actual customer demand is less than the capacity in a manufacturing department in a traditional planning system, the result is a negative variance. Advancing customer planned or future planned demand to utilize the available capacity might level the production schedules in the department and even satisfy the controller's office, but this practice can have only one outcome: excess inventory. So, for a manufacturing company with a requirement of full utilization and actual customer demand that is *less than* departmental capacities, the only options available are to have a negative variance or to produce excess inventory! Materials management, however, doesn't want the inventory because they're measured on turn rate and the manufacturing group doesn't want the negative variance! Even though neither option is preferred over the other, the manufacturing group will usually choose to produce excess inventory to avoid receiving a negative variance. (After all, the manufacturing group is not usually held accountable for the production of excess inventory.) These less-than-ideal outcomes are a source of great conflict — one month, manufacturing is successful; the next, materials management is. In the meantime, unsold inventory continues to accumulate and consume working capital that could be used for more productive purposes.

Departmental manufacturing capacity in the Lean operating model. The Lean operating system treats resource utilization more seriously than traditional planning systems. The Lean operating system can accommodate full utilization when customer demand requires it by putting sufficient resources in place to meet the demand, but it can also accommodate customer demand that requires less than full utilization of resources. Instead of bringing future planned or firm planned orders forward from a future period into the current period and producing inventory ahead of the actual demand as a traditional planning system does, the Lean operating system modifies the production throughput to match customer demand. When customer demand requires less than the full utilization of resources, the Lean operating system reduces line output volume even if this level of production is less than 100% utilization of resources. Throughput modification is accomplished by increasing or decreasing the number of labor resources assigned to the manufacturing processes. By matching labor resources to actual customer demand, production output is reduced. Only the actual units sold are produced. No unsold inventory is produced.

The benefits of matching labor resources to actual customer demand. The Lean operating system constantly seeks to eliminate the seven wastes of manufacturing. Unsold inventory is considered as overproduction in the Lean operating system and therefore one of the seven wastes. In addition to the overproduction, operating resources at full capacity creates additional waste in the form of wait time, transportation, and the working capital investment associated with inventory when customer demand cannot absorb the output. By matching the utilization of resources with actual customer demand, little to no unsold inventory is produced by a Lean manufacturing line. In the Lean operating model, resources = customer demand. Each day only the resources required to match actual customer demand that day are used on a Lean manufacturing line.

The challenges of matching labor resources to actual customer demand. Intentionally using fewer resources versus having full resource utilization regardless of customer demand is one of the major distinctions between traditional planning systems and Lean operating models. In the Lean operating system, the full utilization of resources is of *secondary* importance. This difference alone is enough to cause resistance in production departments. Department managers strive to keep their operators busy so they remain assigned to their respective departments. Maintaining their labor pool is a way to justify their management fiefdom. Less than full utilization of resources negatively impacts the traditional full utilization performance model used by the controller's office when this model is used as a baseline for monitoring performance on the shop floor. The controller's office prefers consistent, standard performance measurements for reporting the company's performance to stockholders.

Recall the three elements of product cost: labor, overhead, and materials. For most manufacturers, the smallest component of product cost is labor. The largest cost component is materials (including the WIP and FGI materials). Most managers in a traditional operating system devote the majority of their time to managing the smallest cost component, labor costs. They concentrate on managing the costs of labor by pushing existing labor to increase their productivity. In seeking full utilization, they rarely if ever consider that material costs represent the majority of product cost. The Lean operating model concentrates on the elimination of material waste. Concentrating on savings in the cost of materials, however, would yield a better return on their investment of management time than the same amount of management time invested in saving labor costs. Labor costs, of course, should not be ignored, but the greatest returns from managerial resources are from concentrating on eliminating the costs of material waste. The Lean operating system recognizes that efforts to minimize material costs result in significantly higher returns on investment and lower product costs compared to the reduction of labor costs. The benefits from a 1% reduction in material costs are likely to be greater than the benefits of a 1% reduction in labor cost.

STANDARD WORK ASSIGNED TO EACH WORKSTATION

Identifying the labor and machine work required for producing a product is an important element of the Lean operating system. Traditional planning systems use *standard time* as the basis for measuring efficiency, the utilization of resources, and the overhead absorption cost calculations for determining burdened labor cost. Traditional manufacturers often use a routing file to determine the standard time for a product. The Lean system uses *standard work* to establish the cycle time of products, identify the work required at individual workstation level, certify operator training requirements, and to ensure the quality criteria at task level. A Lean system requires a detailed definition of the standard work that must performed to complete the production of a product. Once defined, standard work is assigned to every workstation on a Lean manufacturing line (see Chapter 6 for a discussion of how to develop a standard work definition). The standard work assigned to each workstation is static. Operators are required to move from workstation to workstation to perform the standard work rather than relocating the standard work to a workstation that is more convenient for them. Figure 2.3 illustrates the assignment of standard work to individual workstations on a Lean line.

Standard time and utilization in the traditional planning model. Traditional planning systems use standard time to perform capacity planning routines. *Efficiency* is calculated as standard time multiplied by the scheduled quantity divided by the actual run time (efficiency = standard time × scheduled quantity ÷ actual run time). This formula indicates the efficiency for work that has been completed. *Utilization* is calculated by dividing the uptime by the actual time used for production (uptime ÷ actual time). *Uptime* is the time available to the resource to do work in a process. *Actual time* is the time required for a scheduled production quantity. More often than not, once standard times have been recorded the first time in a traditional planning system, they are seldom changed or updated. As long as negative variances are not too numerous, keeping standard times up to date does not receive much priority from the engineering department. The manufacturing environment, however, is very dynamic. The accuracy of standard times begins to be lost almost as soon as they are recorded. How accurate can the efficiency and utilization measurements be if the standard times used are unreliable? Standard times must be kept as up to date as possible. Maintaining them is a huge effort. In manufacturing, the standard time statement is part of a production

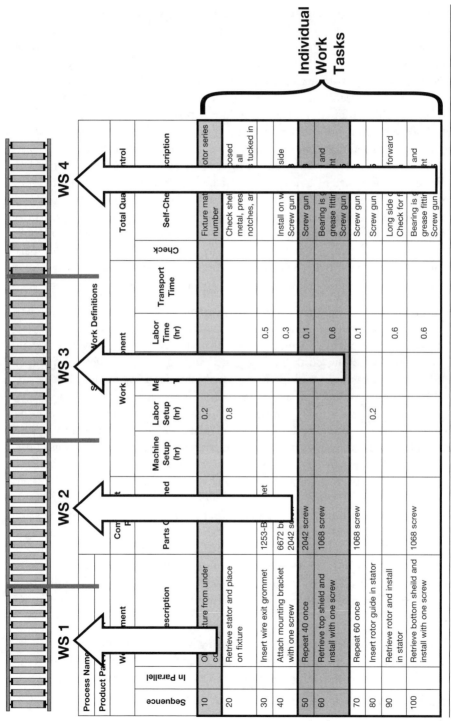

Figure 2.3. Standard work assigned to each workstation. WS, workstation.

order on a routing file. Standard time is used by the cost accounting department when developing a variance report. A negative variance will be created if the amount of time required to produce a quantity exceeds the stated standard time on the routing file. Production managers in a traditional operating system will do almost anything to avoid negative variances. To optimize their chances of achieving maximum utilization and efficiency, they often opt to use techniques such as consolidating production orders into longer production runs to amortize the setup of the machines and labor and managing standard times by slowing down the work to a speed that is intentionally less than the actual required time. These techniques can skew the standard time measurement in their favor. If production is driven by the constant quest to maximize utilization and efficiency, the only possible outcome is unsold inventory. If the three elements of product cost are labor, overhead, and materials, with materials being the largest, other than providing the simplest solution for achieving maximum productivity, what possible logic could there be for producing unsold inventory? If labor is the smallest part of product cost, what logic could there be for concentrating management efforts on maximum utilization and efficiency just to reduce labor?

Standard time and utilization in the Lean operating model. The Lean operating system, of course, cannot completely ignore utilization — it's just more concerned with controlling manufacturing costs. The Lean operating system approaches controlling costs by first concentrating on the largest element of product cost: inventories and their associated material costs. Standard times are still documented in the Lean operating system. The accuracy required in observing the standard time for performing the work for each product in each process is the same as in a traditional planning system. Just as in a traditional planning system, inflated standard times in the Lean operating system result in increased use of resources (labor, workstations, machines, and inventory). Production managers in traditional planning systems like to have inflated standard times. In their quest to increase efficiency and utilization measurements, production managers know they can beat production standards on the shop floor if standard times are inflated. Inflated standard times, however, usually result in producing too much inventory. In the Lean operating system, inflated standard times usually result in having too many labor resources. (What is more costly in Figure 2.4 — materials or labor?) If utilization is no longer the primary performance goal for production managers, the gamesmanship of manipulating standard times will no longer be necessary.

Standard work time in the Lean operating model. When operating a mixed-model product line in which different products are run through the same workstation, products with invalid standard work times quickly affect the balance of the Lean line. Invalid standard work times on a Lean line become very obvious,

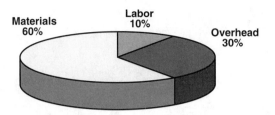

Figure 2.4. The three elements of product cost: labor, overhead, and materials.

very quickly, because some operators are constantly waiting while others are working slower than the flow of the balanced workstations. When an operator on a Lean line runs work through a workstation *faster* than the time allotted to the workstation, the operator has to wait for the operator at the next downstream workstation to catch up because in-process kanban (IPK) discipline requires the operator *not* to run another unit through his workstation as long as the downstream IPK is full. This downstream IPK will remain full until the downstream operator can consume the unit in the IPK by pulling it into his workstation. The operator could move into an adjoining workstation, but the full IPK still prevents him from producing another unit until a signal has been received from the downstream workstation (the empty IPK). Conversely, when an operator on a Lean line runs work through the workstation *slower* than the standard time, the downstream IPK at the workstation remains empty until work on the unit is completed. In the meantime, the downstream operator must wait for the work to be completed by the upstream operator. Other upstream operators also must wait for their IPKs to be consumed. Standard work imbalances can occur all day long. Imbalanced workstations demand immediate resolution. Waiting is non-value-added time! In a Lean operating system, the constant waiting of operators upstream and downstream soon attracts the attention of the management team to the need for immediate resolution of the imbalance. Keeping workstations balanced cannot be forgotten once the Lean transformation project has been completed. Balanced workstations must be a way of life in a Lean operating system.

How an IPK works. The Lean operating system uses simple visual management devices whenever possible. One of those visible devices is the *kanban*, a Japanese term meaning *signal* (or *card*). Lean methodology uses three different types of kanbans to serve as signals: the IPK, the two-bin kanban, and the multiple-card kanban. The IPK is the simplest type of signaling device. On a Lean line, an IPK is placed on the downstream side of each workstation. It is this placement of the IPK that regulates the measured rate of the one-unit-at-a-time flow of products on the line. If the Lean line has multiple processes (e.g., feeder processes), each workstation within each of the processes must also

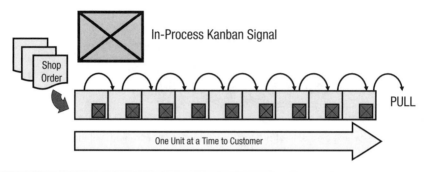

Figure 2.5. An IPK signal as the authorization to do work.

have an IPK located on its downstream side. To be an effective signal, an IPK must be a physical location with a dedicated space for placing in-process units of production. This dedicated space functions as a parking place where a partially completed unit of production can be temporarily placed during the manufacturing process. Depending on the process and the product, IPKs can be of different sizes, shapes, and types. For example, the IPK for a smaller product made on a bench can be a designated space on the bench that is the same size as the product itself. A larger product might have a designated space on the shop floor. Both spaces indicate the status of the IPK. When the unit residing in the space is consumed, the resulting *empty* space becomes the signal to an operator to produce another unit to replace the unit that was just consumed. The empty space is the *authorization* for the operator to produce one more unit. When a partially completed unit is moved into the downstream workstation from the upstream IPK, the resulting empty IPK at the upstream workstation becomes the authorization for the upstream operator to produce another unit. When this upstream operator takes a unit from the upstream workstation, another signal is then given to the next upstream operator and so on and so on upstream though all the processes on the line. The signal is illustrated as a letter X in a rectangle in Figure 2.5. As a unit is completed at each workstation and moves downstream toward completion, every workstation except for the very last one will have a partially completed unit of production in its IPK. Only the IPK at the last workstation will have a fully completed product ready for consumption by a customer (see Chapter 8 for a detailed discussion of the kanban system).

Standard work ensures quality. With the Lean operating system, the time for performing quality inspections was included when the required tasks and times for standard work were recorded. Standard work in the Lean operating model therefore includes the time required for performing the tasks associated with inspections. Performing inspections is critical for achieving parts-per-million

(PPM) quality at the task level. These inspections do not change the form, fit, or function of a product, but until there are no longer any variances in a process, this inspection work must be done by a labor resource. Until variation is impossible, *not* performing quality inspections ensures that variation will be built into a product. This cannot be allowed to happen! Until the time that all processes are 100% fail-safe, performing a quality inspection is the only way to ensure that a defective product will not be placed in a downstream workstation's IPK. Traditional manufacturing systems do not allow for quality inspection time. Unless specifically stated, traditional routing files do not account for the time needed to complete inspections. Commonly used efficiency and utilization performance measures also do not allow time for inspection work. If a defect occurs within a batch quantity, the defective unit(s) will likely be advanced through the remaining routing with the hope that the defective units will be discovered at a downstream quality control station. In this scenario, the costs of rework and scrap can be significant. Quality rework is a common cause of negative variances. On a Lean line, two quality inspections are part of the standard work at each workstation. These two quality inspections limit a defective product to the workstation where the defect is discovered. In the meantime, upstream IPKs fill up and stop the production of all products in upstream workstations.

Standard work balances work assignments. With a traditional operating system, the description of work detail is limited to the contents of the routing file. If the level of work detail on a routing file is defined too broadly, then too much room concerning how the work is to be done can be left to individual interpretation by operators. For example, if a department has ten operators, and each operator can independently decide how the work should be completed, the work might end up being done ten different ways! When this occurs, likely only one of these ten different ways is the *best* way. The other nine have been left to each operator to determine on their own. In a Lean operating system, standard work is defined at the task level using a detailed description of the individual tasks for each process. The individual tasks are assigned in equal amounts of standard time, causing each workstation in a process to be balanced with another. Balancing the work at each workstation by assigning equal amounts of work causes products to *flow* through the processes at a measured rate until the product is completed at the last workstation. Once assigned, operators may perform only the standard work assigned to the workstation. Assigning standard work to each workstation makes interpreting how work is to be done the responsibility of management team members. A sign that individual interpretation of work is occurring is when an operator has chosen to complete all of the manufacturing work for a product at a personal workstation or assembly bench (known as *single-station build*).

Standard work avoids single-station build. In single-station build, an operator independently decides to complete all of the work in the manufacturing process for a product, from start to finish, at a personal workstation. A single-station-build operator takes ownership of a certain area of the shop floor and establishes that space as *his* workstation. A single-station-build workstation often has personal items (e.g., a radio, posters, family pictures, a personal toolbox, cabinets and drawers with hidden stashes of components, etc.). A single-station-build operator might even obscure the view around the workstation by strategically placing shelving, part racks, or other large items such as flat, corrugated material to have the privacy of working at his or her own pace. An operator who performs standard work as a single-station build may or may not be manufacturing a product in the *one best way*. No second or third set of eyes examines the work completed at a single-station-build workstation, so no one knows if the product was completed in the standard time or at the required level of quality. Single-station-build methodology is not used in the Lean operating system. Operators do not own their workstations. The Lean operating system divides standard work into equal amounts and spreads it across multiple workstations. Standard work is attached to specific workstations. Individual operators do not choose the method in which work is done at any workstation. The one best method for completing the work has been predetermined by a member of the management team. Each operator has been trained to complete only the work assigned to the workstation. Operators are assigned to workstations on a daily basis based on customer demand. The Lean shop floor has no single-station-build workstations. Single-station-build methodology promotes the best operator syndrome.

Standard work avoids the best operator syndrome. In the best operator syndrome, an operator is empowered by being recognized as the *best* when compared to all of the other operators in the department. When the best operator syndrome exists, the best operator is not motivated to share information or any of his singular techniques with other operators for fear of losing his superior ranking in the department. Because specialized skills are concentrated in one operator, the best operator becomes practically indispensable whenever a shop floor emergency requires specialized skills. This situation, of course, only enhances the best operator's status. Should the best operator be absent when a shop floor emergency occurs, the situation can be disastrous because in comparison to the best operator all other operators are considered substandard substitutes. In a Lean manufacturing environment, there is no single best operator. Instead, the Lean operating model seeks to have equality of skill sets among all operators. Parity among operators is more likely when the total amount of standard work to be learned is limited to the work assigned to a single workstation. When parity is achieved, shop floor emergencies, absenteeism, and vacation schedules will have no impact on the daily performance of the factory.

Standard work facilitates training new operators. When specialized skills for building a product are concentrated in one person (the best operator syndrome of the single-station-build model), and the standard time for manufacturing a product is lengthy, the time required for training new operators is also lengthy. The learning curve required for a new operator to become proficient in using the single-station-build method takes a long time (after all, learning to become the best operator didn't happen overnight). In the Lean operating system, standard work is assigned to a specific workstation. The standard work is broken into a time equal to the work at a balanced workstation, which provides important training benefits. New operator training is simplified. When standard work is broken into a time equal to the work at a balanced workstation, the learning curve is reduced to the amount of standard time for the work of one workstation. By needing to learn only a single balanced workstation amount of standard work, new operators become proficient much faster than if they are required to learn large groupings of standard time — it's much easier to train new operators to do a balanced amount of standard work at one workstation than to train them to build an entire unit. They're also less likely to produce defective units during the learning curve for the workstation. Working together as a team, with each operator using one workstation's amount of time on building a single unit, causes a series of objective inspections to be performed on the work of other operators. Customers are less likely to receive defective products because quality improves.

Standard work matches resources to demand. Customer demand can expand or contract on a daily basis. Rarely are customer mix and volume the same two days in a row. Traditional planning systems are inflexible when demand varies between planning periods. With a traditional system, if the assigned headcount remains the same, but customer demand falls below the available capacity, there is no flexibility for modifying production output. The only way to fill the gap between demand and capacity is to produce unsold inventory. Rather than loading the manufacturing process to achieve full utilization regardless of customer demand, the Lean operating system has the capability to match customer demand by increasing or decreasing the number of labor resources (up to the designed capacity of a manufacturing cell). When matching resources to demand, it's much easier to add or subtract a human labor resource than to add or subtract a machine or a workstation. If customer demand is *less than* the designed capacity of a Lean line on a given day, the output of the Lean line can be reduced to meet the smaller demand by modifying the number of human labor resources assigned to the line that day. Only the number of operators assigned to work on the line that day needs to be adjusted. Even though fewer operators are assigned to the line, the standard work at each workstation and the designed line rate remain the same. In one-unit-at-a-time production, reduced staffing on a Lean line requires some operators to complete two cycles of work, which will reduce the output of the line that day. This flexibility to add or subtract labor resources so that only customer demand is produced is possible only if standard work is assigned to balanced workstations and operators are required to move to the standard work. They're key requirements.

The advantages of standard work. The goal of a Lean operating system is to increase market share by providing the highest-quality products at the best price, in the shortest delivery time possible, and to achieve the highest customer satisfaction in the industry. To accomplish these goals, a Lean operating system concentrates less on utilization of resources and more on controlling the largest part of product cost: inventories and their associated material costs and lead time. The Lean operating system determines the work and where it is to be done prior to customer demand being introduced to the shop floor. Manufacturing of products is accomplished using the least possible amount of non-value-added time. The shortest possible manufacturing response time and resulting customer-quoted lead time are achieved by producing products in only the sum of their value-added work content time. The Lean operating model approaches efficiency in manufacturing processes by documenting the standard work and standard work times for each process. The standard work of a process is defined at a detailed task level and then grouped into equal amounts of time and assigned to a specific workstation. Individual interpretation by operators and the best operator syndrome are eliminated. The assignment of smaller amounts of standard work at each workstation simplifies the training of new operators. Standard work facilitates PPM quality because inspections are completed as part of standard work. The three-workstation certification of operators in the Lean operating system allows the flexibility to add or subtract labor resources in response to changes in customer demand.

The challenges of standard work. For manufacturers using traditional planning models, assigning standard work to individual workstations and changing the approach to line staffing will shift emphasis away from the full utilization of resources. The differences between the traditional approach and the Lean approach to resource utilization will be noticed immediately. Traditional operating systems leave the interpretation of how work is to be done to individual operators. In the Lean operating model, emphasis on the personal empowerment of individual operators will now be obsolete. Standard work will be assigned to specific workstations. Operators who are accustomed to choosing work based on personal preferences will no longer have that option. At first, management and operators will be threatened by the changes. Expect to see resistance.

When assigning standard work to individual workstations based on the benefits expected from the Lean operating system, a manufacturer should always consider the potential impact on the company — what impact will changing the traditional planning model have on the existing culture of the company?

QUALITY AT THE TASK LEVEL

During a sales pitch to a potential customer, a manufacturer's sales representative might boast about the high quality of the company's products. Customers today are not likely to be impressed because high quality is a now a basic expectation for any product. It's an expectation that has been in effect since the 1980s! Whether a manufacturer uses a traditional planning system or a Lean operating system, having the highest-quality product in the marketplace is no longer a marketing differential — it's an essential for being in the marketplace.

Back at the factory, achieving the level of quality expected by customers is a matter of great focus on the shop floor. Management knows that until manufacturing processes are completely fail-safe, with no possibility of variation, conducting inspections is the only way to ensure that the highest levels of quality are achieved — but inspection work isn't value-added work. It adds time and cost to products. Until fail-safe processes are created, inspections must be a part of the work performed when producing a product. (Inspection work should be a frequent opportunity for elimination as part of a kaizen project.)

Inspections in the traditional operating model. Traditional manufacturers who produce products in batches and route these batches through a series of departments perform inspections *after* the standard work has been completed in a process. A traditional operating system requires the assignment of a third party to have the responsibility for inspecting each product before the production order leaves the manufacturing department. Usually the third party is an inspector from the quality control department. This is a stop-gap solution. Because of the desire to achieve maximum utilization of the manufacturing processes, operators are not responsible for discovering product defects. When products are produced in batches and a single defective unit is discovered, all of the remaining units in the entire batch of products are suspect. The defective batch must be segregated from all other batches and set aside. Labor resources will then be assembled to perform a 100% inspection of the batch to isolate any defective units because the potential exists for every unit in the batch to be defective. Once defective products have been separated from the batch, two alternatives are available to remedy the situation: rework the defective units or scrap them. With either choice, the internal costs related to a quality failure in a batch quantity can be very large.

Rework. Besides the costs for 100% inspection of the batch to isolate the defective units, rework costs include the cost of the standard work needed to rebuild the defective products and the cost of any replacement component parts. If the defective units can be reworked to meet the product specifications, rework often means disassembly of the units, scrapping of the defective material, and replacement with new material. Rework costs could also require the addition of premium transportation costs for new component parts required from a supplier to complete the reworking of units (e.g., if airfreight shipping is required). Rework costs may also include machine time. All of these costs and the time required to perform them are non-value-added expenses. To ensure quality for the customer, however, these costs must be absorbed into the cost of the products.

Scrap. If defective units cannot be reworked, entire units must be scrapped or the labor costs necessary to cannibalize the defective units for reusable components that can be used in the production of other units must be incurred. Scrapping defective products is the worst-case scenario. Even though the costs of both alternatives are high (and painful to incur), no manufacturer ever wants defective products to reach a customer. Manufacturers therefore willingly incur the enormous costs of scrap.

Inspections in Lean manufacturing. Just as in traditional operating systems, defects can occur on a Lean line during the production process. The Lean operating system, however, has a cost-effective approach to ensuring that a defective unit never reaches a customer's receiving dock. On a Lean line, products are produced one unit at a time. An IPK placed on the downstream side of each workstation regulates the flow of products from one workstation to the next. Standard work is assigned to each of the balanced workstations. Standard work includes quality inspections at the individual task level. The standard work at each workstation includes an initial inspection of the previous operator's work, the completion of the standard work assigned to the workstation, and then an additional inspection of the work just completed in the primary workstation. By performing three types of standard work, with two being quality inspections, a PPM level of quality can be attained. (Inspections alone cannot achieve a six sigma level of quality, but a five sigma level can be reached from the series of inspections required by the Lean operating system.) The time required to complete inspections is included in the resource balancing activity. Operators therefore always have time to perform the required inspections that are part of their assigned standard work. Every operator assigned to work on a Lean line must be certified. Certification means that before an operator can be assigned to the Lean line, the operator must be able to perform the standard work at three workstations: their primary workstation and one workstation upstream and downstream from their primary workstation.

Defective products in the Lean operating model. If a defect is discovered from the inspection of a product coming from an upstream workstation, the number of defective products will never exceed the number of workstations upstream from where the defect is exposed. When a defect is discovered from inspection of the work just completed at a workstation, the operator is trained to never place the defective unit into the workstation's IPK. The defect must be resolved at the workstation before the unit can be placed in the IPK. Because no unit is placed in the downstream IPK, all work authorizations upstream come to a stop until the cause of the defect is rectified. In the meantime, all downstream workstations will also stop one at a time as their upstream IPKs become empty.

A Lean operating system resolves defects faster. Because IPK rules dictate a defect discovered in the work done at a workstation *cannot* be placed in the workstation's IPK, the discovery of the defect ensures that the unit will be the last one produced with that defect. If the cause of the defect cannot be resolved at the affected workstation within the predetermined rate of the line, the line will stop. Upstream IPKs will fill up with partially completed units causing the entire line upstream from the defect to come to a complete stop. At the same time, work at downstream workstations will also stop because new units will no longer flow downstream. As soon as the Lean line comes to a halt, management's attention is immediately directed to the first workstation with an empty IPK. This workstation is the source of the problem. By not advancing a defective unit into a downstream IPK, an individual operator has the ability to stop the Lean manufacturing line. Once the defect is resolved, the Lean line can begin to flow again defect free. (The learned discipline of not placing a defective unit in an IPK is the same as the concept of *autonomation* in which (1) the abnormality is detected; (2) additional production stops; (3) the immediate problem is corrected; and (4) the root cause is investigated and a counter measure is implemented.)

The Lean operating system limits the number of defects. Because of one-piece-at-a-time production, balanced workstations, IPK-regulated flow, and the IPK discipline component of training for every operator that mandates defective units can never be placed into a workstation's IPK, when a defect does occur, the quantity of at-risk products is limited to only the partially completed units that are in IPK locations upstream from where the defect was discovered. Rework and scrap amounts are therefore reduced, resulting in correspondingly smaller rework and scrap costs.

A Lean operating system improves operator workmanship. The Lean operating system does not rely on inspectors placed throughout the manufacturing process and at the end of the line to test products and fail the defective ones. The Lean operating system requires operators to be responsible for ensuring that defective products never reach a customer. The operator at each workstation in the Lean operating system is responsible for achieving PPM quality levels. Operators accomplish PPM quality levels by completing the standard work assigned to each workstation, one-unit at a time, which includes performing two quality inspections as defined by the standard work content and quality criteria assigned to the workstation. Using the IPK discipline, operators are trained to stop the Lean line by never placing a defective unit of production in a workstation's IPK. The Lean approach to quality is significantly different from a traditional planning system in which isolating defects prior to shipment to a customer is delegated to an inspector at the end of a manufacturing line. Instead of delegating the responsibility for quality assurance to an inspector, operators at each workstation are responsible for ensuring that defective products are never received by a customer.

The advantages of quality at the task level. Manufacturers using the Lean operating system with three types of work at each workstation, two of which are inspections, can expect to receive significant improvement in the quality of workmanship at virtually no additional cost. Inspections are part of the standard work assigned to each workstation in a Lean operating system. When operators are responsible for achieving PPM quality levels, the costs associated with final inspections, and the resulting discoveries of defects that lead to rework and scrap, can be significantly reduced over time as the Lean operating system becomes fully operational. Although Lean theory considers any inspection to be non-value-added work, as a Lean operating system matures and processes become more robust and fail-safe as a result of the implementation of continuous process improvements and kaizen activities, the number of non-value-added inspections can be reduced or eliminated.

The challenges of quality at the task level. Customer demand can decrease on any given day. When customer demand decreases, a Lean line is likely to be staffed with fewer operators than the number of workstations. When this occurs, each operator on the line must be able to move from their primary workstation to another workstation upstream or downstream on the line in response to an empty IPK. This ability to move from one workstation to another is possible only when operators are capable of performing three different types of standard work and the corresponding inspections across three workstations for every possible product produced on the Lean line. Operators must therefore be trained to perform three different types of standard work and the associated inspections at three workstations for every possible product produced on the line. Operators in the Lean operating system are also required to perform this work at a regulated pace. A successful Lean line flows at a prescribed rate that allows sufficient time for operators to complete the three types of work at each workstation. Maintaining this tempo at each workstation requires a new working discipline for all operators on a Lean line. Each operator must rely on the others to be certified to complete their three types of work at their workstation and to fill their IPKs at the measured rate. The requirement to work together each day as a team is a new experience for many operators assigned to a Lean line. The working requirements of a Lean line may be awkward for some operators who are accustomed to working independently at a comfortable speed in an unbalanced workstation.

KANBAN MANAGEMENT OF MATERIALS, ORDERS, AND WORK

Traditional planning systems and the Lean operating system share a similar challenge. Both systems must have a management strategy for bringing component materials together with the standard work required to produce a product.

The traditional planning system approach to materials management. A traditional planning system is an order-based system. The traditional planning system requires a *production order* to be issued to authorize the use of resources to produce a product. Traditional planning methodology also issues a listing of the *component parts* as an addendum to the production order to authorize the usage of the component parts in the manufacturing processes. Common names for this parts listing are bill of materials (BOM), kit list, pick list, or parts list. The listing identifies the component parts, in the required quantities, needed to produce the product (as well as any subassemblies). The production order and the parts listing package is often called a *shop packet*. The parts list is forwarded to a storeroom or warehouse where the component part requirements are filled by their part number identifiers and the quantity per each. The parts are then sent to the point where they will be used for manufacturing the product specified on the production order. The component parts and their BOM listing are then rejoined to the production order where the issued parts are assigned (or *allocated*) to the specific production order. The parts travel together through all of the manufacturing processes listed on the indented BOM until all of them are consumed and production of the product is complete. Barring any changes in the due date, quantity, or the item to be produced, these parts follow the order throughout the manufacturing process. Once the required components parts have been counted out and issued from the stockroom to a manufacturing department, tracking the usage of the parts is required, which includes individual inventory transactions at each point of usage as the parts are consumed. The component parts that travel with the production order represent an inventory investment allocated to the WIP inventory for the entire lead time necessary to complete production of the product. Not only do allocated component parts represent a WIP inventory investment, but these parts are also no longer available for usage by any other production order. If a production priority requires the redirection of these parts for use on another production order (e.g., a new order), reallocation of the parts from the original production order requires the attention of a planner. The planner must manually deallocate the parts from one order and reallocate them to the new production order. The transaction must be recorded in the planning system's database. Once the inventory transaction is completed in the database, the planner must physically move the reallocated parts to the location of the new production order.

The Lean operating system approach to materials management. In the Lean operating system, all finished goods products are deconstructed into two key elements: the work content (the labor and machine resources) and the materials (the component parts). The standard work content and component parts are then managed individually as two separate systems that function independently. This two-system approach to resource management is a major difference from traditional planning systems. The Lean operating system does not require a production order to authorize the use of resources to produce a product. The authorization to produce another product (consume manufacturing resources) is received using an empty IPK. The Lean operating system does not allocate component parts to a production order. The component parts are handled by a materials kanban system. Although component materials are not allocated to a production order in the Lean operating model, the methodology of the *two-bin* materials kanban system does place the component parts listed on the BOM at the location where they will be consumed into the products during production. Throughout the production process, as long as the component materials remain unused on the shop floor, WIP inventory is not increased or decreased. Material in the kanban system is only recorded as usage when it enters the manufacturing area from the stockroom (or is received directly from a supplier) or is packed off the production line as a finished product. Because the management of work content and material components operates as two different systems, materials residing in the materials kanban system are not affected by changes made to a production order, including the standard work content, the measured production rate, the quantity of materials on the BOM (adding or subtracting), the priority of the customer's due date (expediting or pushing out), or cancelled orders.

Inventory and the two-bin kanban. The two-bin kanban uses a simplified methodology for managing inventory investment strategy and turn rate velocity. In a two-bin kanban system, inventory quantities and the resulting working capital investment are based on the number of days of replenishment time assigned to an individual part. Replenishment time is a statement of the time needed to complete the replenishment cycle of a part: going to the point of resupply for the part and returning to its point of usage. The time required to complete a replenishment cycle therefore dictates the amount of available parts and inventory that must be at a workstation to sustain production during the time it takes to complete the replenishment cycle. The more time necessary for the replenishment of a part, the greater the amount of inventory (longer replenishment times = greater inventory costs). Material quantities are therefore calculated to project the amount of material necessary to maintain production volume and to implement an optimum inventory investment and working capital strategy. The amount of inventory investment is controlled by managing the length of replenishment time assigned to a component part. In most cases, using the two-bin materials kanban system results in having a reduced inventory investment and a faster turn rate.

On any shop floor, changes in production orders related to due dates, the quantities of the item to be produced, customer cancellations, and forecast updates are not uncommon. Other commonly occurring changes are related to the reprioritizing of released orders (e.g., customer expedites), shortages of purchased materials prior to production that cause order startup delays, campaigning of production orders beyond the scheduled due-date sequence to achieve productivity goals, unplanned equipment breakdowns, and personnel unavailability (e.g., due to absenteeism, illness, and scheduled vacations).

The traditional planning system approach to order change management. Because a production order and its BOM are linked in a traditional planning system, any change to one impacts the other. When a change occurs in either one, the other must be changed accordingly so both will match. Typically, two separate organizational groups are responsible for making these changes. Synchronous coordination of the information can therefore be problematic. For example, when a production order changes, the planning system must be made aware of the change so that the next MRP net requirements iteration will be accurate and based on the most current information. The planning system must also update the status of released orders. This same information update scenario is required for any changes made to the materials system. If just one organizational group fails to make a timely update, the data necessary for netting the MRP system will be corrupted. Maintaining feedback to a planning system can be a huge undertaking. Significant clerical resources may be required just to keep up with the volume of changes. Typically, a planner (or expeditor) performs the order maintenance function. In some companies, changes are so common that a full-time planner (or multiple planners) is assigned to handle the daily magnitude of changes to ensure that feedback is given to the planning system. All of this activity on the shop floor is required to maintain the integrity of the planning system file. None of it changes the form, fit, or function of the product. The activity helps maintain the accuracy of the planning system, but none of it adds value to the product for the customer.

The Lean operating system approach to order change management. In a materials kanban system, the components parts system operates separately from the production of standard work. Component parts are not allocated to a production order. Instead, they are placed adjacent to the Lean line where they can be used to produce any product in the workstation. Because the kanban system operates as a separate system independent of the production schedule, changes to production orders have little to no effect on the supply of materials to a Lean line. When material needs to be resupplied, the kanban system provides a simple, physical signal that triggers replenishment of materials. This signal is only generated when an individual component has been consumed. The consumption rate of materials therefore parallels the rate of production. No batching of materials is required. The signal for the resupply of materials is an empty container, a card, or an empty space on the shop floor that serves as notification that the material has been consumed and needs to be replenished. When compared to a computer report that is carried around in the hip pocket of a planner, the kanban replenishment signal is a very tangible sign requiring very little interpretation concerning its accuracy. When the planner is confronted with an empty container, there's little doubt that a material needs to be resupplied. Rather than relying on a demand forecast, the kanban system replenishes a material in the same sequence and at the same rate as it was consumed. The Lean operating system does not require component materials to be allocated to a production order. All parts residing at the workstations where they are consumed are available for the production of any product that moves into the workstations. This parts inventory availability feature provides the Lean line with maximum capability to produce any product at a workstation and allows significant flexibility for meeting customer demand without the need for a planner to deallocate or reallocate materials in the planning system. Inventory transactions are greatly reduced. Transactions aren't even required for normal shop floor activity. Maintaining the numerous inventory transactions for component parts required by the traditional planning system isn't required with a kanban system. Transactions are only required when component materials are moved from a warehouse to a point of usage on the shop floor or when finished products are packed off the end of the line. After initial design and setup, a materials kanban system operates itself, requiring little day-to-day management beyond the introduction of new parts and replenishment time maintenance. Although materials kanban systems are compatible with MRP systems, the kanban system is not forward-looking. A kanban system is designed using historical data rather than forecasted data. (MRP systems use an effectivity system to maintain changes in BOMs.) Because the kanban system lacks forward visibility, changes to mix, volume, and the component content requires monitoring and management by a planner or scheduler so the system reflects the current materials profile.

How the Lean operating system handles order changes. It is not unusual for customers to change their minds about the delivery specifications of their products right up to the scheduled production date of their order. They change the delivery date (move it in or out), the SKU (product type), and the mix and quantity of orders (increase or decrease). Until production actually begins on a Lean line, these changes are easily rescheduled. Because labor and materials resources are considered as two separate systems on a Lean line, changing a customer's order poses little to no problem for the line. The resources required to produce a mix of products are already available on a Lean line to produce any product on any day. Accommodating the deletion of one model for another rarely affects the number of resources assigned to the line that day. In addition, because all component parts located at workstations on a Lean line are available for use on the production of any product that moves into the workstations on the line, feedback to the planning system is not required whenever a change in the SKU product type or the production order sequence is required. Changes in the production schedule in response to changing customer requirements are greatly simplified because inventory transactions to deallocate parts from one order and reallocate them to another are not required. The ability to keep parts available for use on any product on any given day provides significant flexibility to meet changing customer orders in a shorter response time. If the priority of an order changes, the operator at the first workstation on a Lean line can begin producing the newly reprioritized order as soon as an IPK signal is received at the workstation. All the first operator on a Lean line has to do is pull the first requirement in the planner's reprioritized sequence of production orders. No interpretation of priority is required by the first operator. Even an order for a customer-configured item can be introduced onto a Lean manufacturing line by simply changing the sequence of production at the first workstation prior to the start of the next unit of production. Based on inventory investment policy, this flexibility is also available to Lean manufacturers even when producing highly configured SKUs.

The traditional planning system approach to work management. In a traditional order-based system, a production order times the start of manufacturing and authorizes the utilization of manufacturing resources (human and material). Start dates and due dates for production orders in a traditional order-based system are established beginning at the SKU level and are scheduled backward using the indented BOM and departmental lead times of the planning system to issue production orders to individual manufacturing departments. All capacity, workload, and customer order priorities are managed by changing the data parameters of a released production order.

The Lean operating system approach to work management. In a Lean operating system, kanban discipline requires a signal to be given by a downstream workstation before the work on another unit of production can be performed. The IPKs on a Lean line time the manufacturing of products by providing a trigger mechanism to authorize the utilization of manufacturing resources to produce another unit of work at workstations. Depending on the type of workstation, the signal could be an empty container, a shelf, or a space on the shop floor sized to fit the unit of production. IPK signaling on a Lean line is a *pull* system. Customer demand *pulls* one unit of production at a time through a series of balanced workstations. For a Lean line to flow one piece at a time at a specified rate, following IPK discipline as an authorization to work (and to expend company resources) is critical. If IPK discipline is violated, the Lean line will cease to flow, compromising the benefits of the Lean operating system. Using IPKs to manage the standard work of products flowing through a set of linked resources on a Lean line is much easier than using a traditional order-based system. An empty IPK authorizes work to begin on another unit of production. The IPKs provide a simple visual technique for prioritizing the work of a Lean manufacturing line, regulating the flow of planned output, and ensuring the quality of the output of the line. The IPK discipline helps to modulate the speed of a Lean line. Once operators are trained to follow IPK discipline, a Lean manufacturing line can operate with little to no management intervention. A Lean line is essentially self-managing.

IPKs simplify prioritizing orders. Determining the priority of customer orders on a Lean line is considerably simplified using IPK discipline. Unlike downstream operators who simply pull a unit from the upstream IPK, the operator at the first (or gateway) workstation on a Lean line does not have an upstream IPK containing a partially completed unit. The operator at the first workstation, however, must know which product is to be produced next. Lean sequencing methodology determines the order of production for the products to be produced each day. In a Lean operating system, only a designated planner (or scheduler) has the authority to establish the priority of production orders. The designated planner is responsible for communicating the production priority of orders to the first operator on the line. Because products are manufactured one unit at a time, products move down the line in the order of priority established by the Lean sequencing methodology. First-in, first-out (FIFO) sequencing at the first workstation ensures that the priority established by the designated planner is maintained throughout all Lean manufacturing processes on the line.

IPKs simplify scheduling. IPK signaling to authorize production of the next unit of product simplifies scheduling routines. Scheduling of all products begins at the first operation on a Lean line. Operators do not need priority or planning information. Rather than developing separate department schedules for multiple manufacturing processes, the number of scheduling points is reduced to one — the gateway workstation. All that is needed for scheduling the daily demand is the *sequence* in which the products are to be produced. The sequence for manufacturing product orders is prioritized by the planner before the line startup every day. The only thing any Lean line operator needs to do is to respond to their downstream IPK when it becomes empty. Upon receipt of an IPK signal, the operator in the gateway workstation pulls the first product in the sequence and places it on the Lean line. Until a product is introduced to the Lean line at the first workstation, remaining customer demand can be resequenced in any way the planner desires.

IPKs simplify subassembly production. Subassemblies are produced in feeder processes and are supplied to the main production line. Production orders do not have to be launched to authorize the consumption of manufacturing resources by feeder processes. A feeder sequence must follow the same sequence as the main line process. Balanced feeder processes work at the same speed as the main production line and follow the same IPK signaling methodology as the main manufacturing line. The output of a feeder process must be consumed directly into a downstream main line process before a subsequent subassembly production is authorized. As with the main manufacturing line, only the sequence of production needs to be known at the first workstation of a feeder process. Once the IPK signal is received by the first workstation of the feeder process, the next unit of subassembly production is produced in the sequence established by the planner.

IPKs simplify expediting. Customers often change their minds after placing orders with a manufacturer. When a production order must be changed, e.g., a change in the delivery date required by the customer, expediting the order is accomplished by simply changing the sequencing priority of the order before it enters the first workstation.

IPKs improve quality. Adherence to IPK discipline regulates the speed at which products move through the manufacturing processes on a Lean line. Adherence to IPK discipline also improves quality of workmanship because a defective unit is never advanced to the next downstream IPK. Should a defect be discovered, the quantity of defective units will be limited to the immediate workstation and workstations upstream to the gateway workstation.

Some final words about the features of the Lean operating system. The operational features of the Lean operating system must be compared with the features of your company's current operating system. Evaluate the value of the time and resources costs expected to be saved from using the Lean operating system. Also evaluate the quality improvements that are received from the Lean operating system. Compare them to the benefits of maintaining the current operating model. Then make the best decision for your company. Override any sense of loyalty to the old, comfortable ways of doing business. In the final analysis, if your decision is to retain the current operating system, at least the potential cost-saving opportunities offered by the Lean system will be known. When all is said and done, it's your company. As a responsible manager, you must do what is best for your company.

REFERENCE

1. George Koenigsaecker, Leadership and the lean transformation, in *Manufacturing Engineering*, November 2005: Vol. 135, No. 5; available at http://findarticles.com/p/articles/mi_qa3618/is_200511/ai_n15847432/.

3

THE LEAN OPERATING SYSTEM: IDENTIFYING THE BENEFITS

No matter what product a company produces, more competitors seem to enter the marketplace every year. Each of these competitors offers some differentiating attribute that sets them apart from your company. The competition for customers is fierce!

Customers are fortunate when they have numerous sources to choose from in the marketplace when buying products. They become quite fickle when making purchasing decisions and show much less loyalty to long-standing, legacy business relationships. They look for (if not expect) more value-added services when selecting suppliers. The value-added services customers look for are the differentials that separate one supplier from another. These *differentials* include shorter order-fulfillment lead times, higher quality, and lower prices.

As greater numbers of configured products with similar features and price are offered by multiple manufacturers, the products begin to approach commodity status. Once a product is designated as a commodity by customers (or perceived to be), product differentiation becomes more and more critical. If your competitors are offering the same great state-of-the-art technology, quality, and price as your technology, quality, and price, then you must develop some other criterion to differentiate your product from their products. There must be some compelling reason for customers to buy your product over another competitor's product! For example, when a customer perceives that there is no difference between products, but expects rapid delivery, the manufacturer with the ability to respond faster than the competition will get that customer's business.

The Lean operating system provides your company with the capability to shorten order-fulfillment lead times and have higher quality with lower prices — the *differentials* that separate one supplier from another.

UNDERSTAND THE MECHANICS, CHALLENGES, AND BENEFITS BEFORE EMBRACING THE LEAN OPERATING SYSTEM

Reading about the Lean operating system in a trade magazine or hearing about Lean manufacturing at a seminar is very interesting. The benefits of operating a factory with Lean principles seem so easy to understand. Visualizing the Lean techniques at work in their factories is very exciting for manufacturing professionals. The arguments for transforming their factories to Lean make perfect sense! Surely, the transformation process will be just as straightforward as the descriptions of the Lean concepts themselves.

It's one thing to read about Lean and visualize the Lean techniques at work in your company, but it is quite another to actually implement Lean techniques in a real factory that has operated successfully for years with a staff of long-term employees who may have no urgency to change the status quo. Even if the benefits of a Lean operating system are significant, a comfort level with the traditional operating system may have set in, leaving the organization with little energy for change along with a prevailing sentiment of *"If it isn't broken, don't fix it."*

Any number of reasons can cause a manufacturer to be motivated to convert their factory to a Lean operating system: to establish differentiation from the competition; to shorten the response time offered to customers; to improve inventory levels and thereby achieve a corresponding reduction in working capital that would allow more competitive pricing; to achieve the enhanced quality created by PPM quality levels; to improve productivity; to have better floor space utilization; to reduce scrap and rework; to have increased employee participation; or to achieve the simplified administrative routines that are available from implementing Lean manufacturing methodologies. Even though the reasons for pursuing a Lean operating system are valid, the motivation to pursue a Lean operating system for many manufacturers may be related to the prevailing pain threshold in the company. Is the pain threshold for retaining the current operation system higher or lower than the pain of needing to improve the performance in manufacturing? Is the pain of continuing to operate with the current system, no matter how dysfunctional the company might be, easier to bear compared to the pain of changing the operating system and the culture in the company?

A Lean operating system strives to produce products in only the sum of their work content time by eliminating all non-value-added time elements. Once the Lean operating system is successful, the manufacturing response time of a product is greatly reduced. When significant improvement in response time occurs in manufacturing departments and manufacturing lead times are shortened, a reduction in the inventories required to support the manufacturing processes will follow. This inventory reduction liberates cash that can be put to use for a multitude of other uses. The newly available cash asset can either be invested or brought to the bottom line. The initial inventory reductions resulting from the first transformation project are a one-time improvement, but because subsequent inventories can be managed at significantly lower levels, the elimination of additional overhead and inventory carrying costs representing ±12 to 20% of the value of the inventory becomes a recurring benefit year after year.

As lead time reductions continue, additional corresponding inventory reductions can be made. In addition, the balancing of standard work in all processes achieved throughout the factory with a Lean operating system continues to drive WIP requirements down. As WIP levels continue to come down and confidence in line capabilities grows, corresponding reductions in FGI levels also occur.

Chapter 2 reviewed the common features of the Lean operating system and outlined how benefits accrue once a Lean system is implemented. It's easy to see why manufacturers who are continually looking for a better system can easily identify with Lean conceptually. It's easy to see why managers are excited by the potential benefits, but managers who conclude that a Lean operating system offers opportunities for significant improvement for their companies must understand that the simple, common-sense Lean concepts will almost always be in *direct conflict* with their current traditional planning system methodologies (electronic or manual). Being excited and enthusiastic about the spectacular benefits of Lean is easy for change agents, too. Enthusiasm is an excellent attribute, but to maintain momentum for transformation of the company to the Lean operating system, change agents must thoroughly understand *how* the individual concepts of Lean compare to current operating methods, *how* the mechanics of the Lean operating system achieves benefits, and *what* the conflicts will be with the methodology of the current operating system. Managers and change agents must be prepared to neutralize resistance — not everyone will be as excited or enthusiastic about changing the existing operating systems as they are today!

Regardless of the most important benefits expected to be received from a Lean transformation of the company, there must be agreement among the management group that the Lean transformation will deliver those benefits. If agreement cannot be attained, passive resistance from non-agreeing managers may result. Although resistance by these managers probably won't be overt, their support won't be either!

The remainder of this chapter will identify benefits of the Lean operating system. It will then provide a method for assessing the strategic benefits, discuss the factors to consider, and provide the business case for considering a transformation to Lean.

IMPROVED MANUFACTURING RESPONSE TIME TO MEET CUSTOMER DEMAND

The most common reason given by manufacturers for implementing a Lean operating system is the desire to reduce long lead times in their factories. Their manufacturing response time for building configured products is exceeding their customer-quoted lead time. The long manufacturing lead times are forcing them to forecast customer demand and final configurations. The traditional planning/order-launched system is relying on alternate strategies so there's a chance they can respond to customers in a time that is close to the customer-quoted lead time. Quantities of raw materials, WIP, and FGI are being maintained in preparation for the receipt of customer orders for configured products. The buffer inventory strategies usually meet customer demand, but they're an expensive solution for achieving customer satisfaction and managing long factory lead times. Labor and machine manufacturing resources are being committed to the production of products in advance of receiving actual customer orders.

How accurate are forecasts of future demand? Ask any manufacturer this question and notice the answer. The typical response is *not very*! Based on this response, consider that the same forecasts of customer demand and final configurations are being used to drive the planning and scheduling systems to authorize the expenditure of manufacturing resources and to develop production schedules. Remember that in traditional systems the lead time of indented BOMs and the resulting start dates for production orders can exceed the MRP planning horizon. Because of BOM lead times, purchase orders must be placed for materials within suppliers' lead times. Any production orders issued to the shop floor for unsold products require the commitment of materials before actual orders are received. They also require the commitment of labor and machine resources. Costly company resources are being invested in the production of products based on a best guess estimate (hopefully customers will eventually buy the products)!

Forecast-driven schedules with predetermined run quantities translate into large batch lots of products being routed through manufacturing. When actual customer demand is received and the mix and volume are not the same as the forecast, resources have been utilized and unsold inventory has been manufactured.

Unsold inventory that cannot be diverted for use in the production of other products is a major cause of increased inventories. Often unsold WIP inventory completes the manufacturing process and winds up in FGI, the most expensive inventory category.

The Lean operating system can shorten manufacturing response time. A Lean factory that can produce products in only the sum of their actual work content time will achieve significantly shorter manufacturing response times (customer-quoted lead time) than competitors who continue to use traditional methods for routing their products through a functional factory. Shorter manufacturing response times allow faster response to customer demand. Shorter manufacturing response times also allow reductions in the amount of FGI and WIP inventories usually carried as a buffer supply to permit a quicker response to customer demand. When the response time through manufacturing is shorter than the current customer-quoted lead time, there is little need to maintain unsold products in a finished goods warehouse. Having the capability to quickly respond to customer demand is a key market differentiator. In a commodity market, the ability of the Lean operating system to deliver products faster ultimately leads to an increase in market share from customers who have the fastest response time as their primary criteria for making purchasing decisions. When all other product attributes in a market are the same, offering a differential that your competitors do not will increase your company's business with the customers that desire that differential.

Although reducing long lead times is almost universally stated as the number one goal of a Lean business transformation, the Lean operating system has other benefits that may be appealing to manufacturers based on their particular manufacturing opportunities. Sometimes in the urgency to respond to a specific issue such as reducing lead time, in the rush to obtain relief, little thought is given to the other improvements usually received as a result of transforming a factory to a Lean operating system. When received, these unexpected benefits are always a pleasant surprise!

LOWER INVENTORY LEVELS

Over time, various inventory strategies have evolved to accommodate the time gap between the customer-quoted lead time and the actual manufacturing response time. For example, building to a partial level of completion through the common levels of the BOM and then finishing the assembly with additional configurable materials based on the receipt of actual customer demand is a common strategy. Purchasing the necessary component parts inventory based on a forecasted projection of the final configurations customers are likely or expected to order is another inventory strategy used to rapidly respond to customer demand. These historical strategies for meeting unplanned customer demand by building to a partial level of completion or building to a forecasted projection concentrate on improving existing WIP and FGI models. In either strategy, if customers fail to purchase the partially built units or the forecasted configurations, then the result is excess, slow-moving, or obsolete part inventories. Regardless of the chosen strategy, an investment in inventory is always required to make the strategy work. The costs associated with these buffer inventory models can be enormous.

In addition to the component materials consumed by unsold inventory, machine and labor manufacturing resources have been consumed by building products before customers have even committed to purchasing them! If the demand estimates are wrong, then resources that cannot be retrieved have been consumed by unsold inventory that winds up in a warehouse.

Customer-quoted lead time establishes inventory policy. Customer-quoted lead time is the delivery time quoted to a customer when the customer first places a sales order with a manufacturer and no product inventory is available to immediately fulfill the customer's order. The customer-quoted lead time states the lead time required to produce the product from the first level in the indented BOM to the final product at the SKU level. Customer-quoted lead time significantly impacts a company's inventory policy. Generally, the number of days of WIP and FGI inventory maintained is equal to the number of customer-quoted lead time days. The length of the customer-quoted lead time therefore establishes the company's inventory policy — 1 day of inventory is kept in WIP and 1 day of inventory is kept in FGI for each day of customer-quoted lead time. If the customer-quoted lead time is unacceptable to a customer, WIP and FGI inventories are relied upon to compensate for the delivery gap between CQLT and actual manufacturing response time.

The Lean operating system can reduce inventory levels. Because manufacturing response time is reduced by the Lean operating system, the reasons that justify maintaining large amounts of WIP as a mechanism for rapid response are no longer valid. The amount of inventory reduction possible is directly proportional to the length of manufacturing response time. Figure 3.1 illustrates how WIP inventory is impacted by manufacturing response time. Manufacturing response time is the minimum time required to move product through a series of manufacturing processes. If manufacturing response time is less than the customer's expectation of delivery, is keeping any WIP or FGI as a buffer even necessary? In a Lean facility, manufacturing resources are not committed to produce a product until a customer commits to purchasing the product. Lean manufacturers

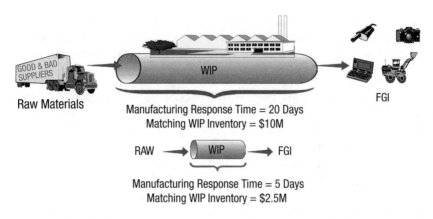

Figure 3.1. Shorter response time means less WIP and less working capital requirements.

continue to reduce the manufacturing response time by having a never-ending goal of making the manufacturing lead time less than customer-quoted lead time.

SMALLER WORKING CAPITAL REQUIREMENTS

Customers expect orders to be shipped within the standard customer-quoted lead time. When the manufacturing lead time is greater than a customer's delivery expectations, customer satisfaction can be adversely impacted. When manufacturing lead time is greater than the customer-quoted lead time, alternative strategies can be used to meet customer demand on time. Some of these alternative strategies include:

- Tell the customer the manufacturing lead time must be accepted *as is*. This solution works if the company has no competition or the company is the only supplier of the product.
- Build WIP inventories of partially completed assemblies or subassemblies that can be fully assembled into a final configuration quickly once an actual customer order is received. WIP items can be converted into finished products in a shorter lead time than the normal customer-quoted lead time. The mix and volume of products to be kept in an incomplete form in WIP, however, might be unpredictable. Keeping WIP inventories can be an expensive solution for rapid delivery of customer demand.
- Ship products from FGIs. Maintaining products in FGI that have been completed in advance of receiving orders is a solution that works well if the products are generic and the order patterns are

predictable, but if products are custom-configured or designed-to-order, the proliferation of models that must be kept in the FGI as a buffer inventory used for rapid response can be a very expensive solution.

The Lean operating system has a strategy for reducing customer-quoted lead time. In a Lean operating system, only the materials needed for the most frequently produced products are purchased. Specialized component parts are not ordered from suppliers until the receipt of a customer's order. The final product configuration must also be known. A highly configured SKU is never produced until actual customer demand for that SKU is in hand. Certain customers will be unwilling to accept the manufacturing lead time plus the supplier lead time needed for receipt of specialized parts needed for their orders. The Lean alternative strategy for these customers is to estimate their needs for highly configured products and then keep the component parts on hand as *raw material only* in anticipation of receiving their orders. These components are maintained in the lowest-cost inventory available to the manufacturer — the raw materials stockroom. Except for the rarest of configurations, the response to most special configurations will be based on the time required to install the specialized components. The amount of inventory kept as raw material is managed to balance response time with inventory investment. Supplier delivery lead time dictates the on-hand quantities of purchased materials to be kept in inventory for this parts inventory strategy.

On-hand inventory affects working capital requirements. Regardless of the strategy chosen to reduce customer-quoted lead time, a manufacturer must determine the appropriate amount of inventory to be maintained to maximize customer satisfaction. Any amount of inventory kept on hand through any stage of completion has an effect on working capital requirements. Working capital requirements can be calculated:

> Working capital = raw materials + WIP + FGI + accounts receivable
> – accounts payable (material purchases)

Cash is typically invested in purchased inventory in the following ways:

- If suppliers expect payment in 30 days (N30), then paid-for purchased materials reside in a stockroom for 30 days before work begins in manufacturing. Inventory older than 30 days represents a cash investment.
- If manufacturing conversion takes 4 weeks, then cash is committed another 4 weeks to support the WIP as it moves through manufacturing.
- If FGI levels are 3 to 4 weeks, then cash is committed for an additional 3 to 4 weeks.

- If invoices are not paid by customers immediately after products have been shipped, then cash is committed to sold, but unpaid-for inventory even longer.

In this typical inventory investment example, cash has been committed for at least 12 to 13 weeks, resulting in an inventory turn rate of four. A working capital requirement of 25¢ for every $1 shipped in revenue is necessary to support this level of committed paid-for inventories. Larger inventory levels require proportionately larger monetary investments. Large inventories not only impact working capital requirements, but they also require space on the shop floor and in warehouses and distribution centers. This space is not without cost. It adds to the overhead costs of doing business. The financial implications can be significant. The trade-off between achieving on-time customer delivery goals and maintaining ideal inventory levels will likely be the subject of much debate. Always carefully consider the amount of inventory to be kept on hand to implement a specific customer-satisfaction strategy.

The Lean operating system reduces working capital requirements. By reducing response time, a Lean manufacturing line can reduce the capital investment required to operate the company. Although reduced response time is a direct benefit for customers, reduced response time through manufacturing also means less company monies are committed to financing buffer inventories. Cash is liberated that can be used for any number of other purposes or brought to the bottom line. Reduced inventories also eliminate additional overhead and inventory carrying costs that can represent ±12 to 20% of the value of the inventories. Inventory reductions resulting from a Lean business transformation are not just a one-time occurrence. Remaining inventories can be managed at significantly lower levels on an ongoing basis.

SIMPLIFIED MANAGEMENT

A key benefit of the Lean operating system is the ability of managers to manage by walking around (MBWA). The attributes of the Lean line make spotting problems easy. By simply walking through a Lean manufacturing facility, managers can easily see what's going on. Supervisory requirements are diminished by the factory layout. Operators working on the Lean line are trained. They are certified to perform the standard work at their workstations. They are also trained to be flexible by moving to other workstations to complete work. They know how to respond to IPK signals. Consequently, they know what to do and when to do it. The one-unit-at-a-time flow of products on the Lean line always indicates the status of the line.

Organization and discipline are important elements in a Lean working environment. A Lean business transformation project supports the simultaneous implementation of the 5S principles. All material locations are clearly marked and maintained. Only the necessary tools, fixtures, gauges, and other resources are located at workstations. Clutter and poor housekeeping habits are not tolerated on a Lean line. Operators are responsible for maintaining their workstations. Time is provided each day to manage workstations. Workstations are organized and operational for the next shift or the next day.

The Lean line is designed to follow the process flow of a product. Reliance on output from a shop floor control system to determine the location or the progress of an order is greatly reduced or completely unnecessary. Each day sequencing boards at the beginning of the line and at feeder processes clearly communicate the product mix to be built that day. At the end of the line, a linearity measurement is kept and the flow rate is posted indicating how the line is doing so far that day. The kanban system indicates how fast material is turning and highlights any potential shortages. At the end of the day, operator flexibility and the IPKs at each workstation will reveal if the line was under- or overstaffed.

In a Lean factory, products are manufactured sequentially and accumulate standard work from each workstation as the unit moves progressively from workstation to workstation until it is completed. *One* is the unit of measure being transferred between workstations. No space is allocated for WIP to accumulate. Accumulation of semi-finished products between workstations is limited to the total number of IPKs on the line. Because of IPK discipline, piles of WIP inventory cannot build up.

Flowing product down a Lean line does not require or advocate assigning operators to a particular workstations or a machine. Operators can be intentionally added to or removed from the line to throttle the line up or down in response to daily customer order requirements.

A variety of different product configurations can be built at any point in time on a mixed-model Lean manufacturing line. If the mixed-product line needs to operate with less than a full complement of human resources, operators will move (or *flex*) from workstation to workstation to achieve the planned daily rate. Flexible, cross-trained operators are the key for achieving productivity in a Lean manufacturing environment.

Because the standard work at each workstation has been balanced, operators on a Lean line are not required to walk along with a unit being produced on a moving line or rush through their work just to keep up. Instead, they are instructed to take the appropriate time necessary to ensure that the unit transferred to the next downstream workstation contains the standard amount of work assigned to their workstation and meets the quality standards defined by the standard work definition. Workmanship quality is greatly enhanced because the time necessary to perform quality inspection work is allowed at each workstation for every product.

Job satisfaction is an intrinsic value for operators working on a Lean line. Operators are required to receive extensive training to perform the standard work assigned to a variety of workstations. They are required to flex up and down to different workstations in response to IPK signals. Operator input and expertise about product production are actively sought during process improvement projects. Operator feedback to production management is encouraged daily. Operator feedback results in improvements being made to the manufacturing process. Operators are encouraged to participate in kaizen activities that focus on a specific reduction in a non-value-adding activity. Operators on a Lean line are highly motivated to complete their work in the assigned time and at the rate designed for the line. Their knowledge of the Lean line's daily goals and production rate helps to promote self-management of the line and reduces the need for constant supervision.

IMPROVED PRODUCTIVITY

Comparing the actual production time of units produced by a manufacturing team with the engineered standard time needed to produce those units is generally accepted as the measurement of a factory's productivity. Improving productivity is not a primary goal for a Lean manufacturer, but the Lean manufacturing methods do cause process improvements that result in increased productivity. Formal improvement strategies such as kaizen often focus on one process at a time in the current manufacturing processes to achieve incremental reductions of wait time, queue time, and other non-value-adding activities. By eliminating wasteful time elements embedded in current manufacturing processes, operators have more available time to actually perform standard work at their workstations. As an example, consider materials handling. Operators on a Lean manufacturing line do not perform material handling activities. These activities are assigned to professional materials-handling personnel. By being able to concentrate only on improving the flow of the products through the facility in only the sum of their work content time, the productivity of operators improves. Productivity improvement is an ancillary benefit of eliminating the non-value-adding time embedded in manufacturing processes!

OPERATIONAL IMPROVEMENTS

By using linked processes and the IPK system, subassembly production planning can virtually be eliminated. Over time, as feeder processes are established on the Lean line, multilevel BOMs can be dramatically compressed or flattened. Lean line output is managed by simply changing staffing (adding or subtracting) on the line to match the required daily production rate. Lean manufacturers drive the production planning process by using a make-to-order production schedule instead of committing manufacturing resources to forecasted demand. On a daily basis, actual customer orders are used to determine the headcount of required labor resources for the production process that day.

The implementation of Lean manufacturing methods and ongoing maturation of the Lean line provides opportunities for simplifying cost accounting methods. As lead time through the facility becomes more consistent, repeatable, and insensitive to volume changes, less complicated, activity-based costing methodologies can be used. Labor costs can be rolled into overhead and applied proportionally to each product based on the number of hours the product spends in the factory absorbing overhead. Unusual, variable overhead costs can be created to account for extraordinary conversion costs driven by the use of special machines or resources.

Because customer demand and corporate mandates increase daily, traditional manufacturing companies are always seeking a better way to meet them. This quest for a better way has caused many Fortune 500 companies to embrace Lean manufacturing strategies to meet the demands of the new e-business economy of the last decade. Meeting corporate mandates for increased profitability, faster delivery times, and lower working capital investment has caused manufacturing management to implement Lean techniques in their constant search to reduce manufacturing lead time, increase capacity, decrease cost, eliminate waste, and reduce working capital requirements. Lean manufacturing is a proven technique. Linking and balancing work processes to enable products to flow one unit at a time through manufacturing results in significant improvements in manufacturing processes. Even though the products might vary in volume, type, and mix, the fundamental Lean techniques always remain the same. By using a basic set of methodologies, Lean manufacturing lines create an optimum flow for any product and production material.

ASSESS THE STRATEGIC BENEFITS

Profit is the measure of successful performance. All companies, whether service- or manufacturing-oriented, are in business to be profitable. The more profitable a company is, the more successful it is. To facilitate survival in the marketplace, management at a successful company constantly looks for ways to gain a larger percentage of the market, to improve the company's profits, and to be accountable to the company's stakeholders (i.e., successful).

Do not undertake a business transformation to a Lean operating system as a program of the month or a trendy, academic exercise! Any manufacturer considering a Lean business transformation should first answer an extremely important two-part question: *what are the specific benefits of a Lean operating system to the company* and *do those benefits justify the business transformation costs*? In other words, is the financial investment of time and human resources and the impact on the culture of the company worth the benefits to be gained from changing the existing operating system?

Likely everyone in the company will have an opinion about the benefits the Lean operating system could offer and the value of changing the current operating system. Of everyone, the Lean business transformation change agent will likely have the strongest opinion about the merits of change, albeit, the least objective one! Expressing opinions and asking questions about the Lean operating system does not necessarily indicate signs of resistance! Asking questions is a valid part of the consideration process. Asking questions indicates interest. Valid questions deserve answers. The people asking questions need answers to assist them in making an informed business decision. Determine your answers as objectively as possible. They must come from an honest assessment of the benefits the company can expect to receive. They must represent your best estimate of the return on investment in financial terms when the benefits are compared to the costs of a Lean business transformation.

Remember: No one wants to be in the 22% group of manufacturers who are dissatisfied with their Lean transformation initatives![1] Every company is unique. Every company has systems that are strong and others that are weak. Every company has different needs and expectations from a Lean business transformation.

Conduct a Strategic Business Assessment

When considering a Lean business transformation, the first undertaking should be conducting a strategic business assessment (SBA) to determine the company's needs and a realistic estimate of the financial benefits to be expected from the transformation. An SBA is an objective, in-depth analysis of current conditions in the company. By using existing performance measures provided in the SBA, goals for improvement can be established and estimates of the benefits to be achieved by the Lean transformation can be made. You may discover that a Lean business transformation in a particular area will *not* yield the magnitude of expected financial benefits. This finding indicates the company performing well in that area.

Even if you determine that a certain area will not benefit from a Lean transformation, the SBA can help direct your attention to other areas that are responsible for poor performance in the company.

Besides providing the expected benefits of the Lean transformation in financial terms, the performance measures of the current operating system recorded in the SBA provide baseline measurements that can be used to develop KPIs (key performance indicators). Should the business transformation go forward, these KPIs will be important for measuring the success of the Lean implementation. They can also be used for measuring results in the key performance areas where improvements from the Lean business transformation are expected to be made.

When the SBA has been completed and the results have been agreed upon by the transformation team, the transformation team can reach a valuable consensus regarding the expected benefits to be achieved from the Lean business transformation. This consensus then becomes the basis for gaining support from the management team. Support by the management team is critical if resistance to change occurs or conflicting objectives arise.

Use a Template to Prepare the Strategic Business Assessment

The SBA template should include a brief description of the expected benefits from the Lean transformation project for each performance area, e.g., lead time, inventory, supplier issues, customer demand (sales), etc. When possible, state the financial benefits in monetary terms. Quality-of-life benefits or differential benefits are difficult to quantify in financial terms. Even if these benefits cannot be quantified in financial terms, they should still be included. The benefits can be significant. State other benefits in units of measure consistent with the problem statement, e.g., from 2 days to 1 day.

- *In the first column:* Under each heading, list the individual KPIs.
- *In the second column:* Record the current-state metric (the actual condition today). The current-state metric then becomes the baseline against which all future progress will be measured in each performance area.
- *In the third column:* For purposes of estimating the benefits, state the KPI goal measurement. For example, for lead time, if lead time today is 20 days, but a competitor's lead time is 10 days, then the goal of the company is to create a differential over the competitor by having a lead time shorter than 10 days. By adding the actual work content times of your product together, your new lead time expectation from the Lean transformation is estimated to be 7 days.

Your estimate cannot be a wish or a wild guess. It must be obtained by adding the sums of the actual standard work content time for each process. Ignore the stated lead time recorded on the indented BOM. Producing products in the sum of their work content time is now the goal of a Lean line.

- ***In the fourth column:*** Record the best estimate of the costs of the current-state metric of the KPI in a performance area. Use the number of days × the 1-day average cost of inventory. Using the same mathematical formula, calculate the savings realized using the goal number of days.
- ***In the last column:*** Subtract the estimated savings realized by the new Lean goal from the cost of the current state metric. The difference is the expected benefit.

When the benefits from each performance area are summed together, the total financial benefit from the Lean transformation can be projected — which is a statement of expectations after the initial Lean transformation is completed.

Complete the Strategic Business Assessment

The resources required to complete the SBA will vary depending on the size of the facility and the number of products and processes. Do not rush the preparation of the SBA. Preparation will require gathering quantitative and qualitative information about the company, the products, the processes, and the customer demand. This information will be obtained from interviews with functional subject matter experts who have the best knowledge on the subject for which benefits are being estimated. In addition to quantitative and qualitative information, also gather subjective information about manufacturing, the administrative systems, and the organization in general. What are the current political issues in the company? Is there competition in the marketplace? Are forthcoming technological changes planned? What is the level of dedication in the company to the success of the Lean project? Is there willingness in the company to make changes?

Construct the SBA as objectively as possible. Use due diligence and extreme thoroughness. Obtaining input from the entire company is essential. Accurately assessing the environment, enthusiasm, and commitment in the company for a Lean project is extremely important. The SBA should be a scientific, conservative business assessment that is designed to *best estimate* the benefits to be received by the company. Although information gathered for the SBA may be general information that is required to estimate the benefits in other areas, always gain consensus about any projected benefits from the person in the organization who is responsible for that performance measurement. Do not exaggerate facts. Intentionally embellishing the facts to gain support for a Lean business transformation is misleading and counterproductive. The potential benefits of a Lean transformation can be confidently stated from an accurately completed SBA. Overstating the potential benefits can ultimately deflate the true value of actual received benefits. (Even your career can be damaged by overestimating the benefits of a Lean transformation and then underdelivering them.) Typically, a successful Lean business transformation yields benefits that exceed the original expectations — which makes inflating benefits unnecessary.

If you have been designated as the Lean change agent for your company and are enthusiastic about implementing Lean in your facility, avoid the temptation to overstate the potential benefits simply to justify a Lean transformation. If the SBA is used as a lever to begin a long-anticipated pet project or to fulfill some other hidden agenda and the results do not meet the stated expectations in the SBA, the Lean transformation project will be considered a failure. The exaggerated SBA then becomes your scorecard for failure. Another unfortunate consequence is being lumped into the 22% group claiming to be unhappy with their Lean initiatives.[1] Based on this failed experience, future attempts to begin subsequent Lean projects may be rejected.

If your company is not prepared to make the necessary changes required by a Lean operating system by challenging the three paradigms of traditional manufacturing systems or the return on investment from the benefits provided by the SBA do not justify the project, then achieving a Lean business transformation will be very difficult. Even if the SBA projects a great return on investment, without the commitment of the entire organization to make the necessary changes, the Lean business transformation will be constantly challenged by those who prefer to retain the status quo. Resistance to change will likely manifest itself in subversion, withholding of information, lack of cooperation, and even outright hostility. Sometimes compromises mandated by a Lean business transformation become contentious. Resistance and compromising can negatively impact projected benefits. Strict adherence to the Lean operating system methods delivers the greatest benefits. As a change agent, be prepared to defend, explain, educate, and reconcile differences and document the impact of any compromise on the projected benefits stated in the SBA. Your best efforts will be required to achieve the optimum results from a business transformation. *Remember*: In the end, as the designated change agent, you are accountable for the success or failure of the Lean transformation.

Table 3.1. The Top Three Business Issues

	Issue
1	Sales group takes too many orders for nonstandard product configurations, causing an increase in factory expediting for the sales group based on quantity with no reward system for sale of standard product.
2	Distribution channel requires consigned FGI to reside in showrooms, causing working capital to be invested too long.
3	Customer order administration and credit approval processes take longer time than the actual manufacturing process.

Table 3.2. Current Sales Facts

Annual Revenue: $75,000,000			
SKUs	250	Daily Rates	400/Day
Product Families	6	Seasonality	May-June/October-November
Shipping Volumes	100,000 Annually	Production Lines	6

USE THE STRATEGIC BENEFITS ASSESSMENT TO MAKE THE BUSINESS CASE FOR A LEAN TRANSFORMATION

Lean methodologies address numerous issues. Typical issues often considered for resolution or improvement with a Lean business transformation include the business areas; sales volume; lead time; labor, inventory, and quality costs; space utilization in manufacturing; processes in manufacturing; supplier management; and customer satisfaction.

Business areas. To improve the company's performance, address three business areas: the sales force, the distribution channel, and customer order administration (Table 3.1). Resolution of issues in these three areas should be a goal of any Lean business transformation. Unresolved issues in these areas will impede, if not stop, advancement to the next level of competitiveness. By listing business issues in your company that must be resolved to improve sales, market share, and profitability, each can then be addressed by using Lean techniques.

Sales volume. Table 3.2 states current facts about the sales volume. Identify product statistics defining the product mix and volume and the current distribution of product variety. Knowing the existing product family makeup and the number of production lines required to produce the current sales volume will be important for designing the future factory. This information will be used later in Lean line design activities to make decisions about future sales volumes, product families, and production rates. Estimate the potential sales volume increase based on the percentage of sales increase expected once the lead time goals of the Lean line are met.

Table 3.3. Current Lead Times in Days and the Reduced Lead Time from a Lean Transformation

	Current	After Lean	Benefit
Order Request to Ship	20	7	13
Elements of Lead Time			
Backlog	5	1	4
Administrative	2	1	1
Process	10	2	8
Inventory	1	1	0
Transportation	2	2	0

Table 3.4. Current Headcount and Compensation Costs

1	Direct Labor Headcount	150 Full Time, 25 Temporary, and 25 Seasonal
2	Annual Compensation	Average Annual Wage = $37,500,
2A	Benefits (%)	with 28.5% Benefit Package
3	Total Compensation	$8,995,000
4	Union	No
5	Overtime (%)	10% = $1,349,250

Lead time. Lead time reduction is the most often-stated goal of a Lean transformation. Usually a Lean transformation project begins on the shop floor because this is where the greatest benefits can be found. In Table 3.3, the process time of 10 days is the longest component of total lead time. This lead time can be reduced by identifying the non-value-added times embedded in the total time and then eliminating them by using Lean techniques. By subtracting the actual work content time of the sum of all processes for a product from the current customer-quoted lead time, the opportunity for lead time improvement can be estimated. The gap in time provides the opportunity for lead time reduction from a Lean operating system. After the initial Lean transformation, conducting continuous improvement activities and future kaizen projects can continue to reduce lead times in administrative and other processes (see Chapter 11).

Labor costs. Table 3.4 states the current headcount and compensation costs. Compensation is based on the average annual wage or salary paid. The overtime differential is the average wage × 1.5%. This information will be used to compare current labor costs with the potential savings to be gained through productivity improvement. Although labor productivity is not a primary goal of a Lean transformation, savings can be expected from having flexible labor resources on a Lean factory floor. Productivity is hard to estimate until the actual amount of standard work can be identified. Before a Lean transformation, labor performs many non-

Table 3.5. Target Days of Inventory, Inventory Valuation, Turn Rates, and Inventory Mix Before and After a Lean Transformation for a Company with Sales of $75,000,000

	FGI	WIP	Raw	Total
Current	10	21	30	61
After Lean	5	5	30	40
Future Lean Low	1	3	15	19
Initial Reduction Target Levels				
From	16%	35%	49%	
To	13%	13%	75%	
Inventory Valuation				
Current	$986,300	$2,071,230	$2,958,900	$6,016,430
After Lean	$493,150	$493,150	$2,958,900	$3,945,200
Future Lean Low	$98,360	$295,890	$1,479,150	$1,873,970
Cost to Carry	$11,836	$35,507	$177,534	$224,876
Turn Rates				
Material COG	$5,760,000	$12,600,000	$17,640,000	$36,000,000
Average Inventory	$956,300	$2,071,230	$2,958,900	$6,016,430
Inventory Mix Target (% of Total Inventory)				
Before Lean	16%	35%	49%	
After Lean	13%	13%	75%	

value-added activities that have been embedded into the traditional planning system model. Even though the time and money to be saved from improved productivity is difficult to state in definitive terms, a conservative estimate of a 1 to 2% savings is a safe projection. The goal for reduction of overtime costs should be 100%, but estimating a 50% reduction is a conservative, safe prediction. Savings estimates at even this level can return significant benefits for the company. When the Lean line is designed to meet customer future demand, there should be no reason for needing persistent overtime just to keep up with productivity goals.

Inventory costs. Inventory reduction and reducing the working capital costs related to maintaining inventories provide some of the greatest expected monetary benefits from a Lean transformation. Days of inventory are determined by current manufacturing lead time in each category. The number of days of inventory by category typically matches the number of days of lead time in each category. For example, if manufacturing response time is 21 days, WIP inventory will also be 21 days. Each day of lead time is supported by a day of inventory. Evaluate the impact of inventory costs and the opportunities for reduction of the current inventory distribution by category. The initial Lean transformation

Table 3.6. Costs of Poor Quality

	Current	After Lean	Improvement	Benefit
First Pass Yield	85%	99%	16%@400/Day	Rework and Scrap
Internal Costs				
Rework				
Workmanship	$40,000	$10,000	75%	$30,000
Process	$7,500	$3,750	50%	$3,750
Supplier Related	$15,000	$7,500	50%	$7,500
Scrap				
Workmanship	$10,000	$2,000	80%	$8,000
Process	$2,500	$1,250	50%	$1,250
Infant Mortality	$12,500	$2,000	85%	$10,500
External Costs				
Warranties	$12,500	$2,000	85%	$10,500
Brand Loyalty Loss	$50,000	$10,000	80%	$40,000

will target inventory reduction in WIP and FGI because Lean reduces lead time in those areas first. (Raw material inventory is not considered during the initial Lean transformation effort. Raw material inventories can only be reduced by the implementation of a supplier partnership program. When a supplier partnership program is implemented at a later time, inventory savings in the raw materials category can be estimated.) The example in Table 3.5 is for a company with total sales of $75,000,000 – profit before taxes (20%) = cost of goods sold (COGS) = $60,000,000 × average material cost = 60% = material cost of $36,000,000 ÷ 365 days per year = average daily cost of 1 day of inventory:

- Daily cost of inventory = days of inventory × average daily cost of inventory
- Annual cost to carry savings = 12%

Substitute actual numbers from your company to estimate the financial impact for your company of reducing lead time.

Quality costs. Table 3.6 states the costs incurred from dealing with the results of poor quality. These costs fall into two cost categories: internal and external. Include the following in your estimate of the costs related to poor quality:

- End-of-the-line failures of attributes before shipment to a customer
- Infant mortality (product failures during the first 2 weeks of service)
- Warranty costs for the product
- Brand loyalty changes by customers

Table 3.7. High-Volume Suppliers: Typical Issues

	Aluminum Inc. Los Angeles	Electronics Inc. Austin	Motors R Us Inc. Miami	Tube & Bar Co. Pittsburg
Typical Lead Time	60 days	30 days	30 days	20 days
Longest Lead Time	75 days	45 days	60 days	30 days
Target Lead Time	30 days	15 days	20 days	10 days
Desired Lead Time	10 days	5 days	10 days	2 days
On-Time Delivery	80%	75%	80%	95%
Quality	90%	90%	80%	99%
Issue	Market Price Dictates Delivery	Small-Volume Company	Transportation	Specialty Products

A Lean operating system directly impacts internal costs caused by poor quality. Workmanship errors caused by operators in the company can be reduced by using Lean techniques. Historically, a 75% reduction of operator workmanship defects has been possible by performing inspections at the individual task level, the level where defects occur. This reduction in workmanship errors is accomplished by using the IPK signaling system and the discipline of never placing a defective unit in the IPK. In a Lean operating system, operators are required to perform three types of work each time they produce the standard work assigned to a workstation. The three-inspection technique required by Lean manufacturing yields a 5 sigma level of quality of approximately 27 defects per 1 million. Improvements in workmanship quality reduce rework and scrap. The Lean operating system has little impact on external factors, such as defects received from a supplier or defects resulting from poor product design. External quality problems can be addressed later by the implementation of a supplier certification program. A supplier certification program can reduce supplier-related quality costs by reconciling buyer/seller specifications and validating suppliers' processes for reliability and repetitiveness.

High-volume suppliers. Identify suppliers from whom the largest volumes are purchased. Volume can be defined by the number of pieces purchased or the amount of annual expenditure. An 80/20 analysis (Pareto analysis) based on purchase price or historical volume purchased can be used to identify the largest-volume suppliers. Identify a realistic desired lead time that reflects a minimum inventory investment. List any supply issues with these suppliers. Table 3.7 lists typical supplier issues. Elimination of these issues should become the goal of a supplier partnership program. Even though supplier certification is a longer-term goal than the typical goals of an initial Lean business transformation project,

Table 3.8. Most Difficult Suppliers: Typical Issues

	Motors R Us Inc. Miami	Lifetime Gear Inc. Kansas City	India Valve Ltd. Delhi
Typical Lead Time	30 days	60 days	45 days
Longest Lead Time	60 days	90 days	75 days
Target Lead Time	20 days	30 days	30 days
Desired Lead Time	10 days	15 days	10 days
On-Time Delivery	80%	75%	90%
Quality	80%	95%	75%
Issue	Plant Distance and Poor Quality	Supply Chain Logistics	Sole Supplier

having dependable, reliable suppliers is critical for the successful operation of a Lean system. When a supplier is certified as dependable and reliable, the amount of replenishment time used for the kanban system can be reduced, creating a reduced need for inventory. A supplier may also be able to bypass stockrooms and replenish materials directly into a Lean manufacturing RIP (raw and in-process) inventory area.

Problematic suppliers. Suppliers in this category might not be high-volume suppliers, but when trying to achieve manufacturing consistency, unreliable suppliers can be the cause of most of the problems. They also might not be very helpful in resolving identified issues. Dealing with problematic suppliers increases costs. The very expensive remedy of keeping excess inventory balances may be the only solution to compensate for their poor quality or poor delivery performance issues (Table 3.8). An initial Lean transformation project might not require resolving difficult supplier issues, but issues with unreliable suppliers will eventually have a negative impact on the performance of the Lean line as well as on the key performance measurements of working capital and inventory.

Supplier management opportunities. Table 3.9 describes three supplier issues, their current-state costs, and the benefits of improving them for a sample company. What top three issues caused by suppliers create recurring problems for your manufacturing group? What specific performance areas need to be improved by these suppliers? Are new suppliers more responsive to your company's needs? Individual suppliers do not need to be specifically identified, but estimating the costs incurred each time one of these issues recurs is important.

Manufacturing utilization of floor space. When Lean manufacturing lines are balanced and linked, less floor space is required for the storage of WIP materials. Unused space has little value, but the benefits of liberated factory shop floor

Table 3.9. Supplier Management Opportunities: Top Three Supplier Issues, Their Costs, and the Benefits from Improving Them

	Opportunity	Cost of Current State	Benefit If Improved
1	On-time delivery performance of sole supplier's deliveries is at 80%.	1-hr line shutdown = $300 last month Performance cost = 10 hours	Downtime reduced by 50%
2	A key component of product is subject to wide swings in price from suppliers.	Commitments to customer product pricing suffer, causing profit loss	Profit improvement by 25%
3	Quality of critical components is poor.	Line shutdown and rework = $25,000/ month	Line shutdown reduced by 75%

Table 3.10. Benefits of Better Floor Space Utilization

	Current	After Lean	Reduction	Benefit
Total Plant	100,000 sq ft	90,000 sq ft	10%	New Product Introduction
Target Area	25,000 sq ft	18,000 sq ft	28%	Plant Expansion

space will soon be appreciated when space is available to introduce new product lines and processes into an established factory without incurring the costs of new construction. A Lean manufacturer who is growing can delay capital expansion for building or leasing a new facility by using existing unused shop floor space (Table 3.10).

Manufacturing process opportunities. Table 3.11 describes three process opportunities, their current-state costs, and the benefits of improving them for a sample company. Using historical information and professional observation, document the three most important improvement opportunities for your manufacturing processes. Although chances are good that you can easily identify many process improvement opportunities, in the beginning, choose only three that have significant costs associated with them. No one likes to be surprised by hearing their area is on a problem list. Meet with knowledgeable persons who have specialized experience in each opportunity area. Record their input. Be certain you have as much information as possible about problems in their areas. Then estimate the benefits you expect when processes in their areas are improved and review the Lean solutions for each problem area with them. Use this review as an opportunity to develop allies for the Lean operating system.

Customer satisfaction opportunities. Table 3.12 lists three typical customer satisfaction opportunities. Based on feedback, list the top three issues causing customer dissatisfaction in your company. These customer dissatisfaction issues

Table 3.11. Manufacturing Management Opportunities: Top Three Process Opportunities, Their Costs, and the Benefits from Improving Them

	Opportunity	Cost of Current State	Benefit If Improved
1	Outside epoxy painting process is used.	Adds 6 days to manufacturing lead time causing market share loss	Increased market share with shorter lead time
2	First-pass workmanship quality defects are excessive.	10% × 200 units per day = 20 units at a rework cost of $50 = $1000/day	Rework reduced to 1% = $900/day savings
3	Excess WIP inventories consume shop floor square footage preventing product expansion.	Excess inventory = $25,000 shop floor Expansion requirements = 5000 sq ft	Inventory reduction = $20,000

Table 3.12. Customer Satisfaction: Top Three Opportunities

	Opportunity	Cost of Current State	Benefit If Improved
1	Improved lead time	Lost sales and market share = $1,000,000 anually	$2,000,000 recovered + increased market share
2	Quality improvement	Quality returns, rework + loss of future business = $250,000 annually (estimated)	Greater sales and profit
3	Improved price competitiveness	Loss of sales = $250,000 annually (estimated)	Increased sales of $250,000

should highlight the historical customer complaints related to competitive differentiation areas. What customer complaints would be resolved by implementing a Lean operating system? Would a shorter customer-quoted lead time take sales away from your company's closest competitor? How much would market share increase by improved product quality? Increased customer satisfaction will result in increased sales and a related increase in market share. Be conservative. Estimate a 1% increase in market share resulting from a business model that consistently delivers faster delivery, improved quality, and a more competitive selling price for customers. A 1% increase in sales represents a significant revenue number for most manufacturers. An initial Lean transformation project might not impact the customer dissatisfaction issues that are related to product attributes (e.g., design, function, personal preferences, etc.), but the Lean operating system can address the complaints about lead time, quality, and selling price that directly impact customer satisfaction. Customer satisfaction opportunities should be a performance measurement of a Lean transformation.

Other issues. Individualize the SBA to identify and quantify the benefits based on issues in your company. The SBA template used in this chapter presents example cost-saving opportunities from commonly collected information. The template is not intended to be all inclusive. The template addresses opportunities that are universal to every company. Other specific opportunities such as setup reduction (SMED), preventative maintenance programs (TPM), and operator training programs may need to be isolated and considered.

Value stream mapping. VSM can also be used to identify improvement opportunities and to quantify the magnitude of current systems. With VSM, a current-state analysis is developed to identify the processes, lead time, and inventory associated with meeting customer demand. Once the current-state map is developed, a future-state map can be developed to project the improvements to be made and what a new operating system might look like.

The most important outcome of the SBA and VSM processes is the quantification of a company's financial opportunity if a Lean operating system were to be implemented. A current-state VSM might not be able to quantify the costs of a traditional operating system in financial terms, but the financial opportunities identified by the SBA can be a statement of the financial goals for the Lean business transformation. The baseline KPI (key performance indicator) values identified by the SBA can be used to monitor progress during the transformation phase of the Lean project.

No one can guarantee a monetary amount of savings or give a firm estimate of the performance benefits to be expected from a Lean business transformation. The SBA only compares the expected benefits of the Lean operating system with the results of your current operating system in realistic monetary terms. The SBA guides you through the decision-making process needed to establish a sound financial justification and the competitive differentials for converting your company's factory to a Lean operating system. You can then determine from the SBA with a degree of accuracy what a Lean operating system would save your company. If the projected savings and the expected benefits identified by the SBA are not large enough or the performance improvements are not significant enough, it's possible your company should *not* make a transition to a Lean operating system. Why waste time on a Lean business transformation if the financial benefits cannot justify the investment in time and energy? If your company decides to maintain the current operating system, then it's good to know what potential savings will be left on the table. If the Lean business transformation is not pursued, you can sleep at night knowing that you performed due diligence when making the best decision for your company.

Some final thoughts. Because the benefits of transforming your company to a Lean operating system dovetail with one another, separating the results of achieving one Lean goal from the results of achieving another is sometimes difficult. Once a Lean operating system is implemented, many manufacturers often find that numerous other unplanned, unexpected benefits are now available to them. Just implementing the Lean operating system frequently results in unanticipated benefits that provide additional differentiations that will separate the manufacturing company from its competitors. Discussions and debates about differing manufacturing methodologies can go on and on endlessly because each manufacturing company is different; each one has a specific reason for considering such an important change as Lean transformation; at any given time each one may be uniquely positioned in their marketplace; some Lean benefits may appeal to the needs of a company's customers more than others, etc. Two things, however, are certain: one or more of the benefits of implementing Lean methodologies must result from a Lean transformation project and there must be a return on the investment of the time and resources required to make the changes required by the transformation project. Simply having your factory serve as a laboratory for an experimental program you read about in a book or practicing a "program of the month" is not a good enough reason to begin a Lean business transformation.

REFERENCE

1. George Koenigsaecker, Leadership and the lean transformation, in *Manufacturing Engineering*, November 2005: Vol. 135, No. 5; available at http://findarticles.com/p/articles/mi_qa3618/is_200511/ai_n15847432/.

4

A LEAN BUSINESS TRANSFORMATION IS NOT A GRASS ROOTS PROJECT — IT MUST BE LED

In 1911, E.M. Forster published *The Celestial Omnibus*.[1] This fictional short story is a good metaphor for any company considering a business transformation to a Lean operating system. The story reminds modern manufacturers of the necessary qualities for managers — a spirit to achieve the benefits discovered in their SBAs and the courage to demonstrate the conviction necessary to achieve these benefits — but these traits of conviction and courage might not be present for a manager who has recently returned from a Lean seminar or a manager who has been coerced by management to lead the company through a transformation project.

The *Celestial Omnibus* is about a young boy who is curious about a sign posted in his neighborhood that points to a cul-de-sac and proclaims *To Paradise*. When running up the alley one evening, the boy finds an omnibus waiting. He takes a risk and boards the omnibus, which carries him into the night sky where he meets characters from fiction and mythology that he has read so much about. When he returns and relays his adventure to his parents, his skeptical parents and their friends dismiss his account as the fiction of a young boy's active imagination.

Executives in many companies react the same way today when hearing about the benefits available with a business transformation to Lean. They're skeptical.

After all, the benefits frequently cited from an implementation of a Lean operating system sound like manufacturing nirvana when compared to the day-to-day Herculean efforts required to meet the demands of the marketplace. How is it possible for any company to achieve the benefits touted by Lean? Like the journey of the omnibus, the advertised benefits might as well be fiction! What's real and what's hyperbole?

It is much easier to embrace the skeptical viewpoint that a Lean operating system promises more than can be delivered or that the effort required for achieving the intangible benefits is too great to seriously consider an actual commitment to projects that may or may not make any substantial improvements for the company. Although many companies around the world extol the benefits of Lean (including your own co-workers), what work is really being done to incorporate a Lean operating system into the daily life of these companies? Lean may be just a flavor-of-the-month program that will soon be replaced next month by a new flavor. Too much faith is required by pragmatists that the benefits identified in the SBA are even possible: "Our company has been working for years to improve with very little to show for all the effort."

Doing little or nothing is easy when faced with a decision of such consequence. Skeptical managers are politically adroit. They very cleverly feign interest in improvement projects championed by their managers, while doing very little to actually improve the current operating system. They publicly praise the benefits of Lean, enlist other managers to sign on to the program, champion projects, have meetings, provide training, and publish results for quarterly goals and objectives reports to appear engaged. It's the politically correct thing to do! It is much safer career-wise to simply read books, go to seminars, proclaim the benefits, and talk the talk than to actually implement any substantive change to policies or procedures in the company. These managers may appear to be enlightened change agents, but their real strategy is to expand the duration of projects long enough to outlast enthusiasm for the program.

In *The Celestial Omnibus*, despite the skepticism of his parents, the boy is still excited about convincing others of the reality of the omnibus. So he invites one of their knowledgeable, well-read friends to ride in the omnibus with him one evening. Although the cynical passenger is truly amazed by the flight of the omnibus and the characters they meet from mythology and literature during their strange journey, he thinks the trip is just too fantastic to be anything more than a dream. He recognizes the characters in his mind, but does not believe they are anything more than just characters in a book. Eventually, he becomes afraid of the height the omnibus has reached, but is so cynical he doesn't believe any of the flight is possible. It must be a dream. So he steps from the omnibus carriage and falls to his death. Unaware of the man's fall, the naïve young boy looks for the man to make introductions to the famous fictional men and women who are coming in a procession to greet them.[2]

Are manufacturing executives today so cynical about the possibilities for improvement with Lean technologies that they just cannot believe what they read, hear, or see? Have they become so comfortable with their lifestyles and positions of authority they cannot risk their comfort zones for significant business improvements? Is it easier to just do nothing rather than assuming the leadership role necessary to bring these improvements to fruition? Any reader can line bookshelves with Lean books and articles. Just to impress friends and colleagues, they can cite success stories from other companies, but to have a chance for Lean success, that same reader must also become a leader to attain great achievements in manufacturing excellence that a Lean business transformation offers. Lean success does not allow a leader to just go along for the ride by merely relating stories from a book or industry magazine.

Forster's fantasy uses the differences between the passenger and the young boy as a metaphor for revealing unimaginative adult pragmatism.[2] The omnibus takes the boy and a well-read, but emotionally bankrupt, passenger to paradise as promised, but only the boy experiences them in his heart. In the end, the boy arrives in paradise and the cynical passenger falls to earth. Only the boy was able to make a connection between the mind and heart.[3]

Many executives are faced with practical decisions about how they will embrace the operating system changes necessary to complete a business transformation to Lean. Like the boy in *The Celestial Omnibus*, some are enthusiastic about the benefits of Lean. They are excited to embark on the journey just for the sake of the adventure itself. They are driven by the excitement promised from the experience. Others, like the passenger, approach the journey to Lean business transformation tentatively, fearful of the unknown and full of misunderstandings. Worse yet, how many will decide to not make the journey at all?

The Celestial Omnibus is a parable about feelings and beliefs. Just as in the omnibus ride to paradise taken by the boy and the friend of his parents, creating a successful business transformation requires a blend of knowledge, enthusiasm, and faith. Most companies have unique cultures and different levels of willingness to embrace change. Usually they have two types of individuals: enthusiastic *boys* who have the spirit, imagination, and vision to see what is possible and *passengers* who might be well read about Lean and talking the talk, but who are lacking the courage necessary to complete a business transformation. These polar points of view are similar to the differing opinions in any company considering the implementation of any major change, Lean or otherwise. Some will always favor change and be able to visualize the future; others will always want to maintain the status quo.

Table 4.1. Institutional Motivation for Change

• To improve sales revenue against new or increased competition	• Cost reduction initiatives to compete in the competitive pressures marketplace
• To improve profit margins	• Desired increase in market share
• To introduce new products	• Merger and acquisition
• Resource availability and staffing turnover	• Changing global performance standards
• Customer demand and improved service	• Expanding markets and distribution channels
• Stockholder return on investment pressures	• Changing employee policies
• Capacity growth	• New market penetration

Undertaking any business transformation with the scope of a Lean transformation and the corresponding impact of the Lean operating system on the organization based solely on fantastic promises and the success stories of competitors would, of course, be naïve. Fortunately, being naïve is unnecessary. Volumes and volumes of publications generated over the years describe implementation history. Sufficient history documented from past factory transformations already validates the results from implementing Lean technologies. The technology, pioneered by numerous companies that have completed Lean transformations since the end of WWII, is already available. There's no need to reinvent the wheel. The technology is proven so using blind faith to begin a business transformation is not necessary. Once armed with an SBA that confirms the financial and qualitative benefits tailored specifically for the company, obtaining buy-in from leadership is the remaining key for moving forward successfully with a Lean business transformation. Learn from those who have traveled the road before you. Do not let fear stop progress in your company. When combined with solid leadership, financial and competitive justification, and good technical guidelines, a Lean business transformation does not have to be a fearful unknown omnibus journey!

THE CHALLENGE FOR EXECUTIVES: BECOMING MOTIVATED FOR CHANGE

Executives, managers, and change agents are motivated to make changes in the way their companies operate for many reasons. The motivation could be related to institutional or corporate goals or to personal reasons or be a combination of both. Institutional changes are to benefit the company as a whole and its stakeholders (Table 4.1). Personal reasons for making changes include those listed in Table 4.2.

Not for lack of trying, the business world is full of failed initiatives. It is common practice for corporate leadership to develop high-level strategies to meet

Table 4.2. Personal Motivation for Change

• Personal power and recognition	• Peer recognition
• Better compensation	• Recognition as an industry leader
• Career growth	• Improved working conditions
• Personal satisfaction and challenge	• Job security
• Pride in work	• Altruism

corporate goals. Politically astute middle management and enthusiastic change agents then quickly sign on to announced projects or initiatives. Corporate strategies offer great opportunities to positively impact a company. Even if a manager or change agent has a separate agenda, neither the clever manager nor change agent wants to be left behind when showing support for any corporate initiative — showing indifference to an executive initiative can lead to an interrupted career.

Yet, as time passes and the promise of the strategy has not been realized, an often-asked question is, "What happened? Why did this brilliant strategy fail?" Great ideas are often launched with much fanfare, but shortly found to be "dead in the water," abandoned and unworkable. Although the reasons for the strategic change might have been excellent, one primary reason for the failure of these corporate strategies could be that the institutional and personal reasons for change did not align one with the other. If institutional reasons do not align with the managers' personal reasons, implementation of strategic strategies has a slim chance of success. Remember the familiar WIIFM question ("What's in it for me?")? Every individual involved in implementation of a strategic strategy must have a stake in the success of the strategy.

As a strategy works its way down through the organization, managers ultimately responsible for implementation of the strategy often may become quite cynical in response to yet another new program of the month. The last thing they need to distract them from the daily accomplishment of their own goals and objectives is one more time-consuming project with uncertain merit and outcome.

If the strategic plan is to capture market share by reducing costs while improving customer satisfaction and profit margins, is it realistic to expect this strategy to be fulfilled without a good execution plan in place? Yet, the *inability* to execute a corporate vision at the operational level is one of the greatest unacknowledged business issues of today. A failed execution wastes time, money, and energy while leadership loses credibility.

Does your strategy match the realities of your capabilities? If your company has consistently shown an inability to execute strategies, what has changed that would make a new strategy more effective than any previous effort? If the execution phase of the strategy is lost by interminable or intentional project creep, what other motivational incentives will challenge managers to embrace change?

At times, managers use the well-known tactic of appearing to support a strategy while quietly maintaining the status quo. If enough managers choose to maintain the status quo, ultimately the new strategy will fail, be forgotten, or be replaced with a newer, more popular "program of the month." As an example of this strategy in action, look no further than a presidential initiative that dies a slow death by thousands of cuts by the legislature! When delay tactics are allowed to operate, company time, money, and energy are wasted and faith in company leadership is diminished. When a company fails to deliver on a strategy, scapegoats are sought and innocents are sacrificed and blame is placed on the strategy itself, which is labeled as flawed. In most cases, a faulty strategy is usually not the cause of failure.

A strategy fails most often because of poor execution, not because the strategy is bad! It is not unusual during the crafting of any strategy for little thought to be given to the implementation of that strategy. Management often assumes that a new strategy will be embraced because they wish it to be so. Lack of a well-conceived execution strategy is the major reason for disappointing results. Remember that 22% of companies pursuing a Lean transformation claimed to be dissatisfied with their results.[4] Could it be that something got lost between their strategy and the execution of that strategy? The failure to execute a strategy can be costly and devastating to a company's competitiveness and sometimes, even its survival. Today, a big difference between a successful company and their competition is the ability to implement business strategies.

A simple answer for ensuring the successful implementation of a corporate strategy would therefore seem to be: first ensure that personal and institutional goals are aligned. Although this sounds like a simple solution, it is *simple* in word only. The odds of aligning personal motivation with corporate goals are significant. Because this struggle exists, implementation of a successful strategy or program can only be realized if some compromise is made, either of personal goals or corporate strategy.

So where should compromise be made? If the choice is for corporate strategy to prevail, then success can only be accomplished by the compromise of personal beliefs or objectives — but compromising personal beliefs or objectives can be subjective and often unpredictable. For some people, the personal compromises required may be of no consequence. To implement a strategy, these people will participate with total detachment. For others, the compromise of personal goals required to implement the strategy is so extreme that their only response is resistance to the strategy.

Depending on the personal interests and motivation of those responsible for the implementation of strategy, predicting attainment of compromise is a moving target. A Lean project leader is wise to know the dynamics of compromise. As resistance to compromise is manifest, learning to act when necessary to control it is critical. Inaction ultimately results in challenges that are so large that the Lean strategy itself may become compromised or cause outright project failure.

EMPLOYEE TYPES

Employee attitudes toward change may be grouped into three general categories: good soldiers, skeptics, and resisters. Most employees do not share identical enthusiasm for change. Expect it. Beyond having a basic understanding of the new operating system and knowing what their roles will be in the new system, having a lot of enthusiasm isn't necessary for most employees. They work for a paycheck and will happily participate in any company-sponsored change. Others may require a higher level of commitment. For others, being fully consumed in the transformation process, the future operation, and the ongoing maintenance of the system after the initial transformation has been completed will be necessary. Knowing where everyone stands in support of a Lean operating system business transformation is important. All employees must fulfill their required roles. In the end, to realize its full potential, the Lean operating system must become a way of life in the company. To successfully manage a transformation project, identifying employees by type is important. To achieve a successful business transformation, knowing employees by type will guide a change agent when resolving important issues regarding the Lean transition process.

Good Soldiers

Good soldiers "go along to get along." They come to work every day and perform according to their job description. They are flexible and will do anything their manager asks of them. Good soldiers rarely ask why. They do not challenge authority or suggest alternative solutions. On payday, they collect their paychecks and go home at the end of the day to relax and enjoy their favorite pastimes. Good soldiers work to live, not live to work. This is a perfectly acceptable business proposition for change agents and employees impacted by the Lean business transformation.

When a new corporate strategy is introduced, good soldiers also readily accept new policies and procedures and require only brief training periods. They ask few questions about new policies and procedures. When given an answer, they usually accept the first response. Not challenging a response or new directive does not indicate good soldiers lack intelligence or are disinterested in the welfare of the company. Good soldiers are simply happy doing their jobs. Some argue they are to be envied for their philosophical approach to work. Their jobs are often not the primary priority of their lives. Work is simply a means to an end for financing life pursuits outside the workplace that are more important to them.

Good soldiers represent the most fundamental relationship between employers and workers: "a day's pay for a day's work." A good soldier is more interested in earning a day's pay than the work they do to earn it. Good soldiers exist at every level of an organization. They are the backbone of a company's workforce. Good soldiers are excellent, dependable, reliable employees. They make up approximately 50% of a company's total headcount. When implementing change, beyond the training required for new procedures, good soldiers require little management time.

Skeptics

Like good soldiers, skeptics are excellent employees. They exist in every organization and can have positions of importance and authority. Often skeptics are long-term employees who have seen many programs come and go. They have become jaded and cynical. Skeptics do not accept change at face value. They almost always challenge an articulated strategy or the stated reasons for a change. Skeptics need to know how the Lean project is any different than other projects that are now long forgotten. Skeptics need to know the reasons behind a change and must have buy-in to the change before accepting it. Their skepticism should be interpreted as informed concern for the welfare of the company and their areas of responsibility. Immediately addressing the concerns and questions of a skeptic with a position of authority is particularly important.

Skeptics usually require more education and time to come around to a new idea. Investing time in training and converting skeptics is always worth the effort. Skeptics must reconcile a new strategy with the current conditions and consider the implications of change and how they might be personally impacted. Once convinced that the new strategy is an improvement over current methods, skeptics become stalwart champions, supporters, and even cheerleaders. Conversely, if not convinced, their skepticism can continue indefinitely, eventually negatively impacting strategy implementation. Continuing to have skepticism is a workable situation so long as this skepticism does not interfere with the forward progress of a business transformation and is not verbalized in an effort to recruit confederates to their point of view. If resistance becomes subversive, a skeptic can become a problem needing action to neutralize the resistance.

In most cases, given an opportunity to express their doubts or an opinion, skeptics are willing to stand down and let the project proceed. They just want to be on the record as being unconvinced of the outcome. If their opinions are honest, heartfelt, and publically expressed so all can hear them, skepticism can even be beneficial. A sincere skeptic can be a sounding board for ideas when the hard truth is needed to test an idea or to break up group thinking. As long as they are verbal and public with their questions and opinions, skeptics will not become resisters to the project.

Efforts to convert a skeptic cannot be open-ended. There is a point of diminishing returns when attempting to bring a skeptic onboard. Every effort should be made to convince a skeptic, but overcoming an individual's skepticism may never happen, even with continuing education, training, and any amount of reasoning. At some point, the conversion effort becomes a sunk cost. The energy and wasted time can be better spent on transformation issues.

If valid, allow skeptics to continue to express their concerns and opinions, but they cannot be allowed to become impediments to progress. When discussing a new strategy, Lee Iacocca, former CEO of Chrysler Corporation, once said, "You can lead, follow, or get out of the way." Iacocca's statement sums up a concise approach for dealing with skeptics when implementing new strategies.[5] Skeptics make up approximately 30% of all employees. At the end of the day, they might have the best interests of the company at heart, but if they do not want to lead the efforts to change a current strategy, skeptics should follow or just get out of the way.

Resisters

Resisters make up the remaining ±20% of the employee population and are the most troublesome category. If not identified, resisters can torpedo any attempt to implement a change or a strategy. Resisters are hardcore proponents of maintaining the status quo. They dismiss any type of change outright. Resisters can be particularly dangerous when a new strategy affects their personal power base or management fiefdom because they often take ownership of their processes and therefore do not want any change. Some resisters have fought for and won their territories over a long period of time and are comfortable with the rewards of their battles. They are not interested in redesigning or rearranging processes. They balk at any attempts by anyone or any strategy that might affect their comfort zones. Resisters often forget they are components of an entire system in which the needs of the organization come first.

The most difficult part of implementing a change or deploying a strategy is identifying resisters. Resisters rarely protest or express their opinions overtly. They are cunning, politically motivated, and smart enough to know that overt resistance can be personally damaging. Resisters use passive aggressive behavior to hide their disdain for change. A resister is always cautious and aware of their audience. Even if resisters have good ideas, they often do not participate in tactical implementation discussions or contribute useful information when discussing a project. In rare instances when a resister must maintain a pretext of participation by making a contribution to the discussion at hand, the resister usually makes a carefully worded restatement of the views of the highest-ranking member of management attending the discussion or a statement that is in agreement with the majority opinion of meeting attendees. At meetings, resisters frequently nod their heads in agreement, particularly when the powerful management or the majority of upper management is in attendance. They often feign interest in the project while silently wringing their hands at the potential damage being made to "their" company or personal fiefdom. In the meantime, they formulate defensive arguments and covertly attempt to organize a confederacy of like-minded resisters.

Rarely can resisters "stay out of the way" by remaining silent about their true feelings. Rarely do they express their true feelings in a public forum. Often resisters spend a great deal of time clandestinely recruiting others to their cause on a one-on-one basis out of public view. They engage in quiet conversations in cubicles, offices, and at after-work events — anywhere like-minded people congregate. They use email and telephone calls during lunch and breaks. The key for resisters is to construct a sizeable-enough coalition of other resisters to delay or kill any transformation to a Lean strategy. As insulation from personal exposure, a resister may also try to enlist the services of fellow resisters to serve as surrogates to champion a public resistance.

By using vacillating statements, fence-sitting, and noncommittal behavior and by keeping their real opinions mysterious, resisters maintain a winning position regardless of the outcome of a project. The last thing a resister wants is accountability for a project. Instead a resister carefully ensures having a position that enables the sharing of any credit that might come from a future success.

Because resisters are rarely obvious and seldom reveal themselves, they are difficult to identify. A resister always plays close to the vest, posturing for a personal position and strategy. Early on, a resister may even be easily confused with a good soldier or a skeptic. As an employee, a resister usually hangs back, saying nothing, while looking for support and assessing the environment for change. As a politically astute manager or change agent, a resister publically supports strategic processes passively, while secretly hiding real contempt for the strategic direction. A resister keeps his month shut in public. Even though skeptics are not easily convinced of the benefits of change, unlike resisters, they are honest enough to articulate their objections and opinions in a public forum.

Assessing employees based on type sounds a bit Machiavellian. Change agents are certainly not psychologists, but knowing where employees stand on their support for any project, Lean or otherwise, is important because all of the factors of emotional motivation will be in play when making a change to Lean. Change agents need to determine where their vision is shared, where support is available, and where resistance is found so they can plan their implementation strategy accordingly. Give individuals the benefit of doubt about their support, but be perceptive enough to know when to cut your loss of time and energy when trying to convince a resister to support the Lean business transformation. At some point, it becomes a lost cause.

Remember a definition of insanity: repeating the same action over and over again expecting a different result. This definition certainly applies to any resister in an organization.

THE LEAN DILEMMA

Understanding the levels of commitment and the types of emotional motivation types attempts to identify team members and visionary supporters to facilitate the changes needed to improve an operating system for a company or to move the company toward becoming more competitive. Companies make huge investments of time and money in efforts to change or manage emotional motivation: a team goes into the woods and falls into each other's arms; team members hold sensitivity sessions and tell each other how much they love each other; they climb ropes to establish trust; they take personality tests to learn how to communicate; and they "form, storm, conform, and norm" to proclaim themselves as a team. Teams compare their favorite books on leadership and debate methods for modifying behavior at the heart level. Usually, a good time is had by all. Everyone feels warm and fuzzy. It is a fine thing to spend the day with work associates and have fun, but when everyone goes home at night, they are still the same people. Feeling more loved seldom changes one's opinion about embracing change in the workplace.

Companies often use contract consultants to deliver these motivational services. Some companies even maintain human resource staffs to develop or sponsor behavior-modification curriculums, sessions, and classroom activities, but employees exposed to this psychological experimentation react the very same way as they do when confronted with any other stimuli for change: they decide to be a good soldier, a skeptic, or a resister.

In most companies, very few resisters make themselves known when the prevailing sentiment is "woe is the person who is labeled a non-team player!" Usually the go-along-to-get-along strategy requires little sacrifice from the resister during these periods of psychological mind games. Resisters, instead, choose to remain under the radar because revealing oneself is not worth the effort required to be identified as one. Many politically astute participants therefore adopt the good soldier approach, hoping to persevere as long as it takes for the next psychological theory of the month to come along. These short-term projects designed to modify behavior seldom achieve their stated goals.

Even after years of trying, most spouses will readily admit that attempts to change the behavior of a spouse are rarely successful, even when using the best logic or coercion techniques. In the business world, debates argue that attempts at using behavior modification techniques should be considered value-added activities, but even when given the benefit of the doubt, attempts to manipulate emotional motivation to achieve consensus among various individuals are often just exercises in futility.

So, if experience teaches us that modifying personal motivation to impact a corporate business strategy is rarely successful, then the only resort for a company is reliance on a rational argument of attaining the practical, objective, and financial benefits of achieving one or more institutional motivations. Each institutional motivation seeks to achieve a common goal: increasing the wealth of the company for its stockholders. Unless a company is in possession of an incredible new technological breakthrough capable of capturing market share, the company can only grow its share of the market by differentiating itself from its competitors to increase wealth. Companies therefore continually seek strategies to increase their share of the market.

Like a pie, the size of any market is finite. Using the pie analogy, company wealth is increased in two ways:

- By growing the market (e.g., attract new customers to the market with innovation and the introduction of new products and services)
- By taking larger slices of the existing pie at the expense of other slices

Innovation and the introduction of new products into the market can be risky for a producer, but great for a consumer. Technological marvels often result from a company's efforts to increase wealth and stay ahead of their competitors by increasing market share. When technology is new, market share growth through innovation is a great strategy, but for producers with mature technology and an established market share, fewer opportunities for wealth growth may be available from innovation and new product introduction. These companies have to rely on strategies that will yield larger pieces of the existing pie.

For a large percentage of companies with mature technologies and stable markets, the only way to gain a larger piece of the pie is to distinguish themselves from their competitors in some way. These companies must offer some advantage over their competitors that will cause more of the existing, finite customer demand to purchase their products instead. More demand equals a larger slice of the pie. In a saturated market, the larger slice comes at the expense of a competitor. To be successful in getting a larger slice of pie, a strategy is needed for offering customers a value-added product or service *differential* that is unavailable from competitors — a strategy that says: "Our company is better than the competitors. Buy our product. Don't buy our competitors' products."

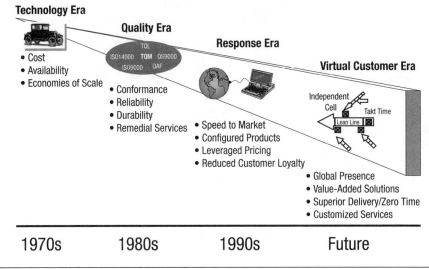

Figure 4.1. The quest for product differentiation.

HOW DOES A COMPANY DIFFERENTIATE ITSELF FROM THE COMPETITION?

Producers know about the simple marketing dynamic of "our company is better than the competitors" and have been searching for ways to differentiate their products and services from their competitors since the beginning of product choices and competition. If a producer is a sole source supplier, getting away with just asking customers to "buy mine" might be possible, but once alternatives become available to customers, producers soon learn that simply asking for business is no longer good enough. Companies have been trying to differentiate themselves from their competition for decades (Figure 4.1).

Technology. Having the best technology was one of the earliest differentials for manufacturers. A manufacturer would claim their product was different than competitors' products because it had better design and manufacturing technology. Better technology translated into better performance, more reliability, or better appearance. Better technology meant a new and improved product that was more efficient and longer lasting than the competitors' products. Naturally, producers battled each other to be the first to incorporate the next new technology into their products just to claim their new model was technologically superior to their competitors' products. Customers needing the latest and greatest product technology always opted for the producer claiming to have the best technology.

New, technologically superior products commanded a higher selling price. Many customers were willing to pay the price just to own the better technology.

Claims of superior technology are still an effective differentiator for producers of goods and services sold today. The battle for technological superiority continues. Look no further than your television set, the Internet, a smartphone, or the Sunday edition of a local newspaper to see advertising for products claiming to have the latest and greatest technology. Think about yourself as a consumer of products. When ready to purchase a product, you want the latest and the best new technology your budget will allow. You want 4G instead of 3G! Sometimes, you may even be willing to sacrifice your budget to get the newest, latest, and greatest technology! Every customer wants the best technology. Who wants to buy last season's outdated or unexciting model?

Unfortunately, offering the best technology available may not be enough of a differentiator for many customers. When they buy a product, the customers just assume they are receiving the best technology available. They do not question if the technology is the latest and greatest. It is just taken for granted that it is. It is crucial for producers wanting to compete in their market to continue to seek and incorporate the latest and greatest technologies into their products. Research and development budgets are driven by the desire of companies to compete on the basis of best technology. Companies with little or no commitment to R&D soon see their market share lost to competitors. If they cannot keep up, they must transition to other businesses or go out of business completely.

Up to and through the 1980s, differentiation of products based on technology alone was sufficient to compete in the marketplace. As long as a producer kept pace with technological changes with an occasional back and forth in short-term leadership change among the competitors in the marketplace, customers were happy. After participating in the same market over a long period of time, producers acknowledged they often shared homogeneous technology with their competitors. Incremental technology improvements were increasingly more difficult to achieve and when they were, they were short-lived. So, to retain customer loyalty and keep market share, producers needed to claim *just enough* technological advancement. Although revolutionary technological changes do occur, temporarily benefiting the inventor, manufacturers sharing the same marketplace will soon find that they are actually using the same technology as their competitors. Products sharing the same technology are candidates for commodity status causing differentiation to become more difficult to claim by the manufacturer.

With the exception of the sales and marketing departments who must continue to create campaigns to package and sell products that have little technological differentiation from their competitors, the slowing of technological change has advantages for the manufacturing shop floor. Machines and processes can run larger batches of products achieving even better economies of scale with less fear of obsolescence. Labor efficiencies and machine utilization can be maximized. Less time is lost to changeover. Inventory is an asset on the balance sheet, so while overproduction increases working capital, it also increases assets camouflaging waste in the system. Factories can run at full capacity to fully absorb overhead costs. The costs of production are passed on to customers who have little choice but to buy what is available in the marketplace. As long as the price between competitors can be justified by perceived technological differentials, customers are satisfied.

Quality. Beginning in the late 1970s and early 1980s, differentials began to evolve. New producer entrants in the marketplace began to appear with the same state-of-the-art technology as existing producers. Technology as a sales differential became even more diluted. Off-shore manufacturers often made up a large part of these new producer market entrants. Along with equivalent and often greater technological features, these producers had a new differential that greatly appealed to customers limited by the technology producers had to offer up to now. That differential was quality. The new products being introduced in the marketplace during this time not only had the great technology of domestic producers, but they now had better quality. The products were more dependable and reliable than domestic offerings. Offshore manufacturers quickly gained a reputation for durability and reliability that existing domestic producers could not match. Japanese automobiles in the early 1980s are an example of this quality differentiator. At one point, domestic automobiles lost 30% of their market share partly because of this quality differential.

Almost overnight, customers had a broader choice of producers from which to choose products along with a new added differential of quality. Customers suddenly felt empowered by the new entrants to the market. By being able to purchase products with a reputation for quality while having the same great technology as domestic products, customers were able to reslice the market pie, redistributing market share between new market entrants and domestic manufacturers. Domestic producers whose primary differentiation had always been dependent on technology were now confronted with meeting a new quality differential by retooling how products were manufactured to improve quality. They might not want to retool, but they had little choice if they wanted to stay in business. Their customers demanded it and the customer was king! With the help of knowledgeable quality experts and the hard work of domestic manufacturers over the last 30+ years, the quality gap has been substantially narrowed or even eliminated in many industries.

If producers do not have solid technology and high quality designed into their products, they cannot expect to participate in the marketplace with competitors that do. Technology and quality are like the pair of jacks required to open in a poker game. If a producer does not have the attributes of quality and technology, market participation will be at a great disadvantage. Lacking these two powerful differentiators, product price and margin reduction may be the only differential a producer can offer customers.

In the 1970s and 1980s, both technology and quality became standard expectations. Once again, in the 1990s, just as producers were becoming comfortable with a renewed dedication to discovering and developing new technologies and implementing newly found quality initiatives, customers once again began to raise the bar for competitors in the marketplace. Customers were no longer satisfied with great technology and high-quality products alone. Great technology was simply expected from all competitors as being part of their products! If a producer did not have the newest technology, the company was not in the running for business. The same was true with quality. Quality was simply expected. Quality attributes were an expected part of a product and taken for granted. In fact, because they were expectations, technology and quality did not receive a second thought. So, the marketplace began to look for a new differentiator to distinguish suppliers.

Companies unable to rise to the double challenge of offering products with state-of-the-art technology and great quality either lost market share, moved on to another business, or simply went out of business. For remaining manufacturers proudly offering these differentials to customers, market leadership and customer preferences continued to be tentative. Because technological and quality differentials were standard attributes that all competitors offered, customers continued to wield great power over their suppliers. They searched for new differentials to help determine which supplier received their next purchase order.

New differentials. Commodity products have equal technology and quality, have many producers, are readily available, and are similar in price. As markets became crowded with high-quality, high-technology producers, companies battled hard for market share as their homogeneous products approached commodity status. As multiple producers offered products that achieved homogeneity with their key quality and technology attributes, customers began to exercise power when negotiating purchase contracts. Because technology and quality were givens that were no longer seen as differentials in the marketplace, customers invented many new differentials. They began to focus their expectations on new differentials such as customized and configured products that could be delivered in standard or even shorter lead time with lower prices; specialized customer service support; improved product attributes; better warranties; and the speed with which products could be delivered to their doorsteps.

Old supplier loyalties were now out the window. If a producer could not meet the new purchase conditions, customers would just go to the manufacturer's competitor. Similar to the 1980s when customers expected quality and technology to be offered as a differentiator, customers now also expected customization, low price, and fast delivery as new differentiators. It was a new era of response to demand and speed to market. It was a new world for producers. Customers would no longer accept what producers defined as a final product. Customers now demanded differentials from producers based on what was important to them. They were insensitive to suppliers needs. If the manufacturer could not satisfy their requirements, customers could shop the world to find it! The virtual customer era was here.

HAVE A STRATEGY OR THROW MONEY AT A PROBLEM?

As a manager or C-level executive of a manufacturing- or service-based company, is it even possible to keep up with the changing differential demands of customers? One thing is for sure, keeping up with the changing demands of customers is no easy task. When confronted with the enormous challenges of pleasing customer demand for faster lead times, configured products, and lower prices, a common strategy for many producers is to just throw money at the problem in hopes of keeping customers happy. For most, this "investment" takes the form of increased inventory levels and a resulting increase in working capital demand. This defensive money strategy has been a reliable solution for meeting on-time delivery of customer demand going back to the response era of the 1980s. Although exhausted managers know the strategy may not be the least-cost solution, they hope to buy enough time until a better strategy is devised, they're promoted or retire and leave resolution to the next generation of managers, or a new strategy becomes institutionalized policy.

Although pouring money into inventories in hopes of providing a buffer between manufacturing capability and customer demands for fast deliveries, short lead times, highly configured products, the best prices, high quality, improved warranties, and increased service after the sale is certainly a strategy, it's not the best solution to meet virtual customer expectations. Inventory investment has cost implications on the balance sheet: increased working capital requirements. Increased inventories also negatively impact customer lead time.

Manufacturing lead time. Manufacturing lead time is the point in time when purchased material enters the manufacturing process until it is converted into a completed product. Since the beginning of the response era of the 1980s, customers have had greater expectations that their orders will be shipped within the quoted lead time or less. When manufacturing lead time is greater than a customer's expected delivery time, customer satisfaction suffers. To avoid that scenario and to have a better chance of meeting a customer's need for a customized product configuration, additional raw material and component inventories are often purchased in advance of demand. To keep customers satisfied, rapid-response manufacturing strategies are formulated. To ship products faster than the time usually required for new production of a configured unit, two popular strategies are used to meet customer demand:

- *WIP.* Build a WIP inventory of assemblies or subassemblies forecasted in advance of demand. This inventory can be completed earlier than receipt of an actual customer order. These items can then be finished in a shorter lead time by using a final assembly schedule. When customer demand is received, prebuilt subassemblies are attached to a partially completed unit to finish the build configuration to meet the customer's demand. If product mix and volume are unpredictable, greater raw material levels in proportion to lead time shortfall are necessary to maintain lead time expectations. The costs of additional raw materials and selected WIP are less than building and maintaining finished units and storing them in a FGI.

- *FGI.* Ship products that have been produced in advance from a FGI. Shipping from FGI is a common solution that works well if products are generic and order patterns are predictable. If the products customers are buying are custom configured or designed to order, predicting the right mix and volume of FGIs for the most expensive categories of inventory can be an expensive guess. For custom-configured or designed-to-order products, producing the most historically popular models is best. With this strategy, however, manufacturers run an increased risk of product obsolescence.

Inventory levels. With current planning systems, inventory levels are determined by forecasting the customer demand to be produced in advance of the receipt of an actual sales order. Quantities of WIP or FGI are calculated sufficient to ensure an ideal customer service response. Because no customer is likely to wait for supplier lead time plus manufacturing's lead time to receive demand, supplier delivery lead time can dictate the quantities of purchased materials necessary to be kept on hand in a store's inventory. Regardless of the customer satisfaction solution chosen, every manufacturer must determine the appropriate amount of inventory to be maintained to provide the customer differential of response time and delivery. The trade-off between customer on-time delivery goals and ideal inventory levels is frequently a debate between manufacturing and marketing. Many variations of inventory strategies have evolved to accommodate the time gap between customer lead time and actual manufacturing response time. Building to a partial level of completion using the common levels of a BOM and finishing assembly with additional configurable materials based on the receipt of actual customer demand is a common strategy. Purchase of the component inventories needed in the stockroom is still based on a forecasted projection of the final configuration a customer might order. As with any forecast, should customers fail to purchase the planned configuration, excess, slow-moving parts or obsolete raw material inventories are a likely result. Regardless of the chosen technique, inventory investment is required. The question is how much is the right amount?

Working capital requirements. Customer response policies are based on the amount of time required to produce products. Longer lead times through manufacturing cause inventory levels to become unusually large and require proportionately greater inventory investments! Of course, the sum of all these inventories has a direct impact on working capital requirements. Inventories not only require space on the shop floor, in warehouses, and at distribution centers, but the space required from them is not free. It adds overhead to the cost of doing business. Inventory always has financial implications!

A throwing-money-at-a-problem strategy causes funds to be invested in purchased inventory:

- If suppliers expect to be paid in 30 days (N30), paid-for purchased materials reside in a stockroom for 30 days before work begins in manufacturing.
- If manufacturing conversion time is 4 weeks, money is committed to WIP for the 4 weeks required to manufacture the product.
- If FGI levels are 3 to 4 weeks, cash is committed for an additional 3 to 4 weeks.
- If invoices are not always paid immediately after products have been shipped to satisfy a customer's demand, cash is committed even longer.

Using this typical inventory investment as an example, money will be committed to the inventory strategy for at least 12 to 13 weeks, resulting in an inventory turn of four. An inventory turn rate of four translates into a working capital requirement of 25 cents of every dollar shipped in revenue to support this level of committed, purchased inventories. What is an acceptable level of working capital for your company?

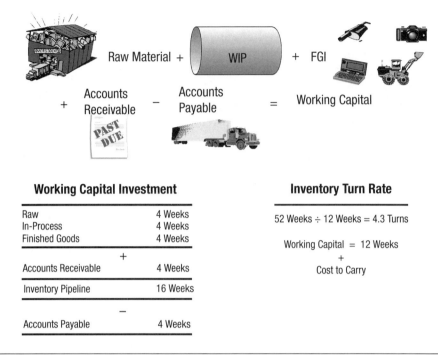

Working Capital Investment	
Raw	4 Weeks
In-Process	4 Weeks
Finished Goods	4 Weeks
+	
Accounts Receivable	4 Weeks
Inventory Pipeline	16 Weeks
−	
Accounts Payable	4 Weeks

Inventory Turn Rate

52 Weeks ÷ 12 Weeks = 4.3 Turns

Working Capital = 12 Weeks
+
Cost to Carry

Figure 4.2. Inventories affect working capital and inventory turn rates.

LEAN STRATEGY AND WORKING CAPITAL

A Lean manufacturing system reduces the working capital investment required to operate a business just by reducing the manufacturing response time. As ongoing lead time reductions are completed by continuous improvement initiatives, so are corresponding inventory reductions and the associated working capital reductions. These reductions in lead time, WIP inventory, and working capital are exciting to consider, but the initial Lean business transformation only gathers the low-hanging fruit of *excess* WIP and FGI inventories. Although any significant inventory reduction is a great payback that is rewarding for the courage required to begin an initial Lean transformation project, long-term benefits must continue to be realized by using ongoing, continuous-improvement (kaizen) initiatives. Figure 4.2 illustrates how inventories affect working capital and inventory turn rates.

Although not as spectacular as the savings realized from the initial business transformation effort, subsequent savings will still continue to accrue. Ongoing reductions in lead time will continue to make the manufacturer more competitive in the marketplace, generating more sales revenue for the company. Continuing reductions in lead time will further reduce working capital and inventories. In addition to the tangible inventory savings, the manufacturer will receive benefits in the form of cost avoidance in the important category of *cost to carry*.

The costs of carrying inventory are incurred just for the luxury of having inventory. Most of these costs are embedded in overhead, the second largest component of product cost. Examples of cost to carry include the lost opportunity of not collecting interest payments on the financial value of the inventory; warehousing; maintaining environmental conditions (e.g., heating and cooling); cycle counting and record keeping; taxes and insurance; internal movement; floor and rack space; scrap and obsolescence; and loss of ROI on the funds used to purchase the inventory. Cost to carry is often difficult to quantify. Many companies therefore estimate this cost as a percentage of total inventory value. Although every company is different because of the cost of borrowing money, common percentages range from 12 to 20%. Imagine the value of annual cost avoidance equal to 12% of your total inventory investment. This invisible benefit will be enjoyed year after year, long after the dramatic savings realized by the initial implementation are history.

A manufacturer may express interest in a Lean operating system to achieve a favorable lead time differential for improving market share, but because lead time, working capital, and cost to carry are so intertwined, the individual benefits obtained from a Lean operating system cannot be separated from one another because Lean delivers improvement in all areas simultaneously. A Lean manufacturer therefore cannot pick and choose which benefits to include with a transformation project.

REFERENCES

1. E.M. Forster. *The Celestial Omnibus.* In *The Celestial Omnibus and Other Stories.* London: Sidgwick & Jackson, 1911.

2. Peter Childs. *The Celestial Omnibus*, as cited in *The Literary Encyclopedia*, January 8, 2001. London: The Literary Dictionary Company; available at http://www.litencyc.com/php/sworks.php?rec=true&UID=1310.

3. E.M. Forster. *The Celestial Omnibus and Other Stories* (1911). London: Snowbooks, 2005.

4. George Koenigsaecker, Leadership and the lean transformation, in *Manufacturing Engineering*, November 2005: Vol. 135, No. 5; available at http://findarticles.com/p/articles/mi_qa3618/is_200511/ai_n15847432/.

5. Media interview; see also *Doing the Lido Shuffle: Lee Iacocca, Bob Lutz, and Bob Eaton*. Copyright © 1998–2000, David Zatz; Copyright © 2001–2010, Allpar LLC; Copyright © 2009, Curtis Redgap. All rights reserved; available at http://www.allpar.com/corporate/bios/lido.html.

PART II
TRANSFORMING
THE BUSINESS

5

THE COMPANY: MAKING THE TRANSFORMATION TO A LEAN OPERATING SYSTEM

The Lean manufacturing model uses a different approach to satisfying customer demand when compared to traditional planned, scheduled, order-launch methodologies. Using a Lean operating model therefore requires a manufacturer to rethink how customer demand is processed through their facility. Recall that a traditional planning system model must be loyal to the three manufacturing paradigms of a planning system: grouping manufacturing resources by function; routing products through departments in batches; and the quest for level production schedules. A Lean operating system does not recognize these three paradigms.

Demand in a traditional model. Planned, scheduled, order-launch factories are organized by individual departments. These departments are grouped together based solely on process similarity. The grouping has little to do with the resulting capacity and little consideration is given to whether capacity is too much or too little. Traditional planning systems also process production orders in batches that are rarely in sync with actual customer demand. Preset batch sizes designed to optimize department utilization are preferred rather than discreet quantities matched to actual customer demand. Traditional systems are driven to produce at a rate equal to the capacity of an individual department with no regard to actual customer demand. When customer demand is less than capacity, the unsold production resulting from the full utilization of excess capacity is consigned to finished goods inventory.

Demand in a Lean model. The features of the Lean operating system concentrate on aligning factory resources with actual customer demand. Little or no consideration is given to department structures, preassigned batch sizes, or routing routines through departments. The benefits of the Lean manufacturing model are a result of the operational features of a Lean system:

- *One-unit-at-a-time production.* There are no preset batch sizes. Production quantity is sized to equal customer demand. Production flows down the Lean line one unit at a time.

- *Balanced resources.* Only the number of resources (people, machines, workstations) required for producing actual customer demand balanced through each set of dissimilar manufacturing processes is used — no more, no less.

- *Linked resources.* All processes required for the manufacture of customer demand are physically linked to one another. Standard work is processed at the same rate of production. Utilization of resources in each process is determined by customer demand, not the stated capacity of the department.

- *Work authorization.* A production order is not required as an authorization to produce the next unit. Because manufacturing processes are linked together and balanced to operate at the same speed, authorization to produce the next unit is from a kanban signal. Units are pulled through the system based on customer consumption of a completed product from a downstream workstation. Lean manufacturing is a *pull* system rather than the push system used in a traditional order-launch model.

- *Standardized workstations.* The standard work content of a product is divided into equal elements of work and assigned to a specific workstation. The work content does not change.

- *Quality criteria.* Quality elements are defined components of the standard work performed at each assigned workstation by the operator. Each operator is required to perform three inspections as part of the standard work at each workstation.

- *Flexible resources.* Resources may be added or subtracted each day as customer demand changes. Only the labor resources (the people) required for meeting customer demand are utilized. Operators are capable of producing the standard work content at three workstations and are trained to be flexible.

- *Materials replacement.* A kanban material replenishment system gives a signal to "replenish at the same rate as consumed." This signal places component materials at work locations in the manufacturing area where they were consumed.

Factory configuration in a traditional model. A traditional scheduled, order-launched, batch-based factory is designed with individual functional departments that are laid out in a configuration that allows using the manufacturing paradigms of grouping resources by function, routing products through departments in batches, and promoting 100% utilization of the resources at full capacity. The scheduled, order-launch, routing-through-department system is a *push* system. Planning system logic (MRP or manual) recommends the generation of sufficient production orders, issued in predetermined batch-size quantities, in response to actual and forecasted customer demand. These production orders are then launched into their gateway work centers. They then follow the scheduled routings and indented BOM as illustrated in Figure 5.1. Orders are scheduled, rescheduled, and expedited through the individual departments based on start and due dates established by the indented BOM and the MRP explosion logic. After production orders are launched, orders routed through imbalanced functional departments are managed based on individual departmental capacity and resource productivity goal performance measurements (utilization and efficiency). The priority of meeting an order due date on time is often less than the focus on meeting individual department utilization goals. When production order due dates are not met on time, expediting becomes the only solution to ensure customer satisfaction goals are met.

Factory configuration in a Lean model. A Lean factory is designed and physically laid out in a configuration wherein the output of one process is immediately consumed into a downstream process to facilitate the operational features of the Lean system. One-unit-at-a-time production is allowed using balanced processes that are capable of producing the preestablished capacity. When customer demand is less than the established capacity, only the number of resources sufficient to meet customer demand are linked together to produce products pulled by the consumption of the standard work completed at downstream workstations. The standard work content of a product is identified and divided equally among all workstations on the line. Dividing standard work content equally among all workstations causes a Lean line to be balanced. Balanced work means the standard work, regardless of the type and standard time of a process, is completed at the same rate at each workstation. A Lean manufacturing line is designed to respond to the consumption of a product by a downstream workstation beginning with the sale of a product to a customer. Because manufacturing processes are physically linked together, in-process, partially completed products residing in upstream workstations on a Lean line "ratchet" downstream one workstation at a time in response to a product being consumed. The consumption downstream becomes the signal for replenishment and serves as the authorization to produce another unit of standard work time at the upstream workstation (Figure

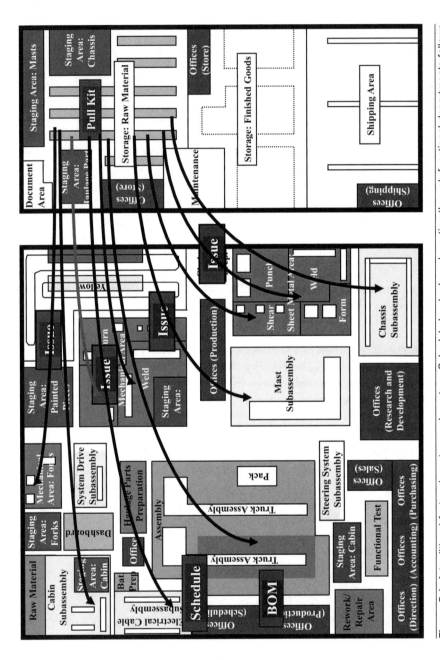

Figure 5.1. A traditional factory layout: a push system. Scheduled order-launch routing through functional departments follows an indented BOM.

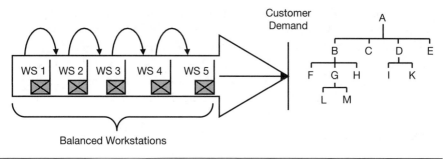

Figure 5.2. A Lean manufacturing configuration: a pull system.

5.2). Because standard work is divided equally among all workstations, all workstations require the same amount of time to complete the next unit of production.

A Lean business transformation is designed to facilitate a logical, orderly, smooth transition from a traditional *push* system factory layout to a Lean *pull* system factory layout capable of delivering all of the benefits of the Lean operating system. To achieve the benefits of Lean, however, implementation of a pull-type system will require completely rethinking the layout of a factory currently using a traditional push-type system. Without a reconfiguration of a traditional factory layout, achieving the full benefits of the Lean operating system will be compromised. The acceptable amount of compromise tolerated is a function of the Lean benefits a manufacturer is willing to live without. It's always a trade-off. What benefits are willing to be sacrificed for the comfort of maintaining the status quo?

CHALLENGES FOR A CHANGE AGENT

As with any project that requires changing an operating system, a Lean transformation needs a champion, a change agent, or a leader. Many of the obstacles awaiting a change agent/Lean champion have already been outlined in Part I: existing paradigms, people issues, and performance measurements. Current operating systems, procedures, and policies are well entrenched in most companies and the Lean operating system technologies will eventually challenge each one of them. In the business world, *antibody* is a popular, descriptive term for a protector of entrenched systems, policies, and procedures. Like antibodies in the human body, these entrenchment antibodies attack the introduction of anything foreign to the existing system. During a Lean transformation, antibodies manifest themselves as skeptics and resisters. Even if these antibodies cannot articulate their reasons for resistance, they will use the existing manufacturing paradigms as their defense to the implementation of Lean initiatives.

When all is said and done, a successful transformation to a Lean operating system *demands* that modifications be made to an existing system. How ready, willing, and able is your company to begin a Lean transformation? Is the company ready to confront the antibodies? If you have been selected as the change agent to lead a Lean transformation, as an individual how prepared are you to defend the necessary changes that must be made?

Assess Readiness

Answers to the questions in the following checklist will give you some idea of how prepared you and your company are to make significant changes to an existing operating system.

Readiness Assessment Checklist

Historical perspective

- How long have you been aware of the current situation?
- How did it evolve?
- How have you been dealing with it?
- What solutions have failed or succeeded?
- What led to the decision to begin a Lean business transformation project?

Overall motivation

- Will the company take ownership of the project and embrace it?
- To what extent does the transformation project respond to a goal that all say is important, but seem to be reluctant to work toward?
- Does motivation in the organization seem to be different in various groups?
- What is your opinion of the possible benefits of the transformation project?
- Where does the transformation project fit in your hierarchy of concerns: is it a top-priority issue or just something that you think the company needs to address?
- What is your motivation for participating in the transformation project: are you enthusiastic or passive?
- Are there other motivational issues?

Overall understanding

- Do you understand the implications of the transformation project for the organization?
- Do key players in the organization have a basic understanding of the specific product or output of the transformation project: who will use it and how will they use it?
- Does the project have a sharply defined outcome?
- Are there measures of success?
- Are there any issues concerning the project that may not be understood?

Climate for change

- Does the company have a culture for change or a culture to maintain the status quo?
- What are the pressures for change in the company and where do they come from?
- Who wants change to take place?
- Who does not care?
- Who is against change?

- Is there overt resistance to change?
- Does the culture in the company support the types of changes that might be required by the project?
- What are other cultural issues?

Resource allocation and level of commitment

- Is the budget for the project clearly stated?
- What is your estimate of the time, energy, and internal support required to carry out the transformation project?
- Are resource commitments from other groups or people required? If so, have they been secured?

Technical capacity and change management skills

- Do you expect to participate in the actual work?
- Do you have the knowledge necessary to carry out the project?
- Do you have the capacity to implement innovation and change: have you demonstrated that you can absorb new ideas and exploit them usefully?
- Does your recent experience indicate you have the ability to carry out the changes and adaptations that will be required by the transformation project?
- Do you have a reputation for finishing projects on time and within budget?
- What are knowledge and skill issues in the company?

Scope, pace, and results

- What do you think is an appropriate scope for the transformation project?
- What pace seems right to you?
- Can you move the project along rapidly?
- Are there any scope and pace issues?
- What are the tangible results of the project?
- How quickly does some type of tangible result need to be seen?

Success factors

- When describing the transformation project, do you and the management team use key words that mean essentially the same thing?
- Are there any solutions that will be unacceptable in the organization?
- Are there any issues related to success that have not yet been addressed?

By answering these questions, can you predict where potential antibodies will be within your organization?

No company or individual will receive 100% positive responses to all of the questions in the assessment. The assessment just helps determine the expected level of support for a proposed Lean transformation project. The answers can also identify issues a company may have when making changes and help Lean change agents be better prepared to defend the transformation project. As a Lean champion, you must agree with the decision to proceed with a Lean project. You and your management team must agree to repair or strengthen any elements identified as being weak by the readiness assessment. In many cases, the Lean techniques will be foreign to the existing operating system. As a Lean champion, not only must you be able to advance Lean methodologies in the presence of antibodies, but for the company you must also be the primary "evangelist" for the benefits of Lean. You must have a thorough understanding of the Lean operating system outlined in previous chapters and how a Lean operating system differs from the current operating system.

Management. Skeptics and resisters will mount passive aggressive attacks on the business transformation behind your back. The Lean champion must continuously bolster management from these relentless attacks. If support from management falters, even transformation team members may become antibodies, greatly diminishing the likelihood of your success as a Lean champion. If a decision has been made to begin a business transformation and you have been assigned the role of Lean champion, leader, or change agent, but the business transformation does not have the support of the entire management team, especially from the top levels at your site, *do not begin* the Lean transformation project. It will fail. If you are the change agent, you will be blamed for its failure.

You. If you have been chosen as the Lean champion, change agent, or team leader against your will or if you do not believe whole heartedly that Lean can make a difference in your company, do yourself and your company a favor — *do not begin* the Lean transformation project. It is far better to spend your time working on smaller incremental changes to the existing manufacturing paradigms seeking improvements. You'll avoid creating the antibodies that can make life miserable. Maybe you'll even improve the existing operating model one more time. Everyone will be happier, too.

Compromising. Every compromise made to maintain the status quo diminishes the benefits received from a Lean operating system. Making too many Lean technology compromises to appease skeptics and resisters will reduce the success of the Lean operating system. Possibly some of the reasons 22% of manufacturers report they are unhappy with their Lean initiatives are the result of yielding too many compromises to the skeptics and resisters during the implementation of their Lean strategies![1] If your company is open to compromise but not ready, willing, and able to make the necessary changes for the implementation of a Lean operating system, *do not even consider beginning* a Lean transformation project. You'll join the ranks of the 22% who are not happy with the results of their Lean initiatives.

Establish Basic Progress Reporting

Achieving measurable results is the primary goal of any business transformation project. When management has agreed to go forward with a Lean transformation project, the potential areas of resistance have been identified, a strategy for dealing with resisters has been developed, and the benchmarks for success have been identified, the next step before beginning the transformation project is reaching a consensus for measuring performance. One component of measuring success should address the opportunities identified by the strategic business assessment. Track and record progress toward achieving these objectives as a key measurement of success. (If the business objectives cannot be established prior to the start of an implementation project, identify them as soon as possible during the transformation process.)

KPIs. Specific business goals that should be tracked frequently to assess the progress from a Lean transformation are referred to as key performance indicators (see Table 5.1 for suggested KPIs). Often KPIs are also prominently posted in employee areas so the entire organization can watch progress being made as a Lean project moves forward. Some manufacturers use a device known as dashboard to follow the progress of a transformation project.

Dashboards. A dashboard is a metaphor for the gauges on the dashboard of an automobile that show the status of operating systems and allow them to be monitored. Seeing multiple dashboards in various locations throughout a manufacturing facility is not unusual. Dashboards can look very impressive. To be effective, dashboards must have the agreed-upon KPIs with accurate information. The information must be updated frequently with the latest information. Maintaining a dashboard can be a major project in itself. If delegated to an employee who has other responsibilities, the dashboard might only be updated as time permits, with maintenance becoming lower and lower in the employee's inbox of priorities. If not maintained on a regular basis, the dashboard eventually may in fact have erroneous or obsolete information. If not current and accurate, dashboards lose credibility. Employees soon lose interest in seeing old information and stop looking at the dashboards. When dashboards are no longer relevant, their display of information simply becomes non-value-added.

Posting KPIs is a good idea, but keep one caveat in mind: a dashboard is highly visible. Sometimes, managers who simply want to impress upper management about how committed they are to the transformation project will abuse the real purpose of a dashboard by adding superfluous items that are unrelated to the agreed-upon KPIs. These items are added to make the dashboard larger and look more impressive. A resistant manager might even use a dashboard as a convenient way to give the appearance of being supportive of change.

Table 5.1. Key Performance Indicators

	KPI	Description	Related to
1	Number of corrective action reports (CARs)	A measurement of problems reported each month from customers (number of quality incidences at customer locations)	Customer satisfaction
2	Number of repeat CARs	A measurement of closures of recurring problems (repeated concerns; closing a CAR means a permanent solution has been found, verified, and implemented; problem will not recur.)	Customer satisfaction
3	Delivery schedule adherence: on-time (%)	[Number of planned deliveries − (number of missed + number of wrong quantity)] ÷ total deliveries	Customer satisfaction
4	PPM (parts per million) external defects	(Quantity of defective units ÷ total quantity supplied) × 1,000,000	Customer satisfaction
5	PPM (parts per million) internal defects	(Quantity of defective units ÷ total quantity produced) × 1,000,000	Manufacturing and quality
6	FTT (first time through)	Percentage of parts shipped to customers that are not rejected for any repair or rework	Manufacturing and quality
7	Repair or rework (%)	Percentage of parts that needed some type of repair or rework before they could be shipped	Manufacturing and quality
8	Scrap (%)	The percentage of parts lost in the manufacturing process (output ÷ input)	Manufacturing and quality
9	OEE (%)	Availability × performance × quality	Manufacturing and quality
10	People productivity	Units made ÷ standard work definition time assigned to making those units	Manufacturing and quality
11	Process cycle effeciency	Value-added time ÷ total lead time	Manufacturing and quality
12	Floor space utilization ($)	Sales revenue ÷ total area	Manufacturing and quality
13	Linearity	Daily rate − absolute deviation ÷ daily rate	Manufacturing and quality
14	Number of recorded injuries (NRIs)	Total number of injuries each month needing treatment by a physician as reported to the U.S. government (often measured as the number of recordable injuries/200,000 hours; measurement made to compare injuries in different companies, e.g., average injury rate in U.S. automotive industry is about 7 injuries per 200,000 hours)	Overhead and safety
15	Lost time rate (LTR)	Actual number of hours or minutes lost to the recordable injuries until physician approves worker to return to work, including restrictions)	Overhead and safety
16	Housekeeping and 6S	Score of 6S (with the sixth S being safety)	Workplace organization and 6S

Table 5.1. Key Performance Indicators (continued)

	Financial Measures	
17	Inventory turnover	Sales ÷ average inventory
18	Return on capital employed (ROCE)	Pre-tax profit ÷ (shareholder's funds + long-term loans + other long-term liabilities) × 100%
19	Return on assets	Net income ÷ average total assets
20	Value added ($)	Value added (sales − purchases)
21	Value added per person (VAPP) ($)	Value added (sales − value of purchased material) ÷ number of total employees
22	Revenue ($)	Total income
23	Revenue per employee ($)	Total income ÷ total number of employees
24	Pre-tax profit per employee ($)	Pre-tax profit ÷ number of employees
25	Investment ($)	New capital investments
26	Exports (% of revenue)	Export sales (in $) ÷ total sales
	Human Resource Measures	
27	Turnover (%)	Employees leaving ÷ total employees
28	Direct ratio	Number of direct employees/number of indirect employees
29	Absenteeism direct (%)	Number of absence days ÷ total number direct employees × working days
30	Training hours per employee	Number of absence days ÷ total number direct × working days
31	Employee growth	Number of total labor and staff employees (includes casual, daily operators and permanent staff)
32	Safety scoring	Safety score per OHSAS 18000
33	Improvements ideas from employees	Number of applicable improvement ideas
	Lean Program Deployment Measures	
34	Trainees completing training	Number of employees who completed Lean training
35	Trainees certified	Numbered of trainees certified in the Lean program
36	Lean penetration (% of total)	(Number of Lean trainees + leadership for Lean + kaizen workshops) ÷ total employees
37	Projects launched	Number of Lean projects started
38	Projects completed	Number of Lean projects completed
39	Savings value ($)	Total cumulative savings for Lean projects and kaizen
40	Actions launched	Number of actions started in the Program Master Action Plan
41	Actions completed (%)	Percent of actions completed in the Program Master Action Plan

DESIGNING THE LINE: DETERMINING PROJECT SCOPE

During the design phase, the Lean champion will need assistance with the tasks necessary to design the line and then to complete the layout design of the factory. A key success factor in any project, including a Lean line design project, is defining size. *Size* or the *scope* of a transformation project must be identified. Staffing needs and team members for the Lean transformation project itself must also be determined.

Interdependencies exist between the staffing needs and the size of the project. Although determining the *right* number of people to assign to a transformation team is dictated by the size of the project, there are no hard and fast rules for developing the scope of a Lean transformation. *Size* is a very subjective term. What determines size? Is it sales revenue? What if sales revenue is large, but the volume of a product is very small? Does product volume dictate size? Is there a magic number that separates large from small? What about square footage (meters) in the factory? Does a physically large plant define size? What about employees? Does the number of people working at a facility determine size?

Traditional descriptions of size are not the best criteria to use for scoping a Lean transformation project. A better basis for determining project size is the number of processes that the Lean line will be designed to handle. The *number of processes* should dictate size because the *work* necessary to mathematically model the Lean manufacturing line is directly related to the number of processes the line requires to produce its products.

Scoping the transformation project. Transformation team members will be required to collect the standard work times for each process of each product. More processes and products will require more data collection time. A good place to start is to use an 80/20 analysis to determine the most likely product mix and volume to be produced on the Lean line. The top 20% of your company's products by volume usually represents 80% of the sales revenue. As the product volume of the remaining 80% of products becomes smaller, the impact of these products on the final Lean line design will become less and less. The remaining 80% of total product volume usually makes up only 20% of the sale revenue. At a certain point, the data collected on small-volume products becomes superfluous, with a diminishing return of information value for the work required to collect any data beyond the top 20% of all those products that make up 80% of the sales revenue. Trying to predict infrequent demand or small-volume products with any degree of accuracy is almost impossible. Additionally, product mixes and volumes eventually running on the line will likely be different from the product data used to design the line anyway. Small-volume products ordered infrequently will have little effect on the accuracy of the line design. It's not worth the time it

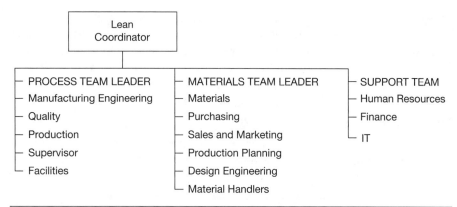

Figure 5.3. Disciplines needed for the members of a Lean transformation team.

takes to document them. The time required to collect this less relevant data only delays design of the Lean line.

Because of the large amounts of information required to model the factory, keep the scope of a Lean transformation *workable*. The goal for designing the Lean line is to collect an appropriate amount of data to represent the products produced most frequently — sufficient data to represent what occurs on the shop floor on most days. As the transformation project moves forward, manage the data collection process. To maintain efficiency, avoid spending time collecting unnecessary data. Collecting unnecessary data places additional demands on the time of team members who have regular work assignments to complete. The last thing a transformation project should become is a never-ending data-collection exercise that leads to participant burnout. Remember the 22% of companies that failed to achieve benefits from a Lean initiative? A major contributor was burned out.[1] Avoid diminishing the enthusiasm of a Lean line design project with data collection that returns little benefit and has the appearance of having no end.

Even though every employee will not participate as a Lean project team member, providing company-wide training about the overall concepts and project goals of the Lean transformation is necessary. Everyone must at least be aware of the Lean concepts and the expected changes that will occur in the various areas of expertise. Understanding the dynamics of operating a multiproduct Lean line is vital. Design the training sessions with the appropriate levels of detail required for project completion. Complete training sessions prior to commencing implementation activities.

Staffing the transformation project. A transformation project is best served by team members who have backgrounds that represent the widest possible spectrum of disciplines in the company (Figure 5.3). In most companies, the multidiscipline manpower needed for completing a transformation project will not just be sitting around on a bench waiting for a new project to come along so there will be something to do. Most employees are usually fully consumed with their own day-to-day responsibilities. Assignment to a new project simply means extra work. For some employees, however, the extra work associated with a new project is not unwelcome because being assigned to an important, high-visibility project provides several intrinsic rewards:

- Public recognition of their skills and competence
- A learning experience for obtaining new skills that can be used for career advancement
- Change that adds excitement to daily routines that may have become repetitious or boring
- The advantages of being a member of a team that is working to achieve an important goal
- An opportunity to share in the satisfaction of a job well done when the transformation project is finished

The intrinsic rewards associated with Lean projects are why they start off with much enthusiasm and excitement. Early in the project, enthusiasm and excitement easily compensate for the extra work and the time away from the team members' primary responsibilities. As the project continues, however, primary job requirements often begin to take precedence over participation in the Lean transformation project. Managers become less and less sympathetic to team members who are working on priorities other than those in their own departments. Lean project assignments can easily fall to the bottom of an inbox and not be completed on time. Over time, fewer team members come to meetings. The high work volume for team members and loss of interest as a Lean project moves forward are primary reasons to carefully consider the scope of a project. Even for the best of transformation projects, enthusiasm will diminish in proportion to the length of elapsed time required to complete the project.

DESIGNING THE LINE: SELECTING THE PRODUCTS

Product selection can be the subject of long, heated discussions. Some team members are inclined to include as many products as possible from every possible product line. Others want to include all unusual or special products because they remember the problems they had the last time those items were manufactured. Although including every product from the company catalog along with every possible combination of customer options will guarantee that the final list of products is as complete as possible, the question becomes *is it practical for the success of the line design*?

When thinking about products to include in the Lean line model, consider the purpose of the completed Lean line. What is it designed to do? Remember that a Lean line design attempts to model what happens on the factory floor *most of the time*. It is a prediction of the product and volume mix ordered most often by customers. Like any forecast or prediction, what happens on the shop floor cannot be predicted with 100% accuracy. Is anyone in the factory clairvoyant enough to project precisely the exact quantity of each product model that will be sold in the future? Can anyone remember a production schedule from a year ago? If anyone could predict the future with 100% accuracy, they would surely be somewhere else more profitable for them than the factory floor. Old-timers might remember a special model production run, but it's unlikely that they can recall the timing or the quantity of the run. Chances are good that the answer to both questions will be *no one can*.

Designing a Lean line to include all possible models offered by a company is unrealistic. A Lean transformation team may try to design the factory to include every possible permutation of every product in the company catalog, but all this ever accomplishes is never-ending discussions and debates about relevance while potentially collecting mountains of data with questionable value. If they try to include all of the special models that may have caused them personal grief in the past, team members can easily become bogged down trying to predict recurring events that might possibly happen in the future. In the end, predicting future events is an exercise in futility. Is it possible that trying to design a Lean manufacturing line to include all of the products, all of the unfortunate incidents, and all of the people, all of the time, may have contributed to the dissatisfaction of those 22% of manufacturers who were unhappy with their Lean transformation projects?[1]

When a Lean line is being designed, first acknowledge that the future cannot be predicted. Then base product selection decisions on the *products that are produced most often* and the *items that make up the majority of the items used* in the factory. This simple technique of focusing on the most-often-produced products and the most-often-used items makes a Lean line transformation project manageable and practical. Also acknowledge that, on occasion, customers will request special orders with special options. There is no way of predicting their timing and volume. Special orders will certainly be an anomaly for a Lean line, but so what? Why design the factory for an occasional anomaly? If special orders are infrequent and their volume is small, a Lean line deals with them easily. Tomorrow, the anomaly will be gone and the Lean line will return to normal operation!

In a Lean operating system, any product is defined as the sum of its *standard work content* and its *parts*. Remember this definition when considering the products to be included in the Lean line design. Both of the elements that make up a product will be designed as a separate system.

The product selection process. Candidate products must be representative of all of the products to be produced on the line. Candidate products must also include every manufacturing process required for each product. When the list of candidate products has been finalized, review the list product by product to confirm that all required manufacturing processes have been identified. Once the representative products to be produced on the Lean line have been chosen from the list of candidate products, the manufacturing processes used to produce the standard work content of each of the representative products must be documented. At this point, however, the processes used to manufacture the products are the most important consideration. The standard work will be identified and documented at a later time.

The product rationalization process. Pareto analysis is a helpful method for selecting products for a Lean line. Vilfredo Pareto, an Italian economist, observed that only a small fraction (typically 15 to 20%) in a population accounts for the major portion of activity (80 to 85%). The Pareto principle is popularly known as the 80/20 rule. A Pareto analysis of the historical sales of all products in a company often reveals a surprising perspective on the models produced most often in the factory. (An 80/20 analysis is also a good starting place for achieving a workable project scope.)

Performing a Pareto analysis. A simple spreadsheet program that lists all possible product permutations in one column and their historical sales volumes in a separate column can be used to construct a Pareto analysis. Select the *Sort Ascending* command for the sales history column and sum the list until 80% of the total sales volume has been identified. Based on Pareto's observation, this grouping of 80% of the sales volume will be represented by approximately 20% of the total SKUs. For most manufacturers, 20% of the possible product permutations will rationalize a more workable number of products for a transformation project and will be significant enough in number to represent the majority of items produced in the factory. As a line capability statement for a newly designed Lean line, an 80/20 mix would mean that 80% of all possible customer demand could be supplied immediately upon receipt of a customer order based on the production of just 20% of the product mix. Conversely, customers will still order SKUs making up 80% of the total products list, but these orders will occur only 20% of the time. Based on this Pareto observation, first-time customer fulfillment policies can be articulated as a delivery strategy. Additional strategies for capturing market share using a rapid delivery differential can be developed by modifying the revenue to SKU proportions with an alternative 85/15, 90/10, or 95/5 strategy. Choosing the alternative strategy to pursue is based on the amount of inventory investment (for the cost of increased component inventories) the company is willing to make to support the strategy. The spreadsheet developed to determine the initial mix of SKUs can easily be extended to determine which products and how many of each will be required to achieve the increased customer fulfillment rate beyond the 80% revenue base. The spreadsheet will allow multiple iterations of mix and volume to determine the ideal mix and volume versus the inventory investment required for alternative policies. Begin with the first iteration of 80/20 and experiment with the higher percentages of sales to test the best proportion for the company. The work content of products beyond the 80% sales relationship will be produced on the resulting Lean line by using a separate parts strategy to meet the higher demand requirements. Using an increased mix strategy can improve market share by increasing speed to market over competitors, but it requires additional inventory investment and incurs the risk of creating slow-moving or obsolete inventories. The risk of increased inventory investment, however, may be worth the trade off for an increased ownership of the market. Although the top 20% of products sold represents 80% of the total mix of products manufactured in the facility, customer demand for the other 80% of products still represents 20% of remaining sales — 20% that cannot be ignored. The Lean line must also be capable of building the sales volume of these products. Remember that part of choosing products for the Lean line design is to identify the manufacturing processes required to produce *all* products. Therefore, for the 80% volume of product SKUs produced, process identification for the Lean line must determine if there are any additional processes not identified by the 20% of product SKU population chosen to be representative of all products. Any products with manufacturing processes that have not been identified in the original 20% of SKUs selected for the line design must be added to the final product selection to be certain all processes are represented.

Based on the premise that the products chosen to be produced on your Lean manufacturing line represent 80% of the sales revenue in the company and are produced with similar processes, how really different are these products from one another? When choosing products based on similarities in processes, certain physical differences can be distracting: color, size, revisions, and customer options. Team members not accustomed to thinking about product designations based only on manufacturing processes may find that product differences are difficult to distinguish if they depend only on a product's appearance. Appearance has more to do with the parts used to construct the product and less to do with the actual manufacturing processes used to manufacture them. When choosing products to represent all the products to be produced on a Lean line, disregard color, size, options, and any other appearance-related characteristics when considering products with similar manufacturing processes. This should help to limit the number of products selected. Once products representing all of the products made in the factory have been selected, the only other factor impacting resources will be the production volume through those processes.

The parts. Parent part numbers must be selected for the design of a Lean manufacturing line to ensure that any location where any standard work is performed is identified. Sometimes parent part number consolidation will be obvious in the total population of products. If the total number of products produced in a factory is small, using an 80/20 rationalization of the parent parts list is unnecessary. For most manufacturers with a lengthy list of end-item products, however, a Pareto analysis of the parent part numbers is the best tool for identifying a carefully condensed selection of products to use in the design of a Lean manufacturing line.

When designing a Lean line, appearance and individual component materials are *secondary* to process identification. Only the processes and product options requiring additional labor, a separate physical location (e.g., a third-party process located outside the factory), or a subassembly process required to manufacture an option should be included in the final product population to be certain all processes have been identified. As long as all manufacturing processes are represented for 100% of the products that could potentially be produced on the line, the 20% of product SKUs and any unique processes represented by the other 80% of product sales will be sufficiently represented for the Lean line design project. Once all processes have been identified, only throughput volume remains to be documented to determine the amount of resources needed to meet customer demand.

DESIGNING THE FACILITY: ESTABLISHING LINE CAPACITY

Think of the design of a Lean manufacturing facility as being the same as building a new physical plant. When standing on an empty lot, a facility engineer must know the answers to two basic questions: what products will be built in the new facility and how many of those products must be produced to achieve the desired sales goals? These same questions must be answered when designing a new Lean manufacturing line. *What to build* has been answered because the representative products identifying all the processes have been selected. Now, the required sales volume for each of the selected products must be identified. The projected sales volume of the selected products is important: not only as a statement of future sales, but also as a statement of the factory capacity needed to produce them. Factory capacity is finite during a specified period of time. At some point, every factory has a saturation point — not one more additional unit can be produced.

A Lean manufacturing line requires its capacity to be expressed as a *daily quantity*: the maximum quantity of sales that can be expected on any given day. This daily statement of capacity is the saturation point of a Lean line. The stated daily sales volume for a Lean line is therefore the *maximum* quantity that can be produced in a single day. The line is incapable of producing one more unit that day. The daily rate of sales is a statement of the production capacity of a Lean line. The stated daily volume (the maximum capacity) of a Lean line is called its *volume at capacity* (V_c). Because V_c states the maximum production capacity on a given day, traditional capacity requirements planning routines become obsolete:

Customer demand $\div$ V_c = number of days required to meet customer demand

When customer order quantities are greater than the stated V_c, additional days of production (not to exceed the V_c) are required to meet the excess customer demand.

Communicating capacity. The volume of sales for a Lean manufacturing line is the stated volume of product that can be produced in 1 day on the line, with a day defined as the number of working hours scheduled in a single 24-hour period. This statement simplifies communicating the capacity of the line. A daily quantity sold in excess of the V_c cannot be produced in the time period identified as a day. Producing a daily quantity in excess of the V_c can only be accomplished by using additional days or by running the line longer than the identified daily time period. Promises made to a customer by the sales and marketing department for volumes in excess of the daily V_c cannot be met. These promises can only be met by using additional days or by running the line longer.

Although V_c is a statement of maximum volume, demand quantities smaller than V_c can be produced on a Lean line. The ability to produce quantities *less than* the line's designed capacity is critical for avoiding overproduction and the resulting inventory (waste) caused by traditional planning systems.

The V_c of a Lean line should not be stated in terms of existing production capacities in the factory or even in terms of the expected sales volume on the first day of line operation. A new Lean manufacturing line should be designed with a sales volume capacity sufficient to produce customer demand at a level *greater than customer demand today*. From the first day of startup of the line, sufficient capacity must be designed into the line to allow production of customer demand that reflects some increase in future sales volume. Projecting greater sale volume assumes that sales volume will increase over time. It's an optimistic statement of the company's future growth potential. Designing a Lean line with enough capacity to meet a future sales volume ensures that constant redesigning will not be necessary each time small, incremental sales increases are realized.

How much capacity? A Lean manufacturing line should be designed with sufficient capacity to support customer demand for 1 to 3 years into the future. The actual time horizon will be a function of the technological lifespan of the company's products. High-tech products are typically reinvented in their marketplace more often than stable, low-tech, commodity-type products. With a 3-year projection, as time passes, and future sales volume projections grow to become today's sales volume, the factory will once again require redesign, but not before the 3-year projection. If the 3-year projection is reached sooner, indications are that company sales have also exceeded original projections, which is not a bad thing! Forecasts are never perfect, but the impact of a faulty forecast on a 3-year projection of sales volume is not as damaging as forecasts with horizons of only a few months that require recurring line redesign.

Projecting V_c. A projection of customer demand and a statement of capacity must be made before the Lean manufacturing line design can be completed. Projecting V_c, however, is usually easier talked about than done. V_c must be established as the result of serious consideration. The first attempt at projecting V_c is frequently completed by estimating the annual sales of a product and dividing that number by the number of scheduled work days in a year to arrive at a daily rate of sales. As the projection moves forward, many variables that can affect future demand are often introduced into the discussion: the product's expected life cycle, the volatility of technological changes in the industry, and unanticipated market share growth patterns. These variables complicate making projections. (When demand is plotted on a graph, the lower the slope of expected demand, the higher confidence is in the demand projection into the future. Conversely, the steeper the slope of expected demand, the lower the confidence is in the accuracy of the projection.) Functional organizational units can be quite anxious about making projections. Sales and marketing is hesitant to make sales projections because they are usually held accountable for them. Manufacturing is extremely cautious about volume projections that might affect the timing of capital expenditures. Projecting future sales and allowing for all the possible variables make achieving a consensus on future demand one of the most difficult tasks to complete in any transformation project. A Lean project manager should expect significant posturing and second guessing before consensus on the final statement of V_c can be reached. After several iterations of volume and product mix have been tried, the final projected daily customer demand (V_c) must be authorized and signed off on by the management team (steering committee).

Sources of Customer Demand Information

Sales history, intuitive knowledge based on previous manufacturing experiences, and forecasts are important sources of customer demand information.

Sales history. Recorded history reveals the reality of past sales, leaving little room for interpretation. Quantities of a product were either sold or they were not. A good starting point for beginning the determination of future V_c is the sales volumes identified by the Pareto analysis when products were selected for the original Lean line design. Sorting historical demand for all products identifies the top ±20% of all products that make up ±80% of all sales revenue. Sales volumes of the remaining 20% volume of products must be taken into account and added incrementally to the 80% volume number to reflect the total historical sales volume to include their impact on resources for all products. Calculating a simple proportion equation to compare the historical 80% volume to the projected 100% volume of future sales can be provided by an extrapolated V_c (80% volume is to historical volume as X is to projected volume). A future V_c for each of the product families selected for inclusion in the Lean line design can now be identified. The sum of the V_c for all selected products should equal the volume required to meet the total projected sales revenue of the company. If, however, only demand identified from historical sales is used to design the new Lean manufacturing line, will a good result be guaranteed? The answer is obvious. Historical sales data alone should not be used to predict future demand. Too many conditions can impact sales. Historical sales provide a good baseline, but more timely information, e.g., updates about current market conditions, new marketing strategies, and anticipated new product introductions, is required to fine tune the baseline historical data.

Intuitive knowledge. The manufacturing group is often the best source of intuitive information. Intuitive knowledge is often referred to as "a gut feeling" or "tribal knowledge." Intuitive knowledge is based on instinct. It cannot be substantiated by facts. Based on the product mix and the quantities running on the manufacturing lines, the manufacturing group can often spot changing product demand trends before the sales and marketing group. The manufacturing group is also more likely to have a high visibility of service and spare part requests. Service and part requests can indicate product preferences or potential shifts in customer preferences for one model over another. Beyond a forecast received from the sales and marketing group, when making projections about the products to produce, the manufacturing group relies on the only tools it has at its disposal: sales history and intuitive knowledge based on past experience. Both are backward-looking, with no visibility into the future. Just as using only historical sales data is risky, so too is using only intuitive knowledge, but do not discount it when making future product projections. Even though intuitive information is subjective, it can be eye-opening when making projections about future sales. Solicit input from individuals who have intuitive knowledge when establishing the future volume for a Lean line design.

Forecasts. For most companies using planning systems, the sales and marketing group is typically responsible for forecasting. Unlike the manufacturing group who relies solely on historical sales information and intuitive knowledge, the sales and marketing group has much better visibility into the future. This group is responsible for marketing programs that can impact daily volumes. From participating in planning sessions and discussing new marketing strategies and shifting customer desires, sales and marketing has knowledge of future corporate sales initiatives. Sales and marketing has first-person relationships with customers. Sales and marketing also has the most objective information for forecasting future sales. Historical sales data is used as a baseline and dovetailed with empirical data and intuitive knowledge from the manufacturing group. Because of their knowledge of projected future demand, input from the sales and marketing group is crucial when establishing the V_c for a Lean line design.

Although the exact mix and volume of products cannot be humanly predicted with 100% accuracy, predictions can be more accurate if they are based on the sales of a family of products rather than the sales of individual product SKUs. When the predicted mix and volume by product family have been determined, simply convert the resulting number into a quantity per day based on the days in a particular period. For example, if the mix and volume of a product family are estimated by month, the estimated daily amount is determined by dividing the monthly estimate by the number of days in that month. *Remember:* The estimated daily amount does not need to be precise. Although the *maximum* projected daily sales volume is used to determine the daily number of resources for each of the manufacturing processes used to design the Lean factory, in day-to-day practice, the resources by process will be recalculated daily based on actual customer demand for that day. The V_c will be modified each day to adjust output of the line to match the actual customer sales that day. Until the sales rate begins to approach the V_c, the Lean manufacturing line will usually produce a quantity less than its stated capacity.

When projecting future sales demand becomes the responsibility of manufacturing, the manufacturing group usually does so because "someone has to do it." This situation often occurs by default — the sales and marketing group has refused to take responsibility for projecting future demand with a sales forecast. Manufacturing groups who develop sales forecasts often weight sales projections too heavily on intuitive knowledge. They're seldom included in sales and marketing discussions. They're unlikely to have enough knowledge of future marketing programs or the visibility of expected marketplace shifts that could impact the projection of future demand. Without sales and marketing input, the manufacturing group has no choice but to rely on a combination of intuitive knowledge and sales history for projections and the subsequent creation of production schedules. Combining history and intuitive knowledge to predict customer demand and subsequently V_c can be quite helpful, but this single-source type of projection is very risky. Historical information can be misinterpreted and market trends can be missed. Making the manufacturing group responsible for projecting future demand is an abdication of responsibility by the sales and marketing group.

Forecasting Future Demand

No matter how scientifically derived, no forecast is ever 100% accurate. The term *forecasting accuracy* is an oxymoron. Even for professionals, forecasting at best is an inaccurate science.

Limit products. Forecasting future sales demand for countless sales catalog end-item product permutations with accuracy is very difficult, if not impossible. Projecting future demand at the end-item level requires knowledge of the individual product models *and* all of the unique component materials for each final configuration of an end item, but if projecting V_c is limited to only a *product family* or if a *representative product model* is used for the line design, accuracy increases dramatically.

Use monetary value. At the corporate production planning level, future sales plans are usually projected in monetary terms (dollars). By knowing the intrinsic dollar value of individual product models, converting sales dollars into units of production is quite accurate. Predicting the volume of sales per product family at the family level is also simpler and more accurate. Projecting units and sales dollars 1 to 3 three years into the future is also much easier and more accurate when V_c is distributed over the product families selected for line design: the V_c reflects the future volume and the product families project the mix of products. Certainly, volumes and dollars can be discussed when each can be related to the other.

Expect inaccuracy. The longer the factory lead time for each SKU, the longer the required forecasting horizon and the less accurate the forecast will be. For example, if an SKU forecast is used to predict all of the permutations of the sales expected *tomorrow*, the forecast will likely be very accurate because the forecasting horizon is so short, but if this same forecast is used to predict the same product mix 6 to 8 weeks into the future, the forecast is likely to be far less accurate. A Lean operating system can accept inaccuracy. Remember the definition of a product in a Lean operating system: *a product is the sum of its work content and its component materials.* A Lean line has processes and resources in place because the line is designed to produce all of the work content of all of the products for all of the product families used for the design of the line. Also, built into the design of the Lean line is the capacity to produce the projected V_c. Because the line has been designed to produce a projected volume and mix of products to meet future customer demand, as long as the daily volume of customer demand does not exceed the *designed* V_c, the manufacturing resources required to produce any mix and volume are available to be applied to the production of any product. Lack of accuracy in predicting a final customer product configuration has little impact on the capability of the Lean line to produce the configuration because of the flexibility provided by the placement of resources required to produce families of products. After all, the real difference in a final product configuration is not the work content, but the component parts! As originally designed, a Lean line can be affected by product mix and sales volume outliers. Fortunately, significant variations occur so infrequently that they can be considered to be production anomalies. Should actual customer demand be different from the products and volumes established during design of the original line, how different is the actual work content from the models used for designing the line and the product the customer has ordered? The line was designed to produce items that are produced *most of the time.* At a minimum, the line is capable of producing 80% of product sales volume represented by only 20% of the product families. When production anomalies do occur, they can being handled on a special-run basis. Performance metrics can be easily suspended on the occasional day when production of a special product is required. This capability for flexibility is a great feature for Lean manufacturers — maximum output can be achieved on most days and there can be a response to unusual customer demand when it occurs. When all of the processes necessary to produce all of the products are available, there is maximum flexibility to produce most models of any type of product on most days. The manufacturing resources of machines, workstations, and inventories are static, but the labor resources can be allocated daily based to match actual customer demand. The only constraint is parts availability. Building actual customer demand instead of a forecasted demand avoids overproduction and unsold finished goods inventories.

Value market intelligence. Forecasting begins by reviewing objective historical data. Then subjective intuitive knowledge is solicited and considered. Usually quantitative, absolute data is more accurate than using subjective information, but historical data is simply a record of actual sales by product mix and volume. For a better forecast, other quantitative and subjective information affecting future demand should be developed and used to fine tune the historical information. Even though market intelligence can be subjective, it is a crucial factor in determining the future capacity of a Lean line. Solicit market intelligence from the sales and marketing group: this group has greater visibility into the future than any other group in the organization. Their input is a very important component of forecasting future demand. The Lean line will be designed to support demand 12 to 36 months into the future. Changes to the daily mix of products or the volume are certain to occur during that time frame. Likely, the precise mix and volume of products used for designing the Lean line will never be seen again. Based on the knowledge of the company's customer base and the variability of the marketplace, the sales and marketing group is in the best position to predict potential mix and volume changes. They have knowledge of product promotions, marketing campaigns, competitive intelligence, and market strategies that will impact the mix and volume of products and product families. Because of its subjectivity, marketing input might not be considered as heavily as historical data, but analyzing the mix of product models and the corresponding demand volumes using sales and marketing information can nonetheless be very valuable. Comparisons may provide surprising insight leading to beneficial modifications to the final list of products to include in the Lean line design.

VOLUME AT CAPACITY: A STATEMENT OF THE SALES PLAN

V_c is first used as a statement of capacity for the design of a Lean manufacturing line. This statement of capacity (or demand) is the *maximum* number of units the company expects to sell on any given day based on a projection of sales 1 to 3 years into the future. V_c must also reflect changing sales revenue following the same proportion as the capacity of the line throughout the planned future period, without exceeding the designed V_c.

V_c *and utilization.* Beginning on day one of operation, and using the projection of future demand, the Lean line will have capacity *in excess* of the expected sales on day one of operation. Managers accustomed to the old manufacturing paradigm of always being 100% utilized will be very tempted to produce the available capacity of the line. If products are built equal to the capacity designed into the Lean line to meet demand 3 years into the future or if products are built in excess of actual demand, then producing excess unsold FGI is guaranteed. To avoid overproduction of products that increase unsold inventory and consume working capital, resisting the temptation to achieve full utilization of the Lean line when customer demand does not require it is critical. Instead, modify resources to match customer demand.

V_c *and sales revenue.* Sales revenue is dynamic. Once the line is operating, current daily sales revenue and customer demand volume will likely fall somewhere in between the startup quantity of the line and the projected future capacity. There is a direct correlation of V_c with sales rate. The sales rate must be the greater goal for the entire company. The sales rate should dictate V_c. After the first iteration of line design (after the initial design period of 1 to 3 years), continue to test the changing rate of sales of the V_c for the Lean line. After 1 year has passed, year 1 becomes a historical number and a new projected sales rate for year 3 can be calculated. The V_c at 3 years out becomes a *rolling* projection of future sales revenue. An ongoing exercise of testing resource utilization will expose potential problems with resources in the future. By projecting demand 1 to 3 years out, response time for the procurement of additional capital expenditures and labor can be managed more proactively.

V_c *and sales revenue projections.* A spreadsheet program that highlights the impact of changes caused by either current daily sales revenue or customer demand volume based on a new sales revenue goal is a simple tool to ensure that sales revenue projections do not exceed V_c (Table 5.2). The current base selling price is extrapolated for expected future volumes based on a stated growth percentage. The sums of these values at the end of the annual sales columns reflect the expected sales of those products for each year of projected sales revenue and volume. The historical sales number from the previous year then becomes the baseline for projecting future sales. Future sales volumes should match or be less than the products and the V_c chosen for the line design. If extrapolated sales revenue (*Daily* V_c in Table 5.2) or unit volume exceeds the V_c, the line may require rebalancing to meet the demands of increased sales or unit volume. If rebalancing the line is required to meet a projected sales volume, the daily V_c spreadsheet will provide an early warning of a capacity shortfall. Use the same spreadsheet and multiple *what if* scenarios to test the impact of different sales revenues on the V_c and ultimately the impact on manufacturing resources.

Making changes in top-level sales revenue is unrealistic if manufacturing resources cannot support the change. Most sales and marketing organizations have little to no visibility into how a proposed change in mix and volume impacts the manufacturing area. Provide the sales and marketing group with a computer-based tool similar to the V_c spreadsheet so the impact of a proposed change can be tested prior to making delivery promises to a customer. Commitments to top-level sales revenue increases can only be made by having corresponding increases in manufacturing resources on the shop floor. The key is seeing these changes far enough into the future to transition the increased resources into manufacturing at a measured rate. Run frequent iterations that compare sales revenue to available manufacturing resources to ensure that the required manufacturing

Table 5.2. V_c Spreadsheet

Projected Growth: 5%　　Projected Annual Sales Rate　　Days in Month: 20

Description	Unit Sales Price	Historical Sales	2011	Revenue	2012	Revenue	2013	Revenue	Monthly Volume	Sales Revenue	Daily V_c
Model 246 Can	$1,025	800	840	$861,000	882	$904,050	926	$949,253	77.2	$79,104	3.86
Model 246 Bottle	$2,050	650	683	$699,563	717	$734,541	752	$771,268	62.7	$128,545	3.14
Model 185 Can	$1,500	575	604	$618,844	634	$649,786	666	$682,275	55.5	$83,204	2.77
Model 192 Bottle	$1,750	490	515	$527,363	540	$553,731	567	$581,411	47.3	$82,722	2.36
Model 154 Can	$2,250	250	263	$269,063	276	$282,516	289	$296,641	24.1	$54,264	1.21
Model 256 Bottle	$1,950	960	1008	$1,033,200	1058	$1,084,860	1111	$1,189,103	92.6	$180,590	4.63
Model 256 Can	$2,100	370	389	$398,213	408	$418,123	428	$439,029	35.7	$74,955	1.78
			0	—	0	—	0	—	0	—	0.00
			0	—	0	—	0	—	0	—	0.00
			0	—	0	—	0	—	0	—	0.00
			0	—	0	—	0	—	0	—	0.00
			0	—	0	—	0	—	0	—	0.00
			0	—	0	—	0	—	0	—	0.00
			0	—	0	—	0	—	0	—	0.00
			0	—	0	—	0	—	0	—	0.00
	$12,625	4,095	1,360	$4,407,244	4,515	$4,627,606	4,740	$4,858,986	395	$683,385	19.75

Historical Sales × Projected Annual Sales Rate

Annual Volume × Unit Sales Price

Third Year Annual Volume ÷ 12 Months

Monthly Volume × Unit Sales Price

Monthly Volume ÷ Days in Month

resources are in position to support increased sales and the corresponding V_c. The farther into the future these comparisons are made, the greater the response time will be to ensure that the manufacturing resources (as well as the projected capital equipment expenditures) are readily available to achieve the new sales revenue projections.

REFERENCE

1. George Koenigsaecker, Leadership and the lean transformation, in *Manufacturing Engineering*, November 2005: Vol. 135, No. 5; available at http://findarticles.com/p/articles/mi_qa3618/is_200511/ai_n15847432/.

6

THE LEAN LINE: IDENTIFYING THE MANUFACTURING PROCESSES

When the products to be built on a Lean line have been chosen and the corresponding V_c statements have been established, the processes each product consumes as it passes through manufacturing must be identified. The Lean definition of a process is very specific: *a physical location where a logical grouping of labor or machine resources performs a sequential series of work tasks necessary to convert raw material into a finished product.* In Lean, processes are specific activities that increase the value of raw material by changing its *form, fit, or function* by the added value of the labor and/or the machine work applied to its conversion.

An easy way to document the processes used to manufacture a product is to use a graphic representation known as a *process flow diagram* (PFD). A PFD illustrates the processes in the same sequence in which they are used for the conversion of raw materials into a completed product. Additionally, any point(s) during production where the output of a subassembly process is consumed into another process can also be easily identified. To prepare a PFD, select one product from the list of product candidates that have been selected for the line design. Visit the shop floor where that product is produced. Start at the last manufacturing process before shipment to a customer (usually the shipping dock) and begin working backward (upstream) documenting the processes as you go. Conclude at the point where only raw materials enter the process and labor is used for the first time. Draw arrows showing where the input from previous processes is consumed.

A PFD must be drawn for every part number chosen for inclusion in a Lean manufacturing line. Although many products may share the same series of processes drawn on a single PFD, compare each PFD to its parent part number to be certain no processes have been omitted. PFDs can be shared, but they must be validated on the shop floor to ensure that all processes have been identified. Capturing all processes where standard work is performed is important because each process will require the assignment of resources when customer demand requires them.

IDENTIFYING THE PROCESSES WITH A PROCESS FLOW DIAGRAM

Preparing PFDs is the responsibility of the process team and should take no longer than a week. In Lean, a product consists of only its labor content and its parts. So, when creating a PFD, ignore any differences in products caused by the use of different purchased materials. Also ignore the different physical sizes of products, colors, and optional parts used on one model and not on another, even if these differences result in a different parent part number (SKU). Concentrate *only* on the processes used to make each specific product. The purpose of a PFD is to document the processes where *labor* or *machine time* is consumed in the manufacture of a product. Identifying the purchased parts used to build the product is the function of the materials system. A PFD only identifies the processes and the sequential use of those processes.

Attach names to the processes on the PFD to help visualize the points where the completed output of one process is consumed into the next. Any work performed as a subassembly at a location separate from the work completed in the main production processes, but consumed into a downstream process, is considered to be a *feeder process*. Output from a feeder process is consumed immediately into the main line as a downstream process. Feeder process work can be done simultaneously while other work is being completed at the downstream process. Any work that can be completed in parallel while other work is being done will shorten the manufacturing response time. Be sure to identify and include feeder processes on the PFD. Also show the specific point in the downstream process where the output of the feeder process is consumed into the next process (e.g., a subassembly). Once the processes have been identified, the final PFD should resemble a fishbone drawing.

Figure 6.1 illustrates a sequence of manufacturing processes along with the sequences of individual feeder processes and where they are used in the downstream main line processes, e.g., the engine is installed before the transmission. Both the engine and transmission are produced in separate feeder processes. Logically, transmission installation cannot occur before installation of the engine,

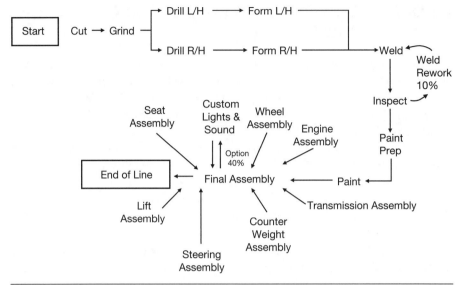

Figure 6.1. A process flow diagram. L/H, left hand; R/H, right hand.

so the output of the motor process must occur before the output of the transmission process can be consumed. Locate feeder processes carefully because the work performed in them is done in parallel to the main assembly processes. Work completed in a feeder process in parallel with work completed in a downstream process greatly reduces total manufacturing response time. Take advantage of any opportunity to relocate work so it can be performed in parallel with the main line work to decrease the lead time for products produced on the line. As more standard work can be completed in feeder processes, the response time through the factory will be reduced as more work is completed in parallel rather than being produced sequentially as steps in the downstream assembly process. The same amount of standard work time is being completed, but in a shorter elapsed clock time, which results in a shorter lead time.

Some words of caution. A commonly made mistake by process teams is documenting an individual work task of a process on a PFD as a process itself. For example, it's tempting to document installing the motor on the frame and attaching the wiring harness as two separate tasks of the assembly processes. *Manufacturing* the motor and the wiring harness was completed in feeder processes. Their *installation* is a work task of the assembly process. Documenting and achieving consensus among team members about *where* processes with standard work are performed is the purpose of a PFD. Documenting standard work *time* for each task of a process occurs later.

DETERMINING THE PRODUCT FAMILIES FOR A MIXED-MODEL PRODUCTION LINE

A Lean manufacturing line is capable of producing one single model with different configurations as well as multiple models that share the same manufacturing processes. Multiple models can be produced on the same Lean manufacturing line so long as the processes needed to manufacture each model differ only by standard work time and appearance. The capability to produce multiple product models sharing the same manufacturing processes is referred to as a *mixed-model* production line. Having mixed-model production capability offers significant benefits for a Lean manufacturer: the ability to produce multiple products using the same manufacturing footprint with a leveling effect on the daily operation of the line that allows for production of seasonal products during periods of alternating demand in mix and volume.

Some products may not appear to be similar when sitting next to one another, but they might be very similar if the processes used to produce them were compared. For example, a lawnmower and a soil tiller appear to be very different products. Perhaps one has a larger engine and is painted a different color. Certainly they have different applications. Upon comparison, however, the processes used to produce each one are very likely to be the same or very similar. The turning tines of the tiller and the spinning blade of the lawnmower have different functions and might be produced in separate feeder processes, but the assembly time to manufacture each one is likely to be very similar. The main assembly process for each product begins with a platform on which wheels and an engine are attached. Even though the platforms have different part numbers and look dissimilar and the engine and the wheel sizes may be different, the work of attaching the wheels and engine to the platform is identical even if the standard work time required for installing each one might be different. One has blades and the other has digging tines to be installed, but the installation process is the same — only the standard times to perform the installation might be different. Both products need handlebars and control cables attached. Both products are packed in corrugated cartons for shipping. Again, the processes are identical — only the work times and materials are dissimilar. Product differences are not based on the manufacturing processes used, but on the component materials (tines and blades) and the standard times used to produce them. As long as the processes are identical, more than one product can be produced on a mixed-model production line using the same shop floor real estate.

Thinking of products according to the sequential processes used to produce them can be difficult. Traditionally, products are seldom grouped into families by manufacturing processes. Usually, the appearance, function, and family designation dictated by the marketing department determine how products get produced on the shop floor. In almost all cases, marketing typically uses parameters for assigning products to a family group that have little or nothing to do with how manufacturing processes are best utilized. Manufacturing simply accepts these family groupings and overlays them directly onto the shop floor. A Lean transformation project requires the manufacturing group to rethink how product families are grouped based on products that share common manufacturing processes rather than the family groupings dictated by sales and marketing requirements.

Manufacturers often claim that their ability to highly configure their products is what makes them unique among their competitors. Being able to promise the availability of a large combination of products is a big differential promoted by the sales and marketing group! Typically the product catalog offers customers numerous product options. The high number of combinations of products and the options often result in a proliferation of product offerings. Each one has an individual end-item part designation (SKU). A review of the total product offerings might reveal that hundreds or even thousands of products are available when in fact the products are very similar. They differ only with the addition of multiple component and cosmetic features. How can all these products be included in a Lean transformation project and still fit within the scope of a manageable project? To achieve a manageable project scope, use a rationalized list of products derived from the total product line to represent all of the products produced. Including all of the products and all of their possible permutations is unnecessary for designing a Lean manufacturing line. So, when selecting products for a Lean line transformation, a manufacturer with hundreds or thousands of unique products must select only a few products that will be representative of all of the products in the customer catalog. Configured part numbers are useful for this rationalization.

Configured part numbers. Many manufacturers use configured part numbers for their product identification. Configured part numbers are designed to identify an exact product model designation (SKU) and to provide the different product options a customer can specify from the customer catalog. Different formats are used for configured SKU numbering, but the logic is usually the same. Most configured part numbers begin by stating an individual model number and any specific characteristics: color, model revision, type, or customer series. Figure 6.2 illustrates a configured part number for a vending machine. Note that the configuration begins by listing product type as **01C**. The **01C** designation is for a can dispensing machine. The product model is **246**. A bottle dispensing machine has a designation of **02C**. The process and standard work time used to produce each vending machine are similar even though each type of machine uses a different dispensing mechanism. Each type of vending mechanism is made from many different parts, but the dispensing mechanism itself is still only a component part of a complete vending machine. The standard time required to

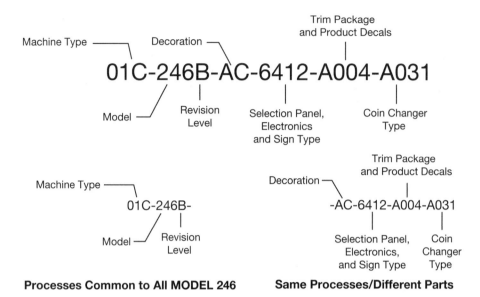

Figure 6.2. A configured parent part number for a vending machine.

install that component part is the same for a can or bottle dispensing machine. The **AC** designation describes the customer decoration for a Coca-Cola machine. **BC** would be for a Pepsi-Cola machine, **CC** would be for a Sprite machine, and so on. The decoration of each customer's configuration does not require a different manufacturing process. The process is *Paint*. The only difference is the different colors in the *Paint* process and the different decals and other styling materials. Even with their different paint schemes, the time required for manufacturing a Coca-Cola and a Pepsi-Cola machine is the same! Regardless of which model of the **246** is produced, the manufacturing *processes* will be identical. Because Lean defines a product as no more than the sum of its work content and its parts, the processes used to produce a model **246** are identical. It does not matter if the vending machine is for Coca-Cola, Pepsi-Cola, or Sprite. It does not matter if the vending machine is for a bottle or a can. Only the parts are different. The time to complete the paint process is the same — regardless of the red, blue, or white paint in the paint gun.

When looking at a lengthy configured part number and the potential number of available options, the number of possible permutations is endless. Very likely the company has sold many of these permutations over the years, but what are the odds that some of these models will never be ordered again — next month, next year, or ever again? Why then would a manufacturer choose to select these infrequent demand or low-volume products as representative products when designing a Lean line? Remember one of the reasons forecasts are always inaccurate: they attempt to project the exact configured product SKUs. (Who could possibly predict which permutation of the thousands offered in the customer catalog a customer might buy?) To select products that best represent what is most often produced on a Lean line, it is better to condense the parent product permutations into a short list that represents the entire product population. Once the product population is condensed, it can be grouped into product families consisting of individual model types that provide a more efficient method of defining what is to be produced on the Lean line.

Manufacturers rarely make only one model of anything. Instead, they make many different products. In some factories, all products may actually share the same processes, yet in others product variety is such that some products share the same processes while others do not. A Lean manufacturer has the option to produce different configurations of the same model on their Lean lines as well as to share production with other product models using similar processes on the same Lean line. Having this option, raises a question: what product models should be selected to share manufacturing on the same Lean line? The answer is obvious: the product models that use the same manufacturing processes. Even though the products look different physically (a lawnmower and a soil tiller), products requiring the same processes can be produced in the same shop floor footprint. When scoping an initial Lean transformation project, avoid the temptation to include all possible product models in the transformation project. Group products into families and design the Lean manufacturing line according to the number of families. Including all models manufactured in the facility is referred to as a *wall-to-wall* transformation project. This approach might be possible for a small- to medium-sized factory with one or few families of products, but for a large manufacturer with multiple product families, a wall-to-wall transformation could present operating system problems if reconfiguring factory processes is later required to eliminate move, queue, and wait times.

DEVELOPING MULTIPRODUCT FAMILIES WITH A MIXED-MODEL PROCESS FLOW DIAGRAM

The capability to produce multiple products on a single line provides advantages for Lean manufacturers. A multiproduct Lean line allows a variety of products to be manufactured using the same shop floor footprint. Even though different products have different PFDs, their processes could still be very similar. A multiproduct Lean line could eliminate the need for separate Lean lines to produce multiple products. Products with similar processes can generally be manufactured sharing the same manufacturing resources (people, workstations, machines, and inventory). The shared resources of a Lean line can therefore reduce or eliminate redundant labor, machines, component parts, planning, purchasing, and supervisory support, avoiding the waste of duplicated resources. Using less floor space can be important for a manufacturer who wants to delay or avoid the costs of a brick-and-mortar expansion as product volume or model proliferation increases.

Family grouping and traditional manufacturing. Producing products by family groupings based on customer types, colors or branding, special features or applications, or sales territory in traditional manufacturing systems is not new. Groupings in a traditional manufacturing facility are usually determined by sales and marketing or financial groups for their own purposes with little or no consideration for the manufacturing similarities of the products. The criteria that facilitate sales and marketing needs do not necessarily match those of manufacturing. On the factory floor, the family designations established by sales and marketing or finance often define how products are manufactured on production lines. If the volume is sufficient, the family designations can even dictate the dedication of manufacturing resources to specific products and production lines. Interestingly, manufacturers rarely challenge sales and marketing family designations even if doing so means keeping redundant resources that must be fully utilized. (*Remember*: Redundant resources and full utilization can result in imbalanced resources and the production of unsold inventory, which are elements of waste in Lean manufacturing.)

Family grouping and Lean manufacturing. Products are also produced by family groupings in a Lean factory, but Lean manufacturers take an active role in determining which products are in each family. Lean production lines are optimally designed to designate families of *similar* products that share common manufacturing processes and materials. Products within a product family are grouped together and manufactured on a single Lean line. The products chosen to be produced on the line are selected for their *process similarities*: process similarity is the common denominator that allows products of the same model to be rationalized down to a few that can be used to represent the production of all models. Not only are products *within* the same product model family excellent candidates for a Lean transformation, but so too are *different* product model families that share the same manufacturing processes. Additional selections are based on similar work task times and the commonality of work steps and materials. Grouping products in this manner ensures that all products in a family move through the factory using shared manufacturing processes.

What about demand cycles? More likely than not, different products will have different demand patterns or sales cycles. If a product line has been dedicated to a few product types and production capacity is matched to customer requirements, fluctuating demand patterns can cause broad swings in flexible operator headcounts. The good news is that a Lean line operates best when manufacturing a variety of products. Manufacturing more product families means more flexibility for operating the line. This flexibility is an important feature when establishing product families that have great swings in demand volume caused by seasonality (e.g., air conditioners, space heaters, and furnaces). The ability to run multiple families of products on a single line reduces the impact of periods of alternating fast and slow demand cycles on valuable manufacturing resources. During periods of seasonal low demand, shared resources do not sit idle and utilize precious factory square footage. When sales shift, and subsequent production slows, the Lean line can easily shift to producing families of products with offsetting seasonal demand.

How to develop a mixed-model PFD. To assist in developing multiple product families based on similarity of manufacturing processes, create a mixed-product (mixed-model) PFD. A mixed-product PFD shows all of the individual manufacturing processes in sequential order for a family grouping of products. As with the single-product PFD described earlier, do not consider physical size, color, or a part used to produce a product. Identify only the processes where work occurs. Limit the number of processes selected for the transformation project by selecting product models that represent all of the products produced (to control the scope of the project), but still provide a significant return on investment and have a completion date that occurs before transformation team members burn out. Begin creating a mixed-model PFD by using a PFD for a high-volume product. Then, one at a time, overlay smaller-volume product PFDs on the initial PFD until all manufacturing processes and their locations have been identified on the new PFD. Figure 6.3 illustrates a conceptual view of how multiple PFDs can be compared to create a mixed-model PFD. When completed, this multiproduct PFD will show products that share similar manufacturing processes while highlighting the other processes used on the lower demand products. It will also assist with the conceptual layout of the manufacturing facility in the final Lean configuration. By projecting beyond the current factory layout, a mixed-product PFD can conceptually visualize the eventual layout of a factory that facilitates a desired one-piece flow of product. Another technique is to plot a line for each PFD in a different color. Begin by plotting the highest-volume product. One by one, follow the processes of each product using a different color for the line. As each process is reviewed, include only the processes not previously plotted. Continue plotting all parent part number PFDs until all processes on the mixed-product PFD have been included. This type of mapping can be done manually with a pencil and paper or with computer programs such as Word, Excel, Visio, CAD, etc. Even a white board with dry erase markers can be used.

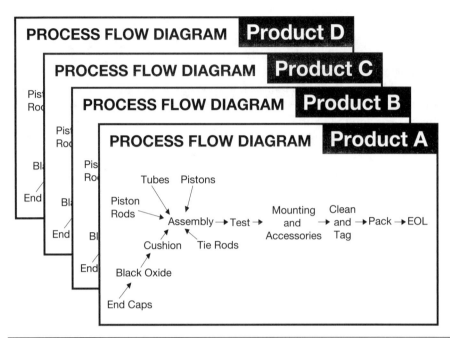

Figure 6.3. Overlay of multiple process flow diagrams to create a mixed-model process flow diagram.

These techniques provide a good visual preview of the relational locations of manufacturing processes in a facility and work well with a *limited number* of products, but for companies having larger amounts of parent products that need to be represented in a single mixed-model PFD, they may be impractical. A more practical way to construct a mixed-model product family for a large number of parent products is to construct a common processes map.

CONSTRUCTING A PROCESS MAP

A process map is a simple matrix with a horizontal axis and a vertical axis. The vertical axis is used to list the products selected for inclusion in a Lean line design. If no product rationalization has been performed (e.g., 80/20) and if the products have substantial customer configurations, the listing may be quite lengthy. The horizontal axis is used to list all of the processes identified from all of the PFDs.

Constructing this process map is the first step in determining product families. Beginning with the first part number (SKU) on the vertical axis (column 1), and using the PFD for the parent product, go along the horizontal axis of the processes and place an X in each cell where the parent product and the process used to produce that model intersect. Complete this part/parent product/process comparison until all products have been reviewed. When this mapping process is completed, parent products sharing the same processes indicated by an X will be revealed. Products sharing the same processes are candidates for membership in the same product family. Once a family has been identified, the sum of the individual volumes (V_c) becomes the stated V_c for that family. The V_c of each product included in a family is cumulative. So, the new V_c is a statement of V_c for the entire family grouping. Figure 6.4 illustrates a mixed-model process map.

After grouping the products based on their similar processes, the initial process map requires input and agreement from everyone who will be affected by transformation of the current operating system to a Lean operating system. Input includes achieving the consensus of dissimilar groups of manufacturing professionals who have different viewpoints and ideas about the families, products, processes, and demands that should be included in the factory transformation. Information about the initial process map can be used to document the results of these numerous debates, educational sessions, negotiations, and reconciliation efforts required to achieve consensus among diverse company disciplines. Individuals with different performance measures, conflicting objectives, and philosophical opinions should have an opportunity to contribute ideas. The time to reconcile all of issues is *before* the transformation project moves forward.

Even though this initial process map displays limited information, it represents the culmination of some of the most difficult information-gathering work for the design of the Lean line for the Lean champion and the team leaders. Likely some groups will be unhappy with the information contained on the initial process map. Resolving multiple cultural issues is one of the most challenging components of a transformation project. This initial process map does reflect the best consensus of a variety of different viewpoints, so congratulations are due to the Lean champion and the process and material team leaders!

At this point, the initial process map displays the products and product families to be included in the design of the Lean line. It also displays the manufacturing processes that are required to convert the products from raw materials into finished products that have been identified using PFDs for each parent product. A projected V_c has been recorded for each of the representative parent part numbers and its product family. Demand has been estimated 1 to 3 years into the future. This initial process map documents the information required for establishing a Lean operating system in the factory. It reflects the *scope* of the Lean implementation project, establishes the *capacity* of the new Lean manufacturing line, and is now the *source document* for capturing future information about the products, processes, and demand for the factory. In addition to identifying product families, the basic process map format can be expanded to include the additional information necessary to complete a Lean line design.

Part Number	Description	PFD History	Family Designation	Track Weld	Finish Weld	Robotic Finish Weld	Powder Coat	Hydraulic Assembly	Roll	Brake	Brake Assembly	Pack
76803	7.6 Steel	AB	Steel	x	x		x	x			x	x
79833	8.2 Steel	AB	Steel	x	x		x	x			x	x
76703	9.2 Steel	AB	Steel	x	x		x	x			x	x
21803	10.0 Steel	AB	Steel	x	x		x	x			x	x
76323	7.6 Poly	AC	Poly	x	x		x	x	x		x	x
74323	8.2 Poly	AC	Poly	x	x		x	x	x		x	x
78546	9.2 Poly	AC	Poly	x	x		x	x	x		x	x
43803	10.0 Poly	AC	Poly	x	x		x	x	x		x	x
76503	7.6 Aluminum	AD	Aluminum	x	x	x	x	x			x	x
78883	8.0 Aluminum	AD	Aluminum	x	x	x	x	x			x	x
76543	8.6 Aluminum	AD	Aluminum	x	x	x	x	x			x	x
76987	9.0 Aluminum	AD	Aluminum	x	x	x	x	x			x	x
58703	10.0 Aluminum	AD	Aluminum	x	x	x	x	x			x	x
76443	7.6 S-Poly	AE	Poly	x	x		x	x			x	x
70987	8.0 S-Poly	AE	Poly	x	x		x	x			x	x
76823	8.6 S-Poly	AE	Poly	x	x		x	x			x	x
72283	9.6 S-Poly	AE	Poly	x	x		x	x			x	x
22345	U/C Ford	AF	Truck	x	x		x	x		x	x	x
22436	U/C Dodge	AG	Truck	x	x		x				x	x
22437	U/C Chevy	AF	Truck	x	x		x			x	x	x
22438	U/C Toyota	AF	Truck	x	x		x			x	x	x

Figure 6.4. A mixed-model process map.

A spreadsheet program is an ideal tool for creating a process map. The format of a process map is the same type of matrix used in popular spreadsheet programs. Table 6.1 illustrates construction of an initial process map using a spreadsheet program to record finalized information. This process map visually identifies products that share the same processes, ignoring size, color, standard time, or existing family designations. Some processes will not have 100% commonality across all products. When completing the line layout, the process map can be used to locate where processes are to be physically located on a redesigned shop floor.

Initially, a process map assumes that the demand volume chosen for each parent part (or family) will be the demand volume throughput for each process included on the process map. The default volume value for each product through each process is 100%. During manufacturing, however, changing conditions can cause this volume to change, increasing or decreasing the V_c from its default value of 100%. Where the throughput volume of a process at the SKU level volume is different, it must be listed separately on the process map. Throughput volume is a critical factor for accurately calculating the production rate of a Lean line. The production rate is also used later to identify the number of resources necessary to achieve the throughput volume of each process. Changes in throughput volume at the process level affect the number of manufacturing resources (people, machines, workstations, and inventory) needed to produce a desired line volume causing the resources assigned to individual processes to change on a day-by-day basis.

HANDLING REWORK, SCRAP, AND PRODUCT OPTIONS ON THE PRODUCT FLOW DIAGRAM

When units of a product move through a manufacturing process and inspection reveals defects, the resulting defective item can be handled in two ways. The first option is to scrap the defective item. This option is, of course, an expensive solution because the costs must eventually be absorbed into the sales price. The second and most frequent disposition for resolving a defect is to repair (rework) the defective item.

Rework

Once a defective item is discovered, it may stay at the workstation where the defect was discovered, be returned to a previous process, or be sent to an off-line process for repair or rework. Repair work requires an assessment for cause of the defect, what rework process is required to correct the defect, completion of the

Table 6.1. An Initial Process Map

Familly Description	Part Number	V_c	Process Identification on Process Flow Diagram							
			Weld		Weld Rework		Assembly		Custom Lights & Sound	
			Machine	Labor	Machine	Labor	Machine	Labor	Machine	Labor
V5A	75903101	2.00								
V6A	76000202	0.40								
A4H	76102402	3.00								
U5	76100002	2.00								
805	72200002	4.00								
806	72210002	6.00								
T5AH	72208902	2.00								
T5LOAH	70524102	0.375								
S5	72208602	1.00								
TM270	71801802	2.00								
G3	70542002	5.00								
G4A	70550402	2.50								
		30.65 = V_c								

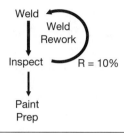

Figure 6.5. A rework loop.

work of the rework process, and retesting the product to ensure it now meets specification. All rework requires additional labor and/or machine time and the material resources needed to complete the necessary work. Upon completion of the rework process, the product can be advanced downstream or returned upstream to repeat the original process or series of processes.

Because standard work at a workstation must be repeated for a reworked item, the volume of each process where rework or reprocessing occurs now changes from 100% of daily volume to some amount greater than 100%. Using historical records, the estimated amount of rework (stated as a percentage) can be documented on the PFD and on the process map so resources can be assigned to perform the work required to complete the rework. To be certain the resources necessary to resolve rework are identified and located, four types of information about a defect must be known:

- Where does the defect occur (at which process)?
- What is the historical (estimated) percentage of rework at that process?
- Where is the defective unit sent to be reworked (at which process)?
- Where does the reworked product reenter the Lean line (at which process)?

The rework and repair process is known as a *rework loop*. Figure 6.5 illustrates a rework loop on a PFD:

- *Inspect* is the process where the defect occurs.
- *Rework* (R) is the historical average amount of rework that occurs at that process (10%).
- *Weld rework* is the process where the product is sent for rework.
- *Weld* is the process where the reworked product reenters the line to be processed a second time.

If the desired V_c throughput is 100 units and the historical rework is 10%, then for every 100 units entering *Inspect*, 10 units will require rework and will be sent to *Weld Rework* for repair. Therefore, the volume of the *Weld Rework* process will be the 10 units received from *Inspect*. Because 10 units are subsequently reworked at *Weld Rework* and returned to *Weld* to be processed a second time, the volume through the *Weld* process (throughput) is now 110 units. Because of the additional 10% reworked units returning to *Weld* and *Inspect*, the production rate is based on 110 units rather than the original V_c of 100.

A defective product may be reworked at any process upstream from where the defect is discovered. A rejected product may also be reworked at the point of failure without being sent to an off-line process. After a unit is reworked, the rejected product is returned to the Lean line, usually to the point where the failure occurred. It is possible that additional processes may have to be repeated if the point where a reworked product reenters the line is upstream from the process where the defect was discovered. When this occurs, the throughput volume of each of the upstream processes must be increased by the rework percentage to account for any reworked volume that has to be processed a second time.

Rework can impact the amount of resources required to produce the desired demand volume. Resources consumed for rework purposes are *always* non-value-added work. Always consider including an estimate of rework in a manufacturing process to be a short-term solution. Eliminating the defects that caused rework to occur in the first place is the best long-term solution. The cost of resources used for rework processes and the increased volume from processing a second time is waste. Usually resolution is through the application of continuous process improvement techniques. Eliminating the waste of non-value-added rework is a perfect application for kaizen activities (and six sigma techniques). Final resolution of more difficult problems uncovered by kaizen might eventually require changing company procedures and policies.

Rework on the PFD. A PFD identifies processes where labor, workstation, or machine resources are utilized and where throughput might be impacted by demand that exceeds 100% of the designed volume of the line. A PFD also documents the location where rework occurs and establishes the magnitude of the non-value-added work. Rework processes are indicated separately on the PFD from the normal processes required to make a product. Although, the location of where labor or machine work is consumed for the production of products is identified on the PFD, many manufacturers overlook identifying rework on their PFDs because rework processes are often not considered to be *normal* processes. Manufacturers tend to think of rework activities as anomalies or exceptions to normal production. Even though rework is a non-value-added activity, it requires resources (people and machines) to perform the work. When creating a PFD, do not overlook the inclusion of rework processes. When diagramming the process

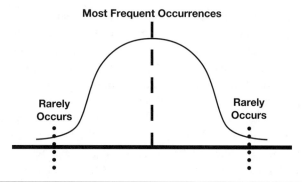

Figure 6.6. A normal defect distribution curve.

flow, document all locations where rework loops occur, but do not try to resolve the causes at this time. Always consider rework processes as abnormal and candidates for elimination by using improvement initiatives.

Estimating rework. An often-used argument for not documenting rework, or even acknowledging its existence, is that rework volume can change daily based on changing conditions. Depending on the type of rework, even the processes affected can be different each day. If no improvements are made, the percentage of rework experienced could be even higher or lower than the stated historical percentage on any given day. Rework is not a hard and fast statistic — nothing is that repeatable. Remember that the rework percentage is used to identify the number of *extra resources* required to produce a stated volume (V_c) and to design a Lean line layout. Therefore, the number of resources required to do the work and the physical placement of those processes must be known. The question often is *can a static rework percentage be applied to a moving target?* The best a rework percentage can ever be is an estimate — an estimate of the future based on history. Use the PFD to identify the most common rework scenario to facilitate determining the resources for a Lean line design. Rely on a normal distribution (i.e., bell curve) to identify the most likely scenario (Figure 6.6). Avoid "analysis paralysis" when trying to make a precise estimate. If rework throughput is overestimated, the worst case scenario is that required resources will be overstated for a day. If the rework percentage is underestimated, the required resources will be understated for a day. A wrong estimate is better than no estimate. If reality later proves that an estimate is incorrect, the rework percentage can be easily adjusted.

Hedging statistics or even ignoring the fact that rework is occurring is not uncommon for some manufacturers. Perhaps they are embarrassed to acknowledge the existence of rework in their factories and the extent to which it impacts operations. Ignoring rework or successfully disguising and reworking production units without assessing the impact on resources may result in searching for solutions to the root cause of rework to never occur. Rework accounts for three elements of the seven wastes of manufacturing: extra processing, additional defects, and extra transportation costs. These three elements all add cost to products. As the first step toward eliminating rework, documenting non-value-added rework to expose hidden rework locations is crucial.

An effort is made to correct most defective products with rework. If the rework is successful, the product is returned to the line and continues downstream toward completion. Sometimes, reworking a defective product is not an option: the product cannot be reworked or performing the rework is financially unfeasible — perhaps the unit cost of the product is too small to merit investing the time, materials, and energy to repair and reprocess it. If a decision is made to forego the rework of a product, the only other alternative is to scrap the product at the point of failure to avoid accumulating any additional costs.

Scrap

When a product is scrapped, it is either destroyed or disposed of in a way that results in a reduction of line output or throughput of individual processes. Just as rework affects volume, so does scrap. Scrap, however, has an added effect: it not only changes the volume of the process where it occurs, but it also affects the volume of all processes upstream from the point where the scrap occurred. Scrapped units must be replaced to achieve the desired throughput at the end of the Lean line. Additional units must therefore be input through each process upstream of where scrap occurs, including the very first process, to achieve the desired throughput at the end of the Lean line. Scrap results in non-value-added work. Kaizen is an excellent technique for reducing or eliminating scrap.

Scrap on the PFD. Scrap causes additional work to be done to meet a required demand. Detection and testing work in excess of the work normally done to meet required quality inspections is also required. Unlike rework, which typically impacts only a few processes, scrap is insidious. It can affect all manufacturing upstream processes from the point of the scrap — extending all the way back into the earliest processes. In addition to the losses incurred from lost materials that cannot be salvaged, the extra work required can significantly impact the amount of resources needed to produce the desired customer volume at each affected process. Managing scrap disposition can also result in a significant investment of management time needed to respond and replan activities to recover from time lost to scrap. The amount of historical scrap (stated as a percentage) must be documented on a PFD at the point where the scrap occurs.

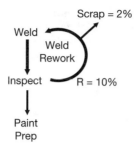

Figure 6.7. Scrap on a process flow diagram.

Determining scrap. Figure 6.7 illustrates how scrap is determined. The desired output of *Weld* is 100 units. Historical rework is 10%. *Weld Rework* yields 2% scrap. So *Weld* must generate a throughput of 112 units to accommodate a 10% rework rate and a 2% scrap rate:

> 100 units of demand + 10 units to be reworked + 2 units to be scrapped = 112

All processes upstream from *Weld* must produce 102 units because 2 will likely be scrapped at *Weld Rework*. Each upstream process must generate two additional units just to compensate for the scrap loss at *Weld Rework*. If any additional scrap occurs at an upstream process, the number of units grows incrementally in relation to the amount of scrap at that process — all scrap is cumulative upstream to the gateway process. To achieve a desired output of 100 units at the end of the line when cumulative scrap occurs upstream at multiple processes, the required input quantity could be significant. If scrap amounts are significant, an increase in the number of resources (labor, machines, workstations, and inventory) may be necessary to compensate for the increased throughput required to overcome the scrap.

Every manufacturing facility has some level of rework and scrap. Rework and scrap are uncomfortable discussion topics for most manufacturers. Unless rework and scrap amounts are documented and recorded, many manufacturers will opt to ignore them, choosing to blend scrap and rework back into the daily production counts at the end of the day. If the time required for performing rework and scrap is not considered on a daily basis, this time can only be made available by taking it away from the resources assigned to the daily production scheduled to meet customer demand. Unaccounted for, significant, recurring amounts of rework and scrap on a daily basis can result in missed schedules, late shipments, and overtime, which are all non-value-added consequences!

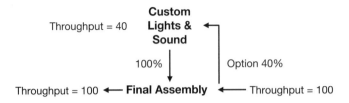

Figure 6.8. An optional process on a process flow diagram.

Product Options

In an environment in which a customer can choose multiple options for products, there may be times when some products do not travel through some processes. For some configurations, the products might be diverted into other processes to receive a special configuration. These special configurations require optional processes. Contrary to scrap and rework, the work required to complete customer-requested product configurations is fully value-added activity. Customers expect to pay for the time and extra work of added features in the purchase price.

Because optional processes are not used on a one-to-one relationship to meet customer demand, throughput volumes and the number of resources assigned to both optional and standard processes are affected. For example, consider manufacturing a fork truck on a Lean line with a desired output volume of 100. Customer demand indicates that 40% of customers will choose to purchase the *Lights & Sound* option for their fork trucks. Only 40% of the fork trucks will require installation of a *Lights & Sound* option. Therefore, the V_c through the *Lights & Sound* optional (feeder) process will be 40 units. The V_c of fork trucks on the main line is still 100 after the 40 units from the optional process reenter the final assembly process and rejoin the original 60 units that have been received directly from *Paint*.

Product options on the PFD. Figure 6.8 illustrates an optional process and how it is recorded on a PFD:

- The desired throughput volume is 100 units.
- *Custom Lights & Sound* is an optional process.
- 60% of the output from *Paint* goes directly into *Final Assembly*.
- 40% of the output from *Paint* goes to the optional process *Custom Lights & Sound*.
- The throughput volume from *Custom Lights & Sound* is 40 units.
- 100% of the volume from *Custom Lights & Sound* goes to *Final Assembly*.

- The input volume from *Final Assembly* remains at 100: 60 from *Paint*; 40 from *Custom Lights & Sounds*.
- The output volume from *Final Assembly* is 100.

If all customers were to choose to purchase the *Lights & Sound* option for their fork trucks, installation of *Light & Sound* equipment would no longer an option, but instead be a standard process requiring value-added resources for 100 units. For some optional processes, manufacturers may decide the costs of maintaining and managing the resources and the shop floor footprint of an option are more than the costs of making the option a standard feature of the product. Not only can an optional feature that becomes a standard feature create a marketing differential, but it may also have a positive effect on the profit margin of the product.

Determining product option percentages. The main line process and the optional process must be documented with the historical percentage for the option and recorded on the PFD for each product that offers it. Wherever optional processes begin, the throughput volume of the main line and the optional processes will be less than 100% V_c. As optional units are completed and rejoin the main line process, the throughput volume of the main line returns to 100%. The sum of the percentages on the main line processes plus the optional process must equal 100%. The amount of resources needed to complete optional processes will vary depending on the volume of products that require the optional process on a given day. All optional process activities must be added to the process map to ensure their impact on the V_c is taken into account when the number of resources required for them is determined.

Rework, scrap, and options and the V_c. V_c is impacted by rework, scrap, and options. The percentage of each must be factored into the V_c quantity for each process and then recorded on the process map in a separate column. Volume changes can ultimately impact the number of resources required. A *Volume Modifier* column is added to the initial process map to record the rework, scrap, and options identified on the PFD (Table 6.2). The percentage will factor V_c up or down to compensate for the percentage of rework, scrap, or options indicated. If rework is 10%, the volume modifier will increase the throughput volume by 10% for the processes where rework occurs. Conversely, the options process is reduced or increased to match the percentage of options produced in the process. Later, the modified volume will be used to calculate the amount of resources necessary to accommodate the changes in processes and volumes.

Table 6.2. A Process Map with Volume Modifier Columns

Family Description	Part Number	V_c	Weld Machine	Weld Labor	Weld Volume Modifier	Weld Rework Machine	Weld Rework Labor	Weld Rework Volume Modifier	Assembly Machine	Assembly Labor	Assembly Volume Modifier	Custom Lights & Sound Machine	Custom Lights & Sound Labor	Custom Lights & Sound Volume Modifier
V5A	75903101	2.00			1.100			0.100			1.000			0.400
V6A	76000202	0.40			1.100			0.100			1.000			0.400
A4H	76102402	3.00			1.100			0.100			1.000			0.400
U5	76100002	2.00			1.100			0.100			1.000			0.400
805	72200002	4.00			1.100			0.100			1.000			0.400
806	72210002	6.00			1.100			0.100			1.000			0.400
T5AH	72208902	2.00			1.100			0.100			1.000			0.400
T5LOAH	70524102	0.375			1.100			0.100			1.000			0.400
S5	72208602	1.00			1.100			0.100			1.000			0.400
TM270	71801802	2.00			1.100			0.100			1.000			0.400
G3	70542002	5.00			1.100			0.100			1.000			0.400
G4A	70550402	2.50												0.400
		30.65												

Weld: Process Causing Rework Must Process Units Twice 10%

Weld Rework: $V_c \times 10\%$ Rework Occurence

Assembly: No Impact on V_c

Custom Lights & Sound: Optional Process 40% of V_c

DETERMINING TAKT TIME

Takt is defined as:

A time/volume relationship calculated as the rhythm, beat, or cadence for each process of a Lean line that is used to establish the amount of resources required to produce the scheduled volume and achieve line balance.

Takt time establishes the *rate* of production at each process on a PFD. During a stated period time, Takt time establishes the frequency of product completion required for one unit of production at a workstation.

Remember that traditional manufacturing paradigms require all functional resources to be grouped into departments and to run at full utilization to be considered 100% productive. Also remember that a Lean operating system uses only the number of resources necessary to meet customer demand as the key to eliminating the waste of unsold overproduction on a Lean manufacturing line. Driving for full utilization of all available department resources is not even considered as a measurable goal for a Lean operating system. Only the resources necessary to produce the daily throughput volume are required. In a Lean operating system, the traditional department structures known today do not exist. For a Lean line to operate successfully, all processes must complete their standard work at the same rate. Even though individual manufacturing processes may have different standard work times, a Lean line breaks all standard work time into equal amounts of work by assigning the resources necessary to produce the required product volume at a desired rate of output.

Takt time per process defines the number of equal groupings of time segments required for each process to achieve the desired output. Each segment of equal time represents one resource: a person, workstation, machine, or inventory. Stated differently, the number of Takt times (how many) required for each process to meet customer demand, i.e., Takt + Takt + Takt = standard time.

Achieving balance among many different processes on a Lean line having a wide variety of different standard work times is accomplished by establishing the number of manufacturing resources to a process based on the Takt time for that process. Takt time is used as the denominator divided into the standard time for each of the processes on the process map. As a result, standard work, regardless of length of time required to complete it, is divided equally into amounts of time equal to the Takt time. Using the desired throughput volume to calculate Takt rate at each process causes each process to complete standard work at the same speed as all other processes regardless of widely variable standard work times. The only difference is the number of resources (Takt times) assigned to complete the standard work at each process. The longer the standard time, the more resources are needed to complete one unit off the end of the line every Takt time. Because each process must complete its standard time work at the required Takt rate for that process, the Lean line is essentially balanced across all processes. By completing standard work at the same rate, no one single process has more capacity than another. Because the Lean line is balanced to a Takt rate of production, process capacities are also balanced allowing no unsold inventories to be accumulated to absorb any excess capacity. Sacrificed with the balance achieved in processes with excess capacity is maximum utilization. Which one costs more — people or inventory? Excess people can be reassigned where they are needed; excess inventory is sent to the warehouse. Balance is at the heart of every Lean manufacturing line.

The concept of balancing work is not new, but the approach of the Lean manufacturing methodologies to use the Takt rate is a newer concept. Instead of balancing lines based on physical considerations such as the length from point A to point B, available square footage or the number of available operators, Lean manufacturing methodology balances work based on the required throughput volume of demand used to calculate the Takt rate for each process. This type of line balancing is often referred to as *Takt line design*. Once throughput volume is defined, the manufacturing processes are divided into equal Takt time amounts of work. A manufacturing process with many different products can have a different standard work content time for each product in the process. By breaking standard work into equal elements of work equal to the Takt time of the process, the output of the final process will be one completed unit of production every Takt time. As each unit is packed off the final process as a shipment to the customer, each upstream process responds by "ratcheting" one new unit into the downstream workstations so one unit begins production of a Takt time amount of work along the entire Lean line.

To achieve this balance, a Takt time must be calculated for each process, independent of all other processes. The reason for separate statements of Takt time is that throughput volume at each process might be affected by rework, scrap, or options. When rework, scrap, or option factors are not present, the Takt time will be the same for all processes. Although Takt times may not always be identical for every process because the V_c for each process can be different, the entire line will still be balanced. Figure 6.9 illustrates how Takt times for each process are required based on throughput volume. Even where throughput volumes are different, the Lean line remains balanced based on the Takt rate established for each process. Takt time is calculated as the available minutes × the number of shifts ÷ the throughput per day, where:

- *Minutes* is the amount of time available to an operator to perform work each day.

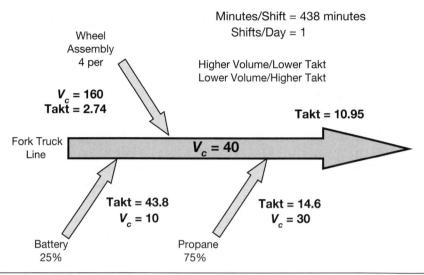

Figure 6.9. Takt times with different throughput volume.

- *Shifts* is number the shifts per day per process.
- *Throughput volume per day* is the V_c factored by any rework, scrap, or optional volume considerations.

Manufacturers commonly refer to the Takt time of a Lean line as if it were a single line. In reality, the Takt time for the entire line is really only the Takt time of the very last process in the line on a PFD. Each process has its own Takt time based on the throughput volume of the process, but the entire line cannot output a unit any faster than the Takt time of the last process, i.e., shipping.

Takt time is a statement of how frequently one unit of production must be completed during the available work minutes per day to achieve throughput volume (Figure 6.10). Takt time is therefore an expression of *rate*. Takt time states that if a required volume is to be produced in a stated time period, then one unit must be completed every X minutes. For example, consider an 8-hour day working one shift. The total available time would be 480 minutes (8 hours × 60 minutes). If the required throughput of a process is 240 units, the Takt time rate is 2 minutes (480 minutes ÷ 240 units). The Takt time states that one unit must be completed every 2 minutes of a 480-minute day to produce a demand volume of 240 units. Takt time is usually expressed in terms of minutes, but can be modified for higher volume products. Takt time is often referred to as the *target* or *goal* rate of a process.

Once the Takt rate for each process has been established, the *flow* of product on a Lean manufacturing line is accomplished by identifying the corresponding

$$\text{Takt} = \frac{\text{Available Minutes} \times \text{Shifts}}{\text{Throughput per Day}}$$

Available Minutes = Effective Minutes per Shift
Shifts = Number of Shifts Worked per Day
Throughput Volume = Daily Volume at Capacity Factored for Rework, Optionality, and Scrap

Figure 6.10. Takt time: a statement of rate that is calculated for each process.

number of resources necessary to meet the Takt time target rate for each process and physically relocating those resources adjacent to where the output of each is consumed directly into the downstream process. The physical location of processes on a final Lean manufacturing line should mirror the mixed-model PFD. Standard time at each process is grouped into elements of work equal to the Takt time of the process. Manufacturing processes divided into equal elements of Takt are balanced regardless of the individual standard time necessary to produce the subassembly (feeder) or final product. A single unit of standard work is performed at a workstation by a person and/or a machine each Takt time. A partially completed unit equal to a Takt time's amount of standard work is then passed to the next resource downstream where another Takt amount of standard work is added. Each unit of work progresses in a flow through all manufacturing processes until the sum of all the standard work has been completed as a finished product.

Balancing work to Takt time and physically linking manufacturing processes together allows the completed output of one process to be directly consumed by another, causing a product to be produced in only the sum of its standard work. Producing products in only the sum of the standard time dramatically reduces manufacturing cycle time. The wastes of wait, move, and queue times are eliminated in a balanced line. Because all processes work at the same Takt rate, the wastes of overproduction, the need for buffer inventories, and transportation costs are also eliminated. Because manufacturing processes are simply divided into equal elements of work, the grouping of similar labor and machines into departments is no longer necessary. Only the resources required to achieve the Takt rate and produce the V_c are located on the Lean line. The Lean line itself is the "manufacturing" department.

MANAGING THE NUMERATORS AND DENOMINATORS OF TAKT TIME

The Takt time formula is straightforward, but important elements should be considered when completing Takt time calculations: working minutes per day; the number of shifts per day; and throughput volume per day.

Working minutes per day. Shift lengths vary among manufacturers for many different reasons, but the most common shift length is 8 hours. Regardless of shift length, this question must be considered: is all shift time dedicated 100% to the production of products? In every company, operators engage in a variety of daily activities that subtract from the time they are available to perform standard work. Non-work activities may vary, but the time used for breaks, lunch periods, required training sessions, periodic employee meetings, and continuous process improvement activities take time away from the production of products. Eliminating these activities may be impossible, but the time for these activities must be identified and deducted from the total amount of daily work minutes available. For example, for a shift that begins at 7:00 a.m. and ends at 3:30 p.m., 8.5 hours are available for performing work. In addition to a 30-minute lunch break, other activities that occur every day further reduce the remaining 8 hours available to perform standard work.

7:00 a.m. to 3:30 p.m. = 8.5 hours
                                – 0.5 hour (lunch period)
                                – 0.5 hour (two 15-minute breaks)
                                – 0.2 hour (12 to 15 minutes for weekly kaizen activities)
                                – 0.05 hour 1 day per month (safety meeting)
                                7.25 hours (435 minutes per day)

Some companies use four 10-hour work days while others have a rotating 5-day schedule with 9-hour days, along with numerous other daily shift routines. Regardless of the shift schedule used, each company must identify the actual work time available each day to perform standard work and deduct the time necessary to do nonstandard work.

When reducing the minutes per day that are unavailable for performing work, it is tempting to discount the effects of personnel fatigue, delays, or other related factors that cause productivity losses. Lean manufacturing methodology acknowledges the existence of these factors, but suggests that they not be considered in the working minutes per day for Takt time calculations. Fatigue, delays, and other similar factors are real factors that can affect the performance of a Lean manufacturing line, and they ultimately increase the number of resources required to meet the daily customer demand, but if personal fatigue, delays, and other factors reduce the available minutes in the denominator of the Takt time calculation, they become embedded automatically in the Lean line design and are invisible to any future improvement initiatives. Personal fatigue, delay, and other factors must be measured independently from Takt time calculations. If measured separately, they become visible to the entire organization. Anything that can be measured can be improved. Modification of resources due to personal fatigue or delays should be measured as *factors of utilization*. Subsequent staffing decisions that assign operators to the Lean line on a daily basis can later be adjusted to compensate for them. These factors should never be accepted as permanent. They should not be embedded in the design of the Lean line as a component of Takt time.

When measured separately, improvements in productivity can be managed as a result of a kaizen or some other type of continuous improvement activity. Lean methodology recommends that a *productivity factor* be added to daily staffing requirements to accommodate the realities of productivity loss. Productivity losses can then be measured and their causes identified and subsequently improved. When built into the design of the line, the factors that cause lost productivity go unseen, unmeasured, and unimproved. If they are included in the Takt time formula, nothing short of a line redesign can change the situation.

Shifts per day. Select the number of shifts the process will operate each day. For Lean line design purposes, using one shift as the factor in the Takt time calculation and extrapolating the necessary labor resources by doubling or tripling the resulting calculated resources based on the number of shifts is often easier. It's also simpler to calculate workstation and machine resources by stating the number of resources for a one-shift operation even for factories that operate multiple shifts. Regardless of the method used, both will yield the correct number of resources required to meet Takt time targets for each process.

For the initial review of resources, the goal of a Lean line is to produce *all demand* on a single shift. By comparing the resources required for a one-shift operation to the existing resources, determining the amount of resources necessary for consolidating the manufacturing operation into a one-shift operation might be possible. If the resources necessary to meet the demand of a second or third shift is possible in the existing shop floor footprint, significant productivity savings can be achieved by a one-shift operation. Aside from the overhead costs saved by not operating a second or third shift, a one-shift line design also allows capacity to be easily doubled or tripled with the addition of shifts should customer demand grow exponentially. Increasing capacity by adding shifts costs less than a brick and mortar factory expansion. Having the ability to control the number of shifts by adding extra shifts in response to increases in demand is also an effective strategy for responding to wide swings in customer demand by ramping up shifts during short periods of unusual demand such as seasonality.

Adding shifts. A Lean line operates like a light switch — either on or off. Running single processes on additional shifts can create excess inventory and add costs from running extra shifts at overtime rates. If a one-shift operation proves insufficient to maintain the Takt rate for some processes, extending available time or building mirrored lines is a good solution. Experiment with the factors of Takt time to make the best business case decision for the company. Insufficient capacity is considered to be an imbalance on the line. For imbalances on a line, Lean methodologies recommend the application of line balancing tools: reduce or eliminate non-value-adding work, relocate work, add resources, or add inventory. If the process has insufficient capacity to meet demand, no Lean technique can create the capacity to fix it! Making a process as Lean as possible can only maximize its efficiency.

Throughput volume per day. Demand volume is important. It ultimately determines the amount of resources required to manufacture that amount of customer demand. Demand volume also becomes a statement of capacity. Daily production of units for sales in excess of the throughput volume per day, V_c, must be manufactured at some alternative date. Remember that a Lean manufacturing line should be designed with the capacity to support demand volume 1 to 3 years into the future. However, by designing a Lean line with a stated future capacity of 1 to 3 years, it will obviously have a capacity sufficient to produce a level of demand volume that is greater than the sales volume today. *Projected future demand* establishes a baseline volume for determining the final throughput volume of each manufacturing process.

Certain activities can alter the baseline demand volume of a process. Account for these activities when calculating the demand volume for each process:

- *Optional processes.* An optional process is a discretionary process chosen by a customer that causes throughput volume to be less than 100% V_c in certain processes. An optional process is used only when customer demand requires its use, e.g., to provide a feature or special functionality to a finished product. Examples of such optional processes include painted vs. unpainted, installed vs. uninstalled, added vs. deleted, or one piece per versus multiple pieces per. For processes that exceed 100%, e.g., products that require two per unit, the option percentage would be stated as 200%; three per unit would be 300%, etc. For volume less than 100%, the percentage is stated as a number representing the number of units estimated to be diverted through the optional process with the balance of units processed normally. The volume of an optional process is calculated using a formula:

$$(T_p) = T_{pOUT} \times \text{option}$$

where:

T_{pOUT} is throughput out of the process upstream of the option process. Option % is the percentage of T_p advanced to the optional process.

- **Rework processes.** A rework process is a process in which defective manufactured products containing absorbed work content are repaired or a process in which identified defects are corrected. Identified rework material can be returned to an upstream process for repair, to be sent to a specifically designated repair process, be sent to an off-line location, or remain at the workstation where the defect was discovered to be repaired. Repair or rework increases the volume of any process where reworking activity occurs. Repair or rework also increases the throughput volume of each process it passes through a second time after reentering a Lean line. The percentage of rework should be reflected on the PFD. The volume will be increased at each process (based on the historical percentage) noted on the PFD: at the process where the defect occurred, at the process where the defect is reworked, and at any additional process where the reworked product reenters the line. The new volume caused by rework at a process is calculated using a formula:

$$(T_p) = T_{pOUT} \times (1 + \text{rework \%})$$

where:

T_{pOUT} is the throughput out of the process where the rework occurred. Rework % is the historical rework percentage indicated on the PFD for the process.

- **Scrap.** In some cases, repair or rework cannot be completed or performing rework might be financially impractical. If a product cannot be reworked, it must be scrapped. Scrapped material is either disposed of or destroyed, resulting in a reduction of the throughput of all upstream processes of an entire Lean line. Not only is the volume of each process where scrap has occurred changed, but the volumes of all upstream processes are also affected. Because scrapped units must be replaced to achieve the desired throughput, additional units must be input through each process. The historical scrap amount, stated as a percentage, is identified on the PFD at the point where the scrap occurs. The required volume for all processes upstream from the point of scrap is calculated using a formula:

$$(T_p) = T_{pOUT} \times (1 + \text{yield } \%)$$

where:

T_{pOUT} is throughput out of the process where the scrap occurred. Yield % is the historical scrap percentage indicated on the PFD for the process where the scrap occurred. This percentage must then be calculated for all processes upstream from the process where the scrap occurs.

Any causes of altered throughput volume must be recorded on the process map and used to modify the V_c of each product affected by options, rework, or scrap because ultimately, the amount of resources required to produce the throughput volume can be impacted by these special processes.

In Figure 6.11, note the line design V_c for a product family is 300 units. Several processes have total quantities less than 300, indicating some products do not use every process. Although all products may be in the same family, all products do not necessarily use every process. These processes are therefore *optional* based on customer specification. Volume through those processes is less than the volume designated for the total product family. Because the volumes are different, the Takt times are also different for these processes. The number of resources required to produce the lower volume may also be less.

In addition to the creation of optional-process maps, similar-process maps can be constructed for the rework and scrap processes. Apply the rework and scrap percentages and resulting throughput calculations to the process map quantities. Note how the Takt times will be different when the volume denominator is changed. The greater the throughput volume, the smaller the Takt time will be. The converse is also true: the smaller the demand volume, the larger the Takt time will be.

Changes in throughput volumes can be easily managed on the spreadsheet process map started earlier in this chapter. Using the *Volume Modifier* column described for Table 6.2, Table 6.3 illustrates how rework, scrap, and optional process percentages impact the volumes of each process on the process map. When writing the formula, use 1 + the percentage change as the multiplier of the V_c for each product using that process. If the process is optional, record only the percentage of products using that optional process. List this quantity as a percent in the *Volume Modifier* column. Rework volumes are added to all processes where the work for reworked units is repeated. The manufacturing process and more than 100% of the V_c is produced as a result of the rework. The rework process V_c is the quantity of the *Rework %* only. Scrap affects all upstream processes and the volume of input must be increased by the *Scrap %* at each process.

Product	V_c	Process A	Process B	Process C	Process D	Process E	Process F	Optional	Process H	Rework
Product 100	120	×	×	×	×	×	×	×	×	
Product 200	50	×	×		×			×	×	
Product 300	40	×	×	×	×	×	×			×
Product 400	30	×	×	×	×	×	×	×	×	
Product 500	25	×	×	×	×	×		×	×	
Product 600	15	×	×	×	×	×	×		×	×
Product 700	10	×	×	×	×	×	×	×	×	
Product 800	5	×	×	×	×	×	×		×	×
Product 900	5	×	×	×	×			×	×	×
Total	300	300	300	250	300	245	220	240	260	65

Figure 6.11. A family of products with different process volumes affecting Takt time.

Table 6.3. A Process Map with Throughput Volume Factored by Volume Modifier for Each Process

Part Number	V_c	Weld Machine	Weld Labor	Volume Modifier	$V_c \times$ Volume Modifier	Weld Rework Machine	Weld Rework Labor	Volume Modifier	10% V_c	Assembly Machine	Assembly Labor	Volume Modifier	10% $V_c \times$ Volume Modifier	Custom Lights & Sound Machine	Custom Lights & Sound Labor	Volume Modifier	40% $V_c \times$ Volume Modifier
75903101	2.00			1.100	2.20			0.100	0.20			1.000	2.00			0.400	0.80
76000202	0.40			1.100	0.44			0.100	0.04			1.000	0.40			0.400	0.16
76102402	3.00			1.100	3.30			0.100	0.30			1.000	3.00			0.400	1.20
76100002	2.00			1.100	2.20			0.100	0.20			1.000	2.00			0.400	0.80
72200002	4.00			1.100	4.40			0.100	0.40			1.000	4.00			0.400	1.60
72210002	6.00			1.100	6.60			0.100	0.60			1.000	6.00			0.400	2.40
72208902	2.00			1.100	2.20			0.100	0.20			1.000	2.00			0.400	0.80
70524102	0.375			1.100	0.83			0.100	0.08			1.000	0.75			0.400	0.30
72208602	1.00			1.100	1.10			0.100	0.10			1.000	1.0			0.400	0.40
71801802	2.00			1.100	2.20			0.100	0.20			1.000	2.00			0.400	0.80
70542002	5.00			1.100	5.50			0.100	0.50			1.000	5.00			0.400	2.00
70550402	2.50			1.100	2.75			0.100	0.25			1.000	2.50			0.400	1.00
	30.65				**33.72**				**3.07**				**31**				**12**

V_c

Sum of $V_c \times$ the Volume Modifier (Volume = V_c + 10% Weld Rework)

Weld Rework = 10% V_c

Assembly = $V_c \times 1$

Custom Lights & Sound = $V_c \times 40\%$

DOCUMENTING THE PROCESS WORK ELEMENTS AND QUALITY CRITERIA ON THE PRODUCT FLOW DIAGRAM

The operational differences of a Lean line provide numerous benefits for a manufacturer. The basis of these benefits is the ability to produce products one at a time in a flow sufficient to meet customer demand, which can only be accomplished by achieving balance at every workstation on the Lean line: equal amounts of work must be designated to each location regardless of the process type. A Takt time establishes the production rate of the line at each workstation. Work equal to a Takt time is assigned to a workstation to define the standard work to be completed. The same elements of standard work are therefore repeated with every Takt time at every workstation. As a unit progresses through the standard work assigned at all the workstations, an additional amount of Takt time work is added sequentially until all the standard work required to manufacture the final product has been completed. Each time a 100% completed product exits the Lean line, all incomplete units remaining at the workstations advance one workstation downstream toward the point of completion. The established Takt time of each process indicates the rate at which the products flow downstream.

Defining the Standard Work of a Product in a Process

The PFD has identified the processes where work is performed sequentially to manufacture a product. The production rate necessary to meet customer demand for these products has been established with the Takt time. At this point in the design of a Lean line, a standard work definition (SWD) listing the work tasks to be completed for each process selected for the Lean operating system must be documented. The individual tasks and corresponding times and work elements required to perform the tasks for each process of each product must now be identified. Because each product chosen to be produced on the Lean line may require different processes with different tasks having different standard times, each product and its corresponding processes, work tasks, and standard times must be documented.

Use a template. An SWD template is used to document the work elements used at each process along with any quality criteria for each task (Figure 6.12). The template for a Lean transformation project can be created using a spreadsheet or word processing program. This template can also be used for future Lean enterprise transformation projects beyond the manufacturing shop floor and as a baseline document for recording improvements resulting from a kaizen process. Detail in an SWD is important. Most companies have some of the information required for the SWD in routing files or on process sheets, but when documenting a process on a task-by-task basis, the SWD requires a greater level of detail

		Standard Work Definitions						
Process ID:								
Product Part Number:								
Work Element		**Work Content**						**Task Quality Control**
Task	**Description**	**Value Added**	**Machine Setup Time**	**Labor Setup Time**	**Machine Run Time**	**Labor Run Time**	**Transport Time**	✓	**Quality Criteria**
Total		0.0	0.0	0.0	0.0	0.0	0.0		

Figure 6.12. A standard work definition template.

than the information provided by most existing routing files or process sheets. All work tasks necessary to manufacture a product must be recorded, including non-value-added work currently being done in the process such as quality inspections, moves, and setups. Until eliminated through an improvement effort, even the time required by a person or machine to perform non-value-added work must be documented. The work tasks on an SWD are used to establish the precise elements of standard work to be assigned to each individual workstation. The standard work times required to complete the work tasks are then summed into groupings of work equal to one Takt time. Grouping work by Takt time causes all processes to be completed at the same speed achieving balance through feeder and main line assembly processes along the entire line. Several types of information are required: product and process IDs, task descriptions and their sequential order, and time measurements.

Identify the product. The SWD establishes baseline work task information for each product. Once documented, the SWD is a primary record of how a specific product is manufactured in a specific process. Later, because the SWD has greater detail than a normal routing file, the manufacturing and design engineering departments can use the SWD as a reference source for future product design improvements.

Identify the process. Use the same names for the processes as used in the PFD. The naming convention is not nearly as important as naming consistency. Determine a preferred nomenclature: Assy or Assm, Grind or Grnd, QA or QC. As process improvements are made as a result of kaizen efforts, document the changes in the SWD. The SWD serves as a permanent record of how a product is made.

Describe the tasks. Describe a task in detail that is as close to a single motion as possible. The design of the Lean line will later require balancing the work being completed in a process by dividing that work into groups equal to a Takt time. Keeping the tasks in smaller elements will facilitate the assignment of tasks to specific workstations in groupings as close to the Takt time as possible. Instead of just recording *Assemble unit*, break the assembly down into individual steps. For repetitive tasks, such as attaching a series of fasteners, use one sequence to document the work, with the next task describing the number of times in the series the sequence is to be repeated. When completing the SWD, there is no way to know which work task will be the last task in a grouping of Takt time. Individually listing work tasks not only facilitates the grouping of work tasks by Takt time, but also assists in the assignment of standard work to a workstation.

Document the order of tasks. Document the sequential order of manufacturing tasks within a specific process. Rather than a 1 … 2 … 3 … 4… numbering methodology, use a numbering convention similar to the one used in the routing file: 010 … 020 … 030 … 040…, which allows the insertion of tasks that may be developed later, e.g., 015 … 025 … 035 … 045 ….

Document each category and type of work. In the SWD, work elements can be identified as one of three different categories: *setup, required,* and *move* (Figure 6.13). Each of these categories can be performed by either a machine or a person. In some cases, people can do work at the same time as a machine, i.e., in parallel. When human/machine work occurs in parallel, record each task with the largest element of time placed in brackets ([ ]). The SWD requires documentation of each category and type of work being performed. The categories break the different types of work into value-added and non-value-added work, with setup and move work always identified as non-value-added work. Later, improvement or kaizen projects can use the SWD to easily identify the non-value-added work tasks as candidates for improvement and possible elimination.

Document the time for each category and work task. Balancing Lean manufacturing processes relies on balancing the work documented on the SWD. For each category and work task, a measurement of the time required to complete the task must be documented. Time measurements must be made for each sequence description and recorded by work category and type in a designated column. Later on, all work (including non-value-added work) defined on the SWD will be divided into groups of standard work equal to the Takt time. Continue documenting each task until all tasks for a process have been identified. With a few exceptions, labor is the smallest of the three components of total product cost: documenting standard time to more than one decimal place is unnecessary. Standard work is performed by human beings. Human beings are not robots capable of duplicating the production of two items in a row in such a small increment of time. The smallest element of work a human can perform is approximately a tenth of a minute or 6 seconds. Just as an entire process *should not be* consolidated into a single large task, elements of work performed in less than 6 seconds should not be documented as stand-alone items. No single task should be recorded as less than 6 seconds (a tenth of a minute). Always round up to the next tenth of a minute. Ensuring that operators can successfully complete a Takt time amount of standard work at their workstations is more important than a finessing a few decimal places by an industrial engineer with a stopwatch and clipboard.

Time measurements: avoid using a stopwatch. Timing a task being done by an operator with a stopwatch can be intimidating. When under observation, the operator may unconsciously speed up or slow down and cause the average time

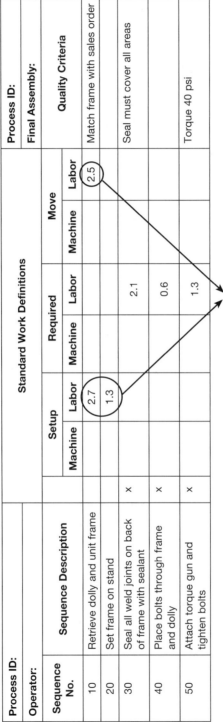

Process ID:							Process ID:
Operator:							Final Assembly:
		Standard Work Definitions					
		Setup		Required		Move	
Sequence No.	Sequence Description	Machine	Labor	Machine	Labor	Machine	Labor	Quality Criteria
10	Retrieve dolly and unit frame		2.7				2.5	Match frame with sales order
20	Set frame on stand		1.3					
30	Seal all weld joints on back of frame with sealant	×			2.1			Seal must cover all areas
40	Place bolts through frame and dolly	×			0.6			
50	Attach torque gun and tighten bolts	×			1.3			Torque 40 psi

Total Non-Value Added Time = 6.5 Minutes
Total Time for the Complete Process = 10.5 Minutes

Figure 6.13. A standard work definition with value-added and non-value-added times identified.

required for the task to be skewed on a daily basis. Unrealistic observed times (high or low) can cause the line to be unbalanced. Always keep in mind the time of day when the standard time is observed. Identify a time that an average operator can repeat each time the work is done and consider that the operator will be repeating the work at the workstation the number of times needed to equal the quantity of the daily customer demand. Ensure that the Takt time can be completed on time and with quality in increments of time no greater than a tenth of a minute.

Use realistic time measurements. To design a Lean line, Lean manufacturing technology requires that generous but realistic standard times be used in the SWD. Hair splitting or recording work times to a multidecimal place level is unnecessary. The final line design is based on an *average weighted time* for all products identified within a product family. The final line will ultimately be staffed with people of varying skills, who work at various speeds. Analyzing the work times for any group of people performing the same task will reveal a normal distribution of actual times: the fastest person, the slowest person, and a majority of people clustered around the mean. Do not design a Lean line using the observed standard time of the fastest or the slowest worker. Design the line so an average person can be successful and productive when performing the standard work assigned to a workstation.

Can the existing time standards be used? Time standards may already exist on routing files, but they may be the *aggregate time* for an entire process (*task-level* detail is required when documenting work for a Lean line). Engineering standards commonly used for developing routing files focus only on a required work category, frequently ignoring setup, move, and quality criteria inspection times. Existing standard times may be unrealistic or incomplete because they were developed to facilitate an efficiency or utilization performance measurement. The standard times may also be out of date, not reflect the current methodologies, or have been set by timing the fastest or the slowest operator. If existing records are used to develop an SWD, be certain that the routing or process sheet time elements and tasks are 100% current and align sequentially with the process tasks and descriptions for products and processes of the SWD.

Document non-value-added work. Non-value-added work must be included in the standard time required to complete a task. Even though it must be performed by a resource (a person or machine), non-value-added work is usually ignored by normal routing files. Non-value-added work is not ignored on an SWD. It's highlighted as a candidate for eventual elimination. Until it can be eliminated through kaizen or some other type of continuous improvement activity, non-value-added work will continue to be a component of response time to customers. Like it or not, non-value-added work must be considered when establishing the lead time for a customer.

Identifying Value-Added and Non-Value-Added Work in the Standard Work Definition Template

The Lean definition of value-added work is simple. If given a choice, customers are usually willing to pay for the time required to perform value-added work because it adds value by changing the form, fit, or function of a product, but what about the work done to confirm or inspect work already completed in a previous manufacturing process or at a workstation? What if a product has a history of failure requiring an extra inspection step before the product can be sent on to a customer with confidence? What about setup and move work?

Once the categories and types of work have been documented, a decision must be made: is an individual task a value-added step or a non-value-added step? Initially, this decision has no impact on the work tasks that are balanced for line design. Regardless of its status — value-added or not — when a Lean line starts up, *all* work documented on an SWD must be performed. The work designated as non-value-added has been automatically identified on the SWD as a candidate for reduction or elimination at a later time. Even though the Lean operating system strives to eliminate it, the non-value-added work must be tolerated until a robust process to eliminate it can be developed. As long as non-value-added work is a component of customer response time, customer-quoted lead time will be negatively affected.

Inspection work. Inspection work does not meet the definition of value-added work because it does not change the form, fit, or function of a product, but until eliminated, inspection work must be documented on the SWD and completed. (If customers knew the cost of quality inspections, they would probably not be willing to pay for them!) In a perfect world, manufacturing processes could only be done one way and the operators doing the work would complete the work exactly the same way every time. Unfortunately, processes are rarely designed to be fail-safe. More common is for manufacturing processes to have some degree of variability. With variability, an individual operator must interpret the best way to complete the work. If experienced and skilled, the operator will likely make the right decision about the one best way to do the work, producing a good unit each time. Conversely, an inexperienced or inadequately trained operator might make a well-intentioned but wrong interpretation and produce a defective unit. Interpreting variable work tasks should not be responsibility of operators. Management is responsible for interpreting variability. Management must define the single correct way to produce a quality unit at each workstation. Engineers work diligently to locate variability and design it out of manufacturing processes, but removing all variability is unlikely. Until a process can be 100% fail-safe, the only practical alternative for managing variability is to require inspections. The ☑ symbol on the SWD indicates to an operator that an inspection is required for that task (see Figure 6.12). For each sequential task description on the SWD, the single, correct way to manufacture the product must be documented on the SWD. Even though inspections are non-value-added activity, they cannot be summarily dismissed. Until variability is eliminated by an improvement or kaizen activity, inspections must be performed to ensure the one correct way to complete a work task has been followed. The time required to perform them must be included in the Takt time amount of work assigned to a workstation. Inspection work is a component of customer response time. It negatively impacts customer-quoted lead time. Although sometimes necessary, inspection work is *always* non-value-added work. (Which solution is less costly for a company: continued inspections or a long-term, cost-effective program to eliminate a faulty or variable process?)

Setup work. A machine or a person can perform setup work. Setup work does not meet the definition of value-added work because it does not change the form, fit, or function, but until eliminated, setup work must be documented on the SWD and completed. Two separate types of setup work are done: *dynamic* and *static*. Dynamic setup for labor is the work done each time required standard work is done. Dynamic setup for a machine is the time required to place material in the machine each time the machine cycle is run. The time required to perform each dynamic setup must be included in the Takt time amount of the work assigned to a workstation. Conversely, static setup work indicates that a manufacturing process must *stop* while the setup work is performed, e.g., the tasks and time associated with the removal of one set of dies and the replacement of a new set of dies. Each should be documented on the SWD for future analysis, but static setup work is *not* documented on an SWD in the same way as dynamic setup time. A static setup is a separate event. For example, when changing over a machine, the tasks, times, and quality criteria for a static setup are recorded, but the setup time is amortized over a preset quantity of products to be added to any dynamic setup time. Dynamic time and static setup time are *always* non-value-added work. Static setup time is always a good candidate for a kaizen or SMED (single-minute exchange of die) project.

Move work. As with setup work (and required work), a machine or a person can perform move work. Also like setup work, move work does not meet the definition of value-added work because it does not change the form, fit, or function of the product. Until it can be eliminated, move work must still be performed and the time required for completing it added to the manufacturing response time through the factory. Move work can also be dynamic or static. Dynamic move work is performed each time a unit is produced. If a transfer conveyor is indexed each time a unit is moved to the next workstation, the move work is dynamic machine time. Static work is not performed until a predetermined amount of product has been accumulated, e.g., a predetermined pallet quantity must be achieved prior to moving products to the next workstation. If work is moved each time a single unit is completed, the move work is dynamic. The move work is static if a full pallet of completed materials must be accumulated before the move work may be done. Move time must be included in the Takt time amount of work assigned to a workstation on an SWD. Move work is always non-value-added work. Move work is a candidate for kaizen and eventual elimination.

Note: When human/machine work occurs in parallel, record each task with the largest element of time placed in brackets ([ ]).

Required work. Required work content alters the form, fit, or function of a unit being manufactured. It's the conversion work that must be completed to transform raw materials into a product that is desired by a customer. Required work always includes the *touch work* conversion processes that add value to a product. A machine or a person can complete touch work. When human/ machine touch work occurs in parallel, record each task as a separate sequence description with the largest time component placed in brackets ([ ]). Required work is *always* value-added-work. It is the *only* value-added work listed on the SWD.

Denote non-value-added work on the SWD. Non-value-added work is waste. As distasteful as non-value-added work is for a Lean manufacturer to accept, non-value-added work must continue to be performed by operators on the shop floor until it can be eliminated. Because of its effect on customer-quoted lead time, eliminating non-value-added work should be the subject of on-going, never-ending, continuous process improvement and kaizen activities. Unless the non-value-added work is low-hanging fruit and easily designed out of a process while creating the SWD, it must continue to be documented and included in the initial Takt design of a Lean line. All non-value-added work tasks must be identified as candidates for elimination with kaizen and other continuous process improvement projects by highlighting each non-value-added task description on the SWD with an asterisk (*) or some other indicator in the *Value Added* column to indicate the task as a process improvement opportunity (see Figure 6.12). For example, once *Setup* and *Move* work are documented, they are easily isolated from the value-added tasks. Continuous process improvement or kaizen teams can then use the SWD to prioritize non-value-added work candidates that have the largest return on investment for elimination. Long term, the goal is to eliminate all non-value-added work in every process. Until the time when all non-value added work has been eliminated, continuous improvement will always be necessary in an organization.

Lean manufacturing methodology requires all work tasks on the SWD identified as non-value-added be documented. Make no judgments or attempts to solve the causes of non-value-adding work tasks at the time the SWD is created. The purpose of the SWD is only to document where non-value-added work elements occur and how much time is consumed to perform the work associated with them. Remain focused on an accurate, thorough collection of work tasks for each process of the SWD. Don't get sidetracked by eliminating non-value-adding tasks. Resolving the causes and developing solutions for eliminating non-value-added work are responsibilities of kaizen and continuous process improvement teams.

THE VALUE OF INFORMATION GATHERING FOR THE PROCESS FLOW DIAGRAM: IDENTIFICATION OF NON-VALUE-ADDED WORK AND QUALITY CONSIDERATIONS FOR KAIZEN ACTIVITIES

Collecting information to complete an SWD requires a significant investment of time and resources. Often the information gathered yields surprising revelations about the company's manufacturing processes. Occasionally, some of these revelations (known as low-hanging fruit) can be resolved quickly and intuitively with little cost. Most others, however, will require time, ingenuity, and the expenditure of resources for resolution. Kaizen activities are well suited for solving more difficult issues and ultimately result in improved or reduced customer response time and customer-quoted lead time. Opportunities for improvement can be quantified from the SWD and used to prioritize kaizen projects:

- *Setups and moves.* In most cases, the realignment of manufacturing processes so the output of a process is consumed directly into another forces the elimination of some setups and moves just because the processes are now located adjacent to one another. Remaining setups and moves are always non-value-adding activities: the times required for them are candidates for reduction or elimination. Challenging setup and move time reductions may require prioritized kaizen projects and further study. For example, SMED (single-minute exchange of dies) is a Lean method used to reduce non-value-added time in a manufacturing process, which provides a faster, more efficient way to convert a manufacturing process running the current product to running the next product.

- **Quality inspections.** Inspections for variations that have been designated as quality criteria on the SWD are non-value-added work. Non-value-added inspection work must continue until the source(s) of variation can be eliminated from a process. If inspection work is required, why does it *not* meet the definition of value-added work? Although this question is the subject of frequent discussions, the answer comes from another question: given a choice, are customers willing to pay for inspection work to be performed? Unless an industry is regulated, customers rarely demand specific inspection work. They simply require the product to perform as advertised. *How* that is accomplished is the responsibility of the manufacturer: conducting inspections to overcome process variability is a choice made by the manufacturer. Over time, use kaizen and poka-yoke projects to make a process fail-safe so no inspection is necessary.

- **Design engineering.** *Engineering throws it over the wall and manufacturing figures out how to make it* is a proverbial lament from the manufacturing group. Often it's a legitimate complaint. It is not uncommon for the design engineering department to be remotely located. Distance from the manufacturing facility compromises the access often required for first-hand observation of how a product is actually manufactured. Design engineers focus primarily on designing individual products and components that meet specific specifications and functionality requirements. Often they do not have knowledge about how the entire product will be used by the manufacturing facility. Tasks in the SWD may therefore be performed simply because engineering lacks understanding of the manufacturing process. Without good communication and visibility between manufacturing and engineering, operators on the shop floor, sometimes by default, must improvise and interpret *how* to put a product together based on personal experience or knowledge. Figure 6.14 illustrates the SWD for a product that was designed without the benefit of engineering having first-hand knowledge about how the product is produced in the manufacturing area. Note the added tasks and inspections required for operators to be certain that the product performs as specified: the excess quality criteria indicate the process has a large amount of variability. Once the SWD has been developed listing the tasks required to produce a product, ensure that the SWD is made available to design engineering so that designers are aware of existing manufacturing processes and have a chance to eliminate the

Process Name: Final Assembly

Product Part Number: Range Top Model 12

Standard Work Definitions

Order	Work Element Description	Parts Consumed	Total Quality Control Self-Check Description
10	Obtain fixture from under conveyor		Fixture matches motor series number
20	Retrieve stator and place on fixture		Check shell for exposed metal, presence of all notches, and wires tucked in
30	Insert wire exit grommet	1253-B grommet	
40	Attach mounting bracket with one screw	6672 bracket 2042 screw	Install on wire exit side Screw gun set to **3**
50	Repeat 40 once	2042 screw	Screw gun set to **3**
60	Retrieve top shield and install with one screw	1068 screw	Bearing is greased and grease fitting is tight Screw gun set to **5**
70	Repeat 60 once	1068 screw	Screw gun set to **5**
80	Insert rotor guide in stator		Screw gun set to **5**
90	Retrieve rotor and install in stator		Long side of shaft forward Check for free turn
100	Retrieve bottom sheild and install with one screw	1068 screw	Bearing is greased and grease fitting is tight Screw gun set to **5**

Figure 6.14. A standard work definition with an unstable process.

non-value-added work elements with improved designs for the next generation of products.

Kaizen activities or a Lean transformation? Many manufacturers claim to have a Lean facility when they are actually only performing a series of kaizen activities to improve a group of disconnected processes. What criteria should be used to select a process (or processes) for a Lean transformation or a kaizen event? Kaizen can work well as a stand-alone technology, but it risks producing sporadic and disconnected improvements throughout the factory floor with no overall benefit for the whole manufacturing process. Lean technology simultaneously streamlines all process required to meet customer demand by balancing and linking processes to one another. Achieving improvements using kaizen activities alone is possible, but Lean methods are improvement activities aimed at reducing customer response time and eliminating the non-value-added work embedded in the standard work times across the entire series of linked processes. Lean requires that priorities for kaizen projects be directed at eliminating non-value-added work and reducing response time, inventories, and working capital. Establish kaizen projects that are prioritized to concentrate on the *greatest* reduction or elimination of individual non-value-added activities that first improve lead time and then reduce working capital. Use the Lean operating system to identify improvement opportunities that yield the greatest lead time reduction, quality improvement, and working capital reduction.

DETERMINING TOTAL PROCESS TIME

When the sequential task descriptions, along with the setup, move, and inspection times, the quality criteria, and the value-added times, have all been documented for a process, the total time for that process for a product can be determined. The total standard work content of a process is the sum of all documented observed times of each work task. Machine and labor times are reported as separate task descriptions on the SWD. The sum of all labor and machine times represents the total time required to produce an identified product in the process. Use the longest times (machine and labor) for the sum of the total time of a process. The longest times represent the best estimate of the response time of a process. Where machine and labor work is performed in parallel, use the longest time as indicated by the brackets ([ ]). Also include non-value-added work times in the sum even though non-value-added work does not change the form, fit, or function of the product. Total process time must include all work times, value-added and non-value-added.

Standard time in a traditional system. Traditional industrial engineering standard time typically does not recognize different categories of non-value-added work. Instead, non-value-added work is ignored or lumped together and labeled as *nonproductive*. It is accounted for as a negative variation in productivity reporting. Often nonproductive work is reported by managers as justification for additional headcounts or for use when purchasing capital equipment. Sometimes, in an effort to reduce non-value-added work or reduce costs, a company campaign to improve productivity is initiated, but often with little idea as to where to begin. Responsibility for the success of the project is usually abdicated to individual managers who are left to their own devices to figure out how to achieve elusive productivity improvements. Some will achieve improvement, but many others will struggle and achieve little. Even if the success of the productivity improvement program is limited, great fanfare is given to the results. After a few months, the productivity improvement program becomes a distant memory and the company returns to business as usual.

Standard time in a Lean system. Total process time, including setup and move work, required work, and the quality criteria, is used to determine the standard times for calculating the amount of resources required to staff a process to achieve the Takt time target. Because non-value-added work has been recorded in a separate column on the SWD, the magnitude of current non-value-added work being done can be easily identified. The sum of non-value-added work on the SWD might be the first time non-value-added work has actually been documented and quantified in great enough detail to distinguish value-added from non-value-added work tasks. The ratio of value-added work to non-value-added work is a good measurement for a kaizen team to use: SWD information can be validated with little subjectivity and used as baseline information for the development of objective-based KPIs. A kaizen project initiated using non-value-added information from an SWD has a better chance of returning long-term recurring process productivity improvements than simply hanging posters espousing productivity around the shop floor. Improvements to the tasks and times will be documented on the SWD and compared with the baseline SWD to establish mathematically based, objective performance measurements. No longer will the "best liar have the best chance" with management when bragging about personal process improvements.

Continuous improvement is a never-ending initiative. Manufacturers know that non-value-added work simply adds time and cost to products. If production costs cannot be reduced, manufacturers may have no choice but to pass these added costs on to their customers. Deal scientifically with the elements of waste without placing blame on operators, supervision, engineering, or a previous group. At some point, excessive time and costs will negatively impact a company's ability to compete effectively based on selling price. There's a threshold beyond which customers are unwilling to pay for costs that do not add value to the product. When this happens, they simply shop their business with competitors, looking for a lower price and faster delivery.

THE LEAN LINE: RESOURCES, LINE DESIGN, AND MANAGEMENT

Information collected so far has identified the processes, the demand for those processes, and the effective minutes available to do work. With this information, the Takt time for each process is calculated (Table 7.1). (Remember from Chapter 6 that Takt time defines the *rate* the line must run to achieve a desired daily output and specifies the *frequency* for the completion of one unit of finished goods.) Standard work definitions (SWDs) have also been developed documenting the individual tasks of standard work in sequential order, the time required to complete the identified tasks, and the quality criteria at the individual task level. With this knowledge, the number of individual resources necessary to produce the customer demand in the various processes can be determined. A resource is defined as:

> *The investment of a person, machine, workstation, or inventory utilized during a manufacturing process to add value to raw materials for the construction of a product or for completing an administrative activity. Resources can be people, workstations, machines, and inventory.*

UTILIZING RESOURCES: THE LEAN APPROACH

All manufacturing operating systems use resources to manufacture products, but Lean manufacturing methodology utilizes resources differently than the order-

Table 7.1. Process Map with Takt Times in Minutes (Takt = Planned Work Minutes × Shifts ÷ Throughput Volume)

Family Description	Part Number	V_c	Weld Machine	Weld Labor	Volume Modifier	Volume Modifier × V_c	Weld Rework Machine	Weld Rework Labor	Volume Modifier	Volume Modifier × V_c	Assembly Machine	Assembly Labor	Volume Modifier	Volume Modifier × V_c	Custom Lights & Sound Machine	Custom Lights & Sound Labor	Volume Modifier	Volume Modifier × V_c
V5A	75903101	2.00			1.100	2.20			0.100	0.20			1.000	2.00			0.400	0.80
V6A	76000202	0.40			1.100	0.44			0.100	0.04			1.000	0.40			0.400	0.16
A4H	76102402	3.00			1.100	3.30			0.100	0.30			1.000	3.00			0.400	1.20
U5	76100002	2.00			1.100	2.20			0.100	0.20			1.000	2.00			0.400	0.80
805	72200002	4.00			1.100	4.40			0.100	0.40			1.000	4.00			0.400	1.60
806	72210002	6.00			1.100	6.60			0.100	0.60			1.000	6.00			0.400	2.40
T5AH	72208902	2.00			1.100	2.20			0.100	0.20			1.000	2.00			0.400	0.80
T5LOAH	70524102	0.375			1.100	0.83			0.100	0.08			1.000	0.75			0.400	0.30
S5	72208602	1.00			1.100	1.10			0.100	0.10			1.000	1.00			0.400	0.40
TM270	71801802	2.00			1.100	2.20			0.100	0.20			1.000	2.00			0.400	0.80
G3	70542002	5.00			1.100	5.50			0.100	0.50			1.000	5.00			0.400	2.00
G4A	70550402	2.50			1.100	2.75			0.100	0.25			1.000	2.50			0.400	1.00
		30.65				33.72				3.07				31				12

	Weld	Weld Rework	Assembly	Custom Lights & Sound
Takt Time	13	143	14	36
Planned Work Minutes	438	438	438	438
Shifts	1	1	1	1
Throughput Volume	33.72	3.07	31	12

launch methodology of traditional planning systems. For designing a new Lean operating system, the process flow of a product, the processes used to complete manufacturing of the product, the standard work at each process for each product, the production Takt rate, and customer demand are required information elements. The remaining information element needed to design and operate a Lean manufacturing line is the amount of resources needed to achieve the daily customer demand: the number of *people, workstations, machines*, and *inventory* resources that must be assigned to each process to achieve the Takt time target.

The primary reason for the existence of a manufacturing facility is to satisfy customer demand by producing and delivering high-quality products in the shortest amount of time possible. Once a company has made the decision to meet customer demand by being a manufacturer, managing people, workstations, machines, and inventory resources as effectively as possible becomes "job number one." The single largest expense for most manufacturing companies is the resources required to operate the manufacturing facility. Managing resources is serious business — if poorly managed, the costs of resources can ruin or seriously handicap even the best of companies.

Over time, if not controlled, wasteful non-value-adding activities silently creep into the manufacturing processes, requiring more and more resources to compensate for them. Slowly, the waste becomes invisible and is simply taken for granted as a cost of doing business. The seven wastes of manufacturing (overproduction, inventory, extra processing steps, motion, defects, waiting, and transportation) are the result of these creeping, insidious non-value-adding activities. Manufacturers know waste is there, but in their day-to-day concentration on meeting customer demand, they cannot see it. Instead, they choose to ignore it because they do not know how to eliminate it. Unfortunately, the costs of waste must be recovered somehow. The fastest, easiest way is to absorb these costs into the selling prices of products. It's a great solution until customers choose not to pay the price of your products and takes their business to a competitor offering a better price. As waste becomes systemic over time, its associated hidden costs become institutionalized and seemingly impossible to eliminate.

Lean and waste. Lean manufacturing methodologies include formal processes that systematically deconstruct traditional manufacturing practices to identify waste so it can be eliminated. When waste has been squeezed out of processes, selling price is no longer the sole competitive differentiator for a Lean manufacturer. Other important differentiators provide additional leverage when deploying strategies for capturing market share: shorter lead time, improved quality, and working capital reduction. A Lean transformation *systematically* seeks to identify and eliminate wastes that have been accumulated in manufacturing costs over time. A Lean operating system eliminates the overproduction of products in a factory caused by a policy of maximum utilization of resources by using *only* the resources necessary to meet customer demand. Because customers rarely order the same amount or variety of products on a given day, instead of using WIP and FGI inventories as balancing mechanisms to offset fluctuations in utilization, a Lean operating system modifies the amount of resources to match changing customer demand each day using flexible resources. Because workstations, machines, and inventory are stationary, inanimate, and inflexible objects, people are the only flexible resource. A Lean system requires the human resources to adjust to changes in customer demand so that the necessary resources required on any given day match the customer demand. When unsold units are not produced, the waste of overproduction is avoided.

Lean = marketplace advantage. Producing products with minimum waste using measured utilization of resources makes sense. Having the ability to avoid the wasteful production of unsold products gives a Lean manufacturer a big cost differential over a non-Lean competitor. Traditional production methods *enable* the production of hidden waste in manufacturing processes. Because waste increases cost, to remain profitable, a non-Lean manufacturer has no choice but to pass on the cost of waste to customers in the price of their product. If selling price is a major differentiator for a customer, a non-Lean manufacturer has little latitude to modify the product's price to meet or beat a Lean competitor. In the marketplace, a traditional manufacturer loses out to Lean competitor who can adjust the cost gap between the profit margin and selling price as a sales differential.

How Lean does it. Lean manufacturing is the production of a product minus all non-value-added work. In Lean, manufacturing a product requires only the sum of its standard work content time and the cost of its materials. Manufacturing response time should not exceed the sum of the work content time of the product: any time in excess of standard work content time is waste. *The goal of a Lean manufacturing line is to produce a product in the sum of its work content time only.* Any non-value-added activity that causes response time to exceed work content time is a candidate for reduction or elimination by a kaizen process.

Lean versus traditional operating system management of resources. Traditional operating systems evolved from the need to maximize the utilization of resources, particularly machines. The approach of traditional planning systems to managing the manufacturing process is very different from the Lean approach. Not until Lean operating systems became popular, causing rethinking of the true costs of utilization and inventory, did manufacturers try to understand the differences between the two systems. A Lean operating system is not difficult to comprehend, but for most manufacturers who have spent their entire careers in traditional operating systems, the different approach required to make a Lean operating system to work in their factories and offices is not intuitive. No consultant, sales person, book, industry article, or seminar can convince a manufacturer of the superiority of a Lean operating system. Management must make the intellectual investment to understand the differences and reconcile how Lean would be an improvement over the current operating method. To better understand the differences between traditional and Lean operating systems, a review of the traditional system will be helpful.

UTILIZING RESOURCES: THE TRADITIONAL APPROACH

Traditional planning systems assume that an infinite capacity of resources is available to manufacturing. Production orders are issued by a planning system to meet customer requirements based on the demand established by a *master schedule*. The frequency of the replanning process is set by the planning group based on the volatility of customer demand. Once the planning system performs time-phasing routines based on the due dates of customer demand, a schedule of work for each individual department is established. The priority of released production orders is determined by its due date and the available capacity in each department. As long as the planned order load does not exceed the stated capacity of a department during the assigned time period, the production plan is considered valid. An individual department manager usually has the final say and as to whether the recommended plan is valid.

The indented BOM establishes start and due dates. To establish correct start and due dates for production orders, which in turn establish the load in each department based on the net requirements, an indented BOM is required. The indented BOM is a key data source for the planning system operation. The indented BOM not only lists the component parts required to manufacture the product, but it also includes department lead times and quantities per each component part required to schedule production of a product. Using the due date of the SKU at the master schedule level as a starting point and using the lead-time offset information for each level in the BOM, start and due dates are established for released orders for each department down through all the levels of the BOM until the start date at the gateway department is established. In traditional manufacturing, the lead time of a finished product is established by summing all of the offset lead times of each department sequentially through all levels of the indented BOM beginning at the gateway department up to the master schedule.

The indented BOM establishes build sequence. The BOM offset function also describes to the planning system how a product is manufactured and electronically communicates the build sequence of subassemblies. Using the offset

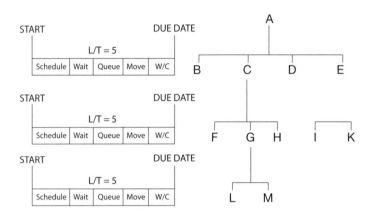

Figure 7.1. An indented bill of materials establishes due and start dates for production orders released in a standard planning system.

lead time recorded for each level of the BOM, and the due and start dates recommended by the replanning process, individual production schedules for every department are developed. The different levels of the BOM represent the sequential build of the product through the manufacturing facility much like a *goes into* chart. On a department-by-department basis, the sum of all orders released by due date establishes the load on that department for that period. Figure 7.1 illustrates how an indented BOM establishes start and due dates for production orders released from the planning system.

The indented BOM impacts the company's organization. The indented BOM is a crucial component for the operation of a traditional operating system that impacts the organization of the manufacturing departments and the management structure of the entire company. Manufacturing departments are often established to mimic the levels of an indented BOM. Similar functions or manufacturing processes are intentionally grouped together in departments to mirror the levels in the BOM. Shop floor layouts use the indented BOM to determine the physical location of the departments in the factory. The structure of data collection and data maintenance responsibilities frequently reflect the structure of the indented BOM. Accommodating database maintenance of the planning system often dictates the organizational structure in a company.

Traditional planning systems require significant information maintenance. The demands of maintaining and operating a planning system require a diverse skills base. Planning systems and individual managers' responsibilities for ROI and utilization of resources in their respective departments contribute greatly to the organization charts in many companies: the organization is designed around responsibilities required for the operation and maintenance of the planning system. Not only is the planning system used for the facilitation of production schedules, but it also requires the development of departmental policies and procedures from engineering, quality control, purchasing, forecasting, shop floor, routings, and capacity planning to cost accounting. Most companies use planning system maintenance requirements to define the responsibilities of individual departments, e.g., BOM creation and maintenance is the responsibility of design engineering, forecasting is the responsibility of sales and marketing, planning and inventory management is the responsibility of materials management, and routing file management is the responsibility of manufacturing engineering. A planning system has a voracious appetite for accurate, up-to-date information. A planning system needs the most current, accurate information to perform the planning function. If the information used to complete the planning routine is incorrect, the planning system's output will be equally incorrect! Successful planning systems require the database maintenance responsibilities to be assigned to a specific department.

Lean challenges traditional organizational structures and planning system information. Implementing a Lean operating system often challenges the indented BOM logic used to establish the departments and the company's organizational structure. Challenging existing departmental roles and responsibilities causes resistance to the potential organizational and structural changes that may be needed by the Lean operating system. Over time, many departments have become dependent on the planning system as a depository for information and to provide feedback from production operations. Their jobs may have been designed around the operation and maintenance of the planning system — they need to input information into the planning system and they need to receive output from it to perform their jobs. Their jobs may have even been justified by the need for data maintenance of the planning system. A Lean operating system does not depend on the output of a planning system to utilize resources to meet customer demand. Reliance on planning system information to operate a Lean manufacturing facility is greatly diminished or completely unnecessary. Once the Lean system is in operation, the departments formerly dependent on planning system information will soon notice the lack of information flowing from the planning system. The reduced dependency on information coming from and going into the planning system may cause great concern about the changing status of the company and the need for some jobs, which, of course, causes great concern for a department manager whose function has been the maintenance of data for the planning system. Some may fear their jobs are going to disappear. Fear created by the change to the Lean system may cause people to go into a job preservation mode. Until an alternative Lean method is developed to replace the data provided by the planning system, the current flow of information must be maintained.

Lean challenges traditional staffing requirements. In many organizations, meeting the increasing needs of traditional planning system information maintenance is a primary justification for expanding departmental staffing requirements. Needing to operate or maintain required planning system information is a good way for department managers to *empire build* the size of their organizational footprint: increased dependence on system output and needing a correspondingly larger staff increases their importance and power. Some may be motivated to grow planning system data requirements to create an even greater need for an increased administrative headcount. Their importance and power have become tied to the existence and size of the planning system. Any incentive to challenge the inputs and outputs of the planning system is nonexistent. Because a Lean operating system requires less traditional information, these department managers often become resistors during a Lean transformation project. They see the reduced reliance on information currently generated by and for their departments as a threat to their status and power.

Traditional modern planning systems significantly impact the departmentalization of the shop floor and the organization of administrative areas, but they give very little attention to ensuring that all manufacturing departments are designed with equal resource capacities. Instead, resources are assigned to a department based simply on its function or the type of work done — similarity of function is the sole reason for assigning resources to a department in a traditional operating system. Using this simple criterion for assigning resources ignores the need for having a balanced capacity among all departments on the manufacturing shop floor. The unbalanced resource capacity leads to some departments having more capacity than others. When the excess capacity in an unbalanced department is fully utilized, production output will be in excess of customer demand. The reverse is true for the departments with less capacity than customer demand. Utilization in those departments is not a problem, but meeting on-time customer demand is! With traditional planning systems, smoothing out these imbalances can only be accomplished by creating buffer inventories or through constant expediting activities to reprioritize customer demand. Neither of these smoothing alternatives changes the *form, fit, or function* of the product. It's non-value-added activity caused by the need of the planning system to achieve 100% utilization in all departments. These overproduction and expediting activities are considered *waste* in a Lean operating system.

ACHIEVING UTILIZATION BALANCE: THE TRADITIONAL APPROACH

Utilization imbalance creates many problems currently seen on the shop floor. Even with a traditional planning system, manufacturing departments seek to achieve balance. Significant efforts are given to rearranging production order loads among the departments with different capacities. Some departments may expedite production orders after they are released to the shop floor. Others may attempt to achieve balance on a default basis by using WIP inventories as their only available balancing mechanism. The shop floor square footage footprint must be increased to accommodate storing the buffer inventories. All departments try to achieve maximum utilization of the resources assigned to them even if it means building unsold inventories, working overtime, or missing customer due dates to make it happen. None of these efforts to achieve resource balance among the manufacturing departments change the *form, fit, or function* of the product. They're considered waste in a Lean operating system.

Utilization and department managers. Maximum utilization of resources allocated to the department is an important component of a manager's annual performance review (and any subsequent pay raise). Managers are therefore highly motivated to achieve maximization of their department's resources. The goal is to achieve a utilization factor as close to 100% as possible: if the department has excess capacity, more work must be added to keep resources 100% utilized. For example, resources underutilized by a planned production order load can be maximized by pulling orders forward from the planning horizon and producing them ahead of their original planned due dates. Running production orders ahead of schedule satisfies the manager's need for departmental utilization, but doing so creates unsold inventory. This 100% utilization strategy is costly if customer demand cannot absorb the output. Because the cost of inventory is more expensive than the cost of labor, a strategy to build excess unsold inventory to achieve utilization goals can cost more than underutilized labor. Even so, the quest for 100% utilization will always trump meeting customer demand in any department with capacity in excess of customer demand. Managers who are measured on the efficiency and utilization (absorption) of their assigned labor and machine resources will do everything in their power to keep their resources as busy as possible. For example, grouping production orders with similar work content together so they can be run sequentially to create longer production runs to reduce inefficiencies caused by changeovers is a common technique. This type of work grouping, known as *batch manufacturing*, is encouraged by the need to achieve maximum utilization. Consider the result of all this production order management activity in departments on a typical shop floor. To maintain database accuracy for the next MRP reschedule, the reprioritizing of production orders requires timely production order status reporting to the planning system. "Gaming" the operating system at the expense of meeting on-time customer demand does nothing to change the *form, fit, or function* of the product being produced. It's all non-valued added activity and considered *waste* in a Lean operating system.

Utilization and the production control group: if manufacturing departments have excess capacity. If the released order load is below the stated capacity of a department, then the manufacturing group will request additional orders from the production control group until full utilization of the department is ensured. The only way the production control group can meet this request is to release firm planned orders in advance of the planning system's recommended release dates (known as *pulling orders forward from the planning horizon*). If no customer demand exists for these orders issued in advance of their recommended release dates, then the result will be overproduction and unsold inventory. Pulling orders forward also results in material shortages or the cannibalization of materials already allocated to other released production orders, leading to excessive expediting activities and premium transportation costs, the need to maintain larger inventories of parts, unsold finished goods that can lead to slow-moving, obsolete inventory, and strained supplier relationships. All of the consequences of pulling orders forward are components of the seven wastes of production. They do nothing to change the *form, fit, or function* of the products being produced.

Utilization and the production control group: if manufacturing departments have limited capacity. In capacity-constrained departments, as the released order load approaches or exceeds the stated capacity in these departments, compromised or even missed due dates are a frequent experience. A capacity-constrained department cannot process the volume of production orders received from the upstream department. Production orders are rarely completed in the sequence necessary to satisfy production priorities downstream. Production orders must constantly be reprioritized to satisfy the downstream processes. If order priorities are uncertain, there is even greater risk for producing customer demand out of sequence, further putting customer due dates at risk. If unsold inventory is produced in a capacity-constrained department, delaying an actual customer production order, then customer satisfaction will the further compromised. Reprioritization of production orders can also cause an increased need for machine setups. When a machine setup is required, even more capacity is lost, resulting a never-ending cycle — constantly attempting to meet on-time delivery of production orders, but always being behind. Capacity-constrained departments always have past-due orders that require the added expense of overtime to meet customer due dates. Working extra shifts and weekends is a way of life in capacity-constrained departments. If a department downstream from a capacity-constrained department needs to maximize utilization, then the pressure on the capacity-constrained department to rearrange its priorities will be relentless. Figure 7.2 illustrates the factory floor expediting of released production orders in an attempt to satisfy the changing priorities and utilization requirements of unbalanced departments. In an imbalanced facility, demand is constantly reshuffled. It's a no-win situation for capacity-constrained departments. In some companies, entire organizations are dedicated to performing the expediting activities required for dealing with the daily rescheduling/rebalancing act occurring on their unbalanced factory floors. None of these activities change the *form, fit, or function* of the product being produced. They're all non-value-added and considered *waste* in a Lean operating system.

ACHIEVING PRODUCTION GOALS: THE TRADITIONAL APPROACH

The struggle to achieve inventory management (or turn rate) and customer service goals versus productivity, absorption, utilization, and efficiency goals has been the source of major conflicting objectives between manufacturing departments and sales and marketing departments for years and continues in most manufacturing companies today. Just observe production planning personnel, expediters, and planners and production managers. Notice the amount of time devoted to winning their respective productivity battles. These victories often come at the expense of meeting customer on-time due dates. Reconciliation of conflicting objectives is a major cause of daily expediting activities. Shuffling production orders to achieve production goals can result in achieving a default resource balance between departments with unequal capacity, but achieving this balance not only creates turmoil on the shop floor, but it also comes at great cost. Shuffling orders and reconciling conflicting objectives do not change the *form, fit, or function* of the product being produced. They're non-valued-added and considered *waste* in a Lean operating system.

Productivity and department managers. Machine setups can be time consuming. Operators and department managers rarely want to perform them. Just as needing to achieve 100% utilization is facilitated by grouping work together, a batch manufacturing strategy enables machines to be more productive. Run quantities are established based primarily on machine productivity considerations and are usually larger and longer than required to meet customer demand. Labor resources are also more efficient when performing repetitious, long runs of the same product. Most companies using a batch manufacturing strategy have

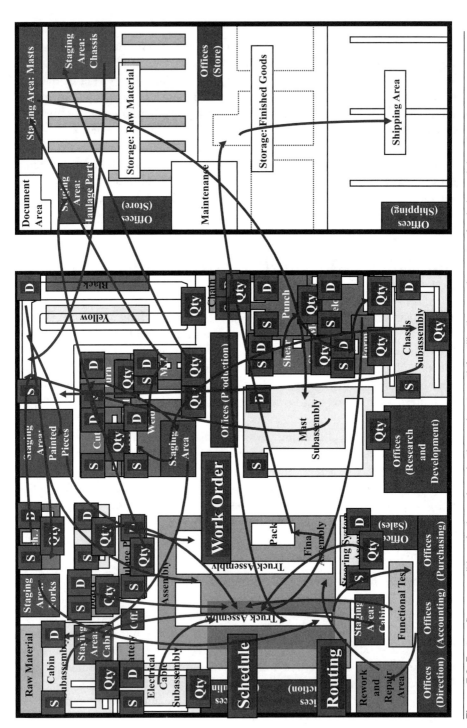

Figure 7.2. Factory floor expedition of released production orders to satisfy utilization requirements of unbalanced departments.

a simple calculation method for setting their batch sizes: "to produce as much as we can as fast as we can." Running large batch quantities therefore usually takes precedence over inventory considerations and customer-demand priorities. After all, inventory management performance measures and meeting customer demand are the responsibility of production planning managers, not manufacturing department managers. Department managers quickly learn to develop individualized inventory strategies to allow smoothing demand fluctuations to achieve their personal absorption goals. For example, they group production orders together to help optimize their departmental performance measures, even if the strategy results in part shortages, missed due dates and late orders, and a resulting high investment of working capital in unsold inventory. They accumulate as many production orders as possible, including orders in advance of their release dates, to facilitate having the ability to *cherry pick* orders and batch them together. They increase the lead time recorded on the indented BOM to cause earlier release of production orders from the planning system. Increasing lead time works great for batching production orders to maximize productivity, but it also results in a longer customer-quoted lead time, which can lead to lost business and sales revenue from customers who demand shorter lead times. Because department managers are not measured on inventory investment or on-time shipments, maximum productivity and utilization always trump all other company performance goals. None of this activity changes the *form, fit, or function* of the product being produced. It's non-value-added and considered *waste* in a Lean operating system.

Productivity and manufacturing costs. Achieving productivity using a batch manufacturing strategy is costly. Machine and labor capacities are prematurely consumed to produce orders that have been incorrectly prioritized in favor of satisfying productivity goals. Parts shortages occur, due dates are missed, and customer orders are late. Unsold inventory causes a higher investment of working capital. The resulting inventory is at risk of becoming slow moving or obsolete if customer demand does not materialize. Expediting and reprioritization activities require management time and effort. None of these costs or activities change the *form, fit, or function* of products produced. They're non-value-added and considered *waste* in a Lean operating system.

Productivity and department managers: if manufacturing departments have excess capacity. Managers of departments with excess capacity devote a significant amount of time looking for additional work to keep their resources productive and utilized. Excess capacity might seem like a good problem to have, but for department managers who must meet their productivity performance goals by running at full utilization, excess capacity can be a managerial headache. Unless resources are kept fully consumed, these department managers will

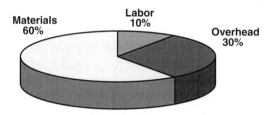

Figure 7.3. Materials: the most expensive element of product cost.

receive a negative variance from the controller's office declaring their unutilized capacity to be nonproductive. Meeting productivity and full utilization goals motivates department managers to waste resources by using their excess capacity on the production of unsold inventory. Materials are expensive. They're the most expensive component of product cost (Figure 7.3). Undisciplined, slow-moving buffer inventories that accumulate in traditional operating systems are costly to maintain and at risk for obsolescence. The activities associated with maintaining excess inventory add lead time and cost to a product, but do not change the *form, fit, or function* of the product being produced. Overproduction of products is non-value-added and considered *waste* in a Lean operating system.

Productivity and department managers: if manufacturing departments have limited capacity. Departments with less capacity than a feeding department have a much different utilization problem than departments with excess capacity. Instead of needing work to keep their resources productive, these managers have a reverse utilization situation. WIP inventory is always in queue waiting to be worked on. The solution for these department managers is to somehow increase the capacity of their departments so the queued inventory can be produced on schedule. Short term (unless a capital investment is received to increase the number of human or machine resources), the capacity of these departments can only be increased by adding extra hours and/or extra shifts. If the real capacity remains unchanged for the long term, these managers will constantly be requested to expedite and reprioritize production orders. Perpetual overtime costs are almost guaranteed because operating for extra hours is the only solution for addressing the capacity constraints. Overtime does not change the *form, fit, or function* of the product being produced. It's non-value-added and considered *waste* in a Lean operating system.

ACHIEVING BALANCE WITH LEAN MANUFACTURING

Lean manufacturing offers an alternative to the traditional operating system solutions. Instead of launching production orders from the planning system into manufacturing and then reprioritizing, rearranging, and regrouping these orders while building unsold inventory as the strategy for achieving the balance of capacities on the shop floor, the Lean operating system balances resource capacities *before* introducing customer demand into the factory. In a Lean environment, expediting and scheduling activities are a waste of time, human effort, and money. They do nothing to change the *form, fit, or function* of the product being produced. They should be eliminated.

Utilization. Lean manufacturing eliminates most of the non-value-added activities caused by the rescheduling and reprioritizing of production orders after they have been issued to the shop floor. Resources are balanced before a production order is issued. Balance is achieved by utilizing only the resources necessary to meet customer demand based on a statement of the daily rate of sales. Rather than operating at 100% capacity at all times regardless of the daily customer demand and shuffling production orders around to maximize utilization of resources, Lean does just the opposite. Lean matches the amount of resources assigned to a manufacturing area based on customer demand: demand = resources. Matching resources to demand often results in *intentional underutilization* of the available resources allocated to a department, which conflicts with traditional operating system performance measurements for resource absorption.

Factory layout. Instead of being organized into departments of like resources, Lean manufacturing processes are physically arranged in a layout based on the sequential flow of the standard work for a product. Often the layout mirrors the mixed-product PFD that details the sequential order of production for the products being manufactured (see Chapter 6). The processes necessary to produce a product are physically located adjacent to one another so that the output of one process is consumed directly into the next downstream process with little to no wait or move time. The manufacturing processes are divided into groups of work equal to a Takt time so that all processes complete their output at the same rate. The number of groups of equal amounts of work is dependent on the standard work content time of each process. This causes the rate of completion to be balanced. Units completed at each process spend little to no time waiting to be worked on at the next process. Grouping similar labor and machines into departments is no longer necessary. Only the resources required to produce the demand are located on a Lean line. Figure 7.4 illustrates a typical Lean line factory model. Excess resources not required for relocation to the Lean manufacturing line are available for the production of any other products not being produced on the lean line.

Labor resources. On most days, the mix and volume of products required by customer demand will likely be different from the quantities used for the initial

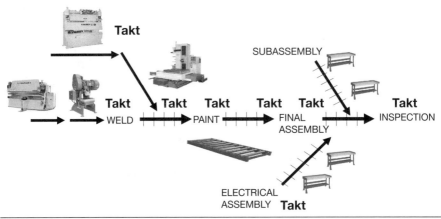

Figure 7.4. A typical Lean factory model.

design of the line. The standard work of each product in each process may also be different. If the mix, volume, or standard work changes, redesigning a Lean line is unnecessary. Although the machine resources on a Lean line are inflexible, when daily requirements change, the human resources on a Lean line can be changed. Only the human resources are flexible enough to meet changing daily demand requirements. The human resources required to produce the products at the Takt rate can be changed. Depending on customer demand on any given day, the daily headcount on a Lean line is variable. Only the number of human resources necessary to meet demand is assigned to the Lean line on a given day (which may result in using fewer resources than the number currently assigned to the department). Figure 7.5 illustrates a balanced Lean manufacturing line.

The ability of the Lean system to assign only the labor resources needed each day to match customer demand challenges current utilization measurements. Current utilization performance measurements are static based on the number of labor and machine resources already assigned to a department. Planned output is based on the full utilization of available capacity. If the available capacity is in excess of customer demand, but the capacity remains fully utilized, then the result can only be unsold inventory. Lean manufacturing discounts the traditional utilization measurement. Lean performance measures do not include utilization as a key performance indicator. Instead, Lean manufacturing performance measurements emphasize quality, response time, and process linearity. As a performance measurement, the underutilization of resources not required to meet daily customer demand is of no consequence.

Production. Products on a Lean line are manufactured one unit at a time at a Takt rate based on an order sequence established by a planner. This physical

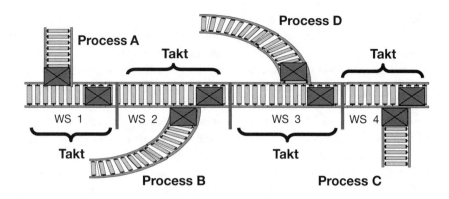

Figure 7.5. A balanced Lean manufacturing line: resources are linked and balanced to produce one unit at a time.

linkage of orders to resources permits work tasks to be distributed, accumulated, and balanced evenly throughout the entire series of manufacturing processes. Each process completes its standard work at the same output rate. As a completed unit of product is consumed by a customer, the entire line ratchets another unit downstream through each process in response to the demand to replenish the consumed unit. This sequential building of one unit of product every Takt time for the duration of available minutes each day results in the daily customer demand being packed off one unit at a time from the last process every Takt time. Even though the Takt time for each process might be different based on process volume, a Lean line is designed so all processes complete standard work at the same speed. Lean lines are often referred to as *flow lines* because products are produced one unit at a time and at the same rate, resembling liquid flowing through a pipe.

Capacity utilization. Lean methodologies approach the utilization of available capacity differently than traditional planning system models. The layout design for a Lean manufacturing factory is done only once. The amount of resources is determined by dividing SWD labor and machine times into groups of work equal to a Takt time. A series of mathematical modeling calculations determines the number of resources needed to meet the designed V_c. These calculations ensure that the optimum number of resources and staff are assigned to each process to meet current demand expectations of the V_c. The calculated resources must also ensure that a capacity sufficient to meet customer demand 1 to 3 years into the future will be available to the line. Once the number of resources is known, the facility is physically rearranged so that the output of each resource is physically located next to the downstream consuming process. Once the Lean line is designed with sufficient resources to meet the designed capacity, using only the number of resources required to satisfy a single day of demand is necessary. All resources work at the same rate based on the process Takt time. Batching or grouping work to achieve efficiency and utilization by an individual department is unnecessary. Individual departments no longer exist on a Lean line. There is only one department in a Lean factory — manufacturing. Planning system-generated shop orders are no longer required to schedule a Lean line. Only the sequencing of demand according to preestablished customer priorities is necessary. No production order is required to authorize work. Lean manufacturing concentrates on meeting daily customer demand with the required resources to complete the standard work using an in-process kanban signal to authorize an additional Takt time amount of work. The standard work content to be completed for any product is designed into the Lean line. When a customer's product enters the Lean line, the standard work will be applied cumulatively through each Takt time until completion. Achieving departmental efficiency, utilization, and absorption goals is secondary to achieving customer satisfaction.

Inventory management. If a manufacturing line is not constrained by imbalanced departments, WIP buffer inventories cannot accumulate. Only a single unit of production at a time ratchets through all the processes and is packed off the end of the line. Wait and queue times required for the normal routing of products in batch-size quantities through the various manufacturing departments is greatly reduced or eliminated. Once manufacturing resources are balanced and physically linked together and manufacturing is in a preset sequence, products are produced on a FIFO priority sequence. Shuffling, expediting, and utilization enhancement activities for production orders are no longer necessary.

Determining the Amount of Resources Needed Using Takt Time

Resources are defined as people, workstations, machines, and inventory. A *people* resource is an operator who manually touches the product and performs a Takt time amount of work. A *workstation* resource is a physical location on the shop floor (the footprint) where an operator completes a Takt time amount of work. A *machine* resource is a device in which the work content cycle time is equal to or less than the Takt time. Machines are considered to be a homogeneous process if they perform the same function at the same cycle time, e.g., stamping. Machines that perform different functions are considered to be a stand-alone process, e.g., drill, grind, form, or weld. An *inventory* resource is the amount of inventory needed to offset imbalances in processes in which the standard or cycle time is greater than the Takt time. Inventory can be used to maintain the targeted Takt time when a process is incapable of achieving the Takt time rate.

Takt time establishes the production rate of a process. The goal of a Lean manufacturing line is to complete one unit of production from every process in its predetermined Takt time. As a unit of production is consumed by customer demand, another unit moves downstream through each process until a product is completed. Standard work times can vary greatly from one process to another. For example, more standard time is required for a person to build a motor assembly in a feeder process than to mount that motor with four bolts onto a frame in the final assembly process. No two processes are exactly the same. No two processes require an identical amount of standard work time for completion. If a process requires standard work content greater than its Takt time, the required work can only be accomplished within its Takt time target by adding more resources. The number of resources required to complete the standard work in its Takt time target can be determined by dividing the standard work of the process by the desired output rate of the process (Takt time). Each resource within a process is the amount of standard work tasks equal to or less than the Takt time: one resource = one Takt time. Standard work assigned to a specific workstation is the basis of the concept of *standardized work*.

Resources and Lean. Obviously, a product cannot be produced if the correct number of operators is not available to staff the workstations to complete the standard work required for the product. If too many operators are assigned, productivity will be sacrificed. If too few operators are assigned, the customer demand for that day cannot be competed in the required Takt time target. In a Lean environment, only the exact number of operators needed to meet customer demand that day is assigned to the line: workstation staffing is determined daily based on customer demand. During the initial line design of the Lean line, the number of workstations required for future V_c was established, but the workstations set in place to meet future volume may not be necessary to produce a smaller volume required today. Because a workstation is an inanimate object, it must be physically located. In the Lean operating system, no rule states that a workstation must be staffed with a human resource every day. If daily customer demand is less than the designed volume of the line, rearranging or removing physical workstations daily makes little sense. Instead, adjusting the number of flexible labor resources assigned to the available workstations is a more logical solution, even though reducing the number of operators means that all workstations will not be staffed on that day. Matching labor resources to actual customer demand instead of the number of physical workstations will cause underutilization of those workstations, potentially generating issuance of a negative variance from the cost accounting group.

Two mathematical values are necessary to determine the amount of resources (people, workstations, machines, or inventory) required to complete the standard work content within the Takt time target for each process identified on a PFD: SWD time and Takt time:

SWD time ÷ Takt time = the number of resources

Remember: SWD time is a measurement of *standard time* and Takt time is a measurement of *rate*.

The numerator. Standard time identified on the SWD for the process required is the numerator (Figure 7.6). SWD time is the sum of *all* labor work, including the non-value-adding time of dynamic setup, rework, move, and any quality criteria inspections. Regardless of the type of work being done, until non-value-added work is eliminated through process improvements or kaizen activities, human and machine resources are still required to do the work. Summing the non-value-added times with the value-added time elements for each process defines the total work content time for a specific product and process combination. Additional factors affecting throughput volume per process are scrap, rework, and options.

The denominator. Takt time for a process is the denominator of the resource calculation. Each process has its own Takt time based on throughput volume. Takt time is a time/volume relationship. Takt time is calculated by dividing the amount of time available to perform work each day by the desired throughput volume of each process. Takt time will be different for every process where the throughput volume of the process is affected by scrap, rework, or optionality. Takt establishes the rate at which a process must complete one unit of production to achieve the designed V_c output. Although the calculation is the same, machine times are calculated separately from labor processes. Labor work content time cannot be co-mingled with machine time because each one can have a separate cycle or standard time for the same process.

This basic formula uses the standard times from the SWD and solves for the number of resources required by defining the number of groupings of work that are equal to the Takt time. Grouping work into equal amounts of Takt time allows a Lean manufacturing line to be balanced to respond to the downstream consumption of one unit of production. Workstations balanced to a Takt time allow the placement of one unit of production into the adjacent downstream workstation at the same rate regardless of how much standard time is required to produce the product in an upstream process (e.g., a feeder process). This balance allows the entire Lean line to flow a product off the end of the line according to the Takt time for the line and permits all upstream processes to produce another unit of production in unison at a rate equal to the Takt time.

Process Name: Final Assembly
Product Part Number: Range Top Model 12

Standard Work Definition

Work Element			Work Content						Total Quality Management
Order	Description	Parts Consumed	Machine Setup	Labor Setup	Machine Run Time	Labor Time	Move Time	Check	Self-Check Description
10	Obtain fixture from under conveyor			0.2					Fixture matches motor series number
20	Retrieve stator and place on fixture			0.8					Check shell for exposed metal, presence of all notches, and wires tucked in
30	Insert wire exit grommet	1253-B grommet				0.5			
40	Attach mounting bracket with one screw	6672 bracket 2042 screw				0.3			Install on wire exit side; screw gun set to **3**
50	Repeat 40 once	2042 screw				0.1			Screw gun set to **3**
60	Retrieve top shield and install with one screw	1068 screw				0.6			Bearing is greased and grease fitting is tight. Screw gun set to **5**
70	Repeat 60 once	1068 screw				0.1			Screw gun set to **5**
80	Insert rotor guide in stator			0.2					Screw gun set to **5**
90	Retrieve rotor and install in stator					0.6			Long side of shaft forward; check for free turn
100	Retrieve bottom shield and install with one screw	1068 screw				0.6			Bearing is greased and grease fitting is tight; Screw gun set to **5**

$\sum$ **STANDARD TIME PER UNIT**

Figure 7.6. Standard work time must include value-adding and non-value-adding times.

Table 7.2. Process Map with Standard Times for Six Different Products with the Same Process

Production Information		Standard Time per Product/Process							
Product	V_c	A	B	C	D	E	F	G	H
Product 1	25	2.6	6.6	4.0	10.5	1.5	30.0	10.0	12.0
Product 2	30	2.7			11.0	1.5	27.5	10.0	14.0
Product 3	50	2.5	4.5	4.0			25.0	10.0	11.0
Product 4	5		7.0	4.0	15.0	2.0	32.0	10.0	16.0
Product 5	12	2.9	5.5		13.0		29.5	10.0	13.0
Product 6	8	3.5		4.0	14.0	1.8	32.0	10.0	15.0

Factories with multiple products. Most manufacturers rarely make a single product only. They produce a wide variety of products having many options that may use different manufacturing processes. As each product moves through the same processes, having different standard times is not uncommon. Most companies therefore operate in a mixed-family environment by selecting a group of representative products with a variety of standard times to run on their Lean lines. Table 7.2 illustrates different products with different standard times for the same process. The resource calculation equation is straightforward, but resource calculations using only the discrete standard time for one product will likely not be accurate enough when producing a family of products. For a *mixed-model* Lean line, using the same group of products as selected to design the line and determining an *average* standard time per process for that product family is more accurate for determining resources. An average standard time per process based on the discrete observed standard times for a representative group of products yields a standard time that is more representative of the actual time of each product in each process. By definition, this average SWD time is unlikely to ever exactly match the actual discrete observed standard time. Using the same logic as when selecting the V_c for a family of products, the resulting average standard time will be representative of all products of a family that are produced in each process *most of the time* on the line. (Unlike V_c, which is estimated, standard work content time is a discrete observed time, but as with V_c, the goal of an average standard time is reasonable accuracy versus precision.)

Determining standard time for mixed-model production lines. Naturally, some products require more standard time to complete while others require less. The products chosen for the design of a Lean line were *representative* of all products to be manufactured on the line and an *estimated volume* was used as a statement of capacity, but unlike the decision process used to select representative products and volume, standard times are *discrete observed values*. For standard times, product and volume estimates are based on what happens in the factory most often. Actual standard times per product in each process are not subject to the same level of subjectivity allowed for choosing representative products and estimated volumes. Standard times are times observed as actual work is performed.

If, however, many products have different standard times, selecting a single time to use in the numerator of the resource calculation is impossible. Using the process map in Table 7.2, look at Process F. Which time should be selected for determining the number of resources for this process? The times range from 25.0 to 32.0 minutes. The best answer is not the fastest time or the slowest, but an average.

Now look at the volume of Product 6. The expected V_c is 8 units per day with a standard time of 32.0 minutes. If the line were designed using the highest standard time of the 32.0 minutes for Process F, along with predicted sales of only 8 units per day for Product 6, resource calculations for all 130 products would be determined based on a standard time of 32.0 minutes. The highest-volume product is Product 3. Product 3 has a V_c of 50 units and a standard time for Process F of 25.0 minutes. Using the higher standard time of 32.0 minutes in a resource calculation would overstate the number of resources required to produce the average mix of products listed in Process F. For example, if the average mix of products on a given day is Products 1, 2, 3, and 5, with standard times of 30.0, 27.5, 25.0, and 29.5 minutes, respectively, and these products are produced in a process designed for 32.0 minutes, each time a product having a standard time less than 32.0 minutes is produced, resources will be idle for 32.0 minutes minus the standard time of Process F for each of the other 117 products. The daily volume for Process F is 117 (Product 1 + 2 + 3 + 5 = 117 units). Each time a unit is produced, idle time is created 117 times during a work shift: 32.0 – 30.0 minutes (Product 1), 32.0 – 27.5 minutes (Product 2), 32.0 – 25.0 minutes (Product 3), and 32.0 – 29.5 minutes (Product 5). Idle time, of course, is *waste*. To make the average standard time as accurate and realistic as possible, the standard time to be used must be *weighted* to reflect the products produced most frequently based on the daily V_c of the products most commonly manufactured: average time is *weighted* toward the products produced most often. The revised average time is known the *standard time weighted* (STW).

Using a 435-minute day to produce a designed line capacity of 130 units, the Takt time would be 3.35 minutes. If the line has been designed using the highest standard time for Process F of 32.0 minutes, the number of resources would be based on the standard time calculation of 32.0 minutes ÷ 3.35 Takt, resulting in 9.55 resources or 9.55 people working at 9.55 workstations (resources/workstations = standard time ÷ Takt time). The time required to build 130 units at 32.0

minutes = 4160 minutes. Using the shortest time for Process F of 25.0 minutes, the time to build 130 units at 25.0 minutes each = 3250 minutes. The difference is 910 minutes or the potential nonproductive time possible each day. Spread evenly over the 9.55 workstations on the line, these 910 extra minutes can result in 95 total minutes of idle time per 435-minute day at each workstation or 44 seconds for each of the 130 units produced each day. Instead of needing all 435 minutes at a Takt rate of 3.35 each day, the daily rate for 130 units at 25.0 minutes would require only a 340-minute day (3250 ÷ 9.55). With this scenario, 95 minutes each day would be lost productivity.

Operators have two options for utilizing this daily idle time of 95 minutes: use the 44 seconds to complete the production of 130 units of work in 340 minutes and be reassigned to another workstation (or go home) or slow their working pace by 44 seconds per unit so their output matches the required daily rate. For most operators, the most popular option is to slow the pace of work. Slowing the working pace is more difficult to detect by management. Each of these options reduces productivity, so neither option is acceptable.

Producing products at a steady rate throughout the day for the entire time of planned effective minutes is preferred. If the Lean line is designed using the shortest time of 25.0 minutes, the line will run too slowly, not only when producing Product 6, but also when producing all products with a standard time greater than 25.0 minutes. Based on the daily mix, Takt time targets will be missed and the output of daily customer demand will be jeopardized. On the other hand, forcing operators to work too fast will compromise quality. A line running too slowly or operators working too quickly will sacrifice optimum productivity and quality.

Humans are not machines and a standard time weighted will never be precise. When selecting a standard time representative of the majority of products produced, develop an *average time* for products using a combination of the high and low standard times with an average mix of V_c expected to be run daily. Perfect numerical productivity cannot be guaranteed, but the time spent selecting the best possible STW is worth the effort. Carefully establish a STW that minimizes idle time and lost productivity.

Representative products and times. When products were chosen for inclusion in the design of the line, the logic used was to select products and volumes representative of all potential products to be produced for the product/volume mix most likely to occur on any given day. The estimated product mix and volume were somewhere between precision and a high level of accuracy, even though estimates are insufficient when predicting customer demand on resources. What customers will buy on any given day cannot be predicted with 100% precision. A similar logic could have been used to choose a representative standard time for resource calculations, but for the mixed-model Lean line, a *weighted* standard time was used to complete the resource calculations for each process. A STW matching the projected mix and volume of products sold and produced most frequently in processes results in the best estimate of standard time for an average population of products, but will still never be 100% precise.

To weight the times, additional calculations are required for each process to establish the standard time weighted. Using the standard times and V_c from the process map in Table 7.2, STW is calculated as:

$$\frac{\Sigma V_c \times \text{SWD standard time}}{\Sigma V_c} = \text{STW}$$

where the numerator is calculated as:

$$\text{Process F}$$

Product 1	V_c 25	×	SWD 30.0	=	750
Product 2	V_c 30	×	SWD 27.5	=	825
Product 3	V_c 50	×	SWD 25.0	=	1250
Product 4	V_c 5	×	SWD 32.0	=	160
Product 5	V_c 12	×	SWD 29.5	=	354
Product 6	V_c 8	×	SWD 32.0	=	256
Σ	V_c 130	×	SWD	=	3595

and the denominator is calculated as:

$$\Sigma \text{ of } V_c \text{ for Process F} = 130$$

The STW is calculated as:

$$3595 \div 130 = 27.6 \text{ minutes}$$

and Takt time is calculated as:

$$\frac{7 \text{ hours} \times 60 \text{ minutes} \times 1 \text{ shift} = 420 \text{ minutes}}{\Sigma \text{ of total Process F volume} = 130 \text{ units}} = 3.23 \text{ minutes}$$

Substituting the standard time used for the non-weighted resource calculation with the new STW, the number of resources for Process F is now calculated as:

$$\frac{\text{STW}}{\text{TAKT}} = \text{number of resources}$$

Rounded up, the number of resources for Process F is 9:

$$\frac{STW = 27.6}{TAKT = 3.23} = 8.54 \text{ or 9 resources}$$

Determining Additional Information Using a Process Map

So far, a process map has been used to accumulate all of the necessary product, process, and volume information collected by the process and materials transformation teams to design the Lean facility. The same process map can now be used to capture additional information necessary for the design of the Lean line.

To document standard work times. The existing process map can now be expanded to document the standard work times from the SWD required for each product at each process. (Remember that the standard work times are *observed* machine cycle or labor times for one unit of production.) The process map can be used to multiply the individual standard work content time by the V_c factored by any volume modifier (rework, scrap, or optionality) previously documented for each product at a process. The sum of required work content times the volume of each product is used to calculate the STW (see STW calculations above). The STW is then divided by the Takt time to determine the number of resources necessary to produce the V_c for that process in the Takt time target. Table 7.3 illustrates a completed process map with the calculations used to determine the number of machine and labor resources required for each process to produce the stated V_c at the Takt rate.

To track the completion of tasks. A process map can also be used as a project management tool by a Lean champion to keep track of tasks assigned to individual process and materials team members. When a Lean transformation project begins and the teams have been identified, required project information is often deconstructed and assigned to individual team members for collection. As individual team members collect information about products, demand, processes, volume modifiers, and SWD times, the data can be posted in an appropriate cell on the process map. As the transformation project advances, incomplete information becomes more and more obvious simply by its omission from its corresponding cell. As team members complete their individual assignments, they can be reassigned to assist in the collection of information missing from the process map. The process map allows the focus of team member efforts to zero in on any remaining missing pieces of information. By concentrating on only the required and missing data, the valuable time of team members is optimized.

To document/validate information. A process map can also document and experiment with multiple iterations of information. Often, project discussions or new information will result in suggestions or alternatives to an original value on the process map. Using the process map as a spreadsheet, multiple iterations of information can be input and tested until the optimum solution is achieved. Returning to the original data, if necessary, is easy. Used as a planning device, a completed process map can test the impact of changes in mix or volume of products on manufacturing resources. Having future visibility of *what if* volumes can help with *make or buy* decisions and the timing for capital equipment expenditures. *What if* scenarios can also be tested by comparing projected sales increases to resource availabilities to project how many and when labor and machine resources should be increased. The resource calculator can be a communication linkage between the sales and marketing and manufacturing departments. These two diverse organizations can use the resource calculator independently to reconcile the production plan with a sales plan so both departments will be synchronized. The sales and marketing and manufacturing groups can validate that the available manufacturing resources can support the sales plan. By including a conditional response signal to volumes increases, the process map can also flag when new resources will be required to meet any future demand volumes and provide sufficient advance timing for negotiating the best contract for the company.

Remember: Standard time weighted is an *average of times* and Takt time is based on an *estimated product mix and volume*. These numbers are *averages* based on absolute values. Attempting to achieve precision when making rounding decisions based on an average quantity often yields diminishing returns for the effort expended. The averages are based on what happens on your shop floor most of the time and the decision to round up or down is subjective, based on personal knowledge and experience with a particular process. Because forecasting with 100% accuracy is impossible, erring on the high side when determining resources is always the best practice. Rounding up quantities of resources addresses several things.

How to handle fractional values. Having a portion of a person, a workstation, a machine, or complete inventory is, of course, impossible. Even if a resource calculation yields a fractional value of 0.1, *round it up* to the next whole number. If a fractional value is less than 0.1, the number of resources may be rounded down. Rounding down, however, translates into having *one less* resource with the remainder of resources calculated to exactly a Takt time. If a value is rounded down, the number of remaining resources will have little latitude for achieving the standard time in a Takt time target. Consider rounding down carefully. It's better to have too many resources than not enough. Resources can always be adjusted after a line is operating smoothly.

Table 7.3. Completed Process Map with Standard Work Times and Calculated Machine and Labor Resources for Each Process

Family Description	Part Number	V_c	Weld Machine	Weld Labor	Volume Modifier	Volume Modifier × V_c	Weld Rework Machine	Weld Rework Labor	Volume Modifier	Volume Modifier × V_c
V5A	75903101	2.00	40	45	1.100	2.20	30	30	0.100	0.20
V6A	76000202	0.40	55	60	1.100	0.44	30	30	0.100	0.04
A4H	76102402	3.00	45	50	1.100	3.30	30	30	0.100	0.30
U5	76100002	2.00	55	60	1.100	2.20	30	30	0.100	0.20
805	72200002	4.00	40	45	1.100	4.40	30	30	0.100	0.40
806	72210002	6.00	35	40	1.100	6.60	30	30	0.100	0.60
T5AH	72208902	2.00	50	55	1.100	2.20	30	30	0.100	0.20
T5LOAH	70524102	0.375	50	55	1.100	0.83	30	30	0.100	0.08
S5	72208602	1.00	55	60	1.100	1.10	30	30	0.100	0.10
TM270	71801802	2.00	60	65	1.100	2.20	30	30	0.100	0.20
G3	70542002	5.00	45	50	1.100	5.50	30	30	0.100	0.50
G4A	70550402	2.50	50	55	1.100	2.75	30	30	0.100	0.25
		30.65				**33.72**				**3.07**

Takt Time	13	13	143	143
Planned Work Minutes	438	438	438	438
Shifts	1	1	1	1
Throughput Volume	33.72	33.72	3.07	3.07
Weighted Time (STW)	45.00	50.00	30.00	30.00
Resources Required	3.46	3.46	0.21	0.21
Resources Available	5	5		1
Utilization	69%	69%		21%
	OK	OK		OK

Manual Input

Resources Required ÷ Resources Available

$$\frac{\Sigma\, V_c \times \text{SWD Std Time}}{\Sigma\, V_c}$$

Final Assembly		Volume Modifier	Volume Modifier × V_c	Custom Lights & Sound		Volume Modifier	Volume Modifier × V_c
Machine	Labor			Machine	Labor		
	330	1.000	2.00		215	0.400	0.80
	400	1.000	0.40		215	0.400	0.16
	360	1.000	3.00		220	0.400	1.20
	340	1.000	2.00		220	0.400	0.80
	360	1.000	4.00		260	0.400	1.60
	320	1.000	6.00		260	0.400	2.40
	300	1.000	2.00		260	0.400	0.80
	300	1.000	0.75		260	0.400	0.30
	400	1.000	1.0		260	0.400	0.40
	425	1.000	2.00		220	0.400	0.80
	360	1.000	5.00		220	0.400	2.00
	300	1.000	2.50		220	0.400	1.00
			31				**12**

14	**14**
438	438
1	1
31	**31**
0.00	**344.70**
0.0	24.1
	25
	96%
	OK

36	**36**
438	438
1	1
12	**12**
0.00	**237.55**
0.0	6.6
	7
	95%
	OK

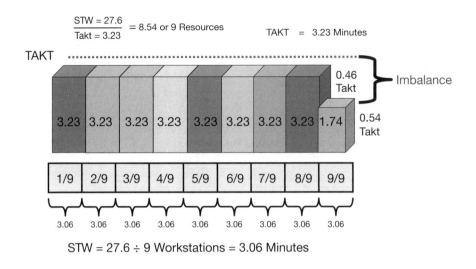

Figure 7.7. Imbalance spread over all workstations.

How to handle productivity concerns. A resource can always be removed, but adding a resource into the design of a factory line later can be difficult. The lowest component of product cost for most products is labor. There is no need to obsess over a few extra labor resources that are a result of rounding. The goal in the end is to make a Lean manufacturing line as successful as possible to produce a product in the Takt time target. Rounding up the number of resources can provide enough extra latitude to achieve Takt time targets, but still minimize excess idle time. Providing this latitude is particularly important when defining human resources. Humans are not machines. Their productivity can vary from day to day. The cost of one additional labor resource will have little effect on total product cost, but having one additional labor resource can make a huge difference when trying to achieve the Takt time target of a line. If the added resource proves to be excessive in the future, the resource can be reassigned with little or no effect on the daily operation of the line.

Figure 7.7 illustrates the balancing effect of a lean manufacturing line. If the STW of 27.6 is divided by the rounded up number of calculated resources, 9 in this example, the resulting standard work assigned to each of the 9 work stations becomes 3.06 minutes (27.6 ÷ 9 = 3.06 minutes). This time is less than the Takt time target which remains at 3.23. By spreading the STW over the rounded up number of resources, the imbalance of 1.74 minutes (0.54) is evenly distributed across all workstations. The difference in time provides extra seconds to the operators, helping to ensure that the Takt time target will be met. In this example, 9 workstations – 8.54 calculated resources = 0.46 of one Takt time or 1.48 minutes.

The 1.48 minutes ÷ 9 workstations = 9.8 additional seconds at each workstation. These 9.8 seconds still represent lost productive time each day at each workstation, but until the 0.54 of Takt time at workstation 9 can be eliminated through kaizen or an improvement project, the Lean line will still be successful. In the long term, the best alternative is to eliminate the 0.54 of Takt time (1.74 minutes of standard time) using kaizen to reduce the number of workstations to exactly 8.

Remember: Assigning *only* the resources needed to produce customer demand within the Takt rate is a key strength of the Lean operating system. The number of resources required to produce customer demand must therefore be determined for *every process* identified on the process flow diagram. When complete, the results of these resource calculations will be expressions of the amount of resources needed per process to produce the V_c in the established Takt time rate. Offsetting unequal standard work times using resource modification is a simple technique that achieves the balance in a Lean operating system. Consider the value of being able to complete all manufacturing processes required to produce a product or subassembly at the same time! Using only minimum resources avoids the production of WIP and FGI inventories. Also do not forget that using only the minimum resources required to meet a volume requirement will challenge the traditional performance measurements of utilization. Until the 1- to 3-year V_c is reached, lower customer demand will always require fewer resources than initially designed into the line to meet the higher future sales volumes.

The Lean approach versus the traditional approach. When comparing a Lean operating system to the three manufacturing paradigms used in traditional planning systems, the ability of a Lean system to adjust manufacturing resources to match customer demand is a major difference between the two systems. Because standard work content is assigned to the individual workstations, flexible labor resources can be trained to move to different workstations as needed to complete the standard work. In traditional planning systems, the standard department structure provides the platform for performance tracking and cost accounting purposes. In a Lean operating system, however, individual departments are not needed to track performance. Performance tracking is done for the entire Lean line as a single unit. Only the *resources required to produce the daily customer demand* are assigned to a Lean line. Excess resources not needed for the production of customer demand are assigned to other production requirements. There is no need to size batches to maximize the utilization of a department, route batches from department to department, or to create buffers of unsold inventories to offset fluctuations in capacity or customer demand. All of the resources required to produce the V_c are in place on a single Lean manufacturing line. A variety of mixed-model products can be produced on this single line sharing these same resources. Each day, a schedule for the number of units to be produced that day, up to the V_c is developed based on the quantity of products that customers have ordered. The schedule can be different each day based on varying customer demand. There is no need, however, to change the physical factory layout. The line remains the same as designed: the number of workstations remains static; only the number of human resources staffing the line is changed to match a change in customer demand.

Balance. Balancing the standard work assigned to a workstation is critical for producing a product in its work content time. A traditional planning system assumes wait and queue times are automatic. Therefore, they are built into manufacturing response time when production orders are routed through departments in batches. As standard work is balanced and assigned to a workstation on a Lean line, the non-value-added elements of wait and queue time are eliminated from manufacturing lead time. Balanced workstations complete work at the same rate, advancing products through each workstation without the need to stop and wait in a queue. Products accumulate the standard work assigned at each workstation until all of the standard work has been completed and the finished product exits the last workstation. By not stopping to wait or build up in a queue, products are completed in only the sum of their *touch* work content time. Completing products in the sum of their work content time results in significant lead-time reductions compared to routing batches of products through the factory. As greater balance is achieved allowing products to flow at the same rate through all processes in manufacturing, WIP inventories serving as a buffer for capacity variations between departments shrink. If the sum of work content time is less than the customer-quoted lead time, the need for buffer FGI inventories can also be reduced or eliminated altogether. As products flow from one process to the next, units of production are consumed immediately in the next production workstation. There is no wait or queue time: the accumulation of inventories is prevented. Overhead costs are reduced by eliminating expediting activities, material shortages, and numerous planning system transactions. As products spend less time in the manufacturing processes, customer-quoted lead times become shorter and shorter. Because work in every process is balanced using a Takt time derived from required throughput volume, small variations in the standard times of different products in different processes have little impact on the ability of a Lean line to manufacture a diverse mix of different products.

Assigning the correct number of resources to all processes so that the Takt time target for each is met is critical. A Lean operating system seeks to achieve the Takt time target for each process. Mathematic calculation of the resources for each process identifies the ideal amount of resources needed to achieve each Takt time target. Too many resources results in waste; too few resources causes Takt time targets to be jeopardized. The ideal ratio of resources to demand is demand = resources.

Defining the Types of Required Resources

After the amount of resources needed to produce customer demand has been calculated and assigned to the process, the types of required resources must be defined. Remember the four types of resources: people (operators), machines, workstations, and inventory (used to offset resource imbalances). A workstation is a physical location on the shop floor where standard work is performed. A workstation is required for each defined labor resource. Each operator must have a designated location where the Takt time amount of standard work can be completed.

People. If the standard time used to determine the amount of resources is the labor time from the SWD, then the human resource calculation establishes the number of people required to complete a volume of standard work in the Takt time target. The initial resource calculation provides a *sanity test* of the accuracy of the labor resource observations and is an early indicator of productivity opportunities. The calculated labor resource headcount (number of people) for the projected future volume of a Lean line should be in proportion to the current headcount at the current volume. For example, if the current production is 100 units per day and the current headcount is 60, then an increase in V_c to 150 units for the Lean line should require an approximate increase in headcount to 90 persons. Comparing the current actual headcount to a future projection of labor resources helps to validate the results of the resource calculations. Because the resource calculations use pure work content from the observed SWD time, a *reduced* proportional head count number is often reported when compared to today's actual headcount. Other factors that affect headcount, such as efficiency and personal fatigue and delay, are not present in the raw resource calculation. While these factors can modify the final resource count (workstations and people), it is best to begin the design of the Lean line with a pure unadulterated resource number to serve as a goal for identifying only the value-added work required for operation of the Lean line. Do not dismiss wide fluctuations in headcount/volume comparisons. A large variation may suggest that a review of the SWD times or the V_c projections may be needed. Human resources in excess of the required resources for a process are a preliminary indicator of a productivity opportunity for that process. Once the SWD times and V_c have been validated for accuracy, summing the number of required human resources for all processes and comparing the results to the existing headcount for those same processes can indicate which processes have the largest proportion of non-value-added time. Inefficiencies for those processes requiring excess resources can then be prioritized for future kaizen activities. When the standard times for an SWD are documented, factors causing inefficiency are not included. An SWD assumes 100% productivity with no time allowed for personal fatigue and delay. Although humans are not machines and experiencing some amount of inefficiency is a realistic expectation, *no inefficiency factors* should be factored into the standard time resource calculation at this time because this calculation will become the *baseline* for future productivity measurements. The initial calculation should be *unaffected* by the subjectivity of personal fatigue and delay factors. Later, if needed, 100% standard times and the final resource calculation result can be increased by a realistic, carefully considered productivity factor to compensate for human inefficiency. Remember, increased resources always add costs to a product. Always consider adding resources very carefully.

Workstations. A workstation must be a designated physical location where human resources are assigned to complete a Takt time amount of standard work. The resource calculation simultaneously defines the required number of human resources and the number of physical workstations. Each human resource requires a physical work location at which they can perform the standard work defined for that particular process. Although individual workstations are a one-to-one match to the number of human resources, workstations may take various forms. For example, if the process is *Assembly* and the product is a kitchen appliance, one workstation could mean one workbench, while another might be a length of roller conveyor sized to the product being produced. Other workstation examples include a ball transfer table or a series of burn-in stations. For larger products, a workstation could be a painted space on the shop floor that is sized to the dimensions of the product. Depending on the product, the manufacturing process could also be a combination of several different types of workstations. The total number of workstations must still match the total number of human labor resources calculated for each process. A workstation must also be placed as close as possible to the next downstream consuming workstation so non-value-added move time between both workstations is minimal or nonexistent. As part of final line design layout, each workstation must be defined by its physical attributes and the dimensions of its footprint on the shop floor. Allowing for ergonomics, optimize the amount of valuable shop floor used and minimize the need for an operator to take extra steps when flexing between workstations. Make every effort to keep the footprint of a workstation as small as is practical based on the size of the product being produced. For example, if the physical dimension of a product is 12 inches wide and 6 inches deep, a 6-foot-wide workbench and the shop floor square footage it requires is unnecessary. Not even considering the wear and tear on the operator by the end of the day, the extra 5 feet is simply excess space that requires movement of 2.5 to 4 feet in each direction, left and right, every other

Takt time, throughout the day, to reach the upstream or downstream workstation. If the V_c is 100 units, this unnecessary activity must be repeated 100 times per day, resulting in wasted movement 100 times a day. In Lean manufacturing, the extra shop floor space used and the repetitive non-value-adding movement of the operator is nothing but *waste*. Even though the company may have numerous workbenches available to the Lean reconfiguration, sizing a workstation to a product may reveal that one workstation ≠ one workbench. For the 12-inch product, two workstations could be created by painting a line down the middle of a 6-foot-wide workbench. The line separates the workbench into two 36-inch-wide workstations that will still comfortably accommodate the 12-inch physical size of the product. Two workstations can now occupy the same shop floor square footage space as the single workbench/single workstation did before. Similarly, if the product is 6 inches in depth, then the space required for a 36-inch-deep workbench would be unnecessary. Workstations must be sized so they are comfortable for the operators using them, but the shop floor space can be greatly minimized by designing the size of workstations to match the size of the work to be performed. Excess workstation space is wasteful. It consumes the valuable square-footage footprint on a shop floor. Consider the financial value of a square foot of shop floor when designing workstations. If the company had to buy or lease the space, what would be the cost for a square foot of factory shop floor space? How much cost (square footage) can be avoided by appropriately reducing the size of workstations to match the size of the work? How much setup and move time could be eliminated by designing minimum-sized workstations and placing them next to one another?

Machines. If the SWD time for a process is for a machine, the resource calculation will determine the number of machines required to produce the designed volume and meet the Takt time target. The number of required machines can be calculated in the same way as human resources and workstations are calculated, without the need for a weighting factor. The cycle time of a machine is always the same. Just as labor resources have a footprint on the shop floor, a footprint must be determined for each machine. The footprint of a machine must also include the footprint of any support equipment, including any ancillary tables, benches, die carts, etc. needed to operate the machine. If the amount of required machine resources exceeds the number of available machines, then additional machines must be added. Machine resources are expensive resources. Purchase of an additional machine includes not only the machine itself, but also multiple cavity dies, workstations, and additional inventory. Additional shifts may be necessary. Unlike the relatively simple act of hiring a human resource, procuring additional machines requires an investment of real capital. As part of final line design layout, the physical footprint of all required machine resources must be located, even if an actual machine has not been received from a supplier or if a machine is projected to enter service at some time in the future. Lean methods can only determine the amount of machine resources required to achieve a Takt time target. Lean methods can make a machine as efficient as possible, but capacity cannot be created where none exists. If acquiring additional machine resources is not an option, then another method to achieve the balance needed to achieve Takt time with an existing machine is to maintain additional inventory to accommodate the difference between Takt time and the cycle time of the machine throughout the day. This solution not only requires additional inventory, but it also requires time to produce the additional units and management time to maintain the inventory.

Inventory. Inventory is an expensive resource. Maintain only the minimum amount of inventory necessary to overcome an imbalance. Selecting the minimum amount of inventory necessary to maintain Lean line production is determined by using a resource calculation. This resource calculation uses the cycle time of the machine process as the numerator and the Takt time of the process as the denominator. The quotient is the number of units of inventory required to ensure that the Lean line continues to flow at the Takt rate. To determine the amount of inventory required to offset imbalances:

$$\frac{\text{Cycle time of machine}}{\text{Process Takt time}} = \text{number of units of inventory}$$

Figure 7.8 compares a dynamic machine to a static machine. It illustrates the impact on inventory by each type of machine.

Inventory for a dynamic process. The machine process of *Paint* is totally automated. A cycle time of 60 minutes is required for one unit to continuously travel the conveyor length through the robotic paint and drying tunnel. This type of process is defined as *dynamic* and describes units continuously moving through a process (Figure 7.8). As an upstream operator hangs one unit on a hook on the conveyor at a rate of one unit per every Takt time, another downstream operator removes a completed unit from the conveyor every Takt time. With a cycle time of 60 minutes and a Takt time of 3 minutes, 20 units of inventory (resources) are required to offset the imbalance of Takt time to machine time for the *Paint* process. For the *Paint* process to achieve the 3-minute Takt time, 20 units of additional inventory must be hung on the hooks attached to the moving conveyor. The speed of the conveyor is adjusted so each paint hook is spaced to exit the *Paint* process every 3 minutes. Even though each individual unit requires 60 minutes to travel the distance through the *Paint* process, 20 units of inventory must remain in the paint tunnel to support the 3-minute Takt time.

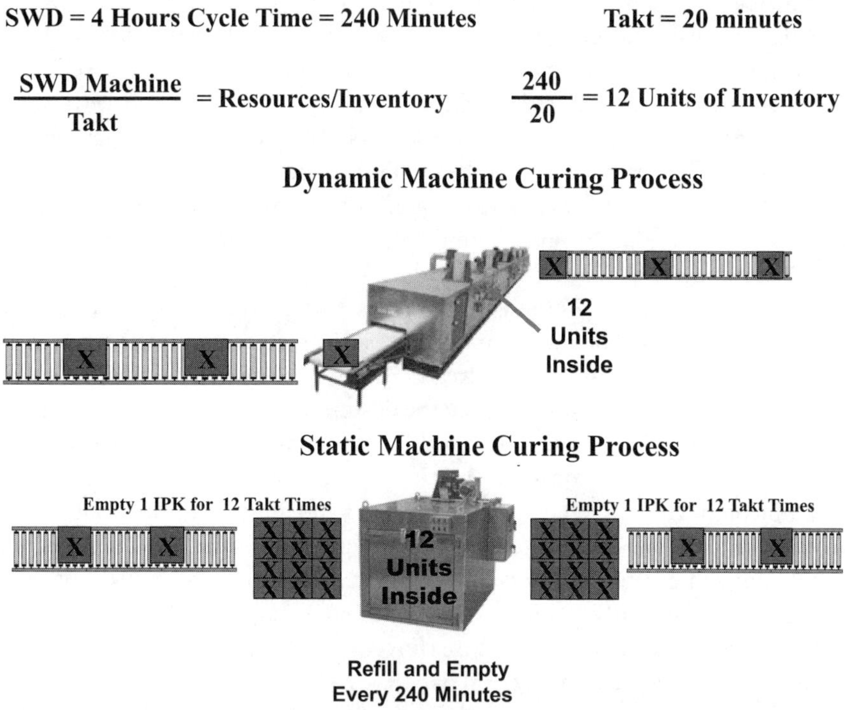

SWD = 4 Hours Cycle Time = 240 Minutes   Takt = 20 minutes

$$\frac{\text{SWD Machine}}{\text{Takt}} = \text{Resources/Inventory} \qquad \frac{240}{20} = 12 \text{ Units of Inventory}$$

Dynamic Machine Curing Process

12
Units
Inside

Static Machine Curing Process

Empty 1 IPK for 12 Takt Times   Empty 1 IPK for 12 Takt Times

12
Units
Inside

Refill and Empty
Every 240 Minutes

Figure 7.8. A dynamic machine versus static machine: impact on inventory resources used to offset machine cycle time.

Inventory for a static process. Another common machine process is *Burn-in*, which is similar to processes used for quality procedures. The type of machine used for *Burn-in* is considered to be a *static* machine. Unlike a dynamic process, units in a static machine do not move during processing (Figure 7.8). If the *Burn-in* process is 60 minutes with a Takt time of 3 minutes, the units of inventory would be 60 ÷ 3 = 20 units. The inventory amount is the same as for the dynamic *Paint* process, but the static machine will require *twice as much* inventory to keep the Lean line flowing at Takt rate. The machine time indicates that 20 *Burn-in* stations or connections are required and the process has been validated that all 20 units must be started at the same time. The 20 units necessary for the *Burn-in* process will therefore require an additional 60 minutes of queue time to accumulate at a Takt rate of every 3 minutes before sufficient units will be available to be placed into the *Burn-in* stations. Once these 20 units have been accumulated, they can be moved into the *Burn-in* station and the 60-minute cycle time can begin processing. Before the 20 new units can be placed in the static machine to begin the 60-minute processing time, the now completed machine load of the previous 20 units must be removed from the machine to be available for consumption downstream at the 3-minute Takt rate interval. During the 60-minute processing time of the static machine, one unit of inventory is consumed every 3 minutes reducing the queue at the downstream workstation while, at the same time, one unit of inventory is being added to the queue every 3 minutes at the upstream queue. At the Takt rate of one per 3 minutes, 60 minutes is required to exhaust the downstream queue of 20 units while replenishment of the upstream queue of 20 units requires the same 60 minutes at a Takt rate of every 3 minutes. Throughout the day, while 20 units are being processed in the static machine every 60 minutes, 20 units of additional inventory on either side of the static process are being accumulated upstream every 3 minutes while a unit is consumed every 3 minutes downstream. Because an upstream and downstream queue inventory is required to balance the 60-minute cycle time to the Takt rate, the inventory quantity for the static machine is therefore double what is required for a dynamic process. The static machine process requiring the loading and unloading of inventory queues repeats itself every 60 minutes throughout the day. Never is the *form, fit, or function* of queue inventory ever changed. The value of these 20 units of inventory in the upstream and downstream queue is considered *waste* by Lean. Not only is this inventory resource expensive, but space is also needed on the shop floor to park this inventory. Movement and handling of inventories by planners and material handlers is also required: inventory = cost.

Assigning the Standard Work to Workstations

The SWDs document the sequential tasks for completing the work of each process. Once the number of workstation resources has been determined, specific work tasks from the SWD to be completed at each workstation, along with the quality inspections identified for each workstation, can be defined. We already know that in a Lean operating system, each workstation performs an assigned series of standard work tasks equal to the Takt time for the work. We also know that assigning standard work tasks to a designated workstation is the only way to achieve the balance that a Lean operating system requires to run at a measured rate. When a Lean system begins operation, each workstation must complete only the work tasks assigned to that particular workstation: nothing more, nothing less. The individual work tasks assigned to each workstation are defined by summing both the value-added and the non-value-added work content time elements of the sequential tasks listed on the SWD until an amount of work equal to (or close to) the Takt time is identified. Once balanced to its Takt time, all workstations complete work at the same speed, with each workstation sequentially adding a Takt time amount of work to a unit of production until a completed unit exits the last workstation. A Lean line therefore indexes one unit through each process one unit at a time at the Takt rate. Balanced workstations allow a Lean line to *flow* from one workstation to the next, throughout the day, and to meet daily customer demand in the *effective* minutes per day. Figure 7.9 illustrates a Takt time of standard work assigned to each workstation using the SWD.

Balancing the Standard Work at Workstations

Perfect balance is the ultimate Lean nirvana. Perfect balance is the goal of a Lean operating system. Unfortunately, the real world is never perfect. Workstation balancing is rarely an exact science. When standard work is assigned to a workstation, breaking standard work precisely at a Takt time is often difficult. Sometimes work cannot be stopped mid-completion (a minimum element of work is a tenth of a minute) and sent to the next workstation. If perfect balance were achieved, all non-value-added work would be eliminated, work standards would be so absolute that operators could be totally repetitive, and all work tasks on the SWD would be *fail safe* with no need for quality inspections. This, of course, would be a perfect world! Even though perfect balance may never be achieved, every effort to achieve the goal of perfect balance should be the focus of all continuous improvement and kaizen activities in the future. Figure 7.10 illustrates unbalanced standard work within a process requiring a series of workstations.

Although it may be impossible to attain perfect balance in all processes, five simple techniques can be used to overcome *minor* imbalances in workstations. These techniques should be the foundation for all future continuous improvement and kaizen projects. The techniques should be completed in a sequential order based on their *cost of implementation*. The least-cost solution is identified as technique 1. All efforts to resolve an imbalance should be exhausted using technique 1 before proceeding to the second or the third technique, and so on. Starting the balancing exercise with technique 1 is not only the lowest-cost solution, but it should also be the simplest solution to implement. Begin each imbalance resolution activity with technique 1 and progress through each additional technique in sequence until an imbalance is resolved.

Technique 1: Look for work content that can be reduced or eliminated. Many work tasks listed on a SWD have been identified and documented separately as non-value-added tasks. Even so, operators are still required to perform these tasks as a part of the Takt time amount of work assigned to the workstation. Setups and moves are *always* candidates for elimination. Quality inspection work is also a candidate for elimination. These tasks have been documented on the SWD. By using kaizen techniques, along with improvements that reduce the work content itself, the elimination of non-value-added work tasks reduces the *elapsed time* required to complete a process. Elimination of non-value-added work also reduces the total *work content time* of a process, its cost, and ultimately,

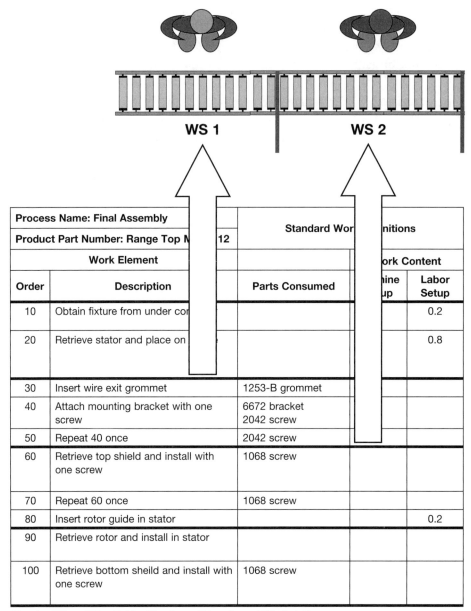

Process Name: Final Assembly		Standard Wor	nitions		
Product Part Number: Range Top N 12					
Work Element				ork Content	
Order	Description	Parts Consumed		ine up	Labor Setup
10	Obtain fixture from under co				0.2
20	Retrieve stator and place on				0.8
30	Insert wire exit grommet	1253-B grommet			
40	Attach mounting bracket with one screw	6672 bracket 2042 screw			
50	Repeat 40 once	2042 screw			
60	Retrieve top shield and install with one screw	1068 screw			
70	Repeat 60 once	1068 screw			
80	Insert rotor guide in stator				0.2
90	Retrieve rotor and install in stator				
100	Retrieve bottom sheild and install with one screw	1068 screw			

Standard Time (W) ÷ Takt = Number of People and Workstations

Figure 7.9. Takt time of standard work assigned to each workstation using the standard work definition.

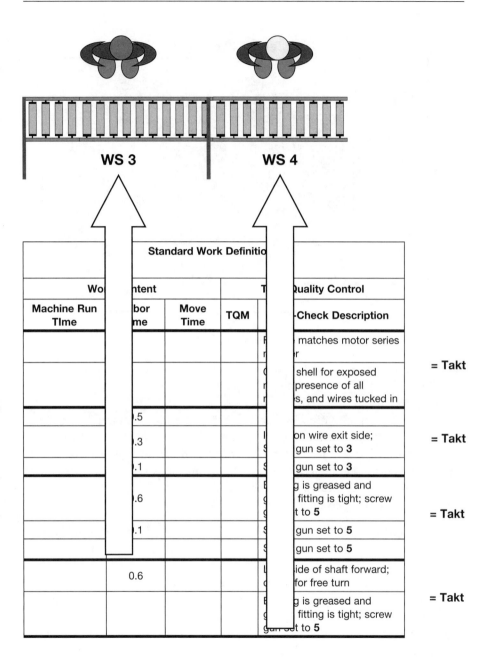

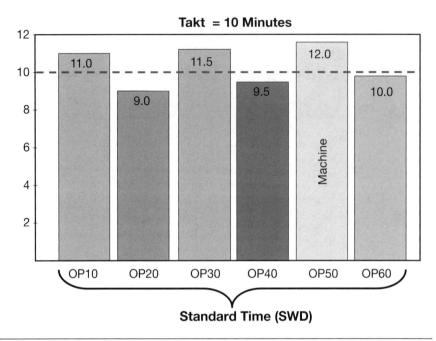

Figure 7.10. Unbalanced assigned standard work and Takt times in a process having a series of workstations.

manufacturing response time. The cost of implementation required to reduce or eliminate work at a workstation is small or nonexistent. Only the creative energy of an operator or kaizen team members is required. Because the cost-to-benefit ratio of reducing or eliminating work can be significant, always use the technique of identifying work that can be reduced or eliminated as the first effort in balancing the standard work content of a workstation.

Technique 2: Relocate work from one workstation to another workstation. Relocating work is a very common technique for achieving workstation balance. It is a common practice in traditional manufacturing systems. Using the SWD as a guide, relocate work by reassigning individual work tasks from one workstation to another, ensuring that relocation of the work is technically feasible and does not adversely affect quality. Most of the time, little or no cost is incurred. Relocation is simply a matter of moving a task from one workstation to another. In some cases, costs such as adding a fixture, a jig, or some other type of equipment may be necessary. Relocation of component inventories to the new workstation may also be required.

Technique 3: Add inventory to an imbalanced workstation. If the first two techniques for eliminating a process imbalance have been exhausted, escalation to the third balancing technique of adding resources as a buffer to maintain the Takt time of the process is required. Imbalance at a workstation can occur in both labor and machine work tasks. Imbalance is caused when the standard time of a process is greater than the Takt time. If the resource constraint is labor, adding an extra labor resource (operator) is a simple solution. When the imbalance is caused by a machine resource, units of additional WIP inventory may need to be placed on either side of a workstation to overcome the imbalance. Adding resources of any kind always increases cost (resources = cost). Exercise caution when making a decision to add resources, especially inventory. If the addition of inventory to buffer an imbalance is necessary, be certain that all efforts to eliminate the non-value-added work or to relocate the work have already been completely exhausted before choosing to add resources as a solution to the imbalance. Adding additional inventory at the workstation often means that additional production time will also be required to manufacture additional units for inventory. These added units must be maintained as extra IPKs, upstream and downstream of the imbalance, to create signals for replenishment and signals for when to stop making units (see Figure 7.8). If adding resources is the next-best solution for overcoming imbalance, avoid the temptation of guessing at the correct amount of inventory to be kept at a workstation. A formula can be used to determine the correct amount of IPK inventory to be added to an imbalanced workstation:

$$\text{Inventory} = \frac{\text{workstation minutes}}{\text{Takt}} - \frac{\text{workstation minutes}}{\text{STW}}$$

$$\frac{438}{10} - \frac{438}{12} = 43.8 - 36.5 = 7.3 \text{ or } 8 \text{ units}$$

$$\text{Time} = \text{STW} \times \text{inventory} = 12 \text{ minutes} \times 8 \text{ units} = 96 \text{ minutes}$$

The calculated number of IPKs must be placed at the upstream side *and* downstream side of an imbalanced workstation to ensure that the Takt time is maintained.

Technique 4: Add resources. Additional human resources, workstations, machines, or inventory resources all add cost to a process and ultimately to a product. Adding a labor or workstation resources is usually less expensive, but adding machine and material resources is always the most expensive solution for solving a line imbalance. If adding machine resources is necessary, always compare the cost of this solution with the cost of just adding inventory. To justify a capital expenditure request to purchase new equipment, the costs of carrying a calculated amount (see equation above) of buffer inventory, along with the costs of managing and storing the inventory, must be compared against the cost of purchasing new equipment. Because imbalanced workstations require more elapsed time each day to process the daily rate of sales during the effective minutes of Takt time, extended work time will be required to produce the buffer inventory. This extra work time must be added either before or after the normal shift time, which causes overtime that results in increased product cost. Depending on the comparison of the cost of inventory to the cost of a machine resource, adding another machine to overcome an imbalance might be less expensive than adding and maintaining the buffer inventory. When choosing to add resources as the solution to process imbalance, comparison of the cost of a new machine resource versus the costs of maintaining inventory will justify the best business solution for the company. Remember that no matter which solution is selected, any additional resource will remain in place every day, consuming costs. Only by eliminating the imbalance itself can the cost of added resources be eliminated. Eliminating the causes of imbalance is the number one reason for sponsoring continuous improvement projects and kaizen teams.

Technique 5: Use mixed-model sequencing. Lean manufacturing lines are almost always mixed-model manufacturing lines. With a mixed model line, no single product standard time was used when balancing the line. Mixed-model Lean lines are designed using some products with greater standard work times than others. A Lean line is balanced using a *standard time weighted* (STW) across a broad population of products weighted toward the *most frequently produced* products. Even with an STW across a broad population of products, the *order* of the models produced can impact the balance on a mixed-product line. Avoid sequential running of products having identical work content times for the process on a mixed-product line. Also, do not group all *low* or all *high* work content time products together and run them back-to-back on a Lean line. A Lean line is better balanced by running *longer* work-content-time products with a standard work time that *exceeds* the Takt time followed by products with a standard work content time that is *less than* Takt time. Over the course of a day, balance is achieved by missing the Takt times for large work content time products and beating the Takt times for shorter work content time products (Figure 7.11). This is accomplished by performing a daily routine in which the order for running product models on the Lean line is established by sequencing large work content time products interspersed between products having a shorter work content time in a process. This sequencing routine also establishes the priority of the products to be produced on the Lean line that day. Responsibility for creating this sequencing document must be assigned to a specific person who has knowledge of the products, processes, and product volumes. The resulting sequencing document

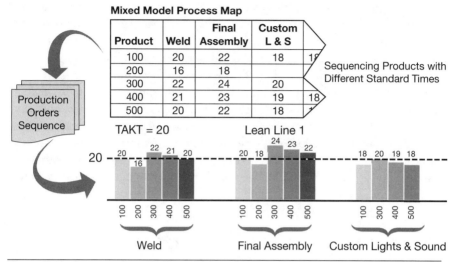

Figure 7.11. Sequenced production mix based on standard times: balance achieved by missed Takt times for longer work content time products and beaten Takt times for shorter work content time products.

must also be tested against the resources to be certain line capacity has not been exceeded. Usually, this work is performed by a planner.

Although Lean manufacturers rarely achieve perfect balance on Lean manufacturing lines in their facilities, the pursuit of perfect balance at each workstation must be a never-ending activity. Daily product mix and volume constantly changes from the mixes and volumes used to design the Lean line. Even if a line is designed to meet a preset mix and volume of sales, a customer will rarely remain committed to their promised mix or volume. Processes are improved. New products are introduced and old ones are dropped. Operators have good days and bad days. Changes occur daily that impact the balance of workstations. Lean lines are designed to produce a mix and volume that happens most of the time, but there is no guarantee that this mix and volume will be what customers want when it comes time to spend their money. Lean lines are based on history, yet they must operate in the here and now. Anomalies in product mix and demand that challenge the design of Lean lines will always exist. Lean manufacturers must always remain as flexible as possible to meet ever-changing customer demand. The key is to design a Lean line reflecting the customer demand that occurs most of the time. Occasionally, on a single day, the daily mix of products may cause the Lean line to miss a target Takt time in several or even all of the processes. It happens on all lines, even a carefully calculated Lean line, but having an average of 95% accuracy in mix and volume prediction is much better than being surprised each day by the changing whims of fickle customers. The Lean line is designed to respond to daily customer changes with a measured systematic response. Tomorrow the customer mix will likely revert to the predicted normal. Most manufacturers can live with a few days of unusual demand out of the ±250 working days per year.

As optimum balance is achieved, the capability to produce product in its work content time will also be achieved. Each small improvement incrementally reduces total manufacturing cycle time and leads to a reduction in response time to customer demand with a corresponding reduction in inventories. A manufacturer's capability to reduce response time and the total cost of production is a powerful weapon in the fight for increased market share. Today, 60 years later, Toyota continues to work on both large and small incremental process improvements. No improvement is too small.

DEVELOPING THE INITIAL SHOP FLOOR LAYOUT

Once a mixed-model PFD has been created, the processes have been identified, and the resource quantities have been calculated, an initial shop floor layout that locates the placement of all the resources is required. The workstation physical attributes (e.g., a 6-foot table versus a 3-foot workstation) have also been defined. The non-value-added setups and moves were identified when the SWDs were created. Setups and move times can be greatly reduced or eliminated just by placing resources and materials in proximity to the point where they will be consumed. Locate feeder (subassembly) processes at points on the line so that partially completed materials can be consumed directly into a downstream process (possible because the processes have been balanced to a Takt time). The final configuration of the resources in the factory layout should facilitate visibility and minimize non-value-added movement and wait time of products, thereby reducing or eliminating any significant amount of setup and move time for products and materials.

The initial Lean line layout is performed by process team members. The initial layout is a paper facsimile of the new facility that illustrates the placement of all resources (workstations and machines) according to the mixed-model PFD. At this point, a paper facsimile is preferable to a CAD drawing. Using a simple paper, perimeter-scaled drawing and scaled footprint cutouts of the resources to record multiple resource location iterations by team members is low in cost and encourages experimentation for determining the ideal placement of workstation and machine resources. To encourage testing and retesting of all ideas for the minimization of shop floor space, setups, and moves from process team members and to facilitate the forward flow of work sequentially through all processes recorded on the mixed model PFD, keep the rules for the new layout out of the factory to only a few.

Although process team members are responsible for the completed line design layout, members of the materials team as well as facility personnel, production management, and anyone else who has a stake in the final design or is interested in the process should be invited to participate. When complete, consensus is required for final acceptance of the new shop floor layout. Team participation and low-cost modeling facilitate achieving a successful Lean line factory floor layout design.

Encourage team participation. To take advantage of the benefits of a Lean transformation, designing the layout of a new factory (or the relayout of an existing factory) requires teamwork. Include shop floor operators who work in the manufacturing area every day. Other employees may also have excellent ideas about how the flow of product through the factory can be improved. Some might have been thinking about improvement ideas for years, but have never had the opportunity to express them. Although the process team is ultimately responsible for the final line design, a layout session is a particularly good time to test all ideas. Allow all interested persons to have their say. The good ideas can then be considered by the process team. Use a conference room table large enough to accommodate seating for all participants in the exercise. A large conference table allows all participants to contribute their ideas. Working around a table is also much easier than leaning over an engineer's computer monitor while a CAD system produces a layout. Locate the perimeter drawing in the center of the table. To encourage contributions, use a large sheet of paper for the perimeter drawing.

Create the model. Begin this process with a large paper layout that shows the perimeter of the new Lean area. Indicate all unmovable objects, such as power tunnels, roof supports, drains, large expensive-to-move equipment, and any other permanent building structures (known as *monuments*) on the perimeter drawing. For each resource (workstation and machine) identified on the process map, prepare a paper cutout of its footprint scaled to match the dimensions of the perimeter drawing. Using the perimeter drawing, begin at the point closest to the customer (usually shipping) and work upstream from the end of the line. Place the scaled shop floor paper footprints following the mixed-product PFD. Continue placing resources on the perimeter drawing until all of the resources that have been calculated on the process map have been placed on the perimeter drawing. Add or subtract any resources not identified on the process map. Test all resource placement ideas that minimize movement and optimize the flow of product from one workstation to another. Also create shop floor paper footprint cutouts for all supporting fixtures, racks, and carts used to manufacture product — even though these items are not manufacturing resources themselves. Fixtures, racks, and carts still require square footage space on the shop floor. Their inclusion can be challenged later to determine if their presence is really necessary or could be eliminated. This is also true for items such as personal toolboxes, chairs, stools, filing cabinets, parts storage, and any other item not necessary for performing the work content assigned to each workstation. Additionally, allocate suitable space to accommodate required material movement, such as space for lift truck aisles and the movement in and out of workstation material containers. Remember that workstations should be designed for minimum movement, yet remain as ergonomic as possible for operators who work there every day.

Make numerous iterations. The most successful line layouts are the result of numerous iterations of the possible arrangements. These iterations occur as participants move around the conference room table and suggest new ideas or changes to previous ideas. Use appropriately scaled paper cutouts to represent the shop floor footprint of the resources to facilitate debate. By moving the simple paper footprint representations of the resources around on the perimeter drawing, participants can get "instant" shop floor modeling. Test alternative ideas instantaneously by simply moving the paper cutouts around until the *ideal* placement of each is identified. Then exhaust all design suggestions from all participants and encourage numerous iterations to reach agreement on the *optimum* factory design more quickly and achieve final acceptance from all participants. Vigorous debate about the *optimum* solution for a layout issue usually results in agreement on the *best* solution. When this process is completed, you will have the new Lean line design for your factory.

Achieve an optimum line flow. In preparation for a new Lean line layout, assume a clean slate and no barriers. Keeping ergonomics, OSHA regulations, environmental and safety considerations, local ordinances, and monuments in mind, do not constrain the design of an optimum line by current legacy workflows or departmental boundaries. For example, the optimum line layout might suggest traversing an existing aisle. An aisle is not a monument, so redirect the aisle if it interferes with the flow of products on the Lean line. In the layout of a Lean shop floor, unencumbered product flow should take precedence over any existing or arbitrary placement of obstructions. Achieving optimum flow of the Lean line is paramount.

Develop the final layout. All resource layout options and factory monuments must be considered when designing the final layout for a Lean factory. Address all disagreements before the design is complete. Once the final layout is completed, obtain agreement on the final design from all process team members. At this point, convert the paper layout and resource cutouts into a formal facility layout drawing (usually done by the manufacturing or facilities engineer using a CAD system). The steering committee must then approve and sign off on the new line layout. For deployment of the final layout, a facility plan must now be created. A deployment plan usually includes the 5S workstation design, scheduling the installation of air and electrical drop lines, relocating workbenches, and contracting with riggers and other contractors. If the new layout requires production to be shut down for a period of time, develop a shut-down schedule to minimize factory down time and to synchronize any final relayout of the new Lean line.

If money were no object, then anything and everything could be moved in a new Lean factory layout (or a relayout), but from a practical standpoint, some items are just too costly to move. The return on investment does not justify relocation of items such as heavy machine tools mounted on engineered concrete pads, processes that are dirty or dangerous, processes that require special venting or maintenance requirements (EPA), and processes that produce loud noise. Relocating processes such as these makes no financial sense. The *ideal* line design might recommend a pure flow through dedicated resources, but an *optimum* final line design will include practical, cost-justified alternative solutions that maximize Lean principals while reflecting good common sense.

IMPLEMENTING THE SHOP FLOOR LAYOUT

During floor layout or when redesigning or relocating workstations, relocate *only* the necessary materials needed for the new Lean line. Move all unnecessary materials away from the line. Make instantaneous decisions. Final disposition of unnecessary materials can be made after the floor layout is completed and the Lean line is operating. When redesigning workstations, use scheduled production shut-down time for locating mechanical services such as air and electrical drop lines, the installation of lighting, and general maintenance of the shop floor not already completed during the original deployment plan.

When a factory is being transformed to a Lean operating system, most resources (workstations and people) will likely require relocation so the new Lean line will resemble the mixed-product PFD. Because resources are already undergoing redesign and relocation, this is the perfect time to implement the 5S initiatives: apply 5S as part of the factory redesign rather than implementing 5S initiatives as a stand-alone project later.

Workstations. Determine workstation size based on the size of the product. Do not provide more space at a workstation than is necessary to perform the standard work for the product. Excess space invites the accumulation of unnecessary materials. Place only the tools required by the assigned standard work at each workstation. Do not allow any unnecessary floor-standing or tabletop tool boxes. Required tools have already been identified by the standard work of the SWD and assigned to the workstation. Use a silhouette board showing all tools required at the workstation. Anything other than the tools needed to do standard work are superfluous and must be removed. Unnecessary tools and equipment take up valuable space and are a waste of resources. Remove unnecessary drawers and shelves from workbenches to eliminate the temptation to squirrel away extra parts, rejected units, and personal items by operators. As part of management by walking around, look for calendars, radios, pictures, and other personal items that are signs of ownership of a work station. On a Lean line, operator flexibility demands that on *any* given day *any* operator will be able to work at *any* workstation. When an operator assumes ownership of a workstation, they are unwilling to move to other workstations in response to the IPK signal. When this occurs, the Lean line is no longer flexible.

Materials. Ensure that all kanban material storage locations are clearly marked and access to material handling equipment is available. Assign a location where operators can access fixtures, gauges, jigs, and tools required to do standard work. Paint the footprint of specialized production materials such as trash receptacles, pallet jacks, fork trucks, and cleaning materials on the shop floor. These specialized items must be returned to their footprint when not in use. None of these materials are allowed to be at a workstation if they are not being used to complete standard work.

Housekeeping. Operators spend half of their waking hours in their workspaces. A clean workspace promotes quality in the products being built and is important for the comfort and safety of operators. A clean workspace also provides an early warning system for potential problems. Good housekeeping on the shop floor makes problems easier to spot. Any item not in its proper place is very conspicuous in a clean workspace. Exposed problems are more likely to be resolved, but hidden ones are not. Looking for problem-solving opportunities is an important part of management by walking around. When calculating Takt time, subtract the time required for cleaning up from the available minutes per day for each process. Making time available to the process removes any excuses for not maintaining good housekeeping at each process.

Meetings. Allow time for meetings at the beginning of each shift to provide operators from both shifts with an opportunity to communicate any information about the operation of process. This time is subtracted from the available minutes per day when determining Takt time for the process. Allowing time for meetings and clean-up activities eliminates excuses for not performing them. Less effective minutes each day will shorten the Takt time and might cause resources to be increased, but the investment is worth it.

MANAGING THE NEW LEAN LINE

So far, the standard work time has been recorded as accurately as possible by observing operators perform their work. These observations were used in the mathematic calculations that determined the number of resources required by each process to meet the Takt time target. From those mathematic calculations, the standard work documented on the SWD was assigned to each workstation in groups equal to a Takt time. Continuous improvement in the form of fine tuning the line by using the balancing tools has begun. Even though objective mathematical calculations were used to determine the resources, one variable common to all line designs still remained: the human resources.

Minor imbalances will *always* exist because a Lean line is staffed by human resources. Why? The reasons are as numerous as the number of human resources! Operators are not machines. They have different working habits. They have good days and bad days. They're preoccupied with problems at home or aren't feeling well. They don't work at the same speed. Some are just naturally faster and others are slower. Generally, the output of most operators varies as the day goes on. They're faster in the morning than in the afternoon. To overcome minor differences in workstation times and natural imbalances between individual operators staffing the line, a *regulator mechanism* is needed to keep the work flowing at the calculated Takt rate for the line. This regulator mechanism is a *production kanban* (also known an in-process kanban or IPK).

Use a Production Kanban

The IPK system is one of the major differences between a traditional planning system and the Lean operating system. Before a Lean manufacturing factory layout can be considered as complete, the physical placement of all IPKs must be completed. The Lean line cannot flow at the balanced Takt rate without the IPK signaling system being in place to regulate the desired speed of the line. Without IPK regulation of the Takt rate, all of the individual differences of the human resources operating the Lean line will accumulate to create significant imbalances. Operators working on the Lean line must be trained in the operation of IPKs. They must follow the established operating rules of the production kanban. Chapter 2 introduced the concept of using the IPK as the authorization for the expenditure of labor, machine, and material resources. The following sections review the IPK discussion in Chapter 2 and describe how the IPK system works to regulate the production rate of the Lean line.

The physical IPK. Once a workstation has been balanced and the standard work has been assigned, a physical IPK is placed on the downstream side of the

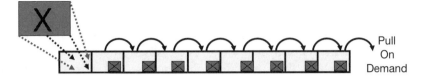

Figure 7.12. Using an in-process kanban as the authorization to do work.

workstation. When an operator completes the standard work assigned to the workstation, this partially completed unit is placed in the space designated as the IPK. Work on the next unit cannot begin until another signal authorizing work is received at the workstation. Until the partially completed unit of production is moved into the adjacent workstation downstream, therefore *exposing* the IPK, the rules of kanban require that the operator cannot begin work on the next unit. Once the unit is moved and the IPK is exposed, the authorization to produce the next Takt time amount of work on the unit waiting in the upstream IPK is given. When the unit is moved from the upstream IPK into the downstream workstation, the upstream IPK becomes *exposed*, thereby authorizing production of the next unit upstream. Only then is the operator authorized to begin work on the next unit. The next partially completed unit is then retrieved from the upstream workstation's IPK and the Takt cycle begins all over again (Figure 7.12). In Lean manufacturing, certain rules are associated with IPK signaling systems. Without the IPK system in place on the line and operator discipline to operate the system, all work content performance variations causing imbalance to occur today will persist, ultimately resulting in the failure of the line: the IPK signaling system is a key component for successful operation of a Lean line.

IPKs are visual. An IPK, empty or full, is a *visual signal* for an operator. As long as a partially completed unit resides in a workstation's IPK, beginning work on the next unit is not authorized. Only an empty IPK authorizes the next Takt time amount of work to begin. An IPK simply provides a temporary parking place for a unit that has been completed faster at the upstream workstation than the downstream workstation can consume it. This empty/full IPK mechanism and the simple work rules associated with an IPK overcome small imbalances at workstations and cause the completion of one finished unit to exit the last workstation every Takt time. IPK authorization of work helps regulate the speed of a Lean line. If left unregulated, imbalances will occur and the Lean line will eventually fail to meet customer demand for the day. At the end of the day, if balanced, a fully staffed Lean line producing one unit at a time, at the Takt rate throughout the day, will yield the required V_c or customer demand for that day. Figure 7.13 illustrates the placement of IPKs at all workstations on a Lean line.

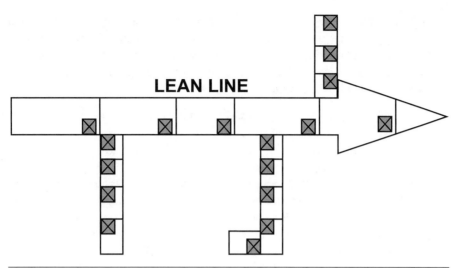

Figure 7.13. An in-process kanban placed at each workstation on a Lean manufacturing line.

IPKs act as a pull system. The IPK mechanism acts as a *pull system*, creating signals upstream from the last workstation (or in a backward direction) all the way back to the first workstation, that authorizes work to begin on the next unit of production at the same speed regardless of the standard work content time of the process. The first workstation therefore works at the same speed as the last! Compare this balanced-workstation pull system to a traditional *push* system of launching orders into production after the BOM explosion of the planning system. Completion of orders is *pushed* through manufacturing by plugging production orders into the available capacity in each department. Balance is of little concern between departments in a traditional system. Customer priorities are often lost in the expediting of production orders. Unsold units that were produced to fulfill capacity imbalances go to a FGI warehouse to wait for a future customer order. Some become slow-moving or obsolete items. WIP inventories accumulate while productivity measurements soar!

IPKs prioritize production. Scheduling production in a Lean factory is greatly simplified once factory layout and kanban signaling begin to pull work through the factory. Production plans are achieved by sequencing customer demand based on FIFO (first-in/first-out) methodology. The IPK signaling system mandates consumption of partially completed units on a FIFO basis from the upstream workstation. In a mixed-model Lean line, it makes no difference which product or SKU resides in the upstream workstation. The operator simply pulls the next unit and completes the assigned work content for that model. Adhering to FIFO discipline is critical for meeting customer order priorities established by the planner. Only by following FIFO methodology can the correct priority sequence be maintained from workstation to workstation. Customer demand is always produced on a Lean line in the same FIFO sequence required by the customer and defined by the planner.

IPKs can also be used for subassembly and feeder processes. A balanced Lean line with IPKs that signal production in feeder processes does not need separate production orders to be launched or batch subassembly production to be scheduled to drive manufacturing in feeder processes. The output of a feeder process is always consumed directly into a downstream process. Feeder processes are physically located adjacent to the consuming downstream process to facilitate minimum movement and little to no queue time in the IPK. Feeder processes are balanced to match the Takt rate on the consuming Lean line. Because a feeder line is balanced with the rate of the downstream consuming process, output from a feeder process arrives at the IPK at the same time as it is needed in the downstream process to be consumed directly into the unit being produced. Subsequent production of the next unit in the feeder process is then pulled by use of the completed subassembly from the IPK at the last workstation, causing a series of IPK signals to flow all the way back to the first workstation of the feeder to authorize the production of another subassembly unit.

IPKs can also handle custom configurations. Customers frequently request special product configurations. Custom orders for most configured products are not a problem for a Lean line. A sales order configuration document (a *configuration traveler*) is sequenced with the product as it advances through the manufacturing processes to notify the operators of the changes required during production of the custom product (any special parts to be used and any custom building required for the custom configuration). Feeder processes are also sequenced in the same order as the consuming downstream processes so that a specially configured subassembly matches the configuration-to-order unit on the main line (Figure 7.14).

IPKs eliminate expediting decisions by operators on the line. The FIFO methodology of the IPK system eliminates the need for operators to make expediting decisions on the shop floor. Operators have no responsibility for maintaining schedules or deliberating priorities. They don't determine the product to produce next or the production order with the greatest priority. Priority changes needed to satisfy changing customer demand are invisible to operators in a Lean facility. They simply pull the next partially completed unit waiting in the upstream IPK. Planners are responsible for making expediting decisions. Priority

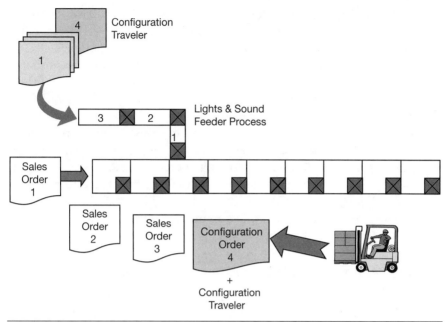

Figure 7.14. A sequenced feeder process with configuration traveler.

changes are accomplished by simply rearranging the sequence of customer orders before a unit enters the first workstation of the Lean line. Once a planner determines the correct sequence of orders to satisfy customer demand, the first operator at the first workstation simply begins production of a unit by pulling the first production order on the sequenced list of orders. Until a production order has been pulled by the operator and standard work has begun at the first workstation, the planner can change the sequence of the orders as many times as necessary to satisfy changing priorities in customer demand. Planners are also responsible for establishing the sequence of feeder lines. Once on the line, the products advance one workstation at a time using the ratchet effect of the IPK pull system.

IPKs require discipline. IPK signaling is critical to the operation of a Lean line. IPKs regulate the speed of the line. They help to smooth out minor factors such as operators working at different speeds, small standard time variations at workstations, and occasional component parts that do not fit together well that cause imbalances. Minor imbalances are common on any manufacturing line, but they still must be controlled. Having shorter standard times at workstations is not a solution. If uncontrolled by an IPK, operators completing standard work faster than the Takt time can accumulate large amounts of WIP. No IPK allows an operator to stay busy at the expense of building units in excess of demand at an individual workstation (known as *pyramid building*). Alternatively, operators slowing down their work pace to match the Takt time to maintain the appearance of balance is not a solution. Neither technique used as an alternative to proper balance is good: speeding up creates inventory and affects cost and slowing down affects productivity. For IPK signaling to be effective, operators must follow IPK discipline. Units cannot be allowed to stack up because one operator works faster than another or because a workstation is not properly balanced. Operators must allow only one partially completed unit of production at a time to be in the downstream IPK. Work cannot commence on the next unit at their workstations until the workstation's downstream IPK is empty. The unit in the IPK must be pulled by the downstream process. The empty IPK is the *only* authorization for an operator to begin working on the next unit.

Use the Managing-by-Walking-Around Technique

The concept of management by walking around (MBWA) isn't new. It wasn't invented by the Lean operating system. MBWA is a popular management technique used by managers in many businesses. It's also a common technique used by Lean operating system managers. How is MBWA different for a Lean manager? What does a Lean manager look for when walking around the shop floor? MBWA for a Lean manager is looking for signs that indicate management intervention is needed. What are these signs? What action should be taken if intervention is indicated?

Observe the IPKs. IPK signaling is crucial for a Lean line to be successful. If the Lean line is not operating as designed, improper use of the IPKs may be the first visual indicator of the viability of the Lean operating system. Any breakdown of the IPK system is an early warning sign of Lean line failure. MBWA is the best method for discovering these early warning signals. Operator discipline to following IPK signaling is the key to making a Lean line flow. Observe the IPKs when performing MBWA. Constant observation of the IPK system will alert a manager to problems affecting the flow and balance of the Lean line. Understanding how the IPK system operates allows many problems observed on the shop floor to be quickly identified.

Observe the processes. Balanced processes are also critical to the success of a Lean line. Going forward, periodic rebalancing will always be necessary to fine tune a Lean line. MBWA can reveal process imbalance opportunities. Constantly seek the perfect balance needed to consistently achieve an established Takt time target. If not monitored, the line may slowly be corrupted over time and become unbalanced. Operators might be picking up bad habits and incorporating them into their work practices. If bad work practices are allowed to continue, operators will interpret silence from management as acceptance of their work practices. Correct operator violations and bad work habits immediately. Explain any observed problems to the operator and provide training as needed to reinforce correct Lean methodology. If bad habits continue uncorrected and imbalances are left unresolved by management, the Lean line will eventually fail. The job of management is to look for signs of imbalance and take immediate responsibility to correct them. MBWA is an excellent way to observe imbalance on the Lean line. All of the work required to transform a facility into a Lean operating system can be compromised if the Lean line is not maintained and improved at all times.

Observe the operators. MBWA requires a manager to look for any key indicator or symptom that the line may be developing imbalances. Certain key indicators are often not easily identified by only casual observation. Identifying them requires paying closer attention. For example, certain operator behaviors can be indicators of imbalance. Behaviors such as nesting, hoarding, cherry picking, and operators acting independently are early warning signals that the line is becoming imbalanced. Learn to recognize these behaviors. They justify close inspection.

Nest builders. Nest building occurs when an operator decides to take ownership of a workstation by just staking a claim to it. Signs of ownership include the presence of personal items such as a calendar, a radio, cooking devices, and other "creature comfort" items. Nest building can be identified by the partitioning off of a workstation from other workstations, e.g., by using paper, cardboard, plastic, etc. In some cases, the partitioning may be done to prevent management from observing the operator, although the operator can still see the approach of management. Nest builders unilaterally decide when and how to do their work. They like batch-unit production. They like to accumulate production units that can be completed quickly, leaving them with free time to pursue activities other than standard work. Nest building is a symptom of an unwillingness to respond to IPK signals. Nest builders are unwilling to move from their nests to properly respond to an IPK signal because they don't want to leave their personal items behind! A Lean line cannot operate effectively if a human resource refuses to be flexible. Remember the Lean rule: *an operator always moves to the work; work does not move to an operator.* Stop nest building as soon as the first personal item appears at a workstation or the first attempt is made to isolate a workstation from other workstations.

Pack rats. Pack rats are always ready for a rainy day. They maintain private caches of parts and materials. Their justification for hoarding these parts often includes a woeful tale about a shortage of parts a long time ago that caused the manufacturing line to stop. Even if the stash of parts has to stay at their workstations for years, pack rats are determined to never let a line stoppage for lack of parts ever happen again! Remember the Lean rule: *on a Lean line, operators build units and material handlers provide parts.* A similar story can justify hoarding tools. This time the tale will describe needing a certain tool to build a special configuration in the workstation a long time ago. Even though this situation happened years before, it could happen again. Pack rats will not be caught flatfooted the next time. Remember the Lean rule: o*n a Lean line, the tools and equipment necessary to produce the products are at every workstation and are provided by the company.* Tools and equipment are company property. Any tool necessary to produce the mix of products designed for the Lean line is already at the workstation, either placed there when the workstation was designed or added during 5S implementation. Stop any hoarding of tools. Look for toolboxes, drawers, shelves, file cabinets, and any other places where tools and parts can be stashed for future use. Continually enforce 5S philosophy: *a place for everything, everything in its place.*

The tenured operator. Because of tenure, longevity, or special skills, some operators think they have paid their dues and earned the right to choose the work they do. Producing many different items is beneath their dignity. These tenured professor operators like to *cherry pick* only units that they like to produce. Tenured professor operators will often stockpile work to complete later at their convenience. Tenured professor operators are also likely to be nest builders so they can maintain a pack rat inventory and be left alone to work on only products of their own choosing. When observing a line, pay close attention to the product mixes in the IPK of a tenured professor operator. Confirm that the daily sequence selected by a planner is being followed on a FIFO basis at the tenured professor's workstation.

The independent operator. Although operators usually have great improvement ideas, they cannot unilaterally incorporate these ideas. Ideas for process improvements can impact an entire line. They must be carefully managed. If an operator acting alone decides to add or delete standard work, stop using a piece of equipment, or reshuffle the work sequence, his workstation may be thrown out of balance and lead to imbalance all along the entire line. Operators should be encouraged to think about improvements, but it must be made clear that any ideas can only be implemented by using the proper procedures for change. An improvement idea must be appropriately addressed during process improvement meetings or a kaizen event. If the idea is adopted, the line can then be rebalanced so all processes will remain in balance.

Prior to the implementation of Lean manufacturing lines, productivity measures promoted utilization and efficiency. Operators were always instructed to build as many products as possible as fast as possible. In companies where absorption was always the primary performance measurement, an individual's ability to work fast was a valuable asset to the company, but with introduction of the Lean line, these same operators are now being trained to work by producing only one unit at a time in response to an IPK signal. As work is completed, it's moved to an IPK. The operators must then wait for more work to come from an upstream workstation or flex to other workstations in response to the IPK signal. When the new Lean line starts up, this new environment will feel unnatural to some operators. Old work habits do not go away just because management says so (speed trumps Takt!). Continue to enforce the discipline for operators to comply with IPK signals. Maintain the discipline of one-piece flow. Do not allow operators to place more than one unit in an IPK. The line should also flow at a Takt rate along all of the workstations. Line imbalance will manifest itself as a breakdown of IPK discipline or it will cause a line stoppage. If upstream operators must always wait every Takt time for work to be completed downstream before receiving an IPK signal, or if work at a workstation is always completed faster than the Takt time, causing the operator to wait, chances are good that the line has an imbalance in the standard work assigned to the workstation. Do not ignore these important warning signs of imbalance. When imbalance is suspected, apply the balancing techniques discussed earlier in this chapter to resolve it: reduce or eliminate non-value-adding work, relocate work, add resources, add inventory, and use mixed-model sequencing.

Going Forward: Avoid Management Indifference

A common mistake when making a transformation to Lean is to assume that the conversion to Lean manufacturing is a project with a beginning and ending date. Nothing is further from the truth in a successful Lean transformation. Lean manufacturing begins with a revolutionary transformation redesign that must become a way of life. Lean must be the chosen manufacturing operating system for running the facility from now on. Although noble, sponsorship from only the grass roots level of the organization will jeopardize the chances for the long-term success of a Lean operating system. The factory conversion to Lean must be championed as a *top-down* activity. The expected benefits must be articulated and woven into the fabric of company culture.

After spending so much time on designing the line, transferring the responsibility for the operation and maintenance of the line to the next generation is easy for transformation team members. They have spent so much time and energy on the transformation project. Allowing the skills and knowledge gained by the original team members to just "walk away" when the transformation project concludes, however, is a terrible waste of talent. Ensure that transformation team members mentor managers and new team members on subsequent Lean line design projects.

The primary reason a Lean line fails after startup is *management indifference* to the warning symptoms of line imbalances. Lean lines do not fail in single day — they fail over a period of time as a result of many small nonfatal actions that were never corrected — as expressed by the idiom *a death of a thousand cuts.* Over time, if management ignores the warning signals, the Lean line will atrophy to the old comfortable solutions and operating systems in place before the Lean transformation. Do not permit indifference to Lean methodology to spoil your success. Allowing indifference to flourish is the first step to returning to the old practices that caused the transition to Lean manufacturing methodologies to be needed in the first place. If this occurs, your company will become a statistic: just another company in the group claiming to be among the 22% who are dissatisfied with their Lean initiatives.[1]

Lean manufacturing is a completely different way of operating a manufacturing company. It requires hard work to implement. The transformation team must be willing to challenge existing manufacturing paradigms. Ongoing successful operation of Lean manufacturing lines requires the commitment to seek continuous improvement using and reusing all of the methodologies employed during the transformation process. Dedication to a Lean operating system will change existing company culture.

REFERENCE

1. George Koenigsaecker. Leadership and the lean transformation, in *Manufacturing Engineering,* November 2005: Vol. 135, No. 5; available at http://findarticles.com/p/articles/mi_qa3618/is_200511/ai_n15847432/.

8

THE KANBAN SYSTEM: A COMPONENT MATERIALS STRATEGY

Lean operating systems define a product as the sum of its work content plus its materials (component parts). Work content is only half of what is necessary to produce a product. Component parts make up the other half. The component parts required for the manufacture of a product can either be fabricated or purchased.

A Lean factory is designed to establish the resources required to produce the work content portion for a family of products. These resources are available to produce the work content of any model of a product family selected for production on the Lean line on any given day. From discussions in previous chapters devoted to producing the work content of products, we know that Lean manufacturers seek to achieve balance across all processes while producing products in only their standard work content time. Manufacturing processes are physically linked together so the output of one process is directly consumed by the next downstream process. The amount of resources required each day are matched to customer demand requirements so demand will be produced *without* building WIP inventories or FGIs to offset imbalances in the manufacturing process. A separate material strategy is necessary to supply the second half of what is required to manufacture a product: the component parts that will be combined with the work content to produce a product. A kanban system is the material strategy used to supply parts to a Lean operating system.

Traditional planning systems. In a traditional planning system, material components identified by the planning system are provided to the manufacturing line by issuing a parts list, a kit build list, or a pick list to a central stores warehouse where the component parts are pulled from a stockroom location and allocated to the corresponding production order. The parts list, pick list, or parts list for kit builds are sent to a stockroom after *exploding* the quantity of scheduled finished goods multiplied by the quantity on the indented BOM. For instance, if a production order is for 10 motor units and the BOM states 1 unit per motor, the stock room will issue 10 armatures, 10 control panels, 10 wiring harnesses, and all other required parts listed on the BOM. Parts with a quantity of more than 1 unit per motor use the BOM quantity per as a multiplier of 10 to calculate the number of parts to be issued. Both production order and allocated parts are then forwarded to the manufacturing area for production. Maintaining traditional planning system accuracy requires feedback communication to the planning system of this activity. Using the pick list method, materials are *chained* to a specific production order. Any future priority change requiring a change in quantity or due date that causes a paper reallocation of materials on the production order must be recorded in the planning system. If production orders are changed frequently, material reallocation expediting activities require extensive database maintenance efforts for planners. If expediting activity is not faithfully documented, the planning system becomes compromised and its databases, including the status of material stocks, will also be compromised.

Lean manufacturing systems. Instead of allocating component parts to a specific production order, Lean manufacturing systems use a *kanban* system as a material handling strategy to make components available to the manufacturing process. Kanban systems are not new. Lean manufacturing did not invent the kanban system. In fact, the two-bin kanban system has been around for years. As with many manual noncomputerized systems, however, the two-bin system fell out of favor with the advent of modern electronic planning systems. Let's review the definition of kanban.

Kanbans. Kanban is a Japanese word meaning *signal* or *card*. Kanban is also a technique used to signal that replenishment is necessary to continue production: a unit, a part, or materials. In Lean manufacturing, kanban may have several variations based on a specific application: the in-process system (IPK; see Chapters 2 and 7), the single-card (two-bin) system, or the multiple-card system. Each variant of kanban has a specific methodology applicable for a specific purpose. Each system has unique properties that work better for each specific application. Common to each of the three systems, however, is that a *signal* of some type is generated to indicate that a material replenishment is required. The difference between the different types of kanbans is in *how* the actual signal is generated and how material replenishment is accomplished.

In-process kanban. An IPK is a clear and visible sign (a designated empty space) at the downstream side of a workstation that signals authorization of the upstream operation to complete another Takt time amount of work. An IPK also signals an operator to flex by waiting to begin work, either at another upstream or at a downstream workstation.

Two-bin kanban. When most people describe a kanban system, they're usually describing the two-bin system. Two-bin systems were present on manufacturing shop floors for years before the advent of computerized planning systems. Japanese manufacturers can be credited with resurrecting and improving earlier two-bin systems by continuing to use them in their post-WWII noncomputerized operating systems. As the Japanese experienced great success with their kanban systems, many manufacturers around the world began to incorporate kanban systems into their operating systems. The methodology of the two-bin system is responsible for the term *Just-In-Time* or JIT. The goal of a two-bin system is for replenishment of material to be received *just in time* for consumption on a manufacturing line — no sooner, no later. In the two-bin system, the last component of the first bin is consumed just as the second bin is received. Material does not sit around in piles waiting to be used. A two-bin kanban material replenishment methodology uses two equal-sized containers that contain quantities sized for the time required to replenish the predetermined quantity of material in the first container. As the first container is emptied by consumption during the manufacturing process, it becomes a signal (a kanban) for replenishment. A second container remains at the workstation to continue to supply the point of manufacturing consumption during the replenishment cycle of the first container. A two-bin system is very simple. Two equal-sized containers are filled with identical parts and equal quantities. Both containers are located at the workstation where the parts are consumed in the manufacture of a product. After using parts from the first container only, the container will eventually become empty. When the first container is empty, this empty container becomes the kanban signal indicating that the container needs to be refilled. While the first container is being refilled, the second container takes its place at the work station and continues to supply parts to the manufacturing process. The line does not stop while waiting for material to be replenished. Eventually, the material in the second container will also be exhausted. As the very last part in the second container is being consumed, the first container has been timed to arrive *just in time* so production can continue. The empty second container now becomes the next signal for replenishment while the refilled first container once again supplies materials to the point of consumption. In the two-bin kanban system, one of the two containers is always being replenished. This usage/replenishment cycle is repeated throughout the day for every part number at every workstation. Containers for parts are clearly visible at workstations; the replenishment activity of material handlers is also quite noticeable. A key benefit of a two-bin system is the capability to use any part for any model of production that comes into the workstation. No reallocation of parts to maintain the planning system stock status report is necessary — parts are no longer allocated to a specific production order. All parts necessary to build the product models designated by the line design are available to the Lean manufacturing line. The logistics to accommodate large movements of batched parts attached to multiple production orders are also no longer necessary. Paperwork required for maintaining planning system databases is greatly reduced. Materials management personnel productivity is improved. Operators do not have to abandon their workstations to look for replenishment parts. Manufacturing processes continue to operate during parts replenishment cycles. If an empty container is impractical as a signal, a card or some other device may be used instead as the replenishment signal. The key is that a *signal* for replenishment is made.

Multiple-card kanban. A multiple-card kanban is a material replenishment technique that uses separate multiple signals, *Move* and *Produce* cards, to communicate the need for material replenishment. Multiple-card kanban signals are typically used with shared manufacturing processes or in independent cells where long setups or great distances between manufacturing processes require lengthy replenishment times.

If a single term in the entire lexicon of manufacturing has been more misunderstood, misused, and misapplied, that term would have to be *kanban*. Often the word *kanban* is attached to any material handling method that just happens to store small parts in containers at a workstation or to describe any system that uses cards to reorder materials. Since its reincarnation by Western manufacturers in the 1970s and 1980s, the two-bin kanban system has arguably been applied incorrectly more than any other system. Kanban has even been used to describe a complete manufacturing line, e.g., a kanban line.

Just as the knowledge of kanban systems has evolved from the first days of the Japanese applications, so too has the evolution to incorrect applications. Current kanban applications did not begin with a misapplication of the original system concepts. The misapplied kanban systems of today are the result of series of minor modifications or compromises — small changes over a long period of time usually made to accommodate some other system or methodology. Soon, the sum of all these small changes to the basic discipline designed into a kanban system become so compromised the system no longer resembles the original system design — except in name only. In a dynamic fast-paced manufacturing environment, the voices of kanban system champions are easily drowned out by louder voices wanting to modify the original kanban system. Eventually, the last defenders of the system move on to other opportunities, leaving behind only a residual of the original kanban system.

THE IN-PROCESS KANBAN

Remember that a traditional planning system uses a production order to authorize work. The amount of work is determined by the quantity of a production order. Consumption of parts is authorized by a pick list or kit build list issued by the planning system and attached to the production order. On a Lean line, an in-process kanban (IPK) authorizes the consumption of parts and the application of labor to produce a Takt time amount of work at a workstation. Manufacturing resources are only expended in units of one Takt time of standard work per workstation. The IPK signal is located on the downstream side of every workstation. The IPK authorizes standard work and parts usage based on the consumption of one partially completed unit downstream.

An IPK is also used to offset minor imbalances on the line by regulating the speed of the line while assuring that the sequence of production is correct by following FIFO (first in/first out) methodology to maintain customer demand priority. The IPK therefore alerts an operator or technician *when* to do another Takt time of standard work or *when* to move to the next workstation to help advance customer units toward completion. The IPK is the mechanism that controls the production rate of the Lean line.

Using the IPK to establish priority. A planner determines the order of manufacture based on customer priorities so that products are manufactured one unit at a time in an established sequence. Customer demand that must be expedited can easily be moved to the front of the line by priority sequencing. The operator in the first workstation needs only to respond to an empty IPK signal by simply beginning production of the next unit in the order chosen by the planner. FIFO methodology ensures that customer demand is satisfied in the priority sequence established by the planner. Spending non-value-added time establishing customer demand priorities is unnecessary for manufacturing managers, production supervisors, and operators. Manufacturing just produces the next order in line or the next unit waiting at an upstream workstation. Setting demand priorities and the manufacturing sequence is the responsibility of planners. Executing the prioritized demand is the responsibility of manufacturing.

USING THE IN-PROCESS KANBAN TO MODIFY PRODUCTION OUTPUT

Remember that when the Lean manufacturing line was designed, a statement of desired line capacity was established. This V_c is a statement of the capacity of the line — theoretically the line cannot produce one unit more than the V_c on any given day. Once established, the V_c should have a volume that can accommodate anticipated customer demand 1 to 3 years into the future (the out years).

Traditional manufacturers tend to obsess about having too little future capacity to meet customer demand, which drives the desire for maximum utilization of the existing resources. Just the opposite is true for a Lean line. When a Lean line begins operation on day one, it has intentional excess capacity by design. If the V_c has been carefully considered and is a valid statement of future demand, line capacity should not become a constraint until a Lean line approaches the out year anniversaries (1 to 3 years later).

No Lean line can create capacity. The potential output of a single resource is finite. Increased capacity can only occur by increasing the number of resources. To increase capacity, a Lean line can only *optimize* the available resources provided to it. As the V_c time horizon approaches, redesign of the Lean line may be necessary (e.g., rebalancing along with new resource calculations). Diminishing capacity is a positive indicator — increasing sales volume is a sign of growth.

If, however, a Lean line operates at a rate equal to the designed capacity of future demand (V_c), while actual customer demand requires less than capacity, excess unsold inventory will be produced. Achieving 100% utilization equal to planned future capacity comes at the expense of increased inventories. A Lean manufacturing line must therefore have a way to reduce output when actual customer demand is less than V_c.

Slow the pace of work or periodically stop work. One method of matching lower customer demand with the output of a Lean line is to slow the working pace of labor resources to reduce the output of the line. Slowing the working pace of labor resources, however, artificially increases the standard time of the products being produced. Another method is to periodically stop work on the line to interrupt its output. Both methods will certainly diminish line output, but they are too subjective to accurately maintain the discipline a manufacturing line requires to operate. Operators who are responsible for managing the speed and output of the line must have a controlled, disciplined method to reduce the output of the Lean line.

Reduce the headcount. A third method of matching customer demand with the output of a Lean line is to reduce the headcount on the line to a number less than the number of available workstations. Reducing the headcount causes a corresponding reduction in line output. It has the same effect as slowing the line down or stopping it, but instead of working slowly or sitting idle, the remaining operators are still required to complete standard work in the Takt time assigned to their workstations. Using this method, line output is reduced because the operator headcount is less than the number of available workstations, causing some workstations to be without an operator for a Takt time. Common terminology for an unassigned, empty workstation is *a hole in the line*. Reduced output is achieved when units of production wait in a hole in the line and miss the Takt time amount of standard work applied for completion of the unit. The unstaffed workstation and the IPK authorization sitting at the workstation cause waiting units of production to require two elapsed Takt times for completion of assigned work. Eventually, the hole in the line will migrate to the last workstation where a unit of production will sit idle for one additional Takt time while the operator flexes into the upstream workstation in response to the empty IPK signal. The amount of output reduction needed is managed by the number of Takt times missed. The number of Takt times needing to be missed is determined by the number of workstation holes assigned to the line each day. Adjusting output of the Lean line is a daily management routine based on the mix and volume of customer demand to be produced that day.

Reducing the headcount: intentional suboptimization. Intentionally suboptimizing the Lean line by reducing the number of operators to less than the number of workstations of a Lean line will reduce its output, but will also cause utilization to be less than 100%. For companies using capacity utilization as a performance measurement, intentionally suboptimizing the output of a Lean line to match the daily customer demand rate will cause rethinking utilization as an effective performance measurement. Some manufacturers have embraced OEE (overall equipment effectiveness) as a performance measurement to monitor their manufacturing effectiveness. OEE is calculated as:

$$\text{Availability} \times \text{performance} \times \text{quality} = \text{OEE}$$

Because a Lean line has been designed to operate at a Takt rate, output can only be matched to customer demand by intentionally reducing its utilization (to suboptimize). The performance component of the formula is calculated as the ratio of actual run rate to ideal run rate (theoretical capacity): 100% performance means a process consistently runs at its theoretical maximum speed. On a Lean line, when customer demand requires the reduction of output, achieving full utilization of a resource can only result in the production of excess unsold inventory. The Lean line prefers to take a hit on utilization rather than to produce the first two *wastes* of manufacturing — overproduction and inventory. The power to make daily and intentional modification of line output to reduce the creation of the most expensive component of product cost makes the OEE measurement ineffective for use with a Takt Lean line design. Remember that product cost has three components — labor, 10%; overhead, 30%; and materials, 60%. Controlling which cost component offers the least-cost option for the business? What is the cost premium for a company to achieve 100% utilization compared to the cost of having excess unsold inventory?

Change the location of physical resources. Still another method of reducing the output of a Lean line is to remove physical resources such as workbenches or machines from the line daily to match decreased customer demand. This method certainly works, but moving physical factory fixtures around on the shop floor daily is expensive, awkward, and time consuming. Rearranging or removing physical resources is not the best choice for managing output.

Reducing output: the best option. Modifying the most flexible resource — the people — is the best option for reducing output. Because customers rarely order the same mix or volume of products two days in a row, determining the required headcount to match actual customer demand is needed on a daily basis for a Lean manufacturing line. When the headcount is reduced to match customer demand that is less than V_c, some workstations will intentionally be unstaffed. As the Lean line flows, incomplete products at the unstaffed workstations will remain idle for one additional Takt time. After one Takt time has been completed and the operator places a partially completed unit in the workstation's IPK, the operator cannot pull the next unit from the upstream workstation and begin another Takt time of work until an IPK signal is received from the downstream workstation. So, when no signal is received, what does the operator do? The operator could just stand in the workstation and do nothing, but on a Lean line the operator relocates to the downstream workstation (a movement referred to as *flexing*); pulls the partially completed unit they just placed in the upstream IPK; and begins the next Takt amount of standard work assigned to that workstation. The act of pulling the partially completed unit from the upstream workstation now creates an empty IPK signal at the previously idle workstation. The ability of operators to flex by moving up and down the line in response to an IPK signal is a requisite for achieving productivity while still meeting customer demand with less than full staffing.

On a Lean line, two things can happen when an IPK is empty and no operator is in a workstation to respond to the IPK signal: the workstation remains empty and a Takt amount of work is missed *or* another operator moves to the workstation to complete the assigned standard work. With the next Takt time cycle, the operator will once again move to the workstation with an empty IPK signal. Figure 8.1 illustrates how operators move in response to one IPK signal during

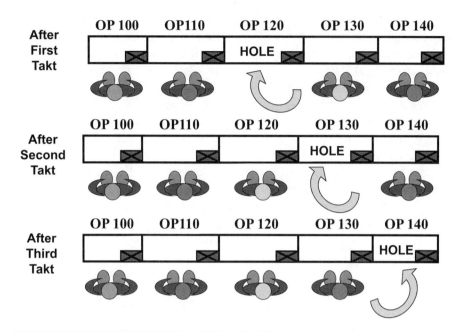

Figure 8.1. Flexible labor resources to match customer demand: operator movements in response to IPK in three Takt times.

three Takt times. This up and down movement in response to IPK signals results in missed Takt times at alternating workstations throughout the day. Missed Takt times all day long throughout a Lean line reduce line output. When managed correctly, at the end of the day, daily customer demand will have been met. This type of Lean line management technique of intentional labor reduction will be ineffective unless operators learn to flex and adhere to IPK discipline. Without IPK discipline, a Lean line will become unbalanced and eventually fail.

   Calculate resources daily. Because the mix and volume of customer demand can change daily, the number of labor resources required to produce that variety can also change. The number of labor resources needed to staff a Lean line must therefore be calculated each day to match the daily mix and volume of customer demand. During original design of the Lean line, a projected V_c was used as a statement of line capacity to determine the number of resources required for the physical layout of the shop floor. A computer-based resource process map was used to calculate the number of resources needed to produce the V_c. Although V_c can be changed each day to determine adjustments needed for labor resources, any changes to V_c will change the Takt time of the line. *The Takt time of a Lean line is static based on throughput volume: it does not change until the line is redesigned!* The Lean line was designed and machine and workstation resources were located on the shop floor based on the established Takt time of the line. In addition, the standard work to be performed at each workstation was assigned based on the Takt time of each workstation. Changing Takt time each day to accommodate fluctuating mix and volume changes in customer demand will also require changing the amount of standard work assigned to each workstation each day to maintain the balance of the line. A better way to determine daily headcount is to divide the *standard time weighted* for the actual daily mix and volume of product by the *effective working minutes per day* rather than using Takt time as a denominator as was done for the resource calculations for line design. *Takt time of the Lean line does not change as daily mix and volume change.* Therefore only the number of flexible labor resources required each day should change. Modify the output rate by staffing the line with only the number of operators needed to meet sales requirements for that day. A formula can be used to determine the daily headcount needed to meet customer demand:

$$\text{Staffing by process} = \frac{\Sigma\ (\text{daily sales SWD labor time})}{\text{available minutes per shift}}$$

Underutilization. Changing staffing daily to match changing demand volume may also require intentional underutilization of a Lean line. For example, if the V_c of a Lean line is designed to produce 30.65 units (31), requiring 35 operators and 35 workstations, but daily sales are only 22.25 units (23), the Lean operating system will require staffing of only 26 operators assigned to 26 workstations: 9 of the available 35 workstations will begin the day as *holes* in the line. The 9 (35 – 26) operators who are not required that day to produce the daily volume of 23 units must be assigned to other duties in the facility rather than working on the Lean line. Even with 9 unmanned workstations, the Lean line with a capacity for 35 units will still be able to produce the required 23 units. Throughout the production day, products landing at one of the nine unstaffed holes will sit idle for one additional Takt time. After each Takt cycle, operators will then *flex* to the unstaffed workstations and perform the required work for the idled unit. During this new Takt cycle, another nine different workstations will become idle. When the production day is concluded, the line will have packed off 8.4 (9) units less than the designed capacity of the line. Using 26 workstations to produce 23 units when 35 workstations are available to produce 31units is, of course, less than 100% utilization. Alternatively, if the potential output of 31 units that can be produced by 35 operators were not reduced to match the customer demand of 23 units requiring only 26 operators, and the excess 9 operators were left assigned to the line to simply achieve a utilization metric, 9 units of excess, unsold inventory would be produced. Because inventory costs more than labor, which one of the two components of cost is best underutilized? When the Lean line is operated with 26 operators instead of 35, the Takt time at each of the 26 workstations does not change. Because operators move *to the work* at a workstation, each of the 26 operators assigned to the Lean line that day therefore remains 100% utilized when completing each Takt time at each workstation. Only the total output of the line is underutilized, not the people. Since partial units of a product cannot be produced, the rounded up sum of completed units (8.4) is 9. Table 8.1 illustrates a daily resource planning worksheet that has been used to calculate the required headcount to match the planned daily rate of customer demand. Every Lean line will require a similar tool to determine daily staffing requirements.

From the discussion above, we know that intentional suboptimization of a Lean line by altering staffing to match reduced daily demand creates holes in the line and that the location of these holes moves up and down the line throughout the day as operators flex into idle workstations. Using the example of 35 workstations with 26 operators, 9 holes in the Lean line are created by not staffing 9 workstations. At the beginning of the day, starting with the first Takt cycle, nine units of production receive no standard work. These units require extra wait time: one Takt cycle must be completed before another operator can flex into the unmanned workstation to complete the work. As operators flex to idle workstations, locations of the holes shift up and down the line. When a hole finally reaches the last workstation on the line, a Takt cycle will be missed: one unit therefore cannot be packed off as a finished unit within the established Takt rate. Missing a Takt cycle at the last workstation is intentional, but acceptable as long as daily customer demand is met. By using this suboptimization technique, at the end of the day, ±25% of the capacity of the manufacturing line has been underutilized (in the form of missed Takt time cycles). Only ±75% of the available capacity has been utilized to meet the required customer demand of 23 units. Total line capacity has been underutilized purposely to achieve the intended outcome of producing fewer units. To achieve a 100% utilization goal, individual operators have not been excused from completing standard work in the designated Takt time target at their workstations. Operators have been 100% utilized individually even though the Lean line itself was not. For each day that full staffing has not been required, the remaining management issue has been to determine where to best utilize the unassigned operators that day. Lean manufacturers must therefore develop proactive strategies designed to best utilize unassigned resources in other areas of the facility when they not needed on a Lean line.

Because the cost of inventory is greater than the cost of labor, the Lean operating system considers underutilizing labor to be the least-cost alternative compared to the costs generated by producing unsold FGI. Table 8.2 compares

Table 8.1. Daily Resource Planning Spreadsheet with Calculations for Staffing a Lean Line to Meet Daily Customer Demand

Family Description	Part Number	Planned Daily Rate	Weld Labor	Volume Modifier × V_c	Volume Modifier	Weld Rework Labor	Volume Modifier	Volume Modifier × V_c
V5A	75903101	1.00	45.000	1.10	1.10	30.00	0.10	0.10
V6A	76000202	0.00	60.000	1.10	0.00	30.00	0.10	0.00
A4H	76102402	2.00	50.000	1.10	2.20	30.00	0.10	0.20
U5	76100002	2.00	60.000	1.10	2.20	30.00	0.10	0.20
805	72200002	4.00	45.000	1.10	4.40	30.00	0.10	0.40
806	72210002	4.00	40.000	1.10	4.40	30.00	0.10	0.40
T5AH	72208902	2.00	55.000	1.10	2.20	30.00	0.10	0.20
T5LOAH	70524102	0.75	55.000	1.10	0.83	30.00	0.10	0.08
S5	72208602	1.00	60.000	1.10	1.10	30.00	0.10	0.10
TM270	71801802	2.00	65.000	1.10	2.20	30.00	0.10	0.20
G3	70542002	1.00	50.000	1.10	1.10	30.00	0.10	0.10
G4A	70550402	2.50	55.000	1.10	2.75	30.00	0.10	0.25
		22.25			**24.48**			**2.23**

Planned Work Minutes	438	438
Shifts	1	1
Throughput Volume	24.48	2.23
Standard Time Weighted	51.0	30.00
Resources Required	2.85	0.15
Resources Available	4	1
Utilization	71%	15%

Actual Daily Sales = 22.25
Line Design V_c = 30.65

Daily Headcount Reduced to match Daily Sales While Increasing Team Utilization

Planned Work Minutes	438	438
Shifts	1	1
Throughput Volume	24.48	2.23
Standard Time Weighted	50.96	30.00
Resources Required	2.85	0.15
Resources Available	3	1
Utilization	95%	15%

Final Assembly Labor	Volume Modifier	Volume Modifier × V_c	Custom Lights & Sound Labor	Volume Modifier	Volume Modifier × V_c
330.00	1.000	1.00	215.00	0.40	0.80
400.00	1.000	0.00	215.00	0.40	0.16
360.00	1.000	2.00	220.00	0.40	1.20
340.00	1.000	2.00	220.00	0.40	0.80
360.00	1.000	4.00	260.00	0.40	1.60
320.00	1.000	4.00	260.00	0.40	2.40
300.00	1.000	2.00	260.00	0.40	0.80
300.00	1.000	0.75	260.00	0.40	0.30
400.00	1.000	1.00	260.00	0.40	0.40
425.00	1.000	2.00	220.00	0.40	0.80
360.00	1.000	1.00	220.00	0.40	2.00
300.00	1.000	2.50	220.00	0.40	1.00
		22		0.40	**9**

438	438
1	1
22	9
343.15	240.90
17.4	4.9
25	7
70%	70%

Daily Headcount Reduced to match Daily Sales While Increasing Team Utilization

438	438
1	1
22.25	8.90
343.15	240.90
17.43	4.89
18	5
97%	98%

Table 8.2. Headcounts for 100% Capacity Staffing versus 73% Capacity Staffing

Resources	Weld	Weld Rework	Final Assembly	Lights & Sound
Resources required for 100% line design volume	4	1	28	7
Resources required to meet 73% capacity daily sales rate	3	1	18	5
Number of persons not required to meet daily customer demand	1	0	7	2

the headcount for staffing a line at 100% capacity with staffing requirements for a 73% capacity.

Manufacturing variances. In traditional cost accounting systems, intentionally creating suboptimized resources causes a manufacturing variance to occur. This variance will be an issue each day that customer demand does not require full utilization of a Lean line. Does the occurrence of a variance on a particular day mean that unassigned operators were of no value that day? If these operators had gone to a break room to read a newspaper or watch TV, they of course would have been of no value to the company, but more than likely plenty of other work was available for the unassigned operators on those days when they were not needed on the Lean line. Traditional cost accounting systems consider inventory as an asset on a balance sheet. Traditional cost accounting systems offer no alternative to negative variances except to require direct labor (operators) to continue producing inventory. The performance of most production managers is not measured by inventory levels, so the excess WIP and FGI units created to achieve optimum utilization have no negative impact on a production manager's productivity performance. Producing extra units instead of receiving a manufacturing variance report from the controller's office is naturally the preferred solution for production managers. The materials manager, however, is responsible for the turn rate and is very concerned about achieving *optimum levels* of inventory. Turn rate and productivity are therefore conflicting objectives that separate a materials manager and a production manager. Achieving performance goals are also the source of much daily debate, conflict, and strife between members of these two functional groups.

Productive versus nonproductive work. The Lean operating system encourages operators to become as flexible as possible so they can be assigned to other production lines or participate in nonproduction-related activities such as training, plant maintenance, and participation in kaizen projects when not required to meet the daily demand of the Lean line. For the traditional controller, an operator is productive only when performing the standard work required for manufacturing a product. For Lean managers, operators are productive *whenever* they add value to the company regardless of whether a product is produced or not. Although corporate controllers and production managers choose the traditional productivity measurements of efficiency and utilization to measure their performance, Lean materials management groups choose the benefits of shorter lead time and optimum levels of inventory resulting from *optimum* utilization of the factory floor as a better measure of production performance. Metrics that measure how well customer demand is met are more important to materials and Lean customer service groups. Any production or nonproduction activity that achieves the goals of on-time delivery and quality are more important than a measurement of the utilization of the resources. The conundrum: when operators engage in activities traditionally considered to be nonproductive, questions and the ensuing discussions will continue — is a direct labor employee only productive when producing a product and is performing work other than the production of inventory on a manufacturing line value-adding to the organization? What adds more cost to a product — inventory or underutilized labor? The conflicting objectives of productive and nonproductive work are major challenges to the long-term success of a Lean manufacturing line. To allow the Lean model to become a way of life in a company, attaining agreement and compromise to resolve conflict among the functional organizations of a company is essential.

THE TWO-BIN KANBAN SYSTEM: DESIGN AND OPERATION

The kanban system most familiar to manufacturers is the two-bin material kanban. For replenishment of parts in the two-bin material kanban system, two identical containers are filled with an equal amount of parts. Both containers are placed at the location where the material is used. Material is consumed on a FIFO (first in/first out) basis. The quantity of parts in each container has been calculated to support production for the time required to complete the replenishment cycle of the first container. During a replenishment cycle, empty containers are refilled at predetermined replenishment locations. Individual parts may have multiple usage points as well as replenishment points. The label attached to each container advises material handlers of the consumption point on the Lean line, the replenishment location, and the container's quantity. Container quantities and consumption and replenishment locations must be identified so material handlers can efficiently refill containers with parts that need to be resupplied to the line. Figure 8.2 illustrates the operation of a two-bin kanban system.

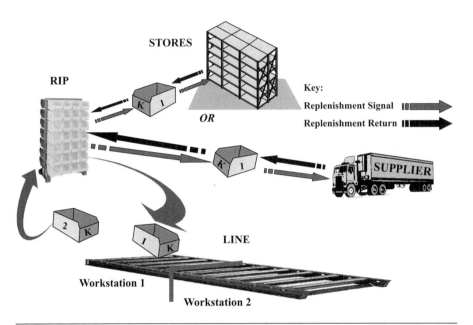

Figure 8.2. Operation of a two-bin material kanban system.

The replenishment cycle. The quantity in each container must be sufficient to supply a consumption point based on the time required to complete a replenishment cycle. Once empty the first container will be refilled. While the first container is being refilled, the second container remains at the workstation providing materials to allow production to continue. Each Takt time, material in the second container is consumed. If the container quantities have been correctly determined — with an amount of inventory equal to the time to perform refill activity — the last part in the second container will be consumed just as the first container is returned from being replenished or before one additional Takt time passes. Signals indicate the need for material replenishment.

The signals. In the two-bin kanban system, a single empty container can signal the need for material replenishment or a single card can be issued to signal the need for material replenishment. When an empty container is used as a signal, the empty container itself serves as the signal that replenishment is required. When a card is used as a signal, instead of an empty container, an identical card attached to each container is issued as the signal that replenishment is required. This system is sometimes known as a *single-card* kanban system because of the card attached to each container used to signal replenishment. In addition to an empty container or a card signaling the need for replenishment of a specific part, anything that indicates the need for replenishment can be a kanban signal, e.g., an empty space on the shop floor that is designated for parts, a flag, an andon light, etc. Other signals may be necessary for extremely large or heavy parts such as cumbersome, unwieldy packing cartons. Although the two-bin kanban system operates exactly the same regardless of the type or size of the signal used, the key for any kanban system is that a signal be generated when replenishment is needed. If the signal is overlooked or ignored, a stock-out situation will occur at the consumption point when the last part in the second container has been consumed.

Raw and In-Process Materials

The initial usage of a part occurs at a workstation where the part is consumed into a manufactured unit of production: the *point of consumption* or *point of usage.* For every point of consumption, there must also be a predetermined location where replenishment parts are stored and retrieved. This is known as the *point of resupply.* One of the most common terms for a point of resupply for line materials is *raw and in-process materials* or RIP. A RIP is the primary replenishment location for the storage of materials used to resupply a Lean line. Another common term used for this point of resupply is *Supermarket.* Supermarket is a descriptive term for a line material replenishment location. Supermarket is also a metaphor for the simplicity of resupplying items used on a day-to-day basis as is done in local supermarkets. Much like a local supermarket, a kanban RIP mantains ample inventories to supply line demands and provides a centralized storage location for a wide variety of items in close proximity to their point of consumption.

For example, rather than keeping a large amount of goods stored in a pantry (the line), a frugal chef is content to let the local supermarket (the RIP) maintain sufficient inventory to supply recipe (product) requirements. When an ingredient is required, the chef makes a short trip to the local supermarket to purchase only what is needed as closely as possible to when it is needed. Ingredients (parts and materials) are kept at a minimum, yet are in close enough proximity to supply the chef's needs on short notice with no inventory investment.

As with a local supermarket, the more frequent replenishment occurs, the smaller the required inventory will need to be. Rapid replenishment of materials causes the turn rate of goods to also be higher. The same dynamic is true in manufacturing. Inventory residing on a line should be rapidly consumed and have a very short replenishment time, resulting in a faster turn rate. RIP inventory quantities are sized so replenishment occurs more infrequently. The use of either *RIP* or *Supermarket* to describe the location of a replenishment inventory is acceptable. RIP, however, is the most frequently used term.

Number of RIP locations. There is no set rule for the number of RIP locations, but having several spread throughout a manufacturing facility is not

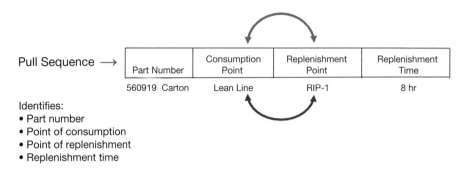

Pull Sequence →

	Consumption Point	Replenishment Point	Replenishment Time
Part Number			
560919 Carton	Lean Line	RIP-1	8 hr

Identifies:
• Part number
• Point of consumption
• Point of replenishment
• Replenishment time

Figure 8.3. Pull sequence for a part illustrating part number, points of consumption and replenishment, and replenishment time.

unusual. The physical location of a RIP resupply point should be located at the shortest possible distance from a point of consumption. Replenishment points in close proximity to points of consumption shorten replenishment cycle times. Because the size of inventory quantities in resupply areas are based on the amount of time required for replenishment, shorter replenishment times mean less inventory. Too many RIP locations can cause a proliferation of the number of pull sequences that must be maintained over time. Managing numerous RIP locations can also cause diminishing returns on the investment of time required to maintain them. The ideal number of RIP locations is based on the total number of parts to be stored, the desired replenishment velocity, and the distance to a point of consumption location in each individual facility. Carefully consider the use of multiple RIP designations.

The Pull Sequence

Each part number selected for inclusion in the kanban system must have all of its individual consumption and replenishment points identified (Figure 8.3). The relationship between a consumption point and a replenishment point in a kanban system must also be identified. This relationship is referred to as a *pull path, pull code, pull sequence,* or *pull link.* An established pull sequence identifies consumption and replenishment locations.

Specific workstation locations for the points of consumption of component materials can be identified using the SWD and based on the standard work assigned to each workstation. Point of resupply information informs the material handler responsible for completing replenishment where to find the replenishment material. In addition to the consumption and resupply points, the amount of elapsed time required to complete the replenishment cycle is also recorded as part of the pull sequence. Replenishment time is the amount of time required for a material handler to receive the signal, travel to the point of resupply, count out the quantity indicated on the kanban container, travel back to the point of consumption, and replace the refilled container on the line. Each time a replenishment time, point of consumption, or point of resupply (RIP) is changed, a new pull sequence must be created.

Pull sequence nomenclature. A point of consumption requires a name designation to be assigned to it. *Line* is a common naming convention for the point of consumption of a part used in a unit of production. *Line* is also used because a particular part is installed into a unit on a Lean *line*. Another common practice is to give the *Line* designation to any other location where a part is consumed with no additional work done to the part, e.g., a feeder process or a service parts center. Using standard nomenclature helps to limit the number of pull sequences created, simplifying the maintenance of pull sequences. Although specific operations or workstations can be identified as separate points of consumption, creating an individual nomenclature for each workstation, combined with their points of replenishment, can create an exponential proliferation of pull linkages. The common name for a consumption point on a Lean line therefore is simply designated *Line*. In a pull sequence where the *Line* signal is replenished at a RIP location, the pull sequence relationship would be stated as *Line/RIP*. Most kanban system users find this generic designation to be sufficient for most applications.

How a RIP resupply works. Using the same two-bin configuration as used for kanban resupply of a line location, a RIP location also contains two equally sized containers with the identical parts as used at the line location. The biggest difference between the *Line* and *RIP* locations is the quantity of parts stored. The RIP location is intentionally sized with larger quantities to reduce the number of replenishment cycles performed by a material handler and to keep sufficient inventory on hand to allow rapid replenishment from a supplier in the event of an unanticipated stock-out condition. Although identified as the point of resupply for a line pull sequence, the RIP is also a point of consumption for inventory consumed to satisfy replenishment on the line. Therefore, a RIP inventory is a consumption point *and* a replenishment point. As with inventory used on the line, a signal for material replenishment of a RIP resupply is generated when the first of the two containers is emptied. As with the line container, the empty RIP container also becomes the kanban signal for RIP replenishment. Using the same rule as for a line kanban, the point of resupply for the RIP location must also identified.

Replenishment of Raw and In-Process Materials

Replenishment of a RIP location can be from a stockroom where purchased materials from suppliers are stored or received directly from suppliers. In the stockroom scenario, purchased materials are delivered to the stockroom by suppliers based on a required due date and in quantities planned by a planning system (MRP) that have been established for the suppliers from forecasted demand requirements. In the second scenario, replenishment of a RIP location is fulfilled directly from a supplier's location. In cases in which suppliers have been certified for reliability of delivery and dependability for quality, the stockroom can be bypassed. Materials can be delivered directly to the RIP point of resupply location. In both of these scenarios, instead of an empty physical container being used as a signal, suppliers as members of the supply chain can be notified of required replenishment by an electronic signal. This signal can take several forms: via the Internet, a smartphone, a fax, or a bar code scan. The signal can also be as simple as a telephone call from a buyer.

Pull Chains

The *pull sequence* identifies the points of usage and resupply for each component material used in the kanban system. The pull sequence has also identified the amount of time required for completing the replenishment cycle. All of this information is placed on a label on each container. When a group of pull sequences describing a series of consumption and resupply points are linked together for one part number, a *pull chain* is created.

A pull chain documents all consumption and resupply points for each individual component identifying the entire supply chain for each item. After the initial line point of consumption into a product being manufactured is consumed, component materials are replenished at a resupply point (e.g., at a RIP). In a pull chain, the RIP location becomes both a point of resupply for the line location and a point of consumption. The pull sequence for the RIP location must identify the location of the point of resupply: either a stockroom or a supplier(s). If a pull chain is extended to include the entire supply chain, additional pull sequences with points of consumption and resupply can be included. Points of consumption and resupply pull sequences can extend all the way back through regional distribution centers and to manufacturers and even to the source of raw materials if desired. A pull chain is a supply chain.

A pull chain must be established for *each* component used in a kanban system. The pull chain therefore identifies the *complete series* of consumption and replenishment point relationships for *each part* managed by the kanban system. In addition to usage and replenishment points, each pull sequence in a pull chain must state the time required to complete one replenishment cycle. For example, a line-to-RIP sequence can be completed very quickly, but the replenishment time for a stockroom or supplier can be longer, stated in days or even weeks. Each pull sequence in a pull chain must therefore state the amount of replenishment time

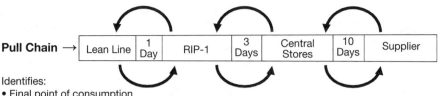

| Pull Chain → | Lean Line | 1 Day | RIP-1 | 3 Days | Central Stores | 10 Days | Supplier |

Identifies:
- Final point of consumption
- Replenishment source back to origin of material
- Total replenishment time

Figure 8.4. Pull chain illustrating total amount of replenishment time for a complete replenishment cycle.

necessary to complete the replenishment cycle for each pull sequence for each part. Figure 8.4 is an example of a pull chain.

Inventory policy. A pull chain is also a statement of inventory policy. Inventory levels for each container are established based on the *amount of time* required to perform the replenishment cycle. When all replenishment times in the pull chain are summed together, the result states the number of days of inventory required to supply that part. The quantity of parts residing in the containers of a pull chain represents the amount of minimum investment that must be maintained to operate the kanban system. To manage the amount of inventory investment kept on the Lean line, the speed of replenishment can be increased or decreased depending on the desired amount of inventory to be maintained: increasing replenishment time *increases* the inventory investment while decreasing replenishment time *reduces* the inventory investment. Because replenishment times have a dramatic effect on inventory quantities and inventory investment, individual pull chains become a statement of inventory policy for each individual part. Inventory investment can therefore be managed by managing the replenishment time of the pull chain. Not all parts are equal. Some are small. Some are more expensive than others. Some are optional. Some are critical to the construction of a product. Some suppliers are unreliable, so buffer inventories of their parts are necessary to ensure supply. Each pull chain replenishment time and the resulting quantities should reflect the desired inventory policy for all variables of all parts. Ultimately, the pull chain is the controller of inventory investment. Pull chain policy is inventory policy.

Decreasing replenishment time will increase the turn rate of parts and reduce inventory investment. At the same time, reduced replenishment time will also increase material handling requirements. Maintaining increased inventories might be desirable to reduce material handling expenses for inexpensive components such as C items. Conversely, frequent replenishment might be more

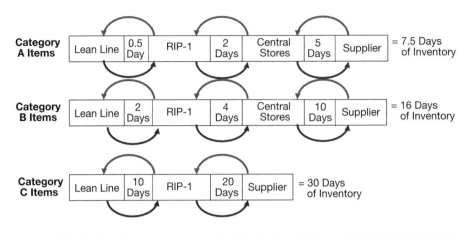

Figure 8.5. A pull chain as a statement of inventory policy.

desirable when maintaining inventories of expensive or fragile components. Manufacturers have many criteria for placing materials into different inventory categories. Each material category should reflect a different investment strategy. Each part category defines the optimum inventory investment strategy when the pull chain has established the total number of replenishment days for each pull sequence of that chain. The greater the sum of replenishment days in a pull chain, the greater the required inventory investment. Figure 8.5 illustrates using a pull chain as a statement of inventory investment.

Using ABC analysis to establish inventory policy. A common technique used extensively by manufacturers for grouping different parts by category is ABC analysis. Lean manufacturing did not invent ABC analysis. ABC analysis has been used to develop different policies for different categories for years. The ABC designation for parts is an excellent way to begin defining categories of inventory investment for a turn rate strategy and assigning pull chains to parts. Parts are assigned an A, B, or C designation based on their cost per unit: an A item is the most costly; a C item is the least costly. Pull chains reflecting a different inventory policy can be assigned to parts based on these ABC classifications. To match the desired inventory investment for expensive parts in the A category, the pull chain for an A item could have less total replenishment days, reflecting a faster turn rate throughout the supply chain and minimizing inventory quantities. Low-cost items assigned C designations (or lower) could have more total replenishment days. The slower replenishment times result in increased investment inventory, but fewer replenishment cycles. The benefit of establishing inventory policy using pull chains is the desired turn rate velocity by part number value is easily controlled by managing the replenishment time of a part.

Limiting the number of pull chains forces parts to be grouped into fewer selected inventory investment classifications. Keeping the number of pull chains to a minimum simplifies management of the kanban system until the optimum inventory turn rate is achieved.

Using Replenishment Time as Inventory Policy

Replenishment time is defined as:

> *The time required to receive the signal (a container), transport the container to a replenishment point, refill the container, and return the container to its assigned location at the consumption point.*

When consumption and replenishment points were established, the time required to physically perform replenishment was also determined. The time required to complete the replenishment cycle was used to determine the amount of inventory remaining in the second container to sustain line production while the first container was being refilled. For example, if V_c is 96 units, shift length is 8 hours (480) minutes, Takt time is 5 minutes, and replenishment time has been determined to be 4 hours (240) minutes, each container will contain 48 pieces of inventory. At a consumption rate of 1 piece every 5 minutes of Takt time, the first container will become empty every 240 minutes or twice per 480-minute day. The kanban system will generate two kanban signals each day: the first at midday; the second at the end of the shift.

Determining inventory investment is simply a matter of multiplying the cost of a material component times the number of pieces of the material in a kanban container. In theory, the only time two full containers are at a point of consumption is on the very first day of system startup. After the first replenishment cycle, only the second container will be at the point of consumption while the first container is being replenished. The second container remains at the workstation point of consumption to support unit production during the replenishment cycle.

We know with a kanban system that the length of replenishment time controls the amount of inventory investment in the system. So if the cost of 48 pieces for a 4-hour replenishment cycle results in more inventory investment than desired, a 2-hour replenishment cycle could be substituted. The full container quantity would then change to 24 pieces and require replenishment every 2 hours (120) minutes. By controlling the cause and effect of replenishment times on inventory investment, the kanban system is used as a *throttle* for achieving turn rate targets. Establishing replenishment times for every consumption point along the length of the supply chain allows inventory investment to become a proactively managed process.

We also know that material handling costs are associated with rapid turn rates. For a container refilled every 4 hours, a single material handler must accomplish a single replenishment cycle every 4 hours. During an 8-hour day, two replenishment cycles will be completed. If that replenishment time is decreased to once every 2 hours, additional replenishment cycles will increase to four replenishment cycles each day. Multiplied times the total number of parts in the kanban system and the number of required replenishment cycles, additional personnel might be necessary to maintain the system. In addition to the cost of additional material handlers, the increased level of physical material handling activity on the shop floor can be significant. An increased velocity of material movement is often associated with increased material handling costs. So a balance must be struck between the amount of material handling and the desired inventory turn rates by making trade-off decisions to balance the costs of inventory investment with material handling.

When establishing a kanban system for the first time, squeezing replenishment times for all items to as small as possible to increase material velocity and reduce inventory investment can be tempting to the materials manager. This strategy, however, has associated handling costs that usually require negotiation and trade-offs. Because of higher cost, it is likely that A items should be replenished more rapidly than C items with lower costs. Achieving optimum balance between inventory investment and material handling costs will frequently require multiple iterations of replenishment times to determine a company's ideal inventory investment strategy.

Container Quantities

The amount of material for each kanban container at each consumption and replenishment point is calculated as:

Daily demand × replenishment time ÷ package size (1) = container quantity

where:

Daily demand. Daily demand is the average daily usage for each part number. Daily rate can be determined by establishing the demand of all parent part numbers using that part and multiplying by the required demand recorded on the BOM:

$$\Sigma \text{ demand} \times [\text{quantity BOM}]$$

This calculation is the product of the MRP system explosion routine for parts quantity requirement generation. Unfortunately, the kanban system cannot predict the future demand of any component part, therefore an historical listing of component parts that have been chosen to participate in the two-bin system can be listed on a spreadsheet program along with historical usage quantities. The out years showing anticipated demand growth can also be listed and tested for future inventory investment. Table 8.3 illustrates a spreadsheet program used to calculate the inventory investment of a kanban strategy.

Replenishment time. Replenishment time is the time required to retrieve the kanban signal (a container), transport the empty container to the replenishment point, refill the container, and return the container to its assigned location at the consumption point. Replenishment time is typically stated in days or a percentage of days: 50% is one half-days' worth of material requiring replenishment twice per day. If daily demand is 100 and replenishment time is stated as 0.5, the quantity of material in the container would be 50 pieces. Replenishment time is 4 hours or one half of an 8 hour shift.

Package size. For most parts, kanban quantities are calculated with a default package quantity of **1**, which will calculate a discrete number based on daily usage and replenishment time. In some cases, however, materials are received from a supplier in packages, e.g., hardware, small parts, partitioned parts, and fragile items. These components are usually items that are difficult to handle on an *each* basis. Because components are supplied with set quantities prepackaged by the supplier, using package size as the denominator in the kanban formula will calculate the number of packages required to cover replenishment time. If no package size is indicated, the default is **1** and a discrete quantity will be calculated. Package sizes are typically used between RIP and stores replenishment points.

Inventory Investment

Once the parts to be included in the kanban system have been identified, and each has been assigned a pull chain establishing the time needed for replenishment, calculating the required amount of inventory and required amount of investment to support that quantity is the first step of managing the inventory to meet turn rate goals and working capital requirements. To make the calculations, a simple computerized program can be used.

To complete the calculations, the standard cost of each component must be recorded along with the pull chain replenishment times assigned to each part number. The quantity of inventory at each point of resupply in the pull chain is determined by multiplying the replenishment time by the daily rate of sales. This calculation is repeated for each replenishment time in the pull chain, e.g., RIPs, stores, and suppliers. The resulting values are summed and then multiplied times the standard cost for the part. This is the cost of the inventory strategy for each individual part number. The grand total cost of all parts is determined by adding

Table 8.3. Spreadsheet Illustrating Calculation of Inventory Investment: Parts, Average Daily Demand Quantities, and Standard Cost

Part Number	Description	Unit of Measure	Standard Cost ($)	Forecasted Daily Requirement	Data Set: 1	Today's Volume 1	2012 2	2013 3	2014 4	Forecasted Monthly Requirement (20 days)
71278501	110" EXT CYL M MH A5	Each	$1662.06	0.063	0.063	0.06	0			
50995003	REPLACED BY50995004	Each	$1625.00	0.038	0.038	0.04	0			
80322	WINCH ASSEMBLY A4	Each	$1595.00	0.038	0.038	0.04	0			
71286201	ATLAS A4H A5 TOPPING	Each	$1534.33	0.025	0.025	0.03	0			
45958	DIGGER DRIVE ASSY A4	Each	$1467.00	0.038	0.038	0.04	0			
71286101	ATLAS TOPPING CYL	Each	$1386.38	0.038	0.038	0.04	0			
70943102	V50C LOWER BOOM CYLINDER	Each	$1299.70	0.011	0.011	0.01	0			
70971302	SATURN LOWER BOOM CYLINDER	Each	$1283.00	0.019	0.019	0.02	0			
71278401	96" EXT CYL A4-A4H	Each	$1279.60	0.063	0.063	0.06	0			
46010	BEARING RING ATLAS	Each	$1205.00	0.063	0.063	006	0			
70741606	CYLINDER, V7-T5 UPPER BOOM	Each	$1200.43	0.024	0.024	0.02	0			
70720205	CYLINDER,T5-V6-V7 LOWER BOOM	Each	$1195.05	0.054	0.054	005	0			
71381602	V50CH UPPER BOOM CYL	Each	$1179.59	0.011	0.011	0.01	0			
71450500	2-3/4 X 96 EXTENSION CYL	Each	$1065.87	0.019	0.019	0.02	0			
70885502	V50C UPPER BOOM CYL G5LB	Each	$1011.40	0.020	0.020	0.02	0			
70720010	V6 UPPER BOOM CYL	Each	$977.00	0.030	0.030	0.03	0			
70716409	V5 UPPER BOOM CYLINDER	Each	$961.41	0.109	0.109	0.11	0			
71298401	GEAR BOX WITH BRAKE	Each	$946.20	0.038	0.038	0.04	0			
46001	V6& TITAN BEARING RING	Each	$92.00	0.054	0.054	0.05	0			
70734308	SATURN UPPER BOOM CYL	Each	$915.10	0.019	0.019	0.02	0			
71320800	GEAR BOX WITHOUT BRAKE	Each	$756.00	0.025	0.025	0.03	0			

the sum of all the totals of all parts together to determine the amount of inventory investment needed to support the strategy identified by the pull sequences. Table 8.4 illustrates a kanban quantity calculator spreadsheet. (Some manufacturers include the process where the part is consumed. They can also include a safety factor, which can be inserted into the calculation to serve as a safety stock by increasing the calculated quantity for each level in the pull chain. Both of these additions are totally optional and are not required to operate a two-bin material kanban system.)

If the resulting grand total reveals an undesirable inventory investment amount, reductions in investment can be made by modifying the replenishment times to shorter, more frequent replenishment. The trade-off for faster replenishment time, however, will be an increase in material handling activity. Individual parts can be reassigned to an existing pull chain reflecting the desired faster replenishment times. If an existing pull chain does not reflect the replenishment speed necessary to provide the desired inventory investment grand total, new pull sequences with shorter replenishment times must be defined.

The day-to-day management of a kanban system requires frequent readjusting of the original pull sequence assignments and replenishment times. New parts will be added, old parts will be phased out with effectivity dating, and parts that vary with seasonality must be managed. Suppliers come and go and kanban strategies change over time. Once the initial kanban strategy has been established, the system will need to be managed every day thereafter. This need for daily management therefore requires hands-on management. A kanban manager position is required once a Lean line begins operation. A computer-based program is also a helpful tool for maintaining a kanban system.

Role of Material Handlers

Like a Lean system, kanban systems are designed to meet the goals and needs of the organization. They rely on the premise that the system is *not* designed to serve an individual agenda. Unless a kanban system is robust, providing service to the organization, its success will be dependent on the last material handler's operation of it. Individuals are promoted, they change jobs, and they retire. Material handlers should therefore be trained to adapt to the operation of the kanban system. To be successful, operation of the system must be disciplined. Material handlers using the system must execute the established rules and procedures of the system. Only then, can these rules reflect the kanban inventory investment policy.

No system is perfect, particularly just after startup. The need for improvement will likely be ad hoc unless there is some formal mechanism for making correction recommendations. A material handler cannot take unilateral actions to change the system according to personal interpretation. If allowed to do so, the

Table 8.4. Spreadsheet Illustrating Kanban Quantities and Inventory Investment

Part Number	Description	Estimated Daily Requirement	Unit of Measurement	Standard Cost	Pull Code	Line Days	Line Qty	Line Exact Qty	RIP Days	RIP Qty	RIP Exact Qty	Stores Days	Stores Qty	Stores Exact Qty	Inventory Extension
71278501	110" EXT CYL M MH A5	2.00	Each	$25.50	A	1	2	2.00	5	10	10.00	10	21	21.00	$841.50
50995003	REPLACED BY50995004	3.00	Each	$47.95	A	1	3	3.00	5	15	15.00	10	32	32.00	$2,397.50
80322	WINCH ASSEMBLY A4	4.00	Each	$249.50	A	1	4	4.00	5	20	20.00	10	42	42.00	$16,467.00
71286201	ATLAS A4H A5 TOPPING	3.00	Each	$28.00	A	1	3	3.00	5	15	15.00	10	32	31.50	$1,400.00
45958	DIGGER DRIVE ASSY A4	0.50	Each	$1467.00	A	1	1	0.50	5	3	2.50	10	6	5.25	$14,670.00
71286101	ATLAS TOPPING CYL	3.00	Each	$97.00	A	1	3	3.00	5	15	15.00	10	32	31.50	$4,850.00
70943102	V50C LOWER BOOM CYLI	4.00	Each	$249.50	A	1	2	2.00	5	10	10.00	10	21	21.00	$8,233.50
70971302	SATURN LOWER BOOM C	4.00	Each	$325.00	A	1	1	1.00	5	5	5.00	10	11	10.50	$5,525.00
71278401	96" EXT CYL A4-A4H	4.00	Each	$175.00	A	1	3	3.00	5	15	15.00	10	32	31.50	$8,750.00
46010	BEARING RING ATLAS	4.00	Each	$89.39	A	1	7	7.00	5	35	35.00	10	74	73.50	$10,369.24
70741606	CYLINDER, V7-T5 UPPER	4.00	Each	$400.00	A	1	4	4.00	5	20	20.00	10	42	42.00	$26,400.00
70720205	CYLINDER,T5-V6-V7 LOWE	4.00	Each	$375.00	A	1	4	4.00	5				42	42.00	$24,750.00
71381602	V50CH UPPER BOOM CYL	2.00	Each	$259.00	A	1	2	2.00	5		*Replenishment Times*		21	21.00	$8,547.00
71450500	2-3/4 X 96 EXTENSION CYL	3.00	Each	$325.00	A	1	3	3.00	5				32	31.50	$16,250.00
70885502	V50C UPPER BOOM CYL G	1.00	Each	$159.99	A	1	1	1.00	5				11	10.50	$2,719.83
70720010	V6 UPPER BOOM CYL	1.00	Each	$175.49	A	1	1	1.00	5	5	5.00	10	11	10.50	$2,983.33
70716409	V5 UPPER BOOM CYLINDE	1.00	Each	$169.99	A	1	1	1.00	5	5	5.00	10	11	10.50	$2,889.83
71298401	GEAR BOX WITH BRAKE	4.00	Each	$249.50	A	1	4	4.00	5	20	20.00	10	42	42.00	$16,467.00
46001	V6& TITAN BEARING RING	3.00	Each	$39.75	A	1	3	3.00	5	15	15.00	10	32	31.50	$1,987.50
70734308	SATURN UPPER BOOM CY	2.00	Each	$249.95	A	1	2	2.00	5	10	10.00	10	21	21.00	$8,248.35
46006	BEARING RING V5	7.00	Each	$49.99	A	1	7	7.00	5	35	35.00	10	74	73.50	$5,798.84
71318000	4 PORT COLLECTOR (PUR	4.00	Each	$139.50	A	1	4	4.00	5	20	20.00	10	42	42.00	$9,207.00

Total Pull Chain Cost $1,999,752.42

Pull Chain A   Line: 1 day → RIP: 56 days → Stores: 10 days system will slowly atrophy into just another informal material handling system with as many methods as there are material handlers. Any improvement process must have structure. A kanban system is no different. Maintaining discipline in the operation of a kanban system adds significant value to a company's product. Capturing good ideas generated by material handlers and implementing them must be done in the context of a kaizen process.

After the initial training of material handlers, the best way to communicate inventory investment decisions to an individual material handler on a day-to-day, hour-by-hour basis is through the labeling of individual kanban containers and cards. Container labels document the decisions made about replenishment time, quantities, and pull sequences. Material handlers are not permitted to unilaterally change these label specifications because a formal procedure is in place to record any changes to a label: unauthorized label changes can impact the inventory investment strategy.

Container labels. Five essential elements of information must be placed on a kanban container label to communicate the inventory policy designed into the kanban system: part number, description, point of consumption, point of replenishment, and container quantity. These five information elements are the minimum requirements. Other optional information items often include a label are bar code, machine cell, machine die, and product grouping for machine setup. If operators and material handlers maintain the integrity of the label elements, along with BOM and item master records maintenance and customer fulfillment goals, desired inventory investment strategies will be achieved. Figure 8.6 illustrates a typical kanban container card.

Establishing Daily Inventory Demand

A common technique for optimizing inventory investment is to review the daily demand quantity used to make kanban calculations. A V_c daily demand quantity has already been established to calculate Takt time and to determine the quantity of manufacturing resources needed to meet that demand. Recall that the Lean line has been designed with a capacity to meet future demand greater than the current demand some 1 to 3 years out. This projected increase in volume could therefore be significantly higher than current demand (e.g., up to 50%) at the time the kanban system becomes operational. Physical inventory and the resulting inventory investment, if sized to meet a future 1- to 3-year demand curve, will be inflated when compared to today's demand. When operating a Lean line, line staffing can simply be reduced to suboptimize output and match daily variations in customer demand. The same, however, cannot be said for inventory management. For inventory, modifying the two-bin kanban system on a daily basis to match changes in customer demand is not practical. Once in place, no mechanism in the

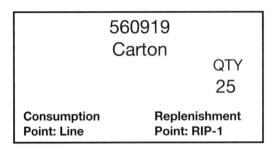

Figure 8.6. Typical kanban container card label illustrating the five essential information elements.

kanban system can respond to daily demand variances. When signals are created as containers are emptied and the quantities in the kanban containers have been sized for a daily demand based on a sales volume that is significantly higher than today's demand, the replenishment quantity will exceed the desired replenishment time. Resulting inventory quantities will then be too large for the current volume and inventory turn rates will be lower than expected.

Determining kanban container size. When designed at the same time as a new Lean factory, a kanban system becomes operational 1 to 3 years before the projected sales volume of factory demand capacity is achieved. To accommodate linear growth in demand volume, the daily demand used for kanban calculations should be modified to reflect the existing sales volume at system startup time. So, if a Lean line has been designed for a future volume of 150 units, but current sales volume is 100, then kanban containers should be initially sized to support a sales volume of 100. If kanban containers are sized to meet a volume of 150 units, replenishment will take 50% longer and material will remain in inventory 50% longer than desired. Excess inventory will have a negative impact on turn rates. Increased costs of inventory must also be reflected in the costs of goods sold, potentially increasing product cost.

Replenishing RIPs. Ideally, the preferred replenishment point for a RIP location is directly from a supplier, but for most manufacturers, the most practical replenishment point is a stockroom. The primary reason a stockroom is preferred over replenishment directly from a supplier is a lack of confidence in the ability of the supplier to reliably deliver products on time while still meeting dependable, repeatable quality criteria. For most manufacturers, meeting quality requirements and on-time delivery dates is just too great a responsibility to leave to a supplier!

Although reliability and dependability concerns do not apply to all suppliers, the fear of shutting down a manufacturing line because of a shortage of purchased materials is one of the main reasons why *just-in-case* inventories are required. If the lack of confidence in on-time supplier delivery dates and quality requirements could be overcome, the amount of purchased materials residing in manufacturing stockrooms could be greatly reduced or even eliminated. Until and unless a long-term reliability and dependability history can be established with suppliers so that deliveries can bypass the stockroom and be made directly into a RIP location, manufacturers must opt for a stockroom. (Establishing reliable delivery and quality criteria with suppliers is the *best* justification for a supplier certification program.)

Supply Chain Management

The two-bin material kanban system can be a model for a supply chain management system. The two-bin kanban system establishes where material is used in manufacturing, where parts are replenished, and if additional replenishment is from a stockroom or a supplier. The initial two-bin system begins with consumption and replenishment points *inside* the four walls of the manufacturing facility. If, however, consumption and replenishment points are extended beyond the four walls of manufacturing to include suppliers and their suppliers, the entire supply chain beginning with the manufacturer and going all the way back to the mining of raw materials can be part of the supply chain model.

Limiting use of the two-bin kanban system to inside the four walls of manufacturing should be the result of a conscious thought process. In the beginning, limiting the process to the factory is a good decision, but as a Lean line becomes more mature, expanding the kanban system beyond the shop floor to include the entire supply chain is a natural progression. The two-bin system then creates a platform for managing materials throughout the entire supply chain. Kanban systems require inventory quantities to be determined by the time required to complete the replenishment cycle from consumption point to resupply point. Replenishment times can range from hours on a line from a RIP to weeks to a stockroom from a supplier located in another country. Careful management of replenishment times can help manage inventory investment. Use suppler certification programs to permit materials to go directly into a RIP on the shop floor instead of needing to be received, inspected, tested, moved, and stored to and from a stockroom, thereby shortening the replenishment times and storage points for inventory. Manage pull chains to reduce the number of supply points where materials are stored. Use the kaizen process to reduce replenishment times.

Electronic management of the supply chain. Kanban signals do not have to be written on the label of a container. The signal can come from other devices: a bar code reader, email, Twitter, or even a fax or telephone call. The critical

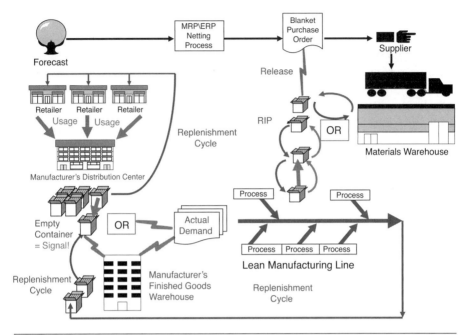

Figure 8.7. Complete supply chain from end customer, to factory, to supplier.

thing is that a signal is generated. The two-bin system can be greatly enhanced by electronic communication devices. Electronic communication transmits information at the speed of light, reducing the transit time needed for receiving a physical kanban signal. A system, however, must be in place to ensure that the information is correct. The two-bin kanban system is the platform for making e-commerce transactions accurate and meaningful for a manufacturer and point of resupply suppliers. Electronic communication-based material kanban systems generate material replenishment signals only in response to real consumption instead of unreliable forecasts of future demand. At manufacturers, balanced and linked manufacturing processes are capable of producing products one at a time in their true manufacturing lead time. Figure 8.7 illustrates a complete supply chain: from the end customer, upstream through the factory, ending at the supplier. The kanban system establishes the series of signals to replenish inventory at the same rate as inventory is consumed.

Without a kanban platform in place, what is the basis for supplier transactions in a suply chain management program? Is it the output of an MRP action item report transmitted at the speed of light only to be retransmitted after the next iteration of an explosion of the MRP? How many cycles of changed purchase order due dates and quantities transmitted at the speed of light would it take before suppliers announced the end of their participation in an MRP experiment? After a time, suppliers would just determine the order replenishment times and quantities based on past history, not on what a purchase order or MRP output recommends.

THE ADVANTAGES OF USING A TWO-BIN KANBAN SYSTEM

Implementing and operating a two-bin material kanban system has numerous advantages:

- No reliance on issuance of a pick list or kit build list to a stockroom to produce a product
- Component materials stored at the workstation point of consumption
- No allocation of materials to an individual production order
- Rapid response to expedited customer demand
- No batch-based system requirement for multiple products be built at the same time in individual departments
- One-product-at-a-time manufacturing at an individual workstation

Inventory maintenance. With a kanban system, the goal is achieving and maintaining a rapid inventory turn rate. Just as with traditional planning systems, the kanban system also requires a high level of inventory accuracy. Inventory must still be accounted for in the two-bin kanban system, but fewer time-consuming transactions are required to maintain inventory accuracy. The first replenishment cycle in the pull chain from a line to a RIP does not even require an inventory transaction (because a rapid turn rate is the goal of line replenishment, stopping to complete a transaction only slows the process). Incoming materials for stockroom and RIP locations, however, *do* require material transfer transactions. Upon receipt of material from a supplier into a stockroom, a *receiving* transaction must be recorded. The RIP location in a manufacturing area and the containers being replenished into the RIP location must also have *receiving* transactions. A normal stock status report from the planning system treats a RIP location as just other type of stock location.

Once material is introduced into a RIP location on the shop floor, it can be consumed in only two ways: as a component in a finished product or as scrap.

As a component. When material is consumed as a component into a finished product, this material must be relieved from the RIP location once the product is packed off the end of the Lean line. Although a single transaction could be recorded for each part number consumed, a more common technique is to use a *backflush* transaction. A backflush transaction *increments* one completed SKU to FGI and *decrements* the WIP inventory (the RIP location) by 1 times (1 ×) the quantity in the BOM. A backflush transaction occurs after all standard work to build a product has been completed and all required materials have been consumed into an end item. For a backflushing transaction to be effective and to maintain a high-integrity WIP inventory, the BOM must be extremely accurate. Errors in BOMs are a primary cause of blackflush errors and inaccurate WIP inventories. Inaccuracies in BOMs result from parts being consumed that were not included in the BOM; parts being listed on the BOM that were not used to manufacture the product; or inaccurate reporting of quantities of material being used. Errors also occur when an operator makes an unauthorized substitution on a Lean line. (If a correct material has been exhausted, and a substitution must be made, the substitution must be approved by the Lean line team lead. Then the kanban system must be updated to record the substitution.)

As scrap. When material is consumed as scrap, the scrap reporting system must be kept current to be accurate. If an MRB process (material review board) is in place, reconcile scrap each day so that an operator at the location where the scrap occurred can provide reasons/solutions for why the scrap occurred. Reconciliation done less frequently sacrifices the ability of management to determine the causes of scrap and to resolve quality or balance issues permanently.

A Simple Physical Signal

We know that the key to a successful kanban system is the presence of a signal. Whether an empty container, a card, or an empty space on the shop floor, the replenishment signal is *physical* — it is a visible, tangible object and therefore difficult to ignore when seen or received. The empty container or the card simply says that more material is needed.

The replenishment signal is nonjudgmental. No interpretation of a report (computer or otherwise) is necessary. No investigation is necessary. No shortage lists or stock status reports are required. No training is required to research a stock-out condition at a point of replenishment. The signal simply requires that replenishment be in the quantity specified and that it occur in the stated replenishment time. The critical issues of material replenishment have been predetermined by the pull sequence, replenishment times, and the resulting calculations of the kanban system. Priorities for refilling material containers are always on a FIFO basis.

Production Flexibility: Maximum Variety Each Day

We know that MRP systems are order-based systems and must follow procedures designed to maintain and operate the system. Once a production order is designated as *released* to the shop floor, manufacturing resources are committed to the production of that product. The issuance of a released production order causes several activities to occur:

- When the planning system completes the BOM explosion process and recommendations for manufacturing are generated, a released production order is created.
- The order status in the planning system then changes from planned to firm planned to released. Once an order is released, manufacturing is committed to producing the product and purchasing is committed to purchasing materials.
- The shop order indicates the product to be produced, the time-phased due and start dates at each department, and the quantity to be produced.
- Component parts required for manufacturing the product must be issued from a stockroom and documented on a pick list. Once the required parts are pulled from the stockroom and issued to the shop floor, the MRP system requires an inventory transaction to change the location of the part from a stockroom to a WIP location. Barring changes in the due date, quantity, or the item to be produced, component materials stay with the order (allocated) throughout the manufacturing process.
- Changes to a released production order, e.g., the due date, quantity, or the item to be produced; a customer cancellation; the demand forecast; the priority of released orders; the need to expedite an order; a shortage of purchased materials; delays in order startups; or the need to group orders out of sequence to achieve utilization goals require informing the planning system so that the next net requirements iteration (explosion) is accurate.

In an order-based system, constant feedback to the planning system is required to update the status of released orders already on the shop floor. Sometimes the changes are so frequent that the majority of the daily activity of a planner is dedicated to maintaining the changes and the resulting feedback to the planning system. At times an expeditor is assigned full time to deal with the magnitude of daily changes.

Updating a planning system with date and quantity changes and cancellations is easily done with a computer at the speed of light. The same cannot be said for changes to issued parts that are physically allocated to a production order in a WIP inventory on the shop floor. Each time a released production order is changed, the parts allocated to the production order must also be changed, which requires physical activity by a person that cannot be done just sitting at a keyboard. Regardless of the change, material handlers must be mobilized to make changes to the parts and material residing on the shop floor. All of this activity is geared toward keeping the order system data accurate for the next MRP iteration. Depending on the volume of changes, updates to production orders may even become delinquent. How much value is added to the product if the changes to the *form, fit, or function* are zero? Administrative costs add no value to the product.

A kanban system in combination with a flexible manufacturing line provides maximum flexibility in meeting customer demand. A Lean manufacturing line does not require scheduling changes to facilitate changes in manufacturing priority. Changing the sequence is all that is required. In addition, the kanban system is not constrained by the need to update and rearrange the parts allocated to individual production orders. Kanban parts located at a workstation are available for use on any product being produced in the workstation. Last-minute changes from customers are easy to respond to on a Lean line.

Kanban management of materials. Component parts selected for inclusion in the initial kanban system have already been determined by using the 80/20 rule: 80% of total sales revenue is generated by the top-selling 20% of SKUs. The parts needed to manufacture the 20% of SKUs therefore dictate the minimum stock-keeping level for materials in a kanban system. By having the component parts available to produce the top-selling 20% of product models every day, the ability to meet customer demand for the 80% of total sales revenue every day within standard lead time is assured. (Obviously, this 20% should mirror the 20% of products chosen for design of the Lean manufacturing line.) Not all parts in the item master, however, are good candidates for a kanban system. Some are better handled on an exception basis. Exception parts are not usually a factor in the total inventory management of parts.

Demand strategy considerations for parts. Having the capability to produce more than the 20% of product models that exceed the 80% sales revenue level is strictly a financial decision. Making this type of strategic decision always requires a trade-off. If the sales strategy is for manufacturing to be more flexible so that customer demand in customer-quoted lead time beyond the 20% level of SKUs can be met, then the cost for keeping materials on hand to produce those products will increase incrementally. Having an ability to respond more quickly to highly configured customer demand beyond the original 20% of SKUs might be an effective strategy to capture market share, but this ability requires higher inventory investment and incurs greater risk of having slow-moving and obsolescent parts and infrequent demand for some products. Because having an ability to respond faster than a competitor in response to changing customer demand is a strategy for increasing market share, ownership of those inventories purchased to support the strategy should therefore be the responsibility of sales and marketing.

Manufacturing should only have responsibility for meeting demand within the standard lead times for a basic mix/volume of 20% of the company's products.

When part strategies conflict. If marketing's strategy is to be "all things to all customers all the time," then every possible product permutation in the customer catalog must be available for delivery within the customer-quoted lead time. Adopting this strategy also means that all possible component parts, in sufficient quantities, must be available at all times for manufacturing of any product model whenever a customer orders one — an unrealistic, extremely expensive inventory investment policy for any company. In addition to the impracticality of such a customer fulfillment policy, this strategy results in conflicting objectives between sales and marketing and manufacturing:

- Revenue volume is the measurement for sales and marketing, but inventory turn rate efficiency (materials management) is the measurement for manufacturing.
- "All things to all customers all the time" with delivery in the standard lead times are desired expectations of the sales and marketing organization, but a material policy based on the 80/20 rule and relying on suppliers to furnish unique components for special customer orders are expectations of the manufacturing organization.

This performance dichotomy is the primary source of disagreement between the sales and marketing and the manufacturing organizations. Loss of sales is often blamed on the manufacturing organization when the production of products beyond the 20% product model parameter exceeds the standard lead time. Yet, component materials purchased in anticipation of a customer-promised order that never materialized, resulting in slow-moving parts' inventories or obsolescence, are blamed on the sales and marketing organization. Which organization should be responsible for material components that are not used or sold? Should manufacturing be held accountable for missed inventory turn rate goals?

Determining a strategy for parts. The best strategy is to reach a compromise between the sales and marketing and manufacturing organizations. The two groups must reach an agreement on what product mix constitutes the 20% of total product models that represent 80% of sales revenue. This product mix will be identified as *standard models.* Manufacturing must then agree to deliver these standard mix products within their standard lead times. A second customer service policy will be necessary for products outside the 20% standard product mix: lead time policy for products outside the 20% agreement will now be standard lead time *plus* the supplier lead time required to purchase specialized component materials. If sales and marketing decides to maintain a parts inventory to produce special products beyond the 20% standard so that delivery can be made in the standard lead time, then the sales and marketing group will be responsible for the increased inventory investment in those component materials. The cost of maintaining these excess components will therefore not be factored into the turn rate calculation for the manufacturing group's performance measurement.

Kanban management of parts on the line. In the kanban system, once parts have been selected and placed on the line at a designated workstation, these parts are available for any product that arrives at the workstation. Kanban parts are not allocated to a designated SKU or shop order. They can be used on any product at any time to meet customer demand. Customer-expedited end items can be introduced onto the line at anytime simply by changing the sequence of production. Part changes are easily accommodated without providing feedback about those changes to released-orders in the planning system. Parts do not need to be deallocated or reallocated to separate production orders. The need for expeditors is greatly diminished. Having this flexibility on any given day offers a tremendous ability to manufacturers who have a goal of meeting customer demand in shorter response time.

Simplified Inventory Turn Rate Management

Once a part number has been selected to be managed in a kanban system, a pull chain must be assigned to the part. The pull chain must contain a series of linked pull sequences that define all the consumption points and replenishment points for the material. The pull chain also defines the time required to complete each replenishment cycle. The kanban system then uses the pull chain to establish the inventory policy for each individual part based on the sum of the replenishment times for the part for each pull sequence.

Management of inventory turn rates and investment strategies with a material kanban system is simple. The pull chain is the statement of inventory policy. The pull chain determines the amount of inventory that must be maintained to supply the kanban system. The quantities of inventory needed and the resulting working capital investment are based on the number of days of replenishment that have been assigned to an individual part: increased time for replenishment increases inventory amounts and inventory investment accordingly. Managing the length of the replenishment time designated for a part therefore controls inventory investment. Once a kanban system has been installed, managing inventory investment is as simple as managing replenishment time. Focus kaizen activities for a kanban system on ways to reduce replenishment times. Reductions in replenishment time equate to reduction in inventory investment.

Simplified Inventory Maintenance Management

Inventory accuracy requirements for a kanban system are as important as the requirements for any other inventory control system. A kanban system, however, requires fewer inventory transactions. The system maintenance transactions normally required for upkeep of the inventory for the real-time environment of a shop floor are reduced. Reduced material input and output transactions result in on-hand inventories being more accurate. Unless mandated by regulation, cycle counting activities and large physical inventories can often be reduced or eliminated.

Management of inventory with a kanban system is a simple matter. The pull chain designates the inventory accounts needed to be maintained for the kanban system. The *Line* inventory and the *RIP* (or *Supermarket*) inventories reside within the WIP inventory location. *Stores* material is maintained in a stockroom. In a kanban system, the only time an inventory transaction is necessary is when material is received into a *RIP* (*Supermarket*), *Stores*, or from a *Supplier*. To encourage rapid turn rates and high velocity, *Line* to *RIP* inventory transactions are not required. By design, this cycle of consumption and replenishment should happen at a very rapid pace. If the kanban replenishment time of the pull chain is sized at a 1-day amount of demand, the replenishment cycle will occur once a day. Recall that the quantity in the kanban container is determined by multiplying the daily demand times the replenishment time.

If completing a transaction for each part number for each cycle from *Line* to *RIP* for a day of demand were required, the number of transactions per day would be equal to the number of part numbers kept at the line location. If a transaction were necessary for replenishment of every part replenishment, rapid turn rates and high-velocity inventory turns would be discouraged. In most instances, these transactions are unnecessary. They also increase overhead expenses and the chance for errors. By simply increasing the number of days of demand kept at a line location, the longer replenishment times will cause signals to occur less frequently: more inventory = less frequent replenishment signals = fewer replenishment cycles.

A typical scenario. If the replenishment time of a RIP container is sized to hold 3 days of daily demand, 3 days of *Line/RIP* replenishment cycles will be supported before the first RIP container becomes empty. Once emptied, this first RIP container becomes a signal for replenishment from the supplier or stockroom. Line production will continue and the *Line/RIP* replenishment cycle will be supported because the second container at the RIP location contains enough material to sustain another 3 days of daily demand before becoming empty. The first RIP container, however, must be replenished and returned to the RIP location *before* 3 days have passed. Depending on the days of inventory sized at the RIP location, the number of transactions is dependent on the number of parts in the RIP location. If sized at 3 days, each part number must be transacted every third day. If sized at 5 days, transactions for each part number will occur every fifth day, and so on. As with Line inventory, more inventory = less frequent replenishment signals = fewer inventory transfer transactions.

A RIP location is usually replenished from one of two designated replenishment points: a stockroom or a supplier. Both of these points are typically located away from the manufacturing shop floor. Even if located adjacent to manufacturing, manufacturing rarely has control of a stockroom. Stockroom material is usually the responsibility of the materials group. The kanban system acknowledges this ownership. Barring an emergency requisition process (e.g., by a second shift), materials stored in a stockroom are commonly unavailable to manufacturing without a requisition. Once an empty RIP container is returned to the stockroom and refilled, a transaction is necessary to decrease the on-hand inventory from the stockroom while increasing the WIP inventory at the RIP location. This transaction routine is also required when the RIP location is replenished directly from a supplier.

Invisible Material Shortages on the Production Line

Part shortages can be a major problem for a manufacturer. The reasons for part shortages are as numerous as there are part numbers: BOM errors, lack of inventory accuracy, late suppliers, faulty part quality, lack of required inventory transactions, unreported scrap, part hoarding, and lack of timely file maintenance. When a part shortage occurs, *expedite* is the word of the day and everyone becomes a firefighter.

After a part shortage, valiant efforts are made to avoid a shortage from ever occurring again. Alternate supplier programs are initiated, with suppliers lined up three and four deep. Parts for orders are staged ahead of production and locked away. Stockrooms become fortresses that are locked to discourage unreported usage. Safety stock procedures are developed and put in place. Planners squirrel away caches of hidden parts even though safety stock inventories are doubling and quadrupling. MRP systems are blamed and said to be invalid. Manufacturing no longer trusts materials management and materials management no longer trusts manufacturing. Gamesmanship and deception become the rule of the day. Fingers are pointed and distrust reigns.

No materials management system in the world can overcome the things that can happen on the shop floor and in administrative offices or predict and overcome the problems responsible for material shortages. Even a kanban system cannot. The kanban system can, however, keep shortages invisible to the

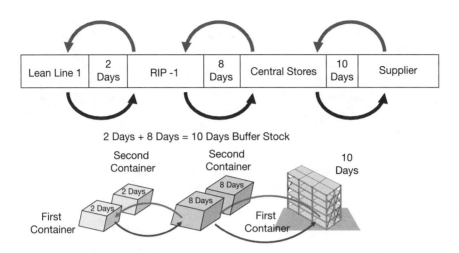

Figure 8.8. Pull chain for a line-to-RIP replenishment cycle with RIP inventory as a buffer for protection against line shortages.

line consumption point, which provides an opportunity for the shortage to be resolved prior to line stoppage by the persons responsible for shortage resolution. This invisibility is accomplished by using a RIP inventory as a safety stock point.

Follow the pull chain illustrated in Figure 8.8: the line-to-RIP replenishment cycle occurs four times before the first RIP container becomes empty. The kanban pull sequence for the RIP container indicates that the replenishment point is *Central Stores*. Based on supplier lead time, there should be 10 days of the required part number in the *Central Stores* stockroom. If for some unknown reason, when attempting to refill the RIP container, no parts are available, there will be a part shortage — even using a kanban system. Any event that caused the shortage is not corrected by the kanban system. The kanban system cannot compensate for BOM errors, poor inventory accuracy, late suppliers, faulty quality, untimely transactions, unreported scrap, hoarding, or poor file maintenance.

In a traditional planning system, all parts in a stockroom must reach a zero inventory level or be consumed at a consumption point or by a kit list before the existence of a shortage is ever discovered. As illustrated in Figure 8.9, in a Lean operating system, a shortage still exists, but the kanban system reveals the shortage first in the stockroom instead of at the *Line* consumption point. Because of line and RIP buffer stocks, manufacturing can continue to produce products at the line location and be oblivious to the shortage that has occurred in the stockroom. The parts at the line location will sustain consumption for 2 to 4 more days before a zero inventory level is reached. The second full container that has been replenished from the RIP can be combined with the parts remaining in the

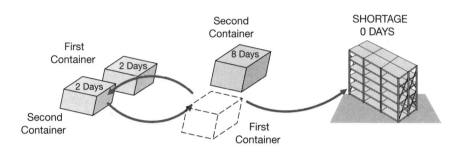

Figure 8.9. Parts shortage revealed by kanban system in stockroom rather than at a line consumption point.

container currently being consumed (0 to 2 days), which allows time for problem resolution of the parts shortage in the stockroom while manufacturing continues to produce products.

At the RIP location, the second container with an 8-day supply can replenish the line containers for four more cycles. If the first RIP container, now residing in *Central Stores* as a physical reminder of the shortage is not replenished from a supplier to the stockroom before 10 to 12 days has passed, the fourth and final cycle from *Line* to *RIP* will occur and cause a line stoppage because of the lack of parts for any product using that part. Although the chance for a stock-out at a line consumption point is always possible, at least 10 to 12 days of inventory are on the line and in the RIP to serve as a buffer inventory and sustain production while resolution of the shortage occurs.

A kanban system cannot eliminate the causes of shortages. Instead, the kanban system concentrates on resolution of shortages by the most appropriate organizational entity — the materials management group. To resolve or eliminate the cause of a shortage, the materials management group must have the necessary information to investigate the root cause of a shortage; to document the frequency of occurrence; and to develop a long-term solution to avoid repetition in the future. A kaizen project (including a Pareto analysis) can help to focus materials management efforts on solving the root causes of shortages. In the meantime, the manufacturing group should concentrate on producing products, not pursuing the resolution of material shortages.

Is RIP inventory necessary? Sometimes, manufacturers implementing a kanban system question the need to have a RIP inventory. A RIP inventory requires a footprint on the shop floor. A RIP is an inventory investment that must be managed. The costs of maintaining a RIP inventory must be weighed against the benefits of maintaining one. If eliminating line stoppages because of material shortages is an important goal, but avoiding the inventory investment costs of

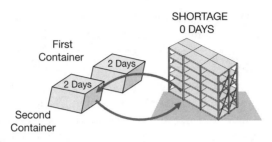

Figure 8.10. Kanban system without a RIP safety stock buffer.

maintaining a RIP is *more* important, implement the kanban system without a RIP inventory (Figure 8.10). It's a simple business decision.

If no RIP inventory is maintained and a line kanban signal is generated, the signal must return directly to the stockroom for replenishment. If as before, if no inventory is available to replenish the line container, how many days can production continue before a line stoppage occurs? With a 2-day replenishment time, remaining parts at the line location should be able to sustain line consumption for a maximum of 2 to 4 days, depending on the timing of the replenishment of the first container. Without an intermediate RIP inventory location, only one line container quantity separates the production line from shutting down due to a part shortage: inventory throughout the system has been exhausted except for one single line container. If achieving resolution of the shortage is possible in 2 to 4 days, and before the line must be shut down, having no RIP point of resupply may be a workable strategy.

Conversely, if short-term shortages are commonplace and frequent, what are the costs of constant stockroom shortages? What is the effect on supplier/buyer relationships? What are the costs of premium transportation charges for overnight shipping of parts? What is the effect on planners who operate in a constant expediting environment? What are the costs of panic responses to shortages and the resulting possibility of line stoppages compared to the cost of having a proactive solution? What is the cost of a line stoppage? Heroic expediting efforts and the electricity associated with crisis resolution may be exciting for some, but are the costs to the quality of life for everyone else worth all the excitement?

Replenishment cycles: the dual role of a RIP. In material replenishment cycles, a RIP location has a dual role: as a safety stock inventory and as an early warning system for potential stock-out situations. The early warning system allows sufficient time for the materials management group to respond to a parts shortage before it stops production. Instead of holding quantities in inventory based on percentages of past usage and projections of variable customer demand, replenishment of a RIP safety stock is based on the actual usage of materials and triggered by an empty container as a signal. Instead of being based on some arbitrary quantity or percentage attached to an MRP order action report as the safety stock, the RIP quantity is based on the time required to replenish the material and replenishment frequency is dependent on consumption rate. To allow the time necessary for resolution of shortages at a RIP location, keep on hand the number of days of replenishment time necessary to permit receipt of expedited shipments from suppliers once shortages are detected in the stockroom, e.g., for a suppler with an emergency lead time of 10 days, RIP replenishment time should be 10 days. When the first RIP container is sent for resupply at the stockroom and no material is available, 10 ten days of inventory must be available in the RIP location for use until material can be received from the supplier.

Inventory investment management strategies: the kanban system. A kanban system provides a buffer inventory designed to reduce or eliminate material shortages on a Lean line. Having a safety stock inventory provides an early warning system of stock-outs. Both require inventory investment costs (kanban = inventory = capital), but material shortages also have costs. Reacting to material shortages after they happen creates chaos. Which cost is preferable? By managing the kanban system, achieving reduced inventory investment goals is still possible. For example, using a pull chain with 2 days of *Line* materials, 8 days of *RIP*, and 10 days of *Central Stores* (stockroom), with 20 total days of inventory, based on a 250-day work year, the turn rate will be slightly over 12 turns (250 days ÷ 20 days = 12.5 turns). If the *Line* inventory is reduced to replenishment once per day and the RIP is reduced to replenishment every 5 days, with the stockroom remaining at 10 days, the total days of inventory will be 16 and the turn rate will increase to over 15 turns (250 days ÷ 16 days = 15.6 turns). In this scenario, the trade-off for a higher velocity of material turn rates with more frequent replenishment times will be an increase in the amount of material handling. The decision as to which is most desirable for the company is the responsibility of the management team. Managing the kanban inventory provides the most proactive solution.

With any inventory strategy, there is always a cost/benefit trade-off. Maintaining an inventory has associated costs, but if the inventory is a critical component, whether costly or not, the expense associated with maintaining the inventory might be considered an appropriate investment to ensure that a stockout does not occur. Maintaining a RIP inventory can be a controlled, proactive, safety stock policy if sized to realistic expectations for emergency replenishment from a supplier. Compare the costs of maintaining the continuity of an operating production line to the costs of expediting parts or shutting down a line.

THE MULTIPLE-CARD KANBAN SYSTEM

Operation of a multiple-card kanban system in manufacturing is similar to the operation of a single-card kanban system (two-bin) in that when a container is emptied at a point of consumption on the shop floor, a signal is generated. Unlike the two-bin system, however, the multiple-card system does not use an empty container as a replenishment signal. Although replenishment materials for a two-bin kanban system and a multiple-card kanban system are similarly maintained in a RIP location in containers, the container itself has no significance in the multiple-card kanban system. In the multiple-card kanban system, containers kept in the RIP for replenishment are based on the quantity calculated to overcome the variables in the *run-to-recovery* time at an independent cell (a machine, fabrication area, remote process, or subcontracted process). An independent cell operates in isolation not linked to any upstream or downstream process. Once empty, a container will be returned to a fabrication area to be used for any non-specific type of production material.

The Move card. In the multiple-card system, the container being used at the point of consumption has a card attached that is removed when material in the container has been consumed at a Lean line location and the container is now empty. The card removed from the container becomes the replenishment signal from the consumption point to the RIP. This card, known as a *Move* card, is the authorization to move material from the RIP stockroom where components are stored to the Lean line point of consumption. Once the move from the RIP to the line has been completed, the *Move* card that was removed from the empty container is reattached to the new container and moved back to the point of consumption on the Lean line. There is only one *Move* card: it's reused each time the replenishment cycle from the RIP to the line is completed.

The Produce card. In the RIP storage location, a second card, known as a *Produce* card, is attached to each stored container. In addition to the five essential information elements required for a kanban card, a *Produce* card has an additional element. A *Produce* card indicates how many cards must be accumulated before a replenishment signal is generated to authorize setup and run in a fabrication or machine cell. This information is stated as **1 of** ___ on the *Produce* card. A single *Produce* card removed from a replenishment container represents one of a predetermined number of cards that when summed are equal to the authorization required to commence production of more parts. All of the *Produce* cards equal to a signal must be accumulated at the designated collection point before replenishment activity may begin. When a new, full container of parts is pulled to the point of consumption, the *Produce* card attached to the container at the RIP location is removed and replaced with the single reusable *Move* card. The *Move* card is reattached to each new full container of parts when it is pulled to the point of consumption. After the *Produce* card has been removed from the container, it is sent to the point of replenishment: a machine, a machine cell, or a remote location. After each line-to-storage replenishment cycle is completed, *Produce* cards are sent to the point of replenishment where they accumulate until there are enough cards to generate a kanban signal.

In an Independent Cell

A multiple-card kanban system is frequently used when manufacturing/fabricating processes must be shared by multiple production areas or in an independent cell where expensive machines with long setup times cause long replenishment times. An independent cell may also include remotely located or subcontracted processes (e.g., plating process). Determining the replenishment time for a shared machine cell or a remote resupply point process is not as simple as counting out a quantity into an empty container at a RIP location. Replenishment time for a component manufactured in a machine cell may include many more variables than just the time necessary to go to the point of resupply, count out the materials into a container, and return to the point of consumption. In addition to travel time, critical replenishment time variables in a shared cell may include existing machine utilization, setup time for the cell, machine cycle time for the item, the number of parts sourced at the machine cell, and wait time at the machine. The time required for setup, run, and travel is known as *run-to-recovery time*. Replenishment quantities from an independent cell must therefore be sized large enough to overcome these variables: they must allow the manufacturing group to continue producing products during run-to-recovery time at the machine cell. Fabricated parts may also be large. Because of the size of fabricated parts and the larger run-to-recovery quantities, multiple containers are frequently required at a RIP location to store sufficient parts to cover the run-to-recovery time of a machine cell.

The multiple-card kanban system is a variation of the two-bin single-card kanban system. Like the two-bin single-card kanban system, each container has a kanban card attached. Just as with the two-bin single-card kanban system, the multiple-card kanban system requires a signal to authorize replenishment with quantities that are based on the amount of replenishment time necessary to refill a container. A secondary inventory also supplies the Lean production line while replenishment takes place. Unlike the two-bin single-card kanban system, instead of a single card (or empty container) creating a signal, the multiple-card system requires the collection of a predetermined amount of individual cards before a replenishment signal is created. Once the predetermined number of cards has been collected, the *total* of these cards creates the replenishment signal. The multiple cards required to trigger a replenishment signal are the source of the term *multiple-card system*.

If a replenishment quantity will not fit into a single container, multiple storage containers will be necessary. For each container required to store the replenishment quantity, a *Produce* card is attached. Unlike the two-bin single-card kanban system in which a single empty container creates a signal, the multiple-card kanban system requires multiple containers to be emptied before a signal is generated. As each container is emptied, the attached card (a *Produce* card) is removed and returned to the point of replenishment. Once the predetermined number of containers has been emptied and the corresponding quantity of *Produce* cards has been collected at the point of replenishment to match the run-to-recovery time, the kanban replenishment signal will be generated.

A machine cell, group of machines, or remote location is usually capable of producing a wide variety of parts. Multiple kanban signals indicating the need to replenish individual part numbers can be received throughout the day from various areas in the manufacturing facility as well as from the Lean manufacturing line. A machine operator or technician working at a remotely located replenishment point therefore has to make several critical decisions each day: what is the correct priority of the components to be produced today; when should the next changeover begin; and how many components must be produced once the changeover is completed? The multiple-card system along with a WAIT/WORK sequencing board can supply the answers to all of these questions.

Determining the production priority of parts in a machine cell or remote location requires the same discipline as determining production priority on a Lean line: it's based on replacing parts in the same sequence in which the materials were consumed and the kanban signals have been received. Prioritizing parts replenishment in a machine cell follows the same FIFO regimen as prioritizing production on a Lean manufacturing line. The FIFO methodology of the kanban system is an ideal priority-setting mechanism for a machine, a machine cell, or a remote location.

For a multiple-card system to operate properly, individual cards must be accumulated at a central collection point as they are removed from empty containers. The best location for a central card collection point is at a machine or in the machine cell where fabrication of a component takes place. Figure 8.11 illustrates a multiple-card kanban system. The WAIT/WORK sequencing board is the collection point for *Produce* cards.

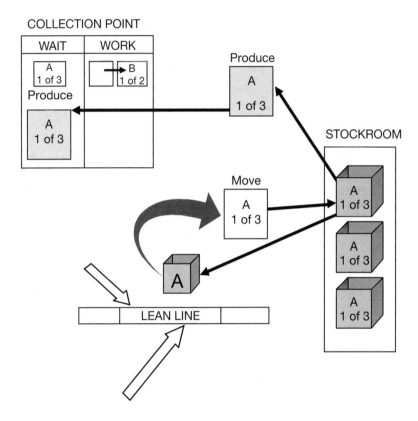

COLLECTION POINT

Figure 8.11. A WAIT/WORK sequencing board and operation of a multiple-card kanban system.

WAIT/WORK sequencing boards. A WAIT/WORK board is a simple board that has been divided vertically down the middle. The word **WAIT** is printed at the top of the board on the left side of the dividing line. The word **WORK** is printed on the right side. Each side of the board has pegs, clips, or hooks to hold *Produce* cards that have been returned from a material replenishment location (RIP). *Produce* cards returning from the RIP location are collected on the **WAIT** side of the board placed randomly and sorted by part number on a separate peg, clip, or hook. *Produce* cards received from throughout the facility are accumulated for each part number until the predetermined number of *Produce* cards has been collected. The predetermined number of cards required to create a signal is recorded on each *Produce* card. If the predetermined quantity of cards is four, the

Produce card will state **1 of 4**. Each card is notated as **1** in a series of cards. The number **4** indicates the predetermined number of cards that must be accumulated on the **WAIT** side of the sequencing board before a kanban signal is created. When the predetermined number of cards has been collected, the complete set of *Produce* cards is transferred to the **WORK** side of the WAIT/WORK sequencing board to become the official kanban signal. This official kanban signal authorizes a setup to be performed in the FIFO sequence in which the *Produce* cards were received and the sum of the quantities on the *Produce* cards for that part to be produced. Once the setup is completed and production is started, the run quantity will be the quantity required to refill the four containers.

When the required number of *Produce* cards has been accumulated, and the card set is moved to the **WORK** side of the sequencing board, random location of the *Produce* cards is no longer allowed. Pegs, clips, or hooks on the **WORK** side are numbered from left to right, top to bottom. *Produce* card sets must be placed sequentially from left to right on the **WORK** side of the board to indicate the order in which the kanban signal was received. Following the left-to-right protocol ensures that parts are replenished in the same FIFO priority sequence in which they were used at the point of consumption.

Establishing Kanban Quantities and the Number of Cards

In the multiple-card system, the kanban signal is determined by the number of *Produce* cards that represents the quantities of materials (and the number of containers) required to cover the run-to-recovery time of a machine, an independent machine, or a remote location. The number of *Produce* cards required to signal production in a multiple-card system has been determined using the variables of run time per piece (Figure 8.12), setup time, and the estimated number of wait days on the WAIT/WORK board. To determine kanban quantity, the variables of individual machines, independent machine cells, and remote locations must also be factored into replenishment time. Also include any additional time such as required travel time to remote locations to ensure replenishment at a point of consumption before a material stock-out.

The formula used is similar to the calculation for two-bin kanban quantities except that replenishment days is the sum of all the times of all the variables: the machines, the independent cells, and the remote locations. The resulting quotient is the number of containers and number of *Produce* cards needed to generate a setup and run signal at a machine or machine cell (see Figure 8.12):

Daily demand × number of replenishment days ÷ storage container quantity
= number of containers and *Produce* cards

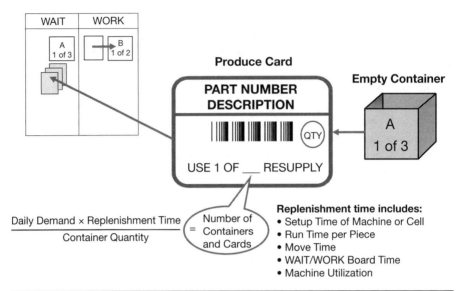

Figure 8.12. Detail of a WAIT/WORK sequencing board for replenishment prioritizing: all *Produce* cards required for a signal must be accumulated before replenishment may begin.

Although calculation of this formula is straightforward, the final answer can be affected adversely when all parts running through a machine or machine cell are included. Additional calculations to assess the *total* utilization of the machine or machine cell must therefore be made. When utilization of a machine approaches ±85%, replenishment days may need to be modified. Assess machine utilization on a monthly basis. The factors needed to evaluate machine and machine cell utilization include:

- Number of machines
- Total number of units run
- Run time per piece
- Work days per month
- Number of shifts per day
- Available minutes per shift
- Setup time
- Number of setups
- Preventive maintenance time and downtime

To determine kanban quantity, the run time per piece must be known. Then total kanban quantity for each part must be calculated and added together to determine the amount of machine time required to produce the desired kanban quantity. When the required machine time to produce the total kanban quantity for all parts is subtracted from the total time available, the difference is the time available to perform setups. Dividing the time to provide setups by the time required to perform a single setup determines the number of setups that can be performed per month or per day. The total quantity of kanban part numbers to be run must not exceed the number of setups that can be made. Based on the utilization of the fabrication machine or cell, ideal kanban quantities might need to be modified to fit into the utilization model developed for a machine or a machine cell. Typically, an iterative process with multiple iterations is required to determine the final ideal kanban quantities. A process map program can be developed to include all of the variables in replenishment days plus the elements of machine utilization to determine the optimum kanban quantities and produce the charts shown in Table 8.5.

Setup time. The greater the number of replenishment days, the larger the replenishment inventory necessary to cover the run-to-recovery time will be. Of all the variables that make up replenishment days, setup time is the variable that provides the greatest opportunity for improvement. If setup time can be reduced, then run-to-recovery time will also be reduced. If run-to-recovery time is reduced, then inventory can be reduced. Theoretically, if a setup can be reduced to a Takt time or less, there is no reason to have a run-to-recovery lot size greater than 1. Unless a machine or machine cell can be dedicated to a Lean manufacturing line and can cycle once every Takt time, reducing setup time should be a constant improvement activity. Expensive machines (e.g., a CNC machine) are frequently shared with many manufacturing areas in a company. No one Lean line or production department should dominate expensive capital equipment with output that must be shared with other areas. In companies where shared machines (resources) exist, whenever a setup is performed, certain lot sizes will need to be produced to recover the cost of setup. (If setup time can be reduced, lot sizes can also be reduced proportionally.)

Just as inventory is considered *waste* that must be reduced or eliminated in Lean, setup time reduction offers an excellent opportunity for a SMED (single-minute exchange of die) kaizen projects. In spite of the attention associated with SMED projects, the business reasons are sound. A SMED project is an excellent activity for a kaizen team that can be prioritized by beginning with the longest setup time.

Although a kanban system is not an absolute requirement for a Lean manufacturing line, it is the perfect companion for a balanced, one-unit-at-a-time manufacturing operating system. Issuing pick lists or kit builds from the planning system in predetermined lot sizes creates special handling issues for a Lean operating system. Anything is possible and any planning system can be modified to use existing pick lists and kit builds, but an argument can be made that a two-bin and a multiple-card system are more responsive to customer demand; reduce or

Table 8.5. Process Map Program Illustrating Variables and Elements of Machine Utilization for Determining Optimum Kanban Quantities: Multiple-Card Kanban (CT, Cycle Time)

28-ton machines	3
Machine setup minutes	90
Total setup/month	14
Total setup minutes/month	1,231
Total setup people needed	1.4
Preventative maintenance minutes/machine	240
Preventative maintenance breakdown/month	720
Days of Wait	3

Days/month	20.0
Available minutes per shift	438
Shifts/day	2.0
Minutes available/month per machine	17,520
Total machine minutes available/month	52,630
Machine run time minutes/month	43,504
Minutes left available/month	7,105
Total machine utilization	0.83

Part Number	Daily Rate	Days of Kanban	Build Quantity	Machine C/T Piece	Total Minutes	Total Shifts	Setups/Month	Parts Container	Cards
C7RCAB0046	300	10	3,900	1.29	5,031	5.7	1.5	150	26
MOLCAB0082	200	10	2,600	1.29	3,354	3.8	1.5	200	13
MOLCAB0083	200	15	3,600	1.18	4,258	4.8	1.1	200	18
C7RCAB0101	200	15	3,600	1.24	4,464	5.1	1.1	100	36
C7RCAB0106	200	15	3,600	1.24	4,464	5.1	1.1	200	18
C7RCAB0107	200	10	2,600	1.24	3,224	3.7	1.5	100	26
C7RCAB0118	400	10	5,200	1.28	6,656	7.6	1.5	400	13
C7RCAB0119	200	10	2,600	1.34	3,484	4.0	1.5	200	13
C7RMEN0630	20	10	260	1.15	299	0.3	1.5	20	13
C7RMEN0632	400	15	7,200	1.15	8,280	9.5	1.1	400	18
Total					**43,504**	**49.7**	**14**		

eliminate the daily expediting of planning system-issued production orders; are simple to operate; and provide maximum flexibility for producing most models on any given day.

9

THE KANBAN SYSTEM: CONSIDERATIONS FOR OPERATING THE SYSTEM

The two-bin material kanban system, unlike traditional planning systems, has no forward visibility for determining demand: it doesn't project future customer demand. During the initial setup of the kanban system, historical and extrapolated information was used to establish the daily demand for kanban container sizing. After system startup, information used for establishing a kanban system began to become more and more inaccurate. Demand is not static. Demand increases and decreases based on the whims of the marketplace and changes caused by adjustments to product mix and volume, technology improvements, the introduction of new models to customer catalogs, and the discontinuance of older models. All contribute to the changing database for a kanban system.

Changes to a traditional planning system are facilitated through database changes required for maintaining the planning system's integrity, e.g., the item master and the BOM. Stand-alone kanban systems, however, do not currently interface with existing planning systems. Maintaining a kanban system is essentially a manual process. To remain current and accommodate all potential changes, the responsibility for maintaining a kanban system must be assigned to a person. To manage the changes in concert with the current planning system, the person maintaining the kanban system must be included in all change control distribution channels.

One way to accomplish kanban system maintenance is to use the action item output from the planning system to monitor the daily volume used for kanban calculations. Net material requirements throughout the manufacturing horizon can be accumulated and divided by the number of days in that horizon, which will give an average daily demand for the part number for that period. A percentage of demand either higher or lower, e.g., ±15%, can be established as the range. If the existing kanban daily demand falls outside the range, making an adjustment may be necessary. For example, a *descending* daily average indicates *diminishing* demand. If confirmed, a corresponding kanban quantity reduction is appropriate. If rising demand is indicated, it must be confirmed: is the increase an incremental shift in product demand or a temporary spike caused by an anomaly of demand? Increased or decreased shifts in demand, along with the addition of new parts and the disposition of discontinued parts, require making individual decisions on a case-by-case basis. These decisions are best made by the person assigned the responsibility for maintaining the kanban system.

Remember that kanban methodology is a materials presentation method designed to *simplify* material handling and inventory management while also providing *maximum flexibility* to meet ever-changing customer demand. Instead of materials being staged in kits and then issued into production to follow a predetermined routing, the materials are physically placed at a point of usage in the manufacturing area. They are replenished only when a signal is generated by their consumption into a product. Because manufacturing materials are located at a consumption point on the line, they are available for consumption in any product that happens to flow down the line. All materials are available for all products. They are not consigned to any shop order or SKU. Materials placed directly on a line at the point where consumed into a product offer a real competitive advantage to a Lean manufacturer.

Once parts have been designated as being part of a kanban system, with daily demand and replenishment frequency recorded, signals generated along the pull chain automatically replenish materials with no input required from a planner or buyer. The only time additional input is necessary is to resolve mix or volume issues for an individual component. Once the kanban system is operational, replenishment cycles can continue indefinitely with little human intervention.

If kanban methodology were expanded to its greatest outlying replenishment points, output from a planning system would be unnecessary to establish demand for material. A supplier would merely respond to kanban signals received from the manufacturer. This would be the case so long as future demand could be accurately projected to determine daily demand for kanban sizing and all suppliers were certified and capable of accepting kanban signals.

If cost were no object, every possible part required to build every possible product configuration would reside on a Lean production line and be automatically replenished by a kanban system. Material handling would be extremely simple. For manufacturers with highly configured products, however, having all of the parts on hand needed to produce all of the possible product configurations in the customer product catalog would be a very expensive policy. To be able to satisfy customer demand for configured products and still be competitive enough to take market share from competitors, while also maintaining a reasonable raw materials inventory investment, having alternative strategies is necessary.

USING FULFILLMENT POLICY TO MEET CUSTOMER DEMAND

Just as the cost of materials handling must be balanced with inventory investment, a similar policy must be considered for meeting *all* customer demand within a stated customer-quoted lead time. The preferred unwritten customer fulfillment policy for most sales and marketing organizations is to be "all things to all people, all the time." In the drive to fulfill this unwritten policy, a common practice for a sales group is to offer customers numerous options on numerous products to close a deal. Sometimes the number of permutations can swell to hundreds or thousands of products. The combinations of options and the resulting products can result in a proliferation of product offerings — each with their own end-item part number (a reason why many companies boast of having thousands of product offerings). This proliferation of end-item products correspondingly translates into needing large numbers of component parts available to the manufacturing group just to service the demand. Having the availability of large numbers of component parts is essential before the sales group can promise delivery within the standard customer-quoted lead time.

Because the success of the sales group is measured by the sales revenue generated, they often have little regard for *how* the configured items they sell get produced in manufacturing — that's a problem for manufacturing to solve! Their policy of "all things to all people, all the time," however, creates a serious conflicting objective for manufacturing: managing the inventory turn rate policy and the inventory level. Materials management is typically measured on inventory turn rates and achieving desired inventory levels. Because the cost of maintaining all possible component parts permutations for all possible customer configurations is prohibitive, a tradeoff decision must be made between 100% customer fulfillment within the standard customer-quoted lead time policy and the inventory investment necessary to achieve the company's inventory policy. Most manufacturers opt for an 80/20 parts strategy to balance their need for reasonable customer service levels with a practical inventory investment. Figure 9.1 illustrates how an 80% inventory investment in total possible parts is the *optimum* customer satisfaction solution.

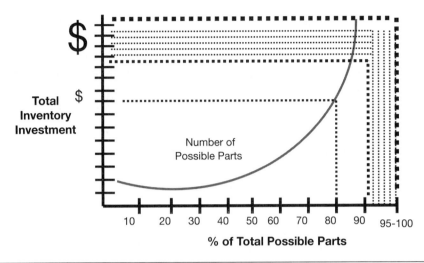

Figure 9.1. Optimum strategy: an 80% inventory investment in the total number of possible parts.

Manufacturers often claim that their products are unique when it is actually the number, variety, and combinations of *parts* and *process options* that can be applied to a standard line of products that are unique. How then, do manufacturers with hundreds or thousands of possible component part combinations decide which parts should be available to meet customer demand on a timely basis? Sales groups who regularly promise delivery of customer-configured products in the standard customer-quoted lead time usually have little knowledge of the required component materials that must be procured from suppliers. The sales group simply assumes all parts are available and in a stockroom inventory just waiting to be used — an option most companies cannot afford. Lean manufacturers who have designed their manufacturing lines with sufficient labor and machine resources to produce numerous configurations on any given day still must have the supplier lead time necessary for the procurement of component parts to be used in specialized configurations. This supplier lead time must be added to the normal manufacturing response time to have a realistic expectation of on-time delivery. Manufacturing may work hard to satisfy demand for highly configured products, but unless heroic expediting efforts are made and increased costs are incurred on the shop floor, meeting customer demand for highly configured products within the normal customer-quoted lead time is highly unlikely. Unrealistic lead time promises made to customers for highly configured products in the standard lead time are the major reason for most expediting activities that take place on the shop floor and throughout the supply chain. Missed delivery promises are also a significant cause of customer dissatisfaction.

The parts strategy. Is it really necessary to have on hand all parts for all possible permutations for all possible product configurations to have a successful customer fulfillment policy? Would stocking the parts necessary to produce a group of products that represents the majority of all products offered be a more practical strategy?

A better option for stocking parts: maintain a component inventory for a representative group of products. Selecting a group of products that represents the majority of the product population chosen for designing the Lean line is a good start for establishing a customer fulfillment policy. Recall that decisions for design of the Lean line selected the parent products that represented all products sold (SKUs, end-items, FGI level). Line design started by selecting SKUs that made up only 20% of the total product permutations, but represented 80% of total sales revenue. To produce 20% of all possible models within a customer-quoted lead time that represents 80% of the total sales revenue chosen for the line design, the component parts required to produce these models must be available at all times. At a minimum, all component parts for the SKUs required by the BOM must also be available to the kanban system so these products are available to be shipped in the standard customer-quoted lead time.

The customer service strategy. Is having a "one size fits all" customer service policy practical or does having multiple policies based on product permutations plus the lead time for vendor-supplied special materials make more sense? Would having one customer-quoted lead time policy for standard products and a second policy for highly configured products requiring purchased parts from a supplier be more practical?

A better option for meeting customer-quoted lead time: have multiple policies. Having a customer-quoted lead time policy for standard products and a separate policy for highly configured products that require low-volume, infrequently demanded parts purchased from suppliers is a better option for most companies. Keeping the parts on hand needed to produce products that are not included in the selected 20% of all SKUs will require maintaining a higher inventory investment in the specialized parts needed for producing the remaining 80% of the other possible product permutations. Choosing to maintain the increased inventories required to meet normal customer-quoted lead time for models beyond the 20% of standard models therefore becomes a financial decision. To be able to ship any of the remaining 80% of potential SKU product permutations within the standard lead time, the same proportion of all possible component part combinations must be stocked to respond to the configured customer demand in the standard lead time. For some manufacturers, this may be a valid customer service strategy. The company, however, must be willing to invest in the inventory required to meet a low-volume, infrequent-demand profile. Every company has to make the decision about inventory investment and customer fulfillment strategy based on their own comfort level. (Does the potential return on investment received from improved customer response for more models delivered in the standard customer-quoted lead time justify the increased cost of inventory? The answer: choose the strategy that is best for the success of your company.)

Using inventory as a strategy to increase market share. Maintaining inventories in excess of the 80% of revenue-generating sales mix in order to meet customer demand for models beyond the 20% of standard models upon receipt of a customer order is a strategy that can be justified. It's just a function of the inventory investment level a manufacturer is willing to incur in order to achieve rapid delivery response. For example, a company wanting to increase its market share by offering faster response times to customers for lower-volume configurations than competitors may view maintaining higher inventories as a necessary investment cost to achieve that goal. It's a valid strategy for increasing market share. To have increased availability for customers, an 85/15 split might be a preferred strategy. A 90/10 split might capture even more market share. Both goals could be justification for maintaining a larger inventory investment. As products approach commodity status, a higher than 80% first-time fulfillment rate will probably be desired. If products can be differentiated from competitors' products with attributes other than price, delivery, and configuration, then an 80% fulfillment rate may be ideal for the market. With every strategic inventory increase designed to meet customer demand within the customer-quoted lead time, however, the cost of maintaining extra component materials increases proportionately: inventory = dollars. A kanban system provides an easy tool for making strategic decisions. Investment values can be easily determined by performing multiple *what if* iterations of the kanban system until the ideal trade-off between speed and investment is achieved.

Establishing fulfillment policy as a strategy to improve response to customer demand. Every company must establish customer fulfillment policy decisions based on a carefully considered customer service strategy. For example, the sales and marketing group prefers a 100% fulfillment policy because their success is measured by the amount of sales revenue generated, but a 100% first-time fulfillment policy can cause a significant increase in inventory investment for the manufacturing group. If adherence to inventory investment goals is the basis of performance measurement, this dichotomy of goals is unrealistic for the organizational unit responsible for meeting inventory investment KPIs. Fulfillment policy should not be established at the plant level. Customer fulfillment policy must be a corporate-level decision. It's a strategic decision that needs the consensus of top management. To resolve conflicting measurement objectives between the manufacturing and sales and marketing groups, an agreement must be reached as to the number of products that are to be designated as standard (e.g., the products used to design the Lean line). A stand-alone customer service policy should then be established for these standard products. Once established, the manufacturing group must agree to produce standard products in the stated customer-quoted lead time of the Lean line. With this agreement, the manufacturing group is now accountable for producing a minimum of 20% of the entire product line that represents 80% of sales revenue (the standard products) and guaranteeing delivery within the standard customer-quoted lead time service policy for the designated products. The manufacturing group will still be responsible for the inventory goals established by the KPIs. Customers still can order nonstandard configured products, but these products will have a separate, stand-alone customer service policy. The lead time for delivery of these products will be longer because it is based on the standard customer-quoted lead time to produce the product on the Lean line *plus* the required supplier lead time for procurement and receipt of any specialized component materials. Sales and marketing can continue selling nonstandard products. The sales group is still responsible for generating sales revenue for the company, but delivery of nonstandard products cannot be promised in the standard lead time. Manufacturing is still responsible for maintaining inventory levels of standard parts and for meeting the customer-quoted lead time for standard products. The only difference is that there are two customer service policies: one for standard products and one for nonstandard products. If corporate strategy is to increase the company's investment in inventory to support an improved response to demand beyond the standard products, then ownership of the resulting component inventories beyond those necessary for the production of standard products belongs to the sales and marketing group. Otherwise, the existing manufacturing performance measurements must be adjusted to reflect the intentional addition of potentially slower-moving inventories. Assuming the inventory investment risk associated with ownership of slower-moving inventories of nonstandard items should cause sales and marketing to carefully consider the consequences of selling highly configured products and instead create incentives to sell standard items. The incentives to sell standard products rather than configured ones include faster customer-quoted lead times, resulting in products being shipped sooner; reduced accounts receivable; and faster payment of commission and bonus payments. Successful salespersons should be more motivated to be better salespersons than to just take an order simply to register a sale. (New Lean performance measurements must be developed to reward the sales and marketing group for selling items from the standard products list.)

FULFILLMENT POLICY: THE CUSTOMER MIGHT BE KING, BUT ARE ALL CUSTOMERS EQUAL?

Since the last time the customer order fulfillment policy was articulated by your company, have customer expectations evolved? If so, it's possible that several fulfillment policies designed for different customers may be required to determine the individual parts strategies for the kanban system and the resulting inventory investment. The Pareto analysis is a good tool for identifying customer categories and possible kanban parts strategies. Other customer categories can be determined based on historical order patterns.

Sales and marketing. The sales and marketing group can sort customers based on the product configurations they order and their total dollars of sales volume. Once again, it is likely ±80% of the total sales dollars are received from only 20% of all customers. The customers creating 80% of your revenue should be cared for very well. The customer fulfillment policy for these customers should include the SKUs that are reflected in the standard lead time policy — the 80/20 policy that guarantees customer satisfaction will be maintained at a high level for the top 20% of customers generating 80% of the company's sales. The most difficult task for manufacturers of highly configured products is keeping the other 80% of the customer base who represents only 20% of total sales happy. The sales and marketing group, however, usually makes little distinction between customers — all are equal in their eyes (and wallets).

Manufacturing. On the shop floor, the customer fulfillment scenario is quite different. Manufacturing does not have the luxury of satisfying all of the customers all of the time (as the sales and marketing group wants them to do) because of the proliferation of possible parts required to do so while still needing to be a good steward the company's financial resources.

Decisions must be made and policies must be established that balance sound inventory investment strategy with satisfying most of the customers most of the time. The decisions and resulting policies should not be made unilaterally — the entire organization must participate in establishing policies that are fair to all KPI groups while maximizing customer satisfaction and achieving financial due diligence goals.

Order policy: for standard product configurations. The component parts in the BOMs for standard product configurations have already been included in the kanban system during its design. These product configurations support the standard product listing. All product configurations in this range of customer demand (the ±80% of sales revenue) should already have an order policy guaranteeing shipment within the customer-quoted lead time. This policy guaranteeing shipment within the customer-quoted lead time is possible because the Lean line was designed to complete the work content of the standard products and the kanban system was designed to include and maintain the component materials necessary to produce all products designated as standard.

Order policy: for higher customer service levels. The cost of maintaining customer service levels above the initial 80% fill rate of standard products can be determined by the increased parts investment required to meet each incremental increase in service level, including the corresponding customer service policy established for each SKU. By working down a list of customers that have been sorted by total sales dollars, order policies can be established based on the time required to procure the parts not kept in the kanban system and the lead time required to purchase them from a supplier. The added lead time must, of course, be added to the customer-quoted lead time of the standard product.

Order policy: profit margin considerations. Establishing an order policy based on product model sales dollars often exposes some of the reasons why manufacturers spend so much time expediting orders. It also raises the following questions:

- Is the time spent expediting highly configured, low-volume products through the manufacturing area worth the sales dollars generated by those products?
- What is the profit margin for nonstandard products with special-order configurations compared to the top 20% of standard items sold?
- Are the markets the company wants to participate in actually being served by the production of nonstandard products?
- In exchange for faster delivery, is switching customers requesting custom orders to products in the 80% satisfaction order policy range possible? Would doing so be more profitable for the company?
- Are the costs of overtime, premium transportation, lost utilization, perpetual expediting, and the impact on quality of life worth the compromised margins returned by small-volume, infrequent-demand products?
- Is loyalty to legacy customers more important than the extra cost and effort required to manufacture their low-volume, infrequently demanded, highly configured products?
- Do the sales dollars generated by the bottom 10% of product configurations represent the current business model and direction of the company?

Keeping nonstandard inventories on hand for longer periods of time to ensure higher customer service levels increases the cost of all products. If the cost of keeping nonstandard inventories cannot be passed on to customers, profitability margins can only decrease. Carefully consider any decision causing the reduction of a profit margin:

- Does the cost of satisfying customers with infrequent, highly configured demand justify carrying the parts inventory needed to meet this demand?
- Does the demand volume of highly configured products merit having the same lead time delivery promise as standard products?
- Has the direction of the company changed so that servicing these customers is no longer cost effective?
- Would it be better to relinquish this business to a competitor so that the company can concentrate on manufacturing the products that yield the best margins?

What about legacy customers? Often a company performs heroically just to satisfy small-volume, infrequent-demand customers because of long-term relationships that date back to the earliest days of the company. These legacy customers may have been very loyal to the company during the early days when the company was just beginning. They probably still are, but it's possible that the marketplace and the strategic direction of the company have grown in a direction different from these legacy customers. Rethinking the company's relationship with legacy customers requires comparing the costs of production to the sales volume generated by them. This comparison may indicate that it is no longer cost effective to produce their small volumes or infrequent, highly configured demand. If retaining loyalty to small-margin customers is preferred to return on investment, then at least the costs will be known and a price for that loyalty can be established.

MATERIALS MANAGEMENT IS HANDS-ON

The two-bin material kanban system is a hands-on system. For the system to be the most effective, it must be designed by responsible materials professionals. Once implemented, day-to-day upkeep of kanban part numbers will be required to ensure system integrity because product mix and volumes change, engineering change notices are received, and labels, containers, and storage racks require physical hands-on maintenance. Without maintenance, a kanban material supply system will become less effective with each passing day.

Kanban system integrity requires the assignment of committed people to the maintenance of the part numbers that reflect the most-current mix/volume relationships and to the physical efforts that are required to handle the parts, labels, containers, and the placement of containers in assigned locations. For the current generation of material handlers who are accustomed to the maintenance of materials channeled through the planning system by the engineering group, the sudden shift to having hands-on responsibility for maintaining the kanban replenishment system and the physical handling of production materials gives new meaning to the term *materials management.*

The commitment required for kanban system maintenance is much different than the commitment required for a computer-driven planning system. In a computer-based system, planning system maintenance is controlled by updating the item master and the BOM. Responsibility for the maintenance of the BOM and item master is typically a function of the design engineering group. When the item master and BOM have been updated in the planning system, the explosion routine will generate the necessary quantity and time-phased requirement action messages for those new components. A kanban system, however, does not rely on the output of a computer-driven planning system routine for maintenance. The number of kanban maintenance updates required on a daily basis might be small, but a human being must *manually* calculate the ideal quantities for the pull chain, fill and label the containers, and then present the material to the point of consumption.

Initial selection of parts. Hands-on management of a material kanban system is especially important when setting up the system for the very first time. When considering parts for inclusion in a kanban system, one of the first decisions to be made is whether certain parts should be in the kanban system in the first place. Some parts are not good candidates for a kanban system. Even though an 80/20 rationalization of parts was used to match the projected sales volume, a significant number of component materials may still be required. If so, for each part number selected for inclusion in the kanban system, a series of separate kanban decisions must be made. For example, if the final kanban part number population is 200 parts, then at least 200 individual decisions must be made about which pull chain best represents the ideal inventory policy for that part along with the container sizes, and the method of material presentation.

One-time/as-needed parts. Very expensive, fragile, or environmentally sensitive parts might be better supplied on an as-needed basis rather than residing on the shop floor in a kanban location. Other parts might be inexpensive, but are too large or cumbersome to be located adjacent to a Lean line, e.g., corrugated containers, large molded parts, pre-cut insulation, and bulky packing materials. Although these materials are relatively low in cost, the footprint required for stocking two "containers" of these items for numerous part number configurations on the shop floor may be impractical. Shop floor space is precious and expensive. The trade-off for the convenience of stocking special parts in the kanban system may not justify the cost of factory shop floor space. Materials in this category should therefore be handled on a *one-time* or *as-needed* basis. Because materials in a two-bin kanban system are automatically replenished when depleted and a signal is generated, one-time-usage materials must be managed *each time* they are consumed. They require more management attention. Responsibility for one-time-usage materials must be assigned to a material handler and sequenced to arrive on the line in time to meet usage at the downstream workstation. One-time-usage parts or other parts intentionally excluded from a kanban system require alternative methods of supply to a consumption point. If there is no kanban container, what is the replenishment signal? A common way for handling a one-time-usage part is to assign the part a separate planner code in the item master so that ordering the part can occur using the existing planning system. When an order recommendation is generated by the planning system, it can be sorted by the planner code with the part order directed to the designated buyer or planner for coordination with a supplier or a production schedule. If the item is a purchased component, the designated planner buys the item as usual and notifies the receiving group of the impending shipment. Notification can be by a separate one-time-use kanban signal or card. When the part is consumed on a Lean line, the card is returned to the buyer for disposition. The buyer either reuses the card in the event that the part is required for future use or destroys the card.

The next decision to be made is related to inventory investment. What is the desired level of inventory investment for each part?

Determine unit cost/the pull chain. Perform an ABC analysis on all kanban part number candidates. ABC analysis will determine the most and least expensive parts based on their unit cost. **A** items are the most expensive; **C** items are the least expensive. Using the resulting ABC designation and the per-unit cost of a part, assign the most appropriate pull chain to represent the desired number of days of inventory investment for that part. If the unit cost of a part is small, assign a pull chain with a greater amount of replenishment time. Replenishment signals will be less frequent for these parts. Larger inventories of inexpensive parts suggest a reasonable investment with less material handling — a smart decision! Conversely, if the unit cost of a part is high, assign a pull chain with the least amount of replenishment time. The inventory investment will be less, and replenishment signals will occur more frequently, causing an increase in material handling. For every part number included in the kanban system, a decision comparing the trade-off between inventory investment and material handling costs must be made.

Every part number in the kanban system must be presented at a point of consumption. Therefore, another important decision concerns how parts will be handled based on their physical size.

Presentation of parts/the replenishment signal. Will the calculated kanban quantity of a part fit into a container? If so, what size container? Most suppliers of part containers make a variety of sizes, colors, and materials, but if a calculated kanban quantity of a part will not fit into one of these standard containers, an alternative way of presenting parts at a consumption point must be developed. If the size and quantity of the parts are too large to put into containers at a work-station, can the parts be placed on the shop floor or on a pallet? If parts are not stored in a container, what will the replenishment signal be?

A materials presentation decision must be made for every part number in a kanban system, which requires a whole new methodology for managing production materials. It requires a hands-on approach to materials management that cannot be delegated to an administrative function. Although a hands-on approach is needed, a shortcut can be used to consolidate the total number of decisions to be made: group the parts by category and apply a pull chain policy based on predetermined category criteria. Generally, the categories used to make kanban decisions are derived using an ABC analysis, a commodity code, or a planner code. To determine the number of kanban containers required to hold all of the parts chosen to be in the kanban system, containers can be assigned an alpha or numeric code indicating size. This code can then be attached to the part numbers in a column on a spreadsheet by individual pull sequence and sorted to determine the number of containers needed.

MAKING THE KANBAN SYSTEM OPERATIONAL

Completing the initial setup of a kanban system can represent a significant amount of work. After pull chain and inventory investment decisions have been made, filling the kanban containers, printing and applying labels to the containers, and presenting the materials must be completed to begin operation of the system. Many companies underestimate the time and physical labor necessary to get the system in place and make it operational. Based on a simple *Line/RIP/Stores* pull chain, at least four containers will require filling, labeling, and presenting at the points of consumption and resupply. Multiplying four times the number of parts in the kanban system and the time required for filing, labeling, and delivering to the points of consumption and supply can add up. Enlist the help of as many people as possible to ensure that the initial setup of the material two-bin kanban operating system is completely in place. After the setup is completed, the daily maintenance routine begins.

Containers, Quantities, and Replenishment Signals

Humans have a tendency to use any space available to them. Nature abhors a vacuum and so do people! Inspect the basement, attic, garage, or storage locker of almost anyone and you will discover this to be true. When making a decision to keep or dispose of something, people often base their decision on the amount of available storage space.

Container size. Just as operators fill empty spaces in their workstations, material handlers on a Lean line have the same tendency to instinctually fill an empty space in a container. Matching a physical kanban container to a calculated kanban quantity is important to ensure inventory investment integrity. For example, at the resupply point, if a kanban container is larger than necessary to hold the calculated quantity, then the tendency will be to fill the container to capacity rather than to change to a container (resize it) that more closely matches the specified kanban quantity. Oversized, overfilled containers can inflate inventory investment! Another temptation is to avoid the cost of purchasing suitable containers by opting to reuse existing containers. If existing containers capacities are not matched with calculated kanban quantities in mind, avoiding the cost of buying new containers may actually increase inventory costs in the long run.

Container color. The color of containers is a matter of esthetics or personal taste. Some kanban practitioners choose to use color as a way to convey the regulations of the kanban system. They have even been known to designate specific colors for certain part categories or pull sequences. The color of a kanban container is not important. A color coding system is a fragile system to maintain. Unless the kanban system is extremely disciplined, if a designated container color is accidently substituted for another color, the color-coding system will be immediately contaminated. Remembering the definition of Lean and that eliminating the wastes of manufacturing means eliminating non-value-adding work, is the time and effort required to maintain a color coding system for a kanban system worth the investment? Will customers think that color-coded containers add value to the products they buy?

Replenishment signals. When setting up a kanban system for the first time, it is imperative to remember the definition of kanban — *a signal.* For replenishment, a signal must be created when a calculated kanban quantity has been reached. Material presentation considerations are secondary to the signal itself. When considering kanban container alternatives, the term *container* is used figuratively to indicate *a signal*, but in actuality, *the signal* can take on different forms by redefining the word *container*. Variations of what represents a replenishment signal are as numerous as the imaginations of the people creating them. For example, if materials are too large to be confined to a container, then mechanisms must be created to generate a replenishment signal when the calculated kanban quantity has been reached. A kanban card can be inserted halfway down into a stack of materials. When the material has been consumed down to the card, *the card* becomes the signal for replenishment. A footprint for two pallets can be painted on the shop floor. When one pallet is consumed and removed, the *empty space* is the signal. A slanted roller rack can have sufficient space for two containers. The space for the second container is painted a different color. When the color is exposed, the *empty space* is the kanban signal. A sight glass on a silo that indicates the silo is *half full* can be the signal. For small parts that require less capacity than the smallest commercially available container, a partition can be placed vertically at the midpoint of the container. When the front half of the container is consumed, *removing the partition* can be the signal. The back half of the container can be tipped forward to serve as a second container. The remaining balance (the back half) should be sufficiently sized to support production until replenishment has been accomplished. A RIP container might be sized to maintain production as long as it takes for a supplier to resupply the material. Regardless of the solution ultimately devised, the critical element is the creation of a signal when a calculated kanban quantity has been reached.

Material Presentation

Kanban system methodology includes the practice of the division of labor theory:

- Operators are best utilized for the manufacturing of products on the line.
- Material handlers are best utilized refilling kanban containers and maintaining inventory and kanban systems.

Operators looking around for parts is a major contributor to lost productivity. Operators on a Lean manufacturing line are not to leave their workstations to go shopping for parts. Replenishment of parts for a manufacturing operation is best accomplished when operators are not disturbed while performing their standard work tasks at a workstation. To work uninterrupted by the need for parts, a methodology for signaling the need for the replenishment of a kanban material container must be in place. The methodology must:

- Notify a material handler when a container is empty and needs replenishment

- Tell the material handler where to place the replenishment material when it is returned to the line

Two methods can be used to notify material handlers that replenishment material is needed: a multicolored light system and a milk run system. Higher-volume Lean lines with numerous workstations are more apt to use a multicolored light system. Lower-volume lines usually opt for a milk run system. Using either system is acceptable.

The multicolored light system. The multicolored light system consists of three colored lights that are mounted next to one another. Typically, the colors are red, yellow, and green. These lights are installed at selected workstations and elevated above the operator's head so they may be seen by any material handler from any location on the shop floor. A switch for each color is located within easy reach of the operator. Each cluster of lights is evenly placed throughout the manufacturing area and adjacent to operators where an empty kanban container can easily be collected when empty. When both kanban containers are full, the green light is illuminated, indicating that a full inventory condition exists. When the first kanban container becomes empty, the operator moves the empty container to the collection area near the light and switches the light from green to yellow. The yellow light notifies a material handler that a material replenishment is required at that location. The material handler then has enough time to collect the container, replenish it with material, and return the filled container back to the consumption point before the second container becomes empty. Once the kanban is replenished, the material handler switches the light back to green, indicating a full kanban location. If the material in the second kanban container at a consumption point is exhausted before a refilled container is returned, a stock-out condition will occur. In this situation, the operator cannot continue to produce product and switches the yellow light to red. If the material is not replenished before another Takt time passes, the Lean line must stop work upstream from that point as each of the IPKs at each workstation fills up. Work downstream from the workstation will also dry up with each consecutive Takt time as the partially completed unit in each workstation IPK is consumed. Some manufacturers do not limit the use of a red light to material stock-out conditions. They expand the use of a red light condition to indicate a manufacturing problem of any type. In these companies, a red light condition is designed to attract immediate attention for resolution of any line stoppage for any reason. Some manufacturing facilities also have an additional red light directly wired into a production manager's or manufacturing engineer's office to ensure immediate attention to a line stoppage.

The milk run system. Signal creation and the movement of containers to a central collection point adjacent to a Lean line are the same in a milk run system

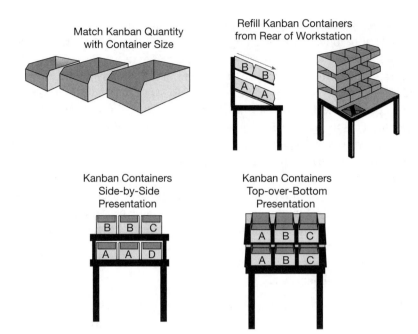

Figure 9.2. Examples of material presentation in a kanban system: placement of containers front to back, with container number one in front and container number two in back, is the preferred method.

as in a multicolored light system. The difference is that there are no multicolored lights in a milk run system. Material handlers simply have a route that runs from one collection point to the next throughout the facility. Empty containers are picked up, returned to the replenishment point, filled, and then returned to the workstation following the predetermined circuitous route. Newly emptied containers are always waiting at the collection points to repeat the cycle.

Workstation design. When workstations are being designed, the location for material containers must be included. When possible, containers should be located front to back with container number one in front and container number two in back. Containers placed side-by-side provide a temptation to take parts from both containers simultaneously as work is completed. If this situation occurs, both containers could potentially become empty at the same time causing a line stoppage until replenishment can occur. If side-by-side is the only alternative, place an indicator on one of the containers to remind the operator about the container to be consumed first. Figure 9.2 illustrates examples of material presentation methods.

Container placement. Material presentation systems must be universally comfortable and convenient for all operators. Avoid placing a container where it interferes with the work of an operator. Place materials as close as possible to an operator, but do not compromise the operator's ease of movement and safety. Consider the average height of operators. Because of Lean flexing requirements, different operators will potentially work at any workstation on any given day. Consider the Takt time of the line and the consequences of physical wear and tear on operators who make repetitive motions many times a day when consuming materials. Locate kanban containers in front of an operator, within arm's reach, to avoid the necessity of turning side to side (or 180 degrees) to retrieve materials. Whenever possible, present replenished materials from the back side of the workstation even though feeding materials from the back side may require additional labeling of the back side of the container to assist material handlers. Slanted flow racks designed to feed materials to an operator are the best method. Ergonomics for operators should always take precedence over the convenience of locating materials for material handlers.

RIP locations. Locate a RIP as close as possible to Lean line workstations. In some situations, finding the best location for a RIP might require creative thinking as well as using creative rack, container, and shelving solutions. A random locator system for materials is not permitted in the RIP location. Each parts container must have its own reserved location in the RIP. Ensure that material handlers and operators are included in any kaizen activities to improve the layout of a Lean line and its supporting material presentation systems. *Remember:* All move and setup work is considered a non-value-added activity.

Kanban Management

Setting up a kanban system for the first time requires a significant amount of decision making and work. Once the setup is completed, the kanban system must be managed on a day-to-day basis. If not maintained and improved, the system will become less effective after the first day of operation.

The kanban manager. To ensure that a kanban system operates at peak efficiency and achieves the optimum inventory investment and the customer delivery strategies desired by the company, a kanban manager must be designated to ensure that all important elements of the system are operational and well maintained. The kanban manager must also develop a methodology to enforce procedures that ensure RIP inventory transactions are made when material is moved into a RIP location so that component parts are recorded as on-hand inventory and are available to the planning system's material planning routines. Additionally, the kanban manager should establish a *backflushing* routine to record material usage from the RIP locations. Backflushing is a formal computer transaction designed to relieve a RIP inventory of component parts upon completion of a finished unit. The backflushing inventory transaction electronically adds one completed SKU to the finished goods inventory while simultaneously relieving the RIP inventory using the part numbers and quantities from the BOM. Backflushing must occur each time a finished unit packs off a Lean line. To ensure accurate inventory balances are maintained, BOMs and inventory levels must achieve 100% accuracy. The term *kanban manager* indicates more than a job title or an organizational level. The term is intended to describe the activities and management requirements needed to operate and maintain the kanban system. Assigning the responsibility for management of the kanban system is more important than the job title. As with any planning system, accurate inventory balances for a Lean line must be maintained at 100% accuracy. To ensure that timely changes are made to the kanban system, the kanban manager must be in the information loop for receiving *all* engineering change notices. A process must be in place to handle implementation of engineering changes to ensure that the BOM is updated and accurate for inventory, planning, and backflushing purposes. Engineering changes to part numbers or BOMs must be reflected in the kanban system to ensure that the most-accurate backflushing transactions are recorded.

Kanban sizing. The kanban system was originally established using static data that was available at that point in time. The manufacturing environment, however, is dynamic. Dynamic manufacturing environments require frequent, ongoing system maintenance. Timely kanban sizing procedures must be established so that kanban pull chains and quantities can be maintained to capture the most current engineering changes, supply replenishment times, packaging sizes, and manufacturing capacity volumes changes.

Inventory velocity. In addition to providing parts, the kanban system should keep part inventories moving through the manufacturing process at the pace necessary to achieve the company's stated inventory turnover goals. Inventory velocity is necessary to manage the inventory investment and minimize working capital requirements. Although the frequency of container replenishment is controlled by a predetermined replenishment time, there is direct correlation between kanban container replenishment time and inventory investment. The key to managing the desired inventory turnover rate is managing the replenishment frequency of kanban containers. While it is tempting to think only of the benefits of reduced inventories and increased turn rates, the kanban system must ultimately establish an equilibrium that balances inventory investment with material handling costs. The process of setting replenishment times and quantities will be iterative until the optimum balance is achieved.

But what if customer demand changes? Kanban quantities were initially calculated to support a stated number of average-day usage. Yet, at times, it's possible that the supply for a calculated number of days will be exceeded by actual customer demand. Any increased customer demand causes replenishment cycles for the line and the RIP containers to occur faster. If the RIP quantity is sufficient, the kanban system can withstand short-term spikes above the daily average of customer demand even if the line kanban is replenished more frequently than designed. If, however, the cycle repeats itself too many days in a row, even RIP and stockroom inventories will eventually become depleted ahead of their planned replenishment time, causing a shortage to occur. If a demand spike is a short-term anomaly, no action may be needed other than a suggestion to the sequencing planner to smooth out the increased demand over a greater number of days if possible. However, if the demand spike is determined to be a leading indicator of a new demand trend, the kanban manager must recalculate the daily rates, replenishment times, container quantities and sizes, material presentation attributes, and sequencing routines. A demand spike may also be an indicator of an individual customer's order pattern. Using the model of an average daily usage rate for calculating the kanban quantity of parts for this customer will be insufficient. Although this customer's ordering cycle may be infrequent, it often occurs with the same demand quantity. The kanban manager therefore has important questions to answer: should kanban inventories of the parts in that amount be kept on hand at all times to meet the infrequent demand of this customer when it occurs versus what the cost/benefit is of maintaining these inventories; does it make sense to keep inventories for several months just so parts will be available when this customer orders them only intermittently during the year? A kanban manager must be alert to demand changes and inventory shortages and be prepared to investigate their causes.

Replenishment time. Inventory investment directly correlates with how often material is replenished: long replenishment times = a greater inventory investment; more frequent replenishment times = a smaller inventory investment. This relationship between replenishment time and inventory investment must be carefully managed and maintained. Speed of kanban container replenishment is a good barometer for assessing inventory velocity. Kanban containers that are replenished *slower* than the stated replenishment time indicate that inventory levels are *higher* than they need to be to support production. Conversely, more frequent replenishment indicates that the replenishment time is *too short* and inventory levels are *lower* than necessary to support production, which causes increased material handling time.

Achieving optimum kanban balance. The only time two full containers should ever reside in a kanban location is at initial setup of the system. After the first replenishment cycle, only one container should be in a kanban location at a time because the second container should always be in the process of being replenished. In an ideal kanban system, materials are in constant motion — either being consumed into production or being replenished. Achieving this optimum balance requires ongoing adjustments. For example, if delivery frequency for RIP replenishment is 5 days, material handling should take 4 to 5 days to fill and return a container to the point of consumption. If the container is consistently being filled every 1 to 2 days, inventory is potentially at half of the amount needed to balance the material handling routines. Rapid container replenishment indicates that the inventory savings obtained from maintaining smaller inventory quantities may be offset by the more frequent material handling costs. A kanban manager must be actively involved in the maintenance and operation of the kanban material system. Monitoring replenishment speed and material usage can only be done on the shop floor. It may be impossible to achieve a perfect balance between inventory and material handling costs, but without an effort to do so, there is no way your company's desired turn rate can be accomplished.

Sequencing Customer Configurations

Pareto (80/20) analysis was used to achieve part number rationalization to select the parts for the kanban system management. Often the greatest amount of a kanban manager's time is spent managing and sequencing the one-time-use parts and all the other parts that *were not* selected for inclusion in the kanban system. The time required to manage these parts is the reciprocal of the initial parts rationalization process: 80% of management's time is consumed in the management of the 20% of the total sales volume. This same 20% of volume represents 80% of the total possible product configurations sold. The parts represented by this product population have intentionally been discounted from the kanban system. When a customer orders a product requiring these intentionally discounted parts, the order must therefore be handled on a case-by-case basis. It's the handling of these specialized product configurations and the required parts that consumes 80% of the kanban manager's time.

Limit special configurations. Obviously, the best solution for managing special configurations and their many required parts is to standardize the product line as much as possible and limit configurations to only a few manageable variations. A standard product line eliminates most one-time-use parts. As a company's product line approaches true commodity status, this solution might be a realistic possibility, but for many manufacturers, this best-solution scenario will never happen because most sales and marketing groups are unwilling to relinquish even the smallest percentage of potential sales to achieve standardization on the factory floor. The sales and marketing group perceives the ability to

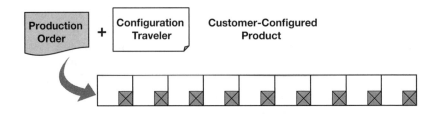

Figure 9.3. Configuration traveler: indicates to individual operators the parts to be installed at a workstation to build a special configuration.

promise highly configured products to be an important competitive differentiation. Promoting the sale of standard items may therefore require establishing new performance incentives that reward the sales and marketing group for selling standard items while making the selling of nonstandard, highly configured items less attractive for performance measurement purposes. Selling standard items might also be encouraged by having a multilevel customer service policy (discussed earlier in this chapter) in which standard products have the shortest lead time while configured products have the standard lead time plus the supplier's lead time. If delivery time is important to a customer, then the customer may give second thought to just how really important the requested special features of a highly configured product actually are.

Managing special configurations in manufacturing. Special products, such as a configure-to-order custom product, may require an additional sales order configuration document (a *configuration traveler*) sequenced to accompany the product as it moves through production. This configuration traveler moves along with the product as it advances through manufacturing and indicates to the individual operators at a workstation which parts are to be installed to build the special configuration (Figure 9.3). One-time-use kanban routines for low- and infrequent-demand products pull the required special component parts into the production process *only* when actual customer demand has been received and sequenced into the production process. A configured product subassembly process is simple when standard parts in a kanban system are used: parts identified on a configuration traveler are simply consumed directly into the configured product and the normal kanban replenishment cycle is completed as needed. Additional management and material handling time will always be required for configured products that require special one-time-use parts. Based on the actual daily customer demand, material handlers will need to know about any special parts to be used and the point of consumption where these parts will be consumed. This information can be presented as a set of sequencing cards on a sequencing board or as a tabular report. The actual material is then placed at a workstation in a designated location so an operator can easily install the special part when the configuration traveler reaches the workstation. On a daily basis, material planners can easily spend a significant amount of time managing special customer orders and one-time-use component parts. To reduce the amount of time required to handle special parts, invest management time in considering adding more part numbers to the standard kanban population. If more components reside in the kanban system, less special handling and materials handling activity will be required.

Handling the costs of highly configured products: the dilemma for the company. If highly configured products are to be offered at the same price *and* with the same delivery policy as standard higher-volume units, then the costs of this strategy must either be absorbed into the standard cost of those products or be charged to the customer at a premium rate to cover the increased costs of production in the standard lead time. If customers are not charged a premium rate, then a company with an "all things to all customers, all the time" customer fulfillment policy has no choice but to absorb the costs of maintaining inventories of the individual component parts along with any expediting and premium transportation costs required to achieve this strategy. If the company is willing to absorb the material costs and can still achieve market share and profit margin objectives, then an "all things to all customers, all the time" customer service policy may be best for competing in their marketplace. The answer is dependent on the best strategy for the company. Often, the best policy is somewhere in between (as long as there is full knowledge of the incremental costs for achieving the delivery policy).

Making customer service and price policy decisions: use the kanban system. The kanban system is an excellent tool for making price and customer service policy decisions. Remember that the initial kanban system began with an 80/20 split to identify the optimum number of parts to include in the kanban system. If the company prefers to have a strategy of achieving a customer first-time fill rate greater than 80%, then a greater number of component parts must be added to the strategy of the 20% top-selling products. The costs of expanding the component part participation necessary to achieve higher first-time order fulfillment strategies can be easily calculated. The costs associated with an 85/15, 90/10, or 95/5 split can then be evaluated and compared with the company's market share strategy. Once the cost of each fulfillment strategy is determined, the best strategy to achieve projected sales or market penetration goals can be established. Quoting the same delivery time and cost for a special configuration product as for a standard item not only causes chaos on the shop floor and for suppliers, but it's also unfair to customers — when required parts for a special configuration are not stocked in inventory, promised delivery dates in the standard lead time will likely be missed. Establishing an alternative order policy that includes the lead time required to receive the specified parts from suppliers and any additional handling costs for processing orders to meet customer demand for one-time-use parts and special configurations is a better customer fulfillment policy than making delivery promises unlikely to be met.

An important goal of a kanban system is to use inventory investment to make the best possible financial and customer fulfillment decisions for the company. The kanban system can be a catalyst for challenging existing policies, e.g., it can be used as an objective cost-estimating mechanism to evaluate a specific order policy. Multiple iterations of inventory investments can be made until the optimum inventory and investment strategy is identified. Although kanban managers are not empowered to make unilateral order policy decisions, they should be empowered to initiate policy change recommendations. Their contributions provide significant value to the customer-quoted lead time decision-making process.

EXTENDING MATERIAL REQUIREMENTS TO THE SUPPLY CHAIN

A longer-term goal of the kanban system is to reduce or eliminate the need for stockrooms. Without stockrooms, suppliers bypass receiving areas and stockrooms and deliver component parts directly to RIP locations on the shop floor. Delivery frequency times can be reduced on the kanban pull chain by the amount of time required to receive deliveries and inspect, locate, and warehouse material inventories. As a result, inventory quantities and working capital requirements are reduced.

Often raw material inventories residing in stockrooms are only buffer safety stocks that serve as cushions against poor quality and delivery unreliability from suppliers. Although the savings of a supplier-to-RIP pull sequence policy are self-evident, poor-quality supplier materials and a history of unreliable delivery performance cause a supplier-to-RIP policy to not be implemented on the same day as kanban system startup. If a supplier's quality has been suspect in the past and reliability in the future is questionable or if a supplier's on-time delivery history is poor, the last thing any manufacturer wants is to have parts from those suppliers delivered directly to a Lean line — supplier failure, whether from quality issues or a lack of parts, can cause line stoppage. Only when reliability and dependability can be proven should a supplier-to-RIP pull sequence be implemented on the factory shop floor.

Unfortunately, some suppliers may never be depended upon to meet price agreements, quality specifications, and delivery promises. Unreliable suppliers must always be closely monitored for purchase order and contract compliance, but opinions about these suppliers should not affect the policies and procedures for all suppliers on the approved supplier list. Supplier policy should not be based on the presumption that all suppliers are unreliable. Although there are exceptions, is making such a broad assumption valid for all suppliers? If this assumption were true, the only policy a company could have would be that *all suppliers cannot be trusted.* Even though most suppliers perform well and are willing to work with their manufacturing customers to improve reliability, historically, many manufacturers still continue to assume that their suppliers cannot be trusted and use an arm's-length relationship when dealing with them. Changing a long legacy of adversarial relationships will require significant effort by both parties to establish mutual trust. (Does having a policy of mistrust really make sense for any company?)

Quality is an expectation, not a differential. Most manufacturing companies continue to tout their ability to provide high-quality products to customers because of the efforts and dedication of their employees and the quality of the raw materials and components provided by suppliers even though they know that customers do not consider quality to be the differential that separates one product from another. Any product purchased today from a manufacturer is automatically assumed to be a high-quality product. Unless specific performance parameters are required, customers usually don't even provide quality specifications for products because quality is simply *an expectation.* The pursuit of quality by manufacturers will continue to be an expectation of customers in the future, requiring manufacturers to develop cost-effective strategies to meet the challenge of sustaining quality as a product differential. In the meantime, competition in the marketplace continues because customers constantly seek manufacturers who can offer newer or better differentials than their competitors.

Specifications. For most suppliers, specifications received from the design engineering group and the delivery requirements of the purchasing group are often the only contact a supplier has with a customer company on a regular basis. Purchase orders are received by the supplier each time a planning system recalculates product requirements or recommends changes to order volumes and due dates. To ensure compliance to engineering design specifications, incoming materials from the supplier are inspected in the customer company's receiving area. To be certain the transaction is correct and the contracted amount of material has been received, accounting procedures for invoice payment require a three-way match: the purchase order is compared to the receiving report and to the supplier's invoice. Any discrepancy must be resolved by the receiving, purchasing, or accounts payable groups. Aside from occasional contact from the supplier about a purchase order or a specification clarification, the entire requisition, order, shipment, receipt, and invoice cycle is usually completed as ordinary day-to-day business. Unless a problem occurs, this cycle can continue for years in each company without any actual contact being made between a customer company buyer and a supplier.

Specifications and delivery dates: considerations for the customer company. How current and accurate are the specifications provided to suppliers? Standards for products within an industry are well known by the manufacturers who produce them. These manufacturers are also well aware of the most up-to-date knowledge about new technologies. The same is true for suppliers. Suppliers know their industry well and maintain a high level of product and manufacturing expertise for the products they sell. So many component materials are used in a manufacturer's products, and how can a customer company's design and industrial engineers who develop specifications for a supplier possibly know the supplier's latest technology as well as the supplier does? When developing product specifications for products, whose product specifications are most likely to describe best how a product is to be manufactured or reflects the latest technology in the industry: the primary manufacturer or the customer? Is adherence to delivery dates used to evaluate the performance of suppliers? Adherence to delivery dates is a fair measurement as long as requested delivery dates are not constantly being moved closer or pushed farther out with every planning system rescheduling. When measuring a supplier's delivery performance, are delivery dates for purchase orders frequently changed? Which date is being used as the baseline for measuring delivery performance? Are delivery date changes communicated to suppliers with enough lead time to allow them to react? Sometimes, a supplier is labeled as poor because the customer's communication was untimely or inaccurate. When this happens, the supplier is held accountable for the customer's error. In this situation, most suppliers don't complain. They're so concerned about losing business that they say nothing and accept culpability for reliability issues when, in fact, the customer company is to blame for a missed delivery date.

Supplier nonconformance to specifications: costs to the customer company. When incoming material from a supplier is rejected for nonconformance to a specification, payment of the supplier's invoice is immediately withheld. Disposition must then be made of the incoming defective material: return the shipment to the supplier; rework the material on-site; or destroy the material. Defective material that escapes detection at the receiving/inspection area may not be discovered until it's in the manufacturing process. Manufacturing support functions then put procedures into place to deal with the defective material. The company's fire fighters swing into action. Buyers get on telephones, premium transportation is requested, planners search for substitute parts, and overtime is approved. Whether a defect is discovered in receiving/inspection or on the shop floor, determining resolution of defective material creates non-value-added activity. All of these procedures, systems, and activities are *reactions* to the defect. They occur only after the defect or damage from it has been discovered. Reacting to a crisis is expensive. It makes products more costly and less competitive.

ENSURING CONSISTENT MATERIAL QUALITY AND ON-TIME DELIVERY

A *reactive* defect-handling policy adds costs to products that can only be absorbed two ways: by reducing the company's margins or by passing the costs on to the customer. Rather than depending on inspections for quality after the receipt of material from suppliers, it's better to establish a proactive policy of certifying suppliers to develop a relationship that improves supplier reliability and dependability at the supplier's site.

Supplier certification is a *preventive* approach to quality. A supplier certification program is based on preventing defects as opposed to detecting them after a failure has occurred. The primary objective of a supplier certification process is to ensure on-time delivery of consistently high-quality material that can be demonstrated by predictable and repeatable conformance to specifications. The basic premise of supplier certification is that by choosing to build conformance to specifications into a product at the supplier's facility, the customer and supplier are working together to establish design characteristics, specifications, testing criteria, and process controls. Failures at the customer's factory will be less likely to occur. The result is a final product that is consistently fit for use, free of defects, and always delivered on time. No matter how valid the reason, customers do not want to pay for supplier activities that add no value to their products.

Implementation of a supplier certification process should result in achieving the objectives of improved quality, delivery performance, and productivity and reduced costs at both companies. Product information is shared. Openly sharing information between a company and its suppliers encourages partnerships and acknowledges suppliers as being an extension of the company's manufacturing process. Having a proactive approach to meeting quality requirements is much better than the traditional arm's-length relationship practiced by many companies today. Having quality *built in* to a supplier's products is a much better strategy than reacting to defects found in inspections or dealing with them after a failure occurs during the manufacturing process.

In addition to the cost reductions achieved by eliminating or reducing all non-value-added activity associated with rejected supplier materials, supplier

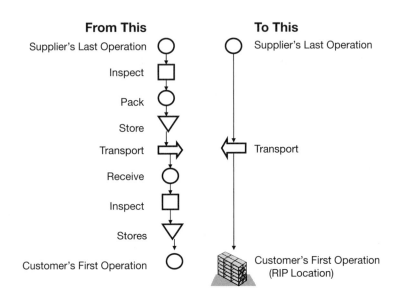

Figure 9.4. Goal of operation to operation: a simple *Line/RIP/Stores* pull chain can become a *Line/RIP/Supplier* pull chain to eliminate stockroom inventory.

certification can reduce the costs associated with maintaining buffer inventories (as WIP or in factory stores) to compensate for poor supplier reliability and dependability. These inventory buffers are often referred to as *just-in-case* inventories. Once a supplier becomes certified by proving materials conform to quality standards and delivery dates are reliable, then the pull chains in the kanban system can be modified to replenish materials directly from the supplier rather from an inventory maintained in a stockroom. Figure 9.4 illustrates that a simple *Line/RIP/Stores* pull chain can become *Line/RIP/Supplier* to eliminate stockroom inventory. Reduction of inspection and handling costs and potential reductions in stockroom inventories contribute to lower total product cost and provide a competitive edge option that could lead to long-term leadership in the marketplace.

Certification of a supplier requires a joint commitment to an ongoing policy of continuous improvement by the customer company and the certified supplier. A continuous improvement policy requires establishing mutually acceptable product specifications and testing processes; performance monitoring and reporting processes; and the improvement activities necessary to consistently meet and improve specifications. Implementing a continuous improvement policy will increase the ability of the company and a supplier to jointly develop stable, repeatable, processes that lead to better quality. Increased reliability of the supplier to meet specifications and the dependability of supplied materials will allow delivery of the supplier's products directly to the shop floor. Document any agreement about specifications and the commitment to work together to resolve quality and delivery issues.

Although the ultimate goal of successful supplier certification is reduced costs, as with any project, certifying a supplier must provide the company with a return on investment for the time, expenses, and personnel dedicated to the certification project. The benefits should positively impact the company and the supplier. The company should have reduced costs from better quality and lower component prices from the supplier. The supplier should receive increased business as result of better quality and more competitive pricing.

Selecting Candidates for Supplier Certification

Establishing a partnership relationship with new suppliers who have little to no past purchasing history with the company is difficult. The first place to look for potential certification candidates is on the list of approved suppliers. Most companies maintain a list of currently approved suppliers or suppliers from whom purchases have been successfully made in the past. Being on the approved supplier list does not mean a supplier provides material which meets all of the quality and engineering requirements all of the time. The material from an approved supplier might, in fact, range from good to poor, but at the very least being on the approved list means a supplier has received a purchase order in the past and has a history of product delivery. After identifying potential certification candidates from the approved supplier list, identify the suppliers who are willing to enter into a partnership and to make the important paradigm shift to a total quality mindset. Being a potential candidate merely indicates the possibility of a future relationship as a certified supplier. Unless a supplier has achieved a qualified or preferred status, efforts to become certified will likely be difficult or impossible to attain.

Begin the selection process with the preferred supplier list. The first candidates for a supplier certification program should be suppliers who have historically demonstrated performance levels that are better than the minimum requirements for being listed on the approved supplier base. Materials from these suppliers are rarely rejected. These suppliers meet quality and delivery requirements consistently. Often, these suppliers are designated as *preferred* (or qualified) in deference to suppliers who are simply *approved*. Beginning with preferred suppliers is not intended to recognize their past service performance history. Supplier appreciation days and supplier-of-the-year programs are designed to do this. Preferred suppliers are simply singled out by becoming the first candidates for certification. Preferred suppliers are the best candidates for ultimate certification.

Critical materials: another consideration in the selection process. In addition to supplier ranking, other criteria should be considered when selecting candidates for certification. These criteria pertain more to a critical material than to the supplier. For example, for several reasons (factors) a particular raw material may have a more significant impact on the success of the operation than another raw material. These factors must be discussed and the consequences of delivery or quality failures of this material must be weighed. The importance of these factors must be determined as the result of a focused decision-making process. Depending on their degree of impact, some factors may have greater product significance than others. Other criteria to consider for suppliers of critical materials include supplier performance, value and volume of the material, frequency of material deliveries, and the storage space required for the material.

The best suppliers. Like preferred suppliers, suppliers of critical materials who provide the best products have a head start in the certification process. Material received from these suppliers may have a better opportunity for the immediate elimination of many non-value-added activities that have been established to deal with the results of poor quality, late delivery, or specification nonconformance normally experienced from other suppliers. Their past performance history of excellent quality and conformance to specification may merit designating some existing quality-appraisal procedures currently in place as unnecessary. By certifying the in-plant processes of these suppliers, extraordinary inspection efforts on the receiving dock can be identified as non-value-added and subsequently eliminated. Only documentation of the reliability and repeatability of their processes would be required for the certification of these suppliers.

The worst suppliers. If critical material is consistently received out of specification or the supplier has a long history of rejections and missed delivery dates, this supplier may actually be a good candidate for a certification effort, particularly if the supplier is a sole supplier of the material. The costs of nonconformance by this supplier are often hidden. They may be borne unequally by several departments throughout the organization. The total cost of doing business with this supplier may even exceed any pricing benefits received from the supplier, but replacing the supplier might not be a feasible alternative. By implementing a partnership process with this supplier, opportunities to reveal inefficiencies and resolve the reasons for nonconformance may represent the best chance for reducing the costs of required inspections of the supplier's material and the resulting high rejection rates.

High-dollar/high-volume materials. Critical materials in this category represent the highest dollar amount spent by the company per year or the largest volume flowing through a receiving or warehouse area. Any delay caused by inspections or rejected materials results in higher inventory carrying costs. (Inventory turn rates are also an important consideration for cost control for these items.) Certification and the subsequent reduction of appraisal and rejection costs leading to an unobstructed flow of material from the supplier to the manufacturer can result in significant savings along the supply chain.

Bulky/large-space-consumption materials. Lot size usually has little correlation with the use of an item on the shop floor, but lot sizes for critical materials are typically established to meet some other criteria unrelated to space utilization. For example, the need for inspection testing of each incoming shipment of a critical material can define the criteria for establishing supplier lot size. Efforts to reduce the repetitive testing required may lead to ordering material in excess of demand beyond the lead time horizon to amortize the testing process on the receiving dock and in the quality control laboratory. Should an increased amortization strategy be used to dictate order quantities, the space in warehouse areas must be increased to accommodate the additional cubic feet required for the storage of these larger quantities. Warehousing costs are expensive. Poor space utilization results in additional handling costs, increased potential for damage, slower inventory turn rates, increased insurance costs, higher interest expenses for borrowed funds, and increased costs for leased space when overflow storage is needed for large, bulky items. Certifying suppliers of large-space-consumption materials provides opportunities for scheduling the delivery of critical materials to more closely follow the demand rate instead of establishing artificial lot-sizing routines designed to minimize repetitive testing costs. Certified suppliers can use a *skip-lot* or a *no-testing* protocol to facilitate more frequent delivery schedules of smaller sizes.

Delivery frequency. The best way to reduce the handing, storage, and distribution costs associated with critical materials is to match the receiving rate to the production rate. Matching the receiving rate to the production rate requires a supplier to have the capability to make more frequent deliveries using a predetermined delivery quantity. Critical materials from a certified supplier can be shipped directly from the supplier to the customer's shop floor without interruptions caused by order confirmations, appraisals, and inspections. At times the production rate may not represent an efficient lot size for an incoming receiving area, which leads to the temptation to change the lot sizing conventions to allow for economies of scale for handling and warehousing — without regard to the opportunities gained from the cost savings of a better flow of material to match the production rate. Replenishment frequency is the primary inventory investment factor in a kanban system pull chain. A certified supplier who can respond to a kanban signal by shipping directly into a RIP location in the replenishment time established by the kanban signal has an advantage for obtaining future business with the customer.

Steps in Supplier Certification

Establishing a supplier certification process requires the customer company and the suppliers to make major changes in how they do business with one another. Supplier certification is a process to establish a partnership with a supplier based on mutual trust and open communication. For most manufacturers and suppliers, the typical relationship is one of distrust. Even if the customer company does not believe it to be true, the procedures for becoming an approved supplier and receiving business and the three-way match after a sale reinforce the belief that suppliers cannot be trusted with purchasing transactions. These procedures cause the entire customer company/supplier relationship to be adversarial. A successful supplier certification process eliminates adversarial relationships. Implementing change is never easy in any company, but the following ten steps can transform an existing supplier/customer relationship into a certified supplier relationship based on trust. The following ten steps facilitate the change process necessary.

Step 1. Select the suppliers, the specific components, and/or the commodity groups to be certified:
- Form a certification team consisting of a buyer, a design engineer, and a quality assurance staff person.
- Select the suppliers and the components based on the documented scope and objectives of the certification program.
- Discuss the certification program with the supplier candidates to determine their interest in participating in the certification process.

Step 2. Exchange information with each supplier selected:
- Invite each supplier to work with the company as a partner to achieve certification of a specific component commodity or product group.
- Explain the certification process and ensure each supplier understands the goals.
- Determine each supplier's willingness to adhere to agreed-upon quality specifications and delivery guidelines.
- Identify the activities and resources required from the company and from each supplier for participation in the certification process.

Step 3. Evaluate each supplier's capabilities:
- Conduct a technical evaluation of each supplier's manufacturing processes to determine compliance with ISO certifications or other stated

manufacturing policies and procedures. Determine each supplier's technical capability. Determine if a supplier is a Lean manufacturer.

- Establish multifunction communication channels and exchange all available information about manufacturing processes. Schedule visits with suppliers as frequently as necessary for the customer company to better understand a supplier's processes and for suppliers to better understand the customer company's use of their products.

Step 4. Determine each supplier's commitment to the certification process:

- Obtain a commitment from each supplier to dedicate the staffing resources necessary to collect certification data and to work with the company's certification team to correct any discrepancies.
- Obtain agreement with each supplier about critical acceptance characteristics, specifications, test methods, and acceptance limits for a product or commodity group.
- Obtain a commitment from each supplier to proceed with a formal certification plan that includes a schedule for review and evaluation.

Step 5. Identify each supplier's improvement opportunities:

- Provide and review the quality and delivery history of each supplier.
- Identify opportunities for process improvement.
- Agree on process improvement goals and assign priorities to action items.

Step 6. Assess each supplier's process capability:

- Identify operating process variables that affect the ability of a process to produce a consistent product according to specifications using cause-and-effect analysis or other appropriate tools.
- Determine if statistical process control, six sigma, or some other appropriate technique is used to control the manufacturing process. Agree to acceptable upper and lower control limits values for critical processes. If not using statistical process control, agree to another acceptable methodology to monitor production control limits.
- Use applicable tools to determine the relationship between process variables and product quality requirements.
- Reconcile testing data with customer data and validate the test equipment calibration program.
- Evaluate supplier performance on the key process control criteria.
- Document, communicate, and review results with each supplier to ensure processes are in control and a component meets the customer requirements each time it is produced.

Step 7. Assess each supplier's process reliability:

- Ensure each supplier documents process control measures and self-inspection systems.
- Ensure data for qualification and certification of each supplier's processes are available for review and audit.
- Ensure each supplier develops, implements, and documents employee training programs on the concepts of supplier certification with particular emphasis on the quality aspects of proper process control systems. Ensure all operators are trained to perform the identified standard work at their workstations.
- Review and document that materials produced in each supplier's process meet agreed-upon quality specifications on a consistent and repetitive basis. Ensure the process is capable of repeating the identical quality specifications each time it is produced.

Step 8. Agree, approve, and document each supplier's certification agreement:

- Ensure an ongoing measurement system based on quality and delivery performance (as KPIs) is implemented after the certification process is completed.
- Ensure measurements are documented, communicated, reviewed, and updated on a continuing basis for corrective action.
- Establish a schedule for periodic audits to verify that procedures, processes, and products conform to agreed-upon requirements.
- Establish a strict change control procedure to ensure the customer company is notified of any process changes prior to their implementation at the supplier's facility. (Significant changes in a process may require recertification.)
- Establish a procedure for the supplier to report any deviations in procedures, processes, or materials to the customer company.
- Ensure written procedures exist to describe the process used for the certification of certified materials, including all criteria, test results, and final approval.
- Establish acceptance criteria for testing required by the customer company and the ISO (and any other manufacturing standards required by any regulating agency) for the acceptance of materials. If required, each supplier must furnish agreed-upon documentation in lieu of acceptance testing at the customer facility with each shipment.
- Document the schedule for periodic testing and audits, including the basis for decertification and recertification.
- Listen openly to each supplier's improvement suggestions and any needs or concerns during the course of certification.

- Consider new business opportunities for certified suppliers and extend the right of first refusal for any new business with the company to them.

Step 9. Recognize certified suppliers:
- Formally recognize suppliers certified for a component or a commodity with an appropriate recognition ceremony.
- Invite certified suppliers to participate in supplier appreciation day activities.

Step 10. Begin a policy of continuous improvement with all suppliers:
- Continue providing any new requirements, specifications, or quality improvements.
- Encourage striving for product improvement and reduced process variability.
- Maintain regular communication through periodic audits and discussion of process changes/improvements.

Certification of all suppliers would be ideal, but for most companies, 100% certification is not a realistic goal. It's not unusual for a company to have a hundred or more active suppliers. For all of them to be willing to participate in a certification project would be even more unusual. An effective certification process consumes a significant amount of time for the purchasing, quality assurance, and engineering groups for the customer company and for its suppliers. Most customer companies cannot make such a significant commitment to their entire supplier base. Even if making a commitment were possible, some suppliers would likely choose not to enter into a certification partnership. The customer company might be a small-volume customer or the current business volume from the customer company may be acceptable as is. These suppliers therefore do not want to change their business models for the sales volume represented by the customer company. They also may not want to make the changes required for certification by shifting the existing quality-management paradigm to focus resources on prevention of defects rather than depending on inspections. In some cases, the supplier may prefer an arm's-length relationship and not be willing to begin an open relationship with the customer company.

Although the cost reductions achieved from eliminating scrap, defect rejections, and other non-value-added costs associated with handling defective materials and the benefits received from shifting to a prevention approach rather than performing inspections to identify defective materials are well documented, some suppliers just will not be ready to make the necessary changes. These suppliers have made a decision that the time and resources investment does not justify the potential gains to be made. Accommodate the decision of these suppliers. Even if all of the desirable suppliers from the approved list do not choose to participate in the certification program, work with as many as possible. Certifying these suppliers will mean better quality and lower costs. Another option, of course, would be to search for alternative suppliers who are more willing to become certified partners.

The Benefits of Supplier Certification

Although anti-trust laws may prohibit guaranteeing all future business to one supplier, particularly if the agreement is to the detriment of other suppliers, the greater likelihood of faster delivery, decreased costs, and higher quality offers clear distinctions that are hard to ignore when a company is evaluating suppliers. Benefits the customer company can expect from the supplier certification program include:

- *Improved quality.* Product quality will be enhanced by the design of stable, consistent, repetitive processes during the manufacture of products at suppliers' facilities.
- *Inventory reduction.* Inventory levels will be reduced because the need to maintain *just-in-case* buffer inventories for the purpose of continuing production in the event of supplier failure will decrease. Dependable, reliable, certified suppliers do not require a manufacturer to maintain buffer inventories caused by inconsistent, unstable manufacturing processes. Stable manufacturing processes at certified suppliers' facilities are capable of being repeated each time materials are produced.
- *Elimination of quality and testing inspections.* On-site inspections will be eliminated. Rather than relying on inspections to look for defects when materials are received or testing products for defects at the end of a manufacturing process, quality attributes are initially specified and then mutually agreed upon by suppliers. Defective materials are never delivered to the manufacturing line.
- *Increased line productivity.* Improved supplier processes will eliminate the non-value-added work associated with defective materials. Disposition of defective products is eliminated (rework on site, returns to suppliers, and destruction of material). Management support functions are not wasted resolving defective material issues; buyer involvement to replace defective materials is unnecessary; and premium transportation and non-value-added expediting activities expenses are avoided.

- *Improved communication.* Information will be shared between the manufacturing group and suppliers. Communication is no longer limited to the buyer and a supplier's salesperson. Direct communication occurs between functional experts at both locations. Engineers and quality managers at both facilities are encouraged to speak directly with one another to communicate quality criteria and product specifications.

Benefits suppliers can expect from the supplier certification program include:

- *Better supplier relationships.* Certification offers suppliers greater opportunities for repeat business. Certified suppliers have a history of dependable quality and on-time reliability based on past deliveries. Although future business cannot be promised to any one supplier, certified suppliers are often given the right of first refusal for any increased or new business. Having the first chance at new business is a supplier's reward for investing their time and energy into achieving certification.
- *Improved competitive position.* Stable, consistent, repetitive, high-quality processes reduce costs for suppliers. Fewer materials will be rejected by the customer company. Productivity will increase. Handling costs will decrease. The cost of finished materials will therefore be less, making their products more competitive in their marketplace.

Some closing thoughts. Rethinking arm's-length adversarial relationships with suppliers and changing to an open dialogue with certified suppliers will yield long-term benefits for both suppliers and the customer company. Process improvements at both locations can be achieved. The free flow of communication encouraged through a partnership association enhances the philosophy of *Do it right the first time:* defects are prevented before they occur. In the long term, the energy used to prevent defects will yield better results than the energy used for the inspection and correction of defects. Supplier certification processes develop relationships based on trust and the recognition that suppliers are the same conscientious professionals as the customer company. Treat certified suppliers located outside the manufacturing facility as an extension of the manufacturing shop floor.

Web
Added
Value™

PART III
EXPANDING APPLIED LEAN TECHNOLOGY THROUGHOUT THE ENTERPRISE

10

BEGINNING THE OPERATION OF A LEAN LINE

The final design of an optimum Lean factory layout includes workstations designed to provide sufficient space for operators to complete their assigned standard work while still being located as close as possible to the upstream and downstream workstations to maximize flexing opportunities. In addition, the correct number of resources calculated as necessary to achieve the Takt time target of the newly designed Lean line indicated on the perimeter drawing has been located for placement on the shop floor. The finished perimeter layout maximizing the flow of products must then be submitted to an industrial engineer to ensure all regulatory, environmental, and safety regulations have been met by the design. Once the final layout is completed and approved, the physical placement of workstation and machine resources can be made on the factory floor. When the resources and kanban materials are in place and operator training has been completed, the manufacturing of products can begin. When the line begins operation for the very first time, certain systems must be validated to ensure the flow of products one unit at a time within the Takt time target can be accomplished on the line.

Layout. The transformation process team is responsible for presenting the original factory layout from the perimeter drawing to the industrial engineer, who will then develop the final CAD drawings for the shop floor layout. Because all EPA, OSHA, and local regulations must be followed, the industrial engineer will ensure that all safety and environmental regulations were considered by the transformation team and that the final layout submitted by the transformation team includes proper aisle widths with adequate access for fork truck traffic and fire exits as well as easy access and sufficient room for employee traffic.

Staffing. Before startup, operators must be trained to work on the Lean manufacturing line to understand the concept of flexing to a workstation upstream or downstream in response to an IPK. They must be trained to understand the rules of the IPK and how IPKs regulate the manufacturing flow of products. Operators must also be certified to perform the standard work assigned to their primary and one-up and one-down workstations. Material handlers need to be trained to be familiar with pull chains and have a method for communicating changes or improvements to the kanban system. Material handlers must also understand the operation of the material kanban system to maintain the inventory investment policy established for the Lean line. Even though sufficient training has been provided, operators working in the new system will still require an adjustment period when the line is started the first time. Operators who have been accustomed to producing as many products, as fast as they can, may feel strange working on a Lean line that requires pacing work based on a unit of Takt time. Ensure that the IPK discipline of producing only one unit at a time when a signal is given is followed and that batching does not occur.

Sequencing demand. When operation of the Lean system begins, customer demand will need to be sequenced into the manufacturing line based on the customer priority established by a planner. The optimum mix of customer demand must be developed to ensure that the volume at capacity (V_c) is not exceeded. Any special customer configurations requiring sequencing at feeder processes need to be sequenced within the mix and volume constraints of other customer demand and one-time-use materials need to be placed at their points of consumption in the feeder processes.

Product selection. Even though the Lean line is designed to be capable of producing multiple products, only a minimum variety of less-complex products should be produced on the line during the first few days of operation. After a few days, as operators become more comfortable each subsequent day, the line can become fully operational, producing the full complement of products selected to be produced on the line. The same is true for the volume of products chosen to be produced. The first few days of operation may not yield the designed volume, but after an initial startup period, the line will be capable of producing the designed V_c.

Beginning on the first day of operation, the newly designed Lean line should follow a structured process at startup to ensure the line achieves full operational performance as soon as possible. Following the schedule of activities listed in the sections that follow will ensure a managed approach is followed to implement the new operating system.

DAY ONE

Beginning at the very first workstation, members of the process and material transformation teams should position themselves to follow the first sequenced product from workstation to workstation as it advances down the line to observe any imbalances or unique production issues unforeseen during line design activities. They should observe the standard work identified for the product at the first workstation, checking each operator's certification to perform the standard work within the Takt time and quality criteria assigned to the workstation to resolve any revealed issues on the spot or before the end of the shift. The team members should also observe that operators can demonstrate that they can perform the three types of work assigned to the workstation within the established Takt time; ensure that operators have working knowledge of the IPK system; and check that the kanban materials used for production are easy to reach and the RIP is located conveniently for refilling kanban materials in the required replenishment time. To ensure the line is operational, process and material team members also confirm that:

- The standard work content assigned to the workstation is as close to the Takt time as possible: neither too short, nor too long.
- Startup performance to Takt time is monitored and response times are noted and documented.
- Operator training on standard workstation definitions is reinforced.
- IPK discipline is in place and each operator's ability to flex downstream and upstream from their primary workstation is confirmed.
- Operator training to obey the IPK signals is reinforced. As line volume increases throughput during the week, be certain flexing occurs in response to IPK signals.
- A pull chain audit of component materials is conducted.
- The material kanban system is tested by intentionally causing a replenishment signal to occur: ensure that the pull chain operates as designed and review the replenishment procedure to be certain material handlers follow the information listed on the kanban label.
- Planner and scheduler responsibilities are reviewed to ensure that manufacturing customer demand does not exceed line's V_c.
- Procedures for sequencing demand into the first workstation have been developed and reviewed. Observe that no established sequencing rules are violated. Add, change, or delete sequencing rules as necessary to maximize the flow of products on the Lean line.
- Sequencing routines on feeder processes are checked to ensure that subassembly items match the sequencing consumption on the main assembly process.

At the end of the first shift, an operator involvement meeting is conducted by transformation team members to get feedback about results of the first day of operation. After reviewing the results and feedback from the meeting, potential modifications to improve the flow of the line are identified, e.g., improvement of workstation and standard work definitions, workstation location and layout, 5S, kanban replenishment cycles, and any pull sequence issues.

DAY TWO

Process and material transformation team members once again station themselves on the line to assist operators in the event of problems and to:

- Identify the procedures for responding to a shortage of parts and to have a practice drill to identify shortcomings in the response procedure
- Designate and establish the team leader role and to identify support organization requirements
- Assign responsibility to develop procedures for sequencing demand to the line and calculating daily staffing requirements to produce the mix and volume of customer demand that day (This must be done on a daily basis before operation of the line begins.)
- Audit workstation definitions for TQC quality checks and to validate workstation balance to the Takt time
- Monitor each operator's flexibility and movement one up and one down from their primary workstation
- Initiate formal employee certification records and to establish training goals for each operator
- Begin baseline measurement of output variance to plan, Takt time, and manufacturing response times (total product cycle time)

At the end of the day, the operation of the line and any improvements in workstation and standard work definitions, workstation locations and layout, 5S, kanban quantities, and pull sequence issues are reviewed at an operator involvement meeting. Solutions for the feedback from the meetings are developed with the implementation teams. During the review, if an issue cannot be resolved or a solution implemented, it is recorded and assigned to a continuous improvement or kaizen team.

DAY THREE

Process and materials team members continue to monitor the operating system on the shop floor and are available for immediate resolution of any issues. Although the shop floor remains the first priority, emphasis now begins to shift from floor operations to enterprise-wide solutions to institutionalize the Lean operating system as a way of life in the company:

- *Shop floor operations:*
  - *Stock-out and line-stoppage conditions.* Ensure that team leaders can document and resolve material stock-out and line-stoppage conditions should they occur; create a procedure to identify the conditions that require a line stoppage issue to be elevated for resolution.
  - *Demand.* Confirm that a valid procedure is in place for sequencing customer demand into the Lean line at the beginning of the line and at feeder points.
  - *Key performance indicators.* Begin collecting the data required for KPI goals; define the procedures for collecting KPI data and identify the responsibility for KPI maintenance; ensure daily performance measurements are reported and maintained on a daily basis.
- *Steering committee:*
  - *Operating system.* Review the overall status of the Lean operating system and the progress on enterprise-wide issues.
  - *Key performance indicators.* Review the KPIs and the status of the transformation progress. Begin corrective actions to bring performance into compliance.
  - *Operator flexibility.* Introduce methodologies to motivate flexibility, e.g., investigate the possibility of implementing a pay-for-skills system.
  - *Strategies.* Develop strategies for managing potential conflicting Lean manufacturing objectives with other corporate support groups: sales and marketing, cost accounting, engineering, quality assurance and control, purchasing, and planning and scheduling; develop strategies for leveraging improvements realized by the Lean operating system.
  - *Operator improvement meetings.* Document feedback and action items generated from operator improvement meetings during line startup.

- *Facility.* Review the status of any incomplete moves, workstation modifications, facility services, or improvement suggestions.
- *Resources.* Assign authority for modification of the number of resources identified by the Lean line design to match the customer demand; develop alternative work assignments for operators not needed to meet daily customer demand; review the need for new machines, fixtures, or facilities and any other capital expenditures necessary to achieve the future V_c; review workstation balance, training, quality, and other issues identified during startup.
- *Time.* Perform total product cycle time and manufacturing response time audits.
- *Line performance.* Review output rate variance, quality measures, inventory levels and working capital requirements, and on-time delivery.
- *Process and materials transformation team meetings:*
  - *Outstanding issues.* Review any outstanding issues identified by the steering committee.
  - *Directives.* Discuss implementation of any directives authorized by the steering committee.
  - *Operator feedback.* Address organizational issues as they are exposed and respond to feedback generated from operator improvement meetings during line startup. Assign responsibility for the resolution of identified action items.
  - *Continuous improvement.* Organize kaizen teams.

DAY FOUR

Even though fewer operational issues should be occurring by day four, process and materials team members should continue to be available to resolve operational issues as they are discovered. When possible, resolution should be immediate or completed before the end of the shift. When the Lean line begins to operate as designed, emphasis for the process and materials teams must shift from the shop floor to the reconciliation of organizational challenges. Organization issues such as policy and procedural changes may be required in some organizational support groups to continue operation of the Lean system. Required organizational changes are necessary to ensure the Lean line continues to operate at the highest performance level possible.

If conflicting issues with support organizations are not addressed, proponents of the Lean operating system may find themselves defending their new policies and procedures for the operation of the Lean line and debating the benefits realized. Based on the organizational challenge, make appropriate resources available to reconcile policy and procedural issues with each individual department impacted by the implementation of Lean manufacturing. In some cases, a simple training session to inform the organization about the Lean operation and benefits may be all that is necessary. Regardless of the scope of changes needed in support areas, identify and implement any modifications to ensure the continuing success of the Lean operating system. Continue discussions with individual departments for as long as it takes to align departmental policy with the Lean manufacturing operation. Areas that may be impacted by the Lean operating system include:

- *Human resources and manufacturing management for operators:*
  - *Flexibility training:* training added to new employee orientation programs for teaching flexibility concepts to newly hired employees and retraining or reinforcement training for existing employees
  - *Motivation:* development of an incentive program to encourage increased flexibility
  - *Operator skills:* posting of a workstation certification matrix listing operator skill levels by workstation
  - *Proficiency training:* establishing continuing proficiency training and certification programs
  - *Process improvement:* continuing activities for process improvement and elimination of non-value-added work; organization of the continuing operation of kaizen teams
- *Materials management: the kanban system:*
  - *Replenishment signals:* establishing replenishment signal systems, e.g., multicolored lights (andon lights), a milk run system, or a combination of systems
  - *Line changes:* developing procedures for the introduction of new components, demand volumes, replenishment times, and the resulting container label system changes
  - *Engineering change orders:* establishing procedures for the incorporation of engineering change orders into the current Lean operating system
  - *Inventory and kanban system operation:* performing periodic pull sequence audits to test the validity of inventory investment policy and the operation of the kanban system
  - *One-time-use materials:* establishing procedures for handling one-time-use materials

- *Line balancing and resource requirements:* developing procedures to incorporate product mix and volume changes into line balancing and resource requirements
- *Planning management/scheduling and sequencing:*
  - *Resource and line staffing requirements:* developing a daily procedure to determine the resource requirements and line staffing
  - *Customer service:* developing an established customer fulfillment policy in conjunction with the sales and marketing group for standard and configured products
  - *Configured products:* establishing policies and procedures for material planning and the logistics for the manufacture of configured products
  - *Finished goods inventory:* developing policies for managing the finished goods inventory and the introduction of demand backlog into the Lean line
  - *Mixed models:* establishing sequencing rules for the production of mixed models and a daily rate policy not to exceed the stated V_c
  - *Performance measurement:* establishing KPI measurements and a system of performance measurement collection and maintenance
- *Suppliers:*
  - *Lead time:* identifying lead time parameters of components for customer-configured products orders
  - *Signaling policies:* developing kanban signaling policies for individual suppliers and commodity groups within the supply chain
  - *Blanket orders:* establishing a blanket order policy with selected suppliers using a kanban signal as a release against a blanket order
  - *Certification:* beginning a supplier certification program and establishing certified supplier conditions and policies
  - *Specifications:* beginning a policy of sharing component specifications with suppliers to leverage the supplier's functional expertise to reduce or eliminate quality defects
- *Quality control:*
  - *Quality criteria:* beginning the development of graphic work instructions that document quality criteria at workstations; training operators to include inspections for quality criteria as part of their standard work at each workstation
  - *Process improvement:* establishing participation in operator-involved programs to foster process change improvements

- *Operational training:* beginning the implementation of Lean operational training programs for operators
- *Performance measures:* defining and beginning implementation of a formal quality performance measures program (to be included in KPIs)
- *Monitoring performance:* beginning the monitoring of established baseline performance levels and reviewing progress to targets
- *Engineering:*
  - *New products:* monitoring the introduction of new products into the Lean line and the impact on workstation balance
  - *Process improvement/standard work definitions:* documenting process improvements and maintaining SWDs
  - *Graphic work instructions:* creating and maintaining graphic work instructions
  - *Change orders:* incorporating engineering change orders into Lean line documentation
  - *Item master/BOM:* maintaining product item masters and the BOM structure
- *Finance and accounting:*
  - *Costing policy:* modifying standard costing policies and procedures to support Lean operations
  - *Costing transactions:* reviewing costing transactions and reconciling the Lean operating system with GAAP guidelines
  - *Capital investment/inventory turn rate:* establishing working capital investment reduction goals and inventory turn rates as performance measures and tracking them as a function of the KPIs
  - *Utilization:* reviewing efficiency and utilization performance measures and their impact on the new Lean performance measures; reviewing policies causing negative variances and modifying performance measures to reflect Lean operating system performance measures

DAY FIVE AND BEYOND

As on previous days, the process and materials teams must make themselves available to resolve any day-to-day issues that may arise. Any issue requiring resolution beyond the end of day five will require documentation as a project for continuous improvement or kaizen teams. Review the impact of the new Lean line on performance metrics and the operation of corporate systems and functional disciplines continues. Begin discussions to resolve issues for all organizational groups required to support the Lean line also continue, with concentration on the organizational functions and departments with standard operating procedures that require modification to ensure that operation of the line does not conflict with individual department performance measurements. Assistance must be given to organizational functions by developing and reconciling the operation of any dual system created during the transition period from a traditional to a Lean operating system.

Periodic joint meetings must continue with the steering committee and the implementation teams to review outstanding issues that were identified during line startup activities, to establish an action item list based on the remaining outstanding issues, and to assign functional responsibility to ensure enterprise-wide implementation.

Implementing a Lean operating system is *not* a short-term project designed to deliver short-term benefits. Transformation to a Lean operating system is the result of a conscious decision about the way business will now be done each day in the company and a statement of how the company will be operated going forward. The goal of the transformation process is to replace existing operating systems with a more efficient system designed to produce configured products one unit at a time in the sum of the unit's standard work content time. Lean technologies and the resulting benefits should not be relegated to only the manufacturing shop floor. Lean technologies can also be applied to any process in the company, including the administrative processes. Although administrative processes may not require a materials strategy, the concept of producing work in its standard work content time applies to even paperwork processes. To be successful, Lean methodologies must become a way of life for the entire company. Lean must be enterprise-wide.

After the initial transformation process has yielded a new operating system in the manufacturing area, to continue successfully, the new system must be reinforced each day. Otherwise, the result will be a slow return to a previously existing operating system, yielding the same performance as before. All employees, especially management, must remain vigilant for any deviation from the implemented Lean methodology. When a deviation is exposed, *no matter how small*, immediate action must be taken to ensure that a slow return to the old status quo does not occur. Commitment to a spirit of continuous improvement must become a way of life for everyone in the company.

DAILY LEAN LINE OPERATION: TEN COMMANDMENTS FOR CONTINUOUS IMPROVEMENT

A Lean enterprise can always be improved. Even Toyota continues to live in the spirit of continuous improvement after 50+ years of operation. After completing the initial transformation project to a Lean operating system, the following "ten commandments" (or daily operating guidelines) are designed to help your company to make the spirit of continuous improvement part of its company culture. Every employee should learn these guidelines and practice them daily until they simply become a way of life in the company.

Commandment 1: Continually Seek Perfect Balance with the Takt Time Target for All Operations

A Lean line seeks to achieve perfect balance to the established Takt time target. Once started, the Lean line requires perpetual rebalancing to maintain maximum results. Many factors cause a line to become unbalanced after initial startup, but the primary reason is indifference! The effort required to design and implement the new Lean line has likely been all consuming and exhausting, so for transformation team members, getting back to work on an inbox of piled up work is tempting. Abdication of responsibility for the line to someone else is easy to justify. When the project is finished, be sure all support systems are prepared to accept hand-off of the Lean operating system. Reluctance to accept change is the first step to returning to the old comfort levels that caused the company to want to make the transition to a Lean line in the first place.

Remember: Silence is acceptance. Monitoring a Lean line is the responsibility of every employee and manager. If a management team member observes a violation of Lean rules and says nothing, operators assume the violation is acceptable behavior. Always practice management by walking around (MBWA), constantly looking for violations of Lean methodology and process imbalance. Imbalance on a Lean manufacturing line is an early warning signal that something is wrong. Several behaviors are warning signs of imbalance:

- *The work mover.* The work mover unilaterally decides when to add or delete a workstation. This habit indicates an unwillingness to be flexible in response to an IPK, choosing instead to bring nonassigned work into the workstation or relocating uncompleted standard work to another workstation ignoring IPK discipline. *Suggestion: Remember the Lean process rule: people move to work; work does not move to people!*

- *The tool hog.* Tools and equipment are company property. The tools required to perform the work at a workstation belong at the workstation, not in personal toolboxes, trouser pockets, lockers, or bench drawers. *Suggestion: Use silhouette boards to enforce the rule that tools and equipment are company property and constantly enforce the 5S philosophy: a place for everything, everything in its place.*
- *The pack rat.* Always ready for a rainy day or stock-out emergency, the pack rat maintains a *just-in-case* private bank of component parts. *Suggestion: Constantly reinforce the rule that operators are responsible only for the standard work at their workstations. Their job is to build products. Only material handlers are responsible for providing parts to the line.*
- *The cherry picker.* Cherry pickers choose to produce only the units they prefer to build. Using seniority or tenure as justification, cherry pickers often think they are entitled to select the work they do. *Suggestion: Monitor the product mix in the IPKs to confirm the established daily sequence is being followed.*
- *The line designer.* Operators often have great improvement ideas, but implementing them unilaterally cannot be allowed. Ideas must be channeled appropriately for implementation. If an operator independently decides to stop using a piece of equipment or to rearrange work, balance of the rest of the Lean line can be adversely affected. *Suggestion: Reinforce the rule that continuous process improvement meetings are the proper forum for process improvement suggestions.*
- *The pyramid builder.* Before the Lean operating system existed, operators were encouraged and rewarded for producing as many inventory units as possible as fast as they could. Old paradigms such as this will not disappear overnight. Compliance to IPKs is the secret to a one-unit balanced flow. *Suggestion: Reinforce the concept of an IPK as the only authorization to produce another unit of production and watch for compliance: producing one unit at a time; moving completed work to the IPK; and not allowing work to pile up in an IPK. A line imbalance is often revealed when the rules of IPK are violated. Do not ignore this important warning sign.*

Achieve balance. To assume the transformation to a Lean operating system is merely a project with a beginning and ending date is a mistake. Nothing is further from the truth! A Lean transformation requires an immediate, revolutionary change in how a company operates. A slow evolution will not get the job done. The need to achieve perfect balance is the reason a transformation to a Lean line must be a top-down activity. Sponsorship from the grass roots level will only jeopardize the chances for long-term success. Every employee must enforce the Lean methods. Implementation of a Lean operating system is the point at which commitment replaces involvement for the success of Lean in your company. As workstations achieve balance, any remaining work not equal to a Takt should be located at the final workstation. Strive to eliminate imbalance at the final workstation by continuously practicing workstation improvement and kaizen activities. Continually seek to resolve imbalance at workstations by using four repeatable balancing tools:

- *Look for work that can be eliminated.* Dynamic setups and moves are *always* candidates for elimination. The time gained can be used to balance the workstation. Use continuous improvement techniques and kaizen to exploit all process improvement opportunities that reduce or eliminate non-value-added work.

- *Relocate work from workstation to workstation.* Identify standard work tasks at one workstation that could be moved to a workstation with less standard work. Ensure that the elements of work to be relocated from one workstation to the next are technically feasible and will not impact the quality criteria identified at either workstation.

- *Add IPKs to an unbalanced workstation.* Additional IPKs at a workstation create additional work authorization signals to overcome the imbalance caused by standard work in excess of Takt time to maintain the flow of product on both the upstream and downstream side of the unbalanced workstation. The addition of an IPK implies that some amount of additional time will also be necessary to produce any additional units for the unbalanced workstation. Remember that an IPK = inventory = investment dollars, so committing inventory to additional IPKs must be done judiciously. Review all calculations and ensure that all efforts to relocate work and eliminate non-value-added work have been totally exhausted before adding inventory at a workstation.

- *Add resources.* Because adding resources is often the most expensive solution to solving line imbalances and should therefore be exercised as a last resort, always compare the cost of adding resources (people, workstations, machines) to the cost of adding IPK inventories to resolve an imbalance. The best business decision should be based on the decision that yields the lowest overall cost for the company: IPK inventory or added machines, workstations, and people.

Consider work content times. On a mixed-model line, the order of product manufacturing can impact line balance. Avoid grouping and running products that have identical work content times. If possible, follow long work content time products with short work content time products. Mixing the sequence of products running on the line throughout the day helps achieve balance of the line and facilitates completing the desired daily rate.

Even though achieving conceptual *perfect* balance is unlikely, seeking the goal of perfect balance at each workstation must be a never-ending, continuous activity. As *optimum* balance is achieved, and the goal of producing a product in its pure standard work content time is approached, total product cycle and manufacturing response times to customers as well as the need for buffer inventories will continue to be reduced. Successful operation of a Lean enterprise requires a dedication to continuously seeking process balance through continuous improvement. For most companies, this level of commitment to continuous improvement will likely require changing company culture. The reward for changing company culture will be the realization of the advertised benefits of a Lean operating system.

Commandment 2: Continually Strive to Eliminate All Non-Value-Added Work Elements to Achieve Minimum Total Product Cycle Time

Non-value-added work does not change the *form, fit, or function* of the finished product. When performed during the manufacture of a product, non-value-added work is either redundant or used for the *convenience* of a manufacturing process and therefore adds no value to the product itself. Instead, it only adds cost. If the costs of non-value-added work were rolled into the selling price of a product and this cost was known to customers, they would refuse to pay the asking price of the product.

Not only does non-value-added work add cost to a product, but it also adds to manufacturing response time. Every product has an individual critical path through the manufacturing processes that requires an absolute minimum amount of time. Total product cycle time is the sum of the minimum amounts of standard value-added time in which a product can be produced (Figure 10.1). The difference between total product cycle time and customer-quoted lead time is the non-value-added time added to the total product cycle time. Customer-quoted lead time includes both value-added and non-value-added time expended during the manufacturing processes. The additional time required to perform non-value-added activities extends the manufacturing response time to customers. If speed of delivery is an important product differentiator for a customer, non-value-added time may be the difference causing lost sales to a competitor who can deliver shorter manufacturing response times.

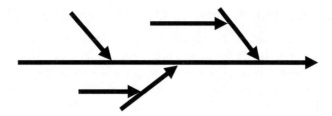

Figure 10.1. Total product cycle time.

Setups and moves. Setups and moves are work elements that are always considered non-value added. Setup work is done in preparation for performing other work. A setup performed each Takt time is a *dynamic* setup. A setup that requires a machine or process to be stopped (an internal setup) while the setup is performed is a *static* setup. In both instances, the time necessary to perform the setup is non-value-added time: while the product is waiting for the setup to be completed, the *form, fit, and function* remain unchanged and completion of the product cannot be advanced. This waiting time adds to the response time for the product. Move work is required to advance a product to the next location. During development of the facility layout, great effort was made to physically locate manufacturing processes as close to one another as possible to reduce or eliminate the time required for movement of material to a downstream location and to ensure that the output of one process would be consumed immediately into the next process. Every opportunity to minimize the movement of products should be exploited. By documenting the move and setup work when creating the standard work definitions, the opportunities for improvement were also identified. Because the times for these work elements were also identified, the improvement opportunity can be quantified and prioritized for reduction or elimination by the kaizen team.

Any non-value-added work that occurs on the longest-time critical path of products has a direct impact on manufacturing response time. Eliminating non-value-added work along the critical path of the total product cycle time always reduces the total product cycle time while simultaneously shortening the manufacturing response time. Continually seeking to eliminate non-value-adding activities is a never-ending activity in a Lean facility that should become part of every job description, from operators to management to the president of the company.

Commandment 3: Strive to Eliminate Process Variability

Variability is defined as: *having multiple procedures for completing the work elements of a process or an individual task, with only one way being the correct way.* Almost all manufacturing processes contain some variability. When performing a process work task that has variability in a traditional operating system, interpreting the *one correct way* to complete the work is often left to individual operators. If the interpretation is made by an operator with extensive experience or a strong skill set, the interpretation is likely to be correct, resulting in a high-quality product. Conversely, if another operator, who may be very well intentioned, but has less experience and training or underdeveloped skills, makes another interpretation of the correct way, the result may be very different. With more process variability, the opportunities for individual interpretations and workmanship-related defects increase. If the correct way to complete work is left to individual interpretation, the impact on product quality can be disastrous.

Determining the *one correct way* to complete work is the responsibility of management, not line operators. Management should identify the variability at every workstation and provide instructions to operators so they can learn the one correct way to perform the standard work needed to complete a process. Until a process can be made 100% fail-safe, with no chance of producing a defect, the best option is to require the operator to perform an inspection at the point where the variability occurs. Unfortunately, this inspection requires work to be done by the operator that is non-value-added — no change is made in *form, fit, or function* and the time required to perform the inspections adds to the total product cycle time — but until a fail-safe process can be developed allowing only *one correct way* to produce a product, inspections are the only way to ensure that process variability is not subject to individual operator interpretation. Inspections require continuous improvement and kaizen projects to achieve a fail-safe level of quality. Once continuous improvement and kaizen projects are successful, opportunities to reduce variability are discovered, quality is improved, and manufacturing response time is reduced.

Graphic work instructions. Until a process can only be performed in only *one correct way*, it is subject to some level of variability. With this in mind, the variability of any process is documented at the task level when the standard work definition is written. The time necessary to perform inspection work to recognize and correct this variability is then included in the Takt time amount of standard work assigned to that workstation. Once standard work for each workstation has been defined, the exact location where variability occurs is identified. Instead of placing a copy of the standard work definition at the workstation, variability is communicated to the operator at the workstation by posting a GWI (graphic work instruction). A GWI is a pictorial representation of the Takt time amount

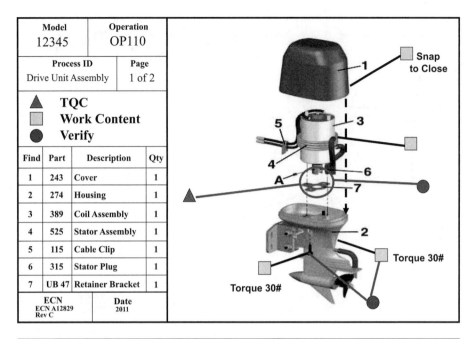

Model	Operation
12345	OP110

Process ID	Page
Drive Unit Assembly	1 of 2

▲ **TQC**
◻ **Work Content**
● **Verify**

Find	Part	Description	Qty
1	243	Cover	1
2	274	Housing	1
3	389	Coil Assembly	1
4	525	Stator Assembly	1
5	115	Cable Clip	1
6	315	Stator Plug	1
7	UB 47	Retainer Bracket	1

ECN	Date
ECN A12829 Rev C	2011

Figure 10.2. A graphic work instruction.

of standard work assigned to the workstation (Figure 10.2). A GWI not only identifies the work to be completed, but it also defines the quality criteria for that workstation. Each workstation must have a GWI so operators know what standard work is to be completed at that workstation and to confirm the *one correct way* to produce the product. Once correct manufacturing instructions have been identified for a work task with variability, operators no longer have any reason to make individual standard work or quality interpretations.

Inspections. Operators are responsible for performing the inspection work required to ensure that a task with variability has been completed according to the GWI. At each workstation where variability occurs, operators are trained to perform two quality inspections in addition to the required standard work assigned to the workstation for every unit produced. These inspections, in combination with the required standard work, identify the three types of work to be done during each Takt time at the workstation. The first quality inspection is of the upstream operator's work. This inspection ensures that the specified quality inspection work upstream has been performed by the operator at that workstation (indicated by a triangle in Figure 10.2). The square indicates the value-added standard work required to be completed at the workstation. The second quality inspection is a visual verification of the operator's own value-added standard

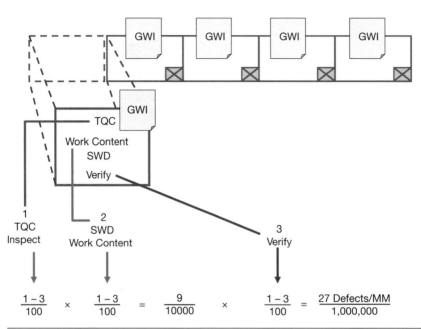

Figure 10.3. The three types of work at a workstation: the work content and the two quality checks required for each Takt time of work.

work to ensure any possible variability at the workstation (e.g., the *Torque 30#* specification) has been inspected (indicated by a circle in Figure 10.2). Both of these quality inspections must be recorded on the GWI for the workstation. The two quality inspections used in conjunction with the assigned standard work illustrated in the GWI in Figure 10.2 can achieve a quality level of 27 parts per million defects. This is equal to approximately a 5 sigma level of quality just by performing quality inspections. Figure 10.3 illustrates the quality checks each operator is required to perform for each Takt time of work at their own workstation. Inspection work, however, is always non-value-added work because no change in *form, fit, or function* is made by performing the inspection. The time required to perform inspections also adds to the total product cycle time and is subject to elimination by continuous improvement or kaizen activity.

Estimates are that 70 to 80% of product cost is determined by the design engineering resources in a company. Reducing manufacturing response time by reducing process variability requires coordination of the design and manufacturing engineering resources of the company. It is common for the design engineering staff to be unaware of how a product is actually put together on the shop floor in manufacturing. The primary role of the design engineering staff is to design a product to meet a prescribed functionality. Often manufacturability is a secondary consideration. It is not unusual for the design of a new product or component to be assigned to multiple design engineers who are responsible for specific components or processes. Once an item has been designed by the engineering team, complete product assembly and how to put the product together are often left to the manufacturing shop floor. Left to manufacturing management, new product or component introductions often lead to interpretation and additional quality elements being added to the standard work definition to compensate for design shortcomings.

Commandment 4: Enforce 5S Housekeeping Practices

Orderliness and neatness are critical requirements in a Lean working environment. An organized, neat work area not only looks good, but it is more conducive to producing quality products. Clutter is not tolerated. Only the necessary tools, fixtures, gauges, and other resources are present at workstations. The workstation is clearly identified and material locations are clearly marked so materials that do not belong in the area are conspicuous. Any item not in its proper place highlights a problem. Improperly placed materials can indicate that an individual operator has made an interpretation about where to store material. Planning system paperwork is minimal because reliance on the output of a shop floor control system to determine the location or progress of an order is limited. Employees take pride in having neat working areas.

The best time to implement 5S is when the physical rearrangement of resources and the deployment of the Lean factory design are underway. Design of the line has identified the number of workstations and labor resources required to produce customer demand in the Takt time target. For every labor resource, there must be a corresponding space, footprint, or workstation where standard work will be performed on the shop floor. As workstations are located on the shop floor, each should be carefully designed, one at a time, at the time of placement. Each individual workstation design should incorporate the 5S guidelines:

Seiri (sorting). Remove all items not used on regular basis. A major component of a Lean line is the removal of items identified as unnecessary for the production of the product: toolboxes, file cabinets, lockers, tables, stools, personal items, cooking appliances, coffee pots, extra desks, tables, shelves, and excess drawers. These items provide opportunities for accumulating unnecessary, unneeded items: parts, tools, and manuals. Accumulating unnecessary items is human nature. Some operators create comfort zones with a "home away from home" by surrounding themselves with a variety of personal items. Others build personal inventories of extra materials and components based on past experiences such as part shortages or unavailable tools or fixtures so they can be prepared just in case a historical emergency is repeated in the future. These items often slowly accumulate over time until these operators do not want to leave their workstations to flex upstream or downstream. Personal workstations conflict with the Lean concepts of balance and flexibility. Reinforce the concept that the company owns the workstations, fixtures, and tools. The individual operator does not.

Seiton (set in order). Identify and arrange the items that belong in each area: *a place for everything and everything in its place.* In addition to the physical layout and location of workstations, locate tools, fixtures, and parts so they are easily accessible to operators. Each item required for production should have an assigned location at the workstation where it is used daily or adjacent to its point of usage. Assigned locations are also important for specific materials not directly used at workstations: pallet jacks, fork trucks, cleaning materials, trash receptacles, and other portable material-handling fixtures. Parking spaces for ancillary support items should be adjacent to the workstation where the items are used most frequently. Indicate the spaces for all ancillary items on the shop floor. If any ancillary item is unnecessary for the production of products, remove it from the shop floor. Enforce the discipline of returning all supporting items to their assigned parking spaces when not in use. Also designate a space for one-time-use kanban materials on the shop floor at the workstations that require them. Provide silhouette boards for tools and fixtures that are located within operator reach; paint squares on the shop floor; suspend air and electrical lines; and have kanban racks and containers placed within easy reach of operators.

Seiso (shining, sweeping). Maintain order, sweep and clean, and shine. The reason for maintaining a clean workplace is obvious: operators take pride in a clean, orderly workplace, which is reflected in the products they build. An equally important reason for maintaining a clean workplace is to provide an early warning system for problems. A cluttered workplace can hide problems: an accumulation of rejected materials may indicate a quality problem; a pile of spare parts may indicate a faulty kanban system; and extra uncompleted units not in the IPK may indicate imbalance on the line. A clean environment makes potential problems more conspicuous. Follow a daily regimen of *shining* workstations. Shining helps to create ownership in equipment and the facility. Inattention to equipment leads to equipment failure. Operators are more likely than anyone else to notice equipment changes: air, oil, and coolant leaks; contamination; or vibration, machine fatigue, misalignment, and maintenance deficiencies. Reinforce continuous improvement with a daily regimen of cleaning. Build in time to perform cleanup at the beginning and end of each shift and deduct the time for shining activities from the available time in your Takt time calculations to ensure that time is made available each day to perform these tasks.

Seiketsu (standardize). Getting the most out of a Lean line requires minimizing individual interpretations. For example, the line's operation has been designed so, on a daily basis, operators can maximize the time building products and minimize the time spent making quality, priority, and quantity decisions. The standard work definition has identified the standard work necessary to produce the products. The individual tasks of standard work, grouped to a Takt time, have been assigned to each workstation and are to be repeated each time a product enters the workstation. Operators have been trained to perform the three types of work at each individual workstation; to respond to decisions using Lean methodology; and to follow the standard work definition and repeat the same set of work rules for each product. The Lean operating system therefore indicates what to do and when to do it, which provides a key benefit for Lean managers who practice MBWA. Because work and procedures have been standardized, a simple walkthrough easily monitors manufacturing processes and spots deviations from standard Lean practices. Operators performing standard work and making standard reactions to deviation will require less day-to-day supervision.

Shitsuke (sustain): Monitoring working conditions is a responsibility shared by operators and managers, but management must immediately respond to rule violations or operators will assume violations are acceptable. A primary reason for MBWA is to observe operation of the Lean system and to watch for possible rule violations. MBWA limits individual interpretations while encouraging operators to propose solutions and elevate problems to the continuous improvement team. Managers have the advantage of seeing the bigger picture of the entire line and must take ownership of problem solving:

- *Work conditions.* Use newly established 5S housekeeping policies, IPK, and flexing rules as a management tool to focus on details. Attention to detail is one of the first things to deteriorate on a Lean line: always look for items that are out of place. Most minor issues can be resolved on the spot. Larger problems may require more time. They must become the subject of continuous improvement or kaizen projects.
- *Operator flexing.* Never stop monitoring the flexibility of labor resources. Having flexible employees and the ability to vary mix and adjust volume on a daily basis based on actual daily demand are key differentiators for the company's competitive advantage.
- *Overtime.* Needing overtime should always be a temporary situation. Overtime should be used only for short-term anomalies to handle unanticipated spikes in demand. Continuing to use overtime as a solution to meet customer demand may indicate a Lean line designed with a V_c that is too small. Determine if demand spikes are short term

or recurring. If increased customer demand is constant, the Lean line may need to be rebalanced.

- **Teamwork.** Engage team members in discussions about line performance. Request ideas for continuous improvement and ensure that team members have a simple, accessible mechanism for suggesting improvements to products and processes. Allow team members to have some control over their own destiny by giving them control over their working conditions while they focus on line performance.

- **Line performance.** Establish performance measurements and then track and publish them. Assign a designated location at the end of the line such as a white board or flipchart to display daily production targets and the actual production performance. Discuss performance and improvement suggestions during formal employee involvement meetings.

- **In-process quality.** Establish and continue emphasizing the value and importance of the three types of work to be completed at workstations: previous operator quality check (TQC), standard work content, and verification. The objective is to catch and fix all defects before they ever reach a QC checkpoint or the last point of rejection on the line. Perform spot checks, e.g., have a team lead or manager select a unit at random from an IPK and verify that the work at that point is being done correctly and that the work is no more or less than it should be according to the standard work for the workstation. Perform spot checks frequently and in full view of operators. Give instant feedback.

- **Training.** Trained employees are a key element to ensure a sustainable Lean transformation. Training must include completing the three types of work at the operator's primary workstation and the work at one workstation upstream and one downstream. As employees receive more training, they become more flexible. As employees become more flexible, the Lean line will be more flexible and can respond to more variability of demand mix and volume.

The methodology of a Lean operating system is powerful, but it is not magical: the results are directly proportional to the commitment of the organization to make the system work.

Even though 5S housekeeping practices add order and discipline to manufacturing and administrative processes, if 5S is implemented as a stand-alone system, the financial benefits will be limited. 5S housekeeping practices are perfect companions for the Lean operating system because the principles of each support the other.

Commandment 5: Ensure Clear and Visible Downstream In-Process Kanban Signals for Every Operator

On diagrams, a common symbol used to depict an IPK is a black ✕ on a colored background, but an IPK can take numerous forms, depending on the physical layout of a line: a painted area on the floor; painted conveyor rails; light systems and flags; an empty workstation; or empty pallets, material carts, and portable workstations. Whatever form is used, IPKs must be clear, visible signals for upstream workstations.

After a Lean line has been balanced and the physical layout has been adjusted to consume the output of one process directly into another, IPKs are the key to making the line flow properly. An IPK authorizes performance of another Takt time amount of work at the workstation; regulates the line to maintain the designed Takt rate; and uses a planner to determine the sequence of production to satisfy customer demand priority, eliminating the need for production orders from a planning system to determine the product to be produced next. A Lean line also challenges the need for production schedules. IPKs are necessary to maintain balance, to ensure the product is produced at the Takt rate, as an authorization to work, and as a signal to operators when they need to flex.

For balance. An IPK provides a temporary location or parking space for a partially completed unit of production until the downstream operator is authorized to pull the unit into the downstream workstation and perform another Takt time amount of standard work. If workstations are properly balanced, a partially completed unit will remain in an IPK for only one Takt time or less. Even with continuous balancing activities, achieving perfect balance on a Lean line is unlikely. If achieving perfect balance for the tasks of standard work were possible, likely operators on the line would still be unable to achieve perfect balance every Takt time because other conditions might also exist that could be causing imbalances. The operation of a Lean line should be like liquid flowing through a pipe. If a pipe diameter is not the same, the flow will become constricted or insufficient to fill the pipe. The most efficient pipe has the same measured diameter for the entire length of the pipe. Unbalanced processes act as a constriction in the line. If imbalance is a recurring situation on the line, partially completed products will temporarily stop production upstream and downstream with every Takt cycle and cause the line to have a jerky-appearing flow. If imbalances occur repeatedly, rebalancing may be necessary, but if they are an anomaly, case-by-case management intervention may be sufficient.

As a signal to produce. Unlike items stored in the two-bin material kanban system, IPKs are non-part-number specific and totally impartial to items placed in them: an item in an IPK is simply the next item sequenced on the line. An empty IPK signals a workstation operator to produce another unit and place it in the IPK at the workstation when completed. As completed units are pulled from the end of the line for distribution to a final customer, a signal is generated at every workstation upstream along the entire length of the line. When the signal reaches the first workstation of the line or feeder process, the first operator simply pulls the next customer requirement in the same sequence as determined by a planner. As long as a partially completed unit resides in an operator's IPK, there will be no signal at the workstation to produce another unit. As long as the workstation IPK has a partially completed unit parked in it, operators are not allowed to pull the next unit from the upstream IPK. If the workstation stops work for any reason for one Takt time or less, one less unit will continue down the line until finally the arrival of a unit into the final workstation at the end of the line is skipped. If the reason for the skipped unit of production is not resolved, the entire line could eventually stop: from partially completed units in IPKs at workstations all the way upstream to the beginning operation on the line and from empty IPKs in all workstations downstream as the units in upstream IPKs are consumed to the end of the line. An unresolved problem at one workstation can easily become a problem for an entire line!

As a signal to flex. Based on the number of workstations being used on a Lean line, a partially completed unit at a workstation without an operator stays at the workstation an additional Takt time until an operator can flex into the workstation and complete the standard work assigned to the workstation before being advanced to the next workstation. Flexing rules and IPKs signal operators when to work at a workstation or when to move to an adjacent workstation by *flexing* upstream or downstream to continue the work on a unit of production. Machines and workstations are inflexible and cannot be modified daily, but labor resources are totally flexible and can easily be adjusted by adding or subtracting operators daily as necessary to match customer demand. Matching required resources to customer demand is not possible without this flexing capability. Customers rarely order the same mix and volume on two consecutive days. To avoid the wastes associated with overproduction and excess inventory, daily staffing decisions are necessary to match labor resources to the actual customer mix and desired volume. By assigning only the number of operators based on the desired daily output of the line, an output range of 50 to 100% of designed volume can be produced without changing the Takt time or standard work assigned to the workstation. At the last workstation on the line, if a partially completed unit remains upstream for one extra Takt time, each Takt cycle, only 50% of the designed V_c will be produced. Operators remain 100% utilized even if all workstations are not fully utilized. Machine and workstation utilization or OEE measurements must be modified to measure the operator (labor) resources separately from the machines and workstation resources. Because flexing allows operators to continue working without remaining idle while waiting for other operators to catch up, productivity goals are facilitated. Having a flexibility signal not only improves productivity, but facilitates the response of the line to daily customer product mix with optimum staffing.

Regardless of the IPK signal type chosen, the paramount rule is the *upstream operator must be able to see his/her IPK signal*. If an operator is unable to see an IPK, there is no way to regulate the line and maintain first-in/first-out sequencing of the line.

Commandment 6: Facilitate the Collection of Continuous Process Improvement Ideas from Everyone Working on the Line

The essence of a Lean line is standardization of methodology, procedures, and operator behavior. Standardization reduces the opportunities for individual interpretation. Once a Lean operating system is in place, individual interpretation by operators is not permitted. The effort required to balance the line, install the kanban systems, and operate the line based on the staffing necessary to produce an established daily rate is the product of facility optimization and line design. Operational discipline, however, does not mean that ideas and recommendations are undesirable. On the contrary, Lean methodology values ideas and suggestions for continuous improvement. Operators who build a product day in and day out often understand the nuances of a product better than the engineers who designed it. Ignoring the immense storehouse of operator product knowledge is equivalent to the eighth *waste* of manufacturing.

Management must provide a formal collection and evaluation mechanism for the expression of ideas and suggestions by operators. A common method is conveniently placing a flipchart (or whiteboard) adjacent to the line so that operators can record their suggestions throughout the day or when ideas occur to them. There is no requirement that operator ideas be fully complete before they are posted on an idea flipchart. Ideas can be developed later during a kaizen project. Continuous process improvement ideas can then be discussed daily or as needed. Remember that Takt time states a time/volume relationship that defines the rate required to build a designated volume of product in the time available. Takt is then used to identify the number of manufacturing resources required to achieve the rate necessary to meet customer demand requirements. A time allowance for continuous process improvement discussions such as 5S or flipchart suggestions can be built into the Takt time calculation numerator as a function of the effective working time (minutes) per day. Meeting time for process improvement ideas must be deducted from the available minutes per day used for the Takt time calculation to accommodate the time used for improvement discussions. This allowance removes any excuses for time being unavailable to discuss process improvement ideas.

Continuous process improvement meetings can be held on a daily basis in the time allocated in the Takt time calculation, usually 3 to 5 minutes per day, or the 3 to 5 minutes per day can be accumulated throughout the week and a 15- to 25-minute meeting can be held on a specified day of the week so support team members can arrange their schedules to be available. Meetings should include a quick review of ideas and can be in a stand-up format at the end of the shift:

- *Leadership.* Meetings should be lead by the team leader of the line. The team leader is a facilitator only and does not pass judgment on any idea presented. Making summary judgments about suggestions will cause team members to remain silent for fear of ridicule. The team leader should be provided with facilitator training. A poor meeting facilitator can cause a continuous improvement process to fail because team participation will cease.

- *Resolution.* Taking action on ideas is crucial for the success of a continuous improvement process. The team leader of the line leads the meeting, but resolution of an idea becomes the responsibility of the individual who suggested it. If this individual does not have the technical expertise to develop a solution for their idea, the team leader should recommend other support staff members to provide assistance. Allow time for the idea to be investigated and appropriate solutions recommended, e.g., during times when the operator suggesting the idea is not assigned to the line because of a less-than-capacity daily rate.

- *Prioritizing.* Ideas should be prioritized. As ideas are recorded on the flipchart, they can often be organized into categories: environmental, safety, quality, esthetics, ease of production, design, and functionality. Separate the ideas by category. Give top priority to implementing safety, quality, and environmental ideas.

- *Follow-up.* A portion of every continuous improvement meeting should be devoted to following up on the status of previous assignments. The team leader should monitor and provide assistance to ensure progress is being made on all assignments.

A continuous improvement process is not designed to be like a suggestion box with ideas that seldom see the light of day. All ideas and suggestions must be addressed, investigated, and resolved. If operators perceive that a continuous improvement process is ineffective or simply a show for top management and visitors, ideas and suggestions will quickly cease and regression to the old methods of individual interpretation and problem solving will quickly replace the improvement process. If operators' ideas are not addressed openly, individual interpretation by operators will slowly cause variability that eventually increases the manufacturing response time, causes quality defects, and increases WIP inventories. This must not happen!

Commandment 7: Ensure Adequate Training to Allow Operators to Flex a Minimum of One Workstation Downward and One Workstation Upward from Their Primary Workstations on Any Given Day

If customer demand is 100% of designed volume, each workstation will be staffed and flexing will not be necessary, but on most days, customer demand will most likely be less than the available (designed) capacity of the line and operators will be required to be flexible to avoid overproduction. Having the capability to increase or decrease staffing to match a daily sales rate requires operators to perform the work assigned to their primary workstations in addition to the work at one workstation upstream or downstream and to flex in response to an IPK signal. Operators must therefore know how to perform the three types of work assigned to at least three workstations (a quality check of work from the previous workstation, performance of the required work at the primary workstation, and self-verification of the work performed at the primary workstation). A successful Lean manufacturing line therefore requires two different categories of training: the ability to perform three types of work for the various product models used to design the line and the ability to flex in response to an IPK signal.

An ability to produce different product models on the manufacturing line. Prior to implementation of the Lean operating system, existing operators may have been assigned to produce only specific products or to perform all of the standard work required for one complete product at a single workstation. On a Lean line, operators are limited to producing only a Takt time amount of work for any product that arrives in their workstation on any given day. When less-skilled operators are not assigned to the line, pair them with skilled operators to learn to build all models.

An ability to flex in response to an IPK. Although flexing is a simple concept, flexing is not intuitive for many operators when starting a Lean line. Flexing may even be unnatural in the beginning because many operators have been conditioned to be productive even during periods of wait time. They prefer to use any wait time to build extra units of inventory in advance of demand so they will have more discretionary time later in the day. This practice of building ahead is also known as *pyramid building*. Pyramid building is an indication of imbalance at a workstation. When a Lean line goes live for the first time, all operators must be already trained to flex. Instead of using wait time to build ahead, operators will be required to flex into another workstation in response to an IPK. The ability to flex is a key to achieving productivity improvement. Ongoing coaching of line operators will be required after startup to instill and reinforce the IPK discipline. Incorporate flex training in new employee orientation programs. Establish a Lean training academy to ensure that all new employees understand the practice of flexing and are ready to work on a Lean line. Prior to assignment, new employees should graduate from the training academy. After graduation, mentoring by certified operators and GWIs and standard work definitions can be used on the line to reinforce the initial employee orientation training.

Identifying operator certification skills. All operators must be certified prior to assignment to the Lean line. Operator certification is defined as *the operator must demonstrate that the work at a certain workstation can be completed within the Takt time target with the quality criteria identified for that workstation.* To monitor the certification skills of operators, post a qualification matrix or an employee certification board in the manufacturing area so management can easily track the certifications of each operator (Figure 10.4). Should reassignment of an operator be necessary to compensate for absenteeism, vacation, or reassignment to other areas in the company, the team leader of the line can easily identify operators who are qualified to fill in for an absentee.

Productivity measurement considerations. By design and definition, a Lean line beginning with day one of operation has a capacity sufficient to meet demand estimated from 1 to 3 years into the future. During the 1- to 3-year period when customer demand is not equal to line capacity, the Lean line will have excess capacity. If output of the Lean line is not adjusted to match actual sales, but is allowed to run at the higher designed capacity during the projected sales period, unsold inventory will be produced. Unless the traditional measurements of utilization are changed to reflect the adjusting of output to match demand by the Lean line, the temptation to run the line at capacity will be great. To avoid utilization of excess capacity, which causes production of unsold inventory and inflation of working capital, work-in-process, and finished goods inventory investments, new productivity (utilization) performance measurements must be developed to measure operator (labor) resources separately from machine and workstation resources. A Lean manufacturing line has the capability to reduce its output to match customer demand. Having the ability to modify the number of operators assigned to a production line on any given day to match output to the daily rate of sales is fundamental to the successful operation of a Lean line and your company's ability to manage inventory investment. Traditional planning systems are

Line		Chassis Line									Bucket Assembly					Final Assembly		
Process	CHP-1	CHP-2	CHP-3	CHP-4	SF-1	WH-1	HA-1	OR-1	OR-2	TA-1	BP-1	BP-2	CG-1	CGB-1	BI-1	AE-1		
A Shift																		
Lorne																		
Ben																		
James																		
Richard																		
Bill																		
Mike																		
Tom																		
Chad																		
B Shift																		
Rick																		
Anthony																		
Bob																		
Rod																		
Scott																		
Jody																		

◉	In-training	●	Qualified	●	Master

Figure 10.4. Sample employee certification board for tracking the certifications of each operator.

simply not designed to allow a manufacturing resource to run at any capacity other than full capacity at all times. This inability to manage line output to match demand is why traditional planning systems continue to generate overproduction, the number one cause of *waste* in manufacturing. Without the output rate modification capability of a Lean line, traditional manufacturers will have no choice but to continue filling their warehouses with finished goods inventory whenever customer demand is less than line capacity.

Performance measurement considerations. Intentionally staffing a Lean line with fewer operators than the workstations available to meet the design capacity effectively *suboptimizes* the line. Because the number of operators on a Lean line can be different each day, cost accounting departments may categorize operators not assigned to the line as underutilized and issue a negative variance report to their department managers. In addition, current cost accounting methodology considers unsold inventory as an asset on the balance sheet. Therefore, matching production rates to sales rates lower than available capacity will require a review of cost accounting methodology to allow labor resources to be less than 100% utilization compared to the value of unsold work-in-process and finished goods inventories. Performance measurements for a Lean line will need to be modified to reward compliance to customer demand rather than the simple utilization of resources. Reductions of inventories will be reflected in the amount of cash available on the balance sheet. Inventory reduction also reduces working capital. Working capital funds liberated from inventory investment can then be diverted to a myriad of other investment opportunities for the company. Measurement of Lean line performance is better determined by how linear the production output is compared to the scheduled daily rate measured against the actual production rate that day. Production of fewer units than scheduled or the units produced in excess of the daily rate are summed and compared to the scheduled quantity, ignoring the pluses or minuses, to achieve an absolute value: the linearity goal for a Lean line is 90% or better.

Commandment 8: Reward Achievement of Performance and Flexibility Goals to Reinforce Desired Behavior

The Lean operating system recommends having incentives that reinforce and reward the disciplines necessary to perpetuate and institute Lean as a way of life across the enterprise. Performance measurements and KPIs must be established to provide incentives in the organization to promote and improve the Lean operating system (also known as a balanced scorecard).

Performance measurements. Linearity, flow rate, and on-time delivery are the three key performance measurements for a Lean manufacturing line.

- *Linearity.* Linearity is an output measurement that compares the number of units scheduled to be produced with the number of units actually produced. Actual output that deviates from planned output (more or less) is recorded as an absolute value (neither positive nor negative) and posted daily, weekly, and monthly. Linearity is calculated by subtracting the actual output from the scheduled output:

Actual = 44	Schedule = 40	Difference = 4
Actual = 44	Schedule = 48	Difference = 4

  For a measuring period (typically a month), sum the differences (absolute deviations) and scheduled quantities for the period. Subtract the sum of the differences from 1 and divide the result by the sum of the planned quantities. Multiply this result by 100 to determine the percent of linearity: the desired goal for linearity is 90%.

$$\text{Linearity} = \left[\frac{1 - (\Sigma \text{ differences})}{(\Sigma \text{ planned}))} \right] \times 1000$$

  Figure 10.5 illustrates the daily linearity measurement postings required to calculate daily and monthly linearity: the daily rate of scheduled units, actual production minus quality rejections, absolute deviation, and the sum of absolute deviations.

- *Flow rate.* Flow rate defines the number of units expected to be produced during a specified time frame of the available work minutes of the day. Flow rate is usually measured at the end of a line on a daily basis (or on a weekly basis in a low-volume environment), but if desired, flow rate can also be measured throughout the day at different workstation points along the line to monitor the rate of production to project whether or not the scheduled daily rate of production will be achieved in the scheduled time available. If close monitoring of the flow rate indicates that achievement of the daily rate is in jeopardy, early detection will allow sufficient opportunity to make the necessary adjustments or corrections to the line to bring the flow rate back into compliance. The flow rate is determined by using a simple calculation:

  Flow rate = daily scheduled units ÷ scheduled time per day

  At any point in time, the flow rate can be applied at any workstation on the line and monitored to determine if the scheduled daily rate is being met. If, for example, a shift has 7 effective hours (or 420 minutes) and the scheduled daily rate is 360 units, 360 units should be

Output Rate Variance Report							
Month:							
Day	**Daily Rate Sequenced**	**Actual Units**	**Team QC Rejects**	**Absolute Deviation**	**Sum of Absolute Deviation**	**Daily Linearity (%)**	**Month-to-Date Linearity (%)**
1	25	24	3	4	4	84.00	84.00
2	25	24		1	5	96.00	90.00
3	25	26		1	6	96.00	92.00
4	25	25		0	6	100.00	94.00
5	25	24		1	7	96.00	94.40
6	25	23		2	9	92.00	94.00
7	25	27		2	11	80.00	93.71
8	25	22	3	5	16	90.00	92.00
9	25	27		3	19	86.67	91.74
10	30	26		4	23	100.00	91.15
11	30	30		0	23	96.67	92.07
12	30	31		1	14	100.00	92.50
13	30	33	3	0	14	96.67	93.14
14	30	29		1	25	90.00	93.42
15	30	28	1	3	28	93.33	93.17
16	30	28		2	30	96.67	93.18
17	30	29		1	31	92.00	93.40
18	25	24	1	2	33	88.00	93.33
19	25	22		3	36	92.00	93.08
20	25	23		2	38	88.00	93.03
21	25	25		0	38	92.00	93.33
22	25	24		1	39	100.00	93.45
23	25	26		1	40	96.00	93.55
24	25	27		2	42	92.00	93.49
25	30	28	2	4	46	86.67	93.19
26	30	31		1	47	96.67	93.33
27	30	26	3	7	54	76.67	92.65
28	30	29		1	55	96.67	92.81
29	30	30		0	55	100.00	93.08
30	30	28		2	57	93.33	93.09
31	30	31		1	58	96.67	93.22
Total	**855**	**830**	**15**	**58**	**58**	**93.22**	**93.22**

Figure 10.5. Daily linearity measurement postings required to calculate daily and monthly linearity.

Lean Line Flow Rate Board						
Daily Flow Rate					**Quality Issues**	
1st Shift Hours	**Daily Rate**	**Line Rejects**	**Actual Qty**	**Comments**		
1			0			
2			0			
3			0			
4			0			
5			0			
6			0			
7			0			
8			0			
Total:	0	0	0			
2nd Shift						
1			0			
2			0			
3			0			
4			0			
5			0			
6			0			
7			0			
8			0			
Total:	0	0	0			
Daily Total:	0	0	0			

Figure 10.6. Sample chart for recording flow rate measurements.

completed by the end of the 420-minute shift: the flow rate for this volume is 51.4 units per hour or 0.85 units per minute. If the shift starts at 7:00 a.m., 51.4 units must be completed by 8:00 a.m., 102.8 units by 9:00 a.m., 154.2 units by 10:00 a.m., and so on throughout the day until the end of the shift. Figure 10.6 illustrates a sample chart for recording flow rate measurements on a Lean line. If the flow rate trend indicates the time to produce the daily rate is longer or shorter than planned, management can investigate any problems causing a deviation from the flow rate during the day to correct problems before the end of the shift.

- *On-time delivery.* The goal for on-time delivery to customers is 100%.

Flexibility measurements. For a Lean line to achieve the flexibility necessary to modify output to match customer demand, operators must be able to flex from their primary workstations to one workstation upstream and one workstation downstream. This three-operation flex pattern is the minimum basic skill level required to produce a quality product while avoiding overproduction and unsold inventory. The Lean line cannot be successful without operators having three-workstation flexibility. Although some operators may prefer to work at only three workstations, as the Lean line matures, operators are encouraged to expand their flexibility beyond the basic three-workstation requirement by obtaining certification for multiple operations: more certifications at more workstations make operators and the line more flexible. (*Note*: Broader certification is always encouraged, but working on a Lean line does not require certification beyond three workstations.) Operators who are certified for multiple operations are obviously more valuable because they can be assigned wherever they are needed on any given day. Multicertified operators also ensure that the Lean line can continue to be operational even in the absence of other operators. The Lean operating system recommends having incentives that reinforce and reward the performance disciplines that perpetuate and institute Lean as a way of life across the enterprise. More flexible operators should also be rewarded for their ability to perform work in more than three workstations with an incentive program that encourages flexibility. Establish certification milestones and provide incentives for operators to become certified at as many workstations as possible. Use an operator qualification board/matrix to document the certification of each operator. Based on a predetermined plan, as operators achieve stated certification milestones, certain rewards can be initiated.

Commandment 9: Match Output of the Line to Daily Sales by Modifying the Number of Assigned Operators Every Day

A significant differential of a Lean operating system is the ability to modify the output of the Lean line by building only the products sold each day even if that volume is less than the stated line capacity. The ability to modify output is accomplished by the capability of a Lean line to staff the exact number of labor resources required on the line to produce only what has been sold that day. It's possible that the staffing on a Lean line will not the same any two days in a row. Headcount is completely dependent on the amount of product to be produced to meet customer demand that day. For example, if a Lean line has 10 workstations capable of producing 100 units a day, but only 80 units have been sold that day, the Lean line can be *intentionally* suboptimized by staffing with only 8 operators who are capable of making only 80 units that day. If the line is capable of producing 100 units with a full complement of operators, and it is not suboptimized, the result will be the production of 20 unsold units (the difference between the 100 capacity and the 80 sold). These unsold units are overproduction that only absorbs working capital and inventory investment.

Before labor resources can be modified, several factors influence the required number of operators to be assigned. Total product cycle, manufacturing response, and Lean response times have been defined for each product manufactured on the Lean line. Once these response times have been identified, they must be managed by management in the manufacturing area, the demand planner, and master scheduler to ensure that these times are met. If these favorable response times are not monitored, customer response times can slowly return to the lead times quoted by the traditional operating system.

Resources. The planning team must establish customer order requirements on a daily basis. Customer order requirements are first compared to current on-hand finished goods inventories. If the customer demand must be produced, then the BOM is exploded to define component and subassembly requirements beyond those components maintained in the kanban system. Requirements for these materials are also tested against the current on-hand materials inventory. If materials are not available at the time of production for a customer's requirement, production may be needed to be rescheduled for that requirement until materials can be received from suppliers. Once the availability of materials has been confirmed, the Lean line capacity must be tested to ensure that sufficient capacity is available for production of the demand (unnecessary if the total demand for the day does not exceed the designed V_c of the line). Next, the requirements are entered into a daily demand planner (or daily planner). The daily planner includes labor and machine times for each product family from the standard work definition. Customer demand volume is then multiplied by standard labor and machine times and the results are summed to define the number of labor and machine resources needed to meet the demand. The needed resources are then compared to the available resources and a percent of utilization is identified. To avoid overtime or flexing resources across break and lunch times, the percent utilization should be less than 100%, e.g., 85 to 90%. Ideally, the percent utilization is between 50 and 85%. If the daily planner indicates the daily mix and volume will cause utilization to exceed 100%, three rescheduling alternatives are possible:

- *Modify the variables.* Modify one or a combination of the two variables that impact utilization: mix and volume. Recalculate the new product mix and volume combinations. (Labor and machine times for each product in each process is static based on the standard work definition.) Continue iterations of mix and volume until the best utilization of resources is achieved, which may require making a decision to resequence certain SKUs or quantities to a later date.
- *Increase line capacity.* Increase the capacity of the line for a single day by working through break and lunch periods, first determining if manufacturing has the available labor resources needed to cover break and lunch periods. If lunch and break periods are not sufficient, additional time may need to be added to the end of the shift. If daily line capacity continues to be chronically short, it may be time to rebalance the line by adding additional resources to meet the new V_c.

- *Increase working time.* Increase the available minutes per day by working extra time to increase the capacity of the line long enough to achieve the required output (a short-term solution). The additional available minutes to do work each day can be added to the numerator of the daily resource calculation to test the impact on resources. Labor utilization can approach 100% utilization, but machine utilization is ideal at 85%.

Daily resources should be calculated prior to the start of every shift to test the impact of customer mix and demand on the labor and machine resources and to help determine the ideal demand sequence for the day. A spreadsheet can be developed to perform the daily resource calculations.

Manufacturing response time. Manufacturing response time is an important component of finished goods inventory policy. A FGI may be required when manufacturing response time is *greater than* customer-quoted lead time. If manufacturing response time is *less than* the customer-quoted lead time, maintaining an FGI may be unnecessary because the factory can respond faster than the customers' delivery expectations. Even with a Lean line, *commodity products* may require an FGI because customers usually expect delivery times that are shorter than the manufacturing response time. If a product is considered a commodity with little to no differentiation value for response time, maintaining a finished goods inventory may be the only way to satisfy the customer expectation of immediate shipment. Even if manufacturing response time can produce products *in time* to meet promised shipping dates, a FGI for products requiring immediate shipment may be required to satisfy customer expectations. So, even with the power of a Lean manufacturing line at a company's disposal, the competitive environment will always dictate finished goods inventory strategy. Seasonal sales or sales patterns that exceed manufacturing capacity, quick-turn spares, short-response order requirements, engineering changes, obsolescence, customer relations issues, and marketing strategies are additional considerations for any FGI policy. Although the marketplace establishes FGI inventory levels for every company, the Lean manufacturer can usually maintain customer satisfaction and still manage smaller FGI quantities.

Product sequencing. After the daily rate has been validated for materials and labor resources, apply the predetermined sequencing rules to develop an ideal production sequence. Limit the number of sequencing rules to a simple, logical, workable few: one to five sequencing rules should be enough for most manufacturers. Configured products requiring sequencing must be synchronized with a configuration traveler at the beginning of the feeder process to correspond with the introduction of the product to the first workstation. Keep the number of sequencing points to as few as possible to avoid additional sequencing and resequencing. As long as a product has not been pulled into the first workstation, customer demand can always be resequenced and order quantities adjusted to respond to changing customer requirements. The ability to wait until the last possible moment to commit manufacturing resources to produce customer demand is a powerful tool for maximizing customer satisfaction. Once an order has been introduced into the manufacturing pipeline, chaos on the Lean line can be avoided by freezing sequenced SKU mix and volume. Once daily sequencing has been established, post the sequence on a sequencing board adjacent to the first workstation of the Lean line. After posting, only the designated planner for the line is permitted to change the sequence on the board. If problems occur, notify the authorized planner immediately to resequence and update the sequencing board. If feeder processes have been sequenced to correspond with products the main line, those feeders must also be resequenced.

Operator staffing. During the Lean line design activity, a mixed-model line was designed and established. Even though the line was designed to produce a future V_c, typically 1 to 3 years into the future, the line was never expected to be operated at full capacity on day one of its operation. It's possible the product mix and volume now being produced on the line are different than the mix and volume chosen for the line design, but for most companies, there is no change or the change is very small. Once the Lean line is operational, constantly redesigning/rearranging resources or changing the Takt time on the line every day to meet minor changes in demand and volume is impractical. The only reasonable alternative to adjust to mix and volume changes is to modify the staffing of the line that day to match the changes in mix and volume. Instead, change *line staffing* to modify the output. So, once the daily mix of products has been validated for materials and sequencing rules, determine the corresponding number of required labor resources each day for each process on the line to match the daily mix and volume of customer demand. A formula can be used to determine the labor resources to assign to each process on the line each day to match daily customer demand:

$$\Sigma \text{ (Daily rate} \times \text{SWD labor time)} \div \text{effective hours} \times \text{shifts}$$
$$= \text{number of labor resources}$$

Once the labor requirements for each *process* have been defined, the total quantity of labor for all processes can be summed to identify the required headcount for the entire line that day. Figure 10.7 illustrates a summary of the labor resources for a series of individual processes required for one Lean manufacturing line (a chassis line). The total headcount for each process on the chassis line has been

Daily Resource Planner Line Summary

	Chassis Prep	TA-1	CSB-1	Boom Install	Accesories/ Electronic	Test Unit	SF-1	OR	BP/ CG	BI	WH	Actual Total	Efficiency Factor	Line Total
Chassis Line														
Labor	3.5	0.7	0.5	0.5	1.3	0.2	0.7	0.7	0.8	0.9	0.9	10.8	15%	(12)

Daily Resource Planner Line Summary

Chassis Line			
Labor	10.8	1.15	(12)
Aerial Line			
Labor	4.9	1.15	6
Auger Line			
Labor	3.0	1.15	3
Hydraulics			
Labor	0.2	1.15	0
Small Parts			
Labor	1.0	1.15	1
Daily Assembly Total			(23)

Sum of Labor Headcount for All Lines

Figure 10.7. Sample daily labor rate summary of the labor resources required for the chassis manufacturing process and other processes used on the line to meet a day of customer demand.

factored up by an efficiency factor of 15%. Figure 10.7 also summarizes the head-count for other Lean processes for a total headcount in the factory that day for that mix and volume of products.

Although a Lean line can be operated up to its designed capacity as long as there is customer demand for the output, 24 to 36 months should elapse before the designed volume is actually reached. Recurring demand in excess of the designed capacity (V_c) may require the line to operate for a short period of time with extra hours or shifts, but if daily demand routinely exceeds the designed V_c, redesigning and rebalancing of the line may be necessary. Conversely, a Lean line should *never operate below 50%* of its designed capacity because quality can be adversely impacted. The smallest amount of product that can be produced on a Lean line is 50% of the designed V_c. If a line runs below 50% capacity, operators are required to flex beyond the one-up/one-down minimum flexing requirement, which requires them to make redundant inspections of their own self-inspections. Redundant inspections increase the risk of an operator missing defects previously inspected by him/her.

Commandment 10: When Confronted with Options, Always Choose Simple versus Complex and Resolve Lean Manufacturing Issues with Lean Manufacturing Techniques

Manufacturers today are blessed with a broad array of inexpensive technology, ranging from low-cost software products that offer solutions for a multitude of problems to inexpensive, disposable hardware products. This technology has been available for many years and newer versions continue to be introduced on a regular basis. Availability and low cost make resisting the temptation to solve manufacturing problems with the latest, greatest technological solution extremely difficult for the current generation of practitioners.

Modern planning systems are good examples of great technology, but how effective are they in most companies? If they were operated as designed, modern planning systems would closely resemble a Lean operating system, but instead they are often modified to accommodate an existing operating system or satisfy a strong-willed organizational need. Policies such as batch sizes, department rout-ings, and minimum run quantities then become embedded in the mathematical logic of the planning system. Even the best planning systems encourage modifica-tion by providing ample planning parameters that are designed to satisfy com-pany policy and operating procedures at the expense of standard operating logic. The capability for maximum flexibility is often touted by sales people as a major differential between competitive planning systems. Once the modified planning system becomes operational, the policies and procedures included in the system serve to satisfy strong company political influences. Managers, supervisors, and planners spend most of their daily activities reconciling planning system logic with dynamic activity on the shop floor. Even a small oversight in planning system data maintenance quickly widens the gap between what the system displays and what reality actually is on the shop floor. Over time, the planning system becomes so far out of sync with the shop floor that all credibility is lost. Soon, the magic solution to manufacturing problems is to purchase and install a new planning system. Then the cycle repeats itself over and over again.

Technology is powerful, but technology tools are usually not the ultimate solution to all manufacturing challenges. Any technology implemented in a vacuum as a solution will fail. Technology tools must be coupled with managerial intelligence and sound analysis. Technology actually has a strong role in resolving problems in a Lean operating system. An excellent example is the software tools that can be developed to transform the existing operating system to Lean and then operate the new system on a daily basis. These tools include line design, kanban sizing, daily resource planning, and linearity performance measuring.

Recall that the essence of Lean thinking is *simplicity*. The line has been designed with a labor capacity to produce a future volume of representative products. The standard work content required to build these products has been divided into groups of work equal to a Takt time, a statement of rate. A manufactured product is nothing more than the sum of its labor and materials. Work is standardized at each workstation. Products are produced sequentially through the manufacturing processes in sums of work equal to the Takt time, a straightforward line balancing technique. Line balancing is not a high-technology solution. It has been around since Henry Ford's first assembly line. A kanban system provides the parts necessary to produce selected products. A series of signals replenishes materials at the same rate as they are consumed. Once installed, a series of action/reaction steps are defined for operators on the line. These actions/reactions then become part of the day-to-day operating environment.

Less reliance on complex computer routines to operate the line often causes conflict between a Lean line and modern ERP/MRP systems. Avoid the temptation to make Lean line and kanban systems conform to requirements of an ERP/MRP system. It will be strong. The shop floor control and capacity planning execution components in the Lean operating system are the biggest causes of disconnects with a modern ERP/MRP system. Shop floor control and capacity planning considerations have been addressed by building capacity and control systems into Lean line design. The line has been designed for a maximum capacity (V_c) that cannot be exceeded. This V_c is the statement of capacity. Demand is stated each day in a quantity that does not exceed the defined capacity. Production flow is controlled by processes that are aligned in the sequence used to produce the product. IPK signals are located at each workstation on a balanced Lean line to authorize the expenditure of resources. Customer priorities are determined by the sequencing routine introduced at the first workstation. Sequencing has replaced production order management routines, and lead time is the total product cycle time. Start and due dates and production order quantities from stand-alone departments are no longer needed from the ERP/MRP system. These predesigned techniques replace the need for complex and burdensome shop floor control routines. Discipline on a Lean line must be maintained, but compared to the complexity of maintaining a large planning system, maintenance is simple and straightforward. Once implemented, the Lean line just needs to know what to make today!

Simple solutions to problems are always better than complex solutions. Rather than relying on variance reports and historical information from the day before or last period, use MBWA to evaluate the operation of the line. Simply walking the line and observing key signals can provide a manager with information adequate to evaluate line performance: is the sequencing being followed; is flexing occurring; are units being produced one at a time within the Takt time target; is the flow rate being achieved; are quality parameters being met; are the rules of 5S being followed? A computer report is unnecessary to observe these things. Enforce Lean rules when a violation is observed to send a clear message to operators that management is serious about the success of Lean manufacturing and how the line is performing.

Other things to consider when using MBWA are the manufacturing design; ergonomics; clear visibility of signals, configured item travelers, and sequencing boards; and the ability for management to have line-of-sight visibility:

- *Design.* A large part of product manufacturing cost (up to 70 or 80%) can be attributed to design engineering, but design engineers are rarely located in a manufacturing facility so they often design components to meet specifications, with little knowledge about how the component will be used in manufacturing. A major contributor to this statistic is the additional non-value-added work performed by manufacturing to produce a product or component design created by design engineering. Document the standard work definition including the quality work, so design engineers can use the information to improve next-generation product designs.

- *Ergonomics.* Reducing injuries is an important reason to pay attention to the ergonomics of a Lean line. Design of the line focused on reducing manufacturing response time and improving ergonomics for operators. Check for proper lighting and environmental comfort. Ensure that workstations remain as close together as possible to shorten non-value-added move time and to facilitate using IPKs and easy material handling. If suitable for the product, use simple conveyance systems, e.g., roller conveyors, ball transfer tables, jib cranes, roller carts, or arms-length hand-offs to the next workstation. Paced conveyors are not recommended unless they are capable of indexing by an individual operator.

- *IPK signal visibility.* Ensure that visual signals, configured item travelers, sequencing boards, and IPK signals are easily visible to operators. Travelers detailing production of configured items should accompany the unit as it advances down the line. Use sequencing boards to indicate the sequence of production for the entire Lean line. The key to sequencing, which is determined only by the production planner, is to inform the first operator on the line or a feeder line of the next unit to start down the line. Keep IPKs as simple as possible. Sometimes the location of a process requires an alternative signaling method such as an andon light or audible signal rather than a simple parking space on the shop floor to transmit the IPK signal. Avoid the temptation to install complex high-tech lights, whistles, or bells: electronic signals should be the exception, not the rule. Limit alternative IPK signaling systems to monuments and independent or shared processes that cannot be easily relocated.
- *Line-of-sight visibility.* Being able to observe the entire Lean line from any location in the factory is an important adjunct to MBWA. Line-of-sight visibility of a Lean line from any vantage point helps identify problems and facilitates their speedy resolution. In some cases, the line of sight is blocked by workstations and unnecessary production materials. Enforce 5S. Look for racks, file cabinets, tool boxes, lockers, desks, corrugated material, and personal items being used to block the line of sight or obscure non-value-added activity.

When issues occur that cause product flow problems or the Lean line to become imbalanced, use simple Lean balancing tools to bring the line into balance:

- Look for work that can be eliminated.
- Relocate work from workstation to workstation
- Add IPKs to unbalanced workstations.
- Add resources to solve line imbalance.
- Mix the sequence of products running on the line.
- Resize kanban signals to solve material shortage problems.
- Continue to educate and train new operators.
- Reward operators for flexing.

Beware of reverting to the old methodology of building inventories to achieve balance and hide manufacturing problems. Of course, this can only happen when operators ignore IPK discipline. Building inventory is the easiest solution to overcome manufacturing problems, but reliance on buffer inventories to overcome manufacturing issues will be fatal for your Lean line. Work toward implementing a new set of performance measurements and KPIs based on quality, delivery, and line linearity. Challenge efficiency and utilization measurements that perpetuate building inventories and accent imbalances in manufacturing processes.

Some final thoughts. Once a Lean line is operational and the company is receiving the expected benefits, moving on to other projects is tempting because original team members and line designers expect the line to operate on its own. The time after a successful line startup is often a dangerous time for the long-term establishment of any Lean line. A Lean operating system is not a magic bullet for operating a manufacturing facility and a transformation alone does not guarantee long-term success. The Lean operating system is just another way to operate the facility. Like any system, to maintain peak performance, the Lean operating system must be managed and maintained. Regardless of how much hard work and effort were expended to implement the line, rebalancing processes, calculating kanbans, and having continuous improvement implementation and training activities will always be necessary. An often-made mistake is assuming management and maintenance of a Lean line will become the responsibility of the Lean coordinator or a participating member of the transformation project team. Another mistake is assuming the plant manager or vice president of operations will manage, operate, and improve the system all by themselves. Abdicating managerial responsibility for maintenance and continuous improvement of the Lean line is often a fatal mistake. For the long-term success of a Lean transformation, all functions and individuals in a manufacturing facility are responsible for the operation, continuing improvement, and success of a Lean operating system. Lean thinking in an enterprise cannot be accomplished by one person. It must become a way of life throughout the enterprise. The proponents of Lean who were recruited during the transformation process must continue to expand their knowledge and skills after line startup.

Web
Added
Value™

11

TAKING LEAN TECHNOLOGY TO THE NEXT LEVEL

The costs of operating a physical plant can be huge: land, taxes, utilities, payroll, personnel issues, union relationships, regulatory compliance issues, product quality issues, inventories, transportation, maintenance, and customer satisfaction, just to name a few. Applying Lean manufacturing technology helps keep many of these costs as low as possible.

Most Lean transformations begin on the manufacturing shop floor. The reason is simple. Manufacturing is the organizational unit where the most money is spent. Often manufacturing is the largest organizational area and represents the largest single business investment of the entire organization. In addition to being the largest cost center, manufacturing requires the support of many other groups that exist to provide service, information, and feedback. It's safe to say that many of manufacturing's problems are transferred to these support groups for resolution. Achieving economies of scale by controlling manufacturing and support group costs, increasing speed to market, and improving quality in manufacturing are just three reasons why most companies begin a Lean business transformation in their manufacturing organizations. Reduction in manufacturing costs offers them the largest return on investment for the time and costs associated with the Lean transformation effort. Manufacturing also receives the greatest benefits from the cost savings that result from the Lean transformation.

Although the financial benefits in the manufacturing area alone may justify a Lean transformation project, other benefits make beginning a transformation in manufacturing worthwhile. Manufacturing response time (the sum of the standard time of all processes required to move products through the manufacturing pipeline) is greatly reduced after a Lean transformation project is completed. Faster manufacturing completion time for customer demand offers a huge competitive benefit for a company. Reduced manufacturing response time means shorter customer-quoted lead time. If a customer's supplier selection criteria include the shortest lead time, the Lean manufacturer will often become the supplier of choice for this customer. When the customer purchases the Lean manufacturer's products instead purchasing a competitor's products, the Lean manufacturer's share of the market increases.

Although the natural relationship between Lean technologies and manufacturing may imply a Lean transformation is nothing more than a manufacturing program, this assertion is incorrect. Just because Lean technologies are almost always initiated in the manufacturing area does not mean Lean is only a manufacturing program. Misinterpreting what Lean is often misleads organizational groups outside the manufacturing area to think Lean is a technology that cannot provide benefits to their discipline. Just the opposite is true. A successful Lean transformation on the manufacturing shop floor almost always leads to changes in procedures and policies in numerous other areas throughout the company. Although these changes are necessary to support the new Lean manufacturing operating system in manufacturing, the changes in policy and procedure will highlight important improvement opportunities for functional departments that can ultimately be beneficial for the entire company.

LEAN IN ADMINISTRATIVE AREAS

Let's review the definition of Lean:

> Lean technology is a series of scientific, objective techniques that causes work tasks in a process to be performed with a minimum of non-value-adding activities and results in greatly reduced wait, queue, move, and administrative time and other delays. A Lean facility is capable of producing a product or service in only the sum of the value-added work content time required to change its form, fit, or function. Lean operating systems seek to identify and eliminate all non-value-adding activities in the design, production, supply chain management, and other activities used to satisfy customer requirements.

Notice that the definition of Lean is not manufacturing specific. It describes work tasks as being part of a *process* performed with a minimum of *waste* and capable of producing a *product or service* in the sum of its value-added work content time. Instead of being limited to only the production of discrete products, Lean can also be applied when performing service or administrative functions. Although visualizing the application of Lean technology to the labor (human and machine) associated with a manufacturing facility might be easy to do, visualizing its application to the service requirements of that same business often requires a leap of imagination.

Review the definition of a process:

> *A process is series of actions carried out to achieve a particular result. A process may also be a physical location where a logical grouping of labor or machine resources performs a sequential series of work tasks necessary to convert raw material into a finished product. Processes are specific activities that increase the value of raw materials by changing their form, fit, or function by adding the value of labor and/or machine work.*

All companies, of course, are not manufacturing organizations. Many, such as banks, brokerage firms, hospitals, insurance providers, distributors, etc., sell their products directly to customers as services that have work routines consisting of a *series of actions carried out to achieve a particular result.* Service companies offer products that are not created by a manufacturing process, but instead are products that provide incremental intellectual property that can be used to increase the value of the customer's service or manufactured product. Service products and routines are also subject to having waste levels similar to those in the manufacturing processes on the shop floor. Sometimes waste in service routines and administrative functions is difficult to see.

Human resources in service routines. Whether working in an office or on the shop floor, human work habits are the same. As a way to make their day-to-day life easier, humans prefer to develop nice, comfortable, safe working routines that make their jobs repeatable and easier to perform. Just as in a manufacturing environment, the service sector likes to create comfortable routines that group work together by function by forming departments, e.g., purchasing, accounts payable, order entry, customer service, engineering, shipping, production planning, etc. Each function then becomes a specialty service headed by a manager who is responsible for utilization of the resources assigned to the specialty service/department. (Sound familiar? This management routine is exactly like the traditional manufacturing processes prior to the design of the new Lean facility.) As an example, human resources in an office and human resources on the shop floor often share similar procedures that cause non-value-adding activities and failure rates to occur. Because of these similarities, the same techniques and tools used to design the Lean factory floor can be used to eliminate non-value-added work in service routines and functional support office requirements! Even though companies providing service products and manufacturing products are very different, all of the benefits realized from a Lean transformation on the shop floor are available to service products, routines, and support organizations: better quality, shorter response time, less inventory, and more productive use of space.

Raw materials, inventory, and quality in service routines. In the service industry, the description of raw materials is different; inventory does not look the same as the piles of inventory seen on a shop floor; and quality attributes are different than those for a manufactured product. Raw material inventory in the service industry is more likely to be intellectual property, documents, or financial instruments that represent money or a financial opportunity. Unlike the partially completed, tangible units of WIP production in manufacturing, the WIP inventory in a service routine is usually a queue of documents in a computer program or an inbox waiting to be processed as a batch. Like the tangible units of WIP production inventory on the shop floor, however, unfinished WIP service routines can represent large sums of money just sitting in a non-value-added queue waiting to have work done. Just like manufactured products moving through the factory, service routines waiting in a queue add to the response time. Longer response times translate into longer lead times. When customers expect fast service, rapid delivery of a service can be a marketing differential just like faster manufacturing response time can be for a manufacturer.

WORKING STYLES IN ADMINISTRATIVE AREAS

Like operators in the manufacturing environment, most service providers want their workspaces to suit their personal style or the way they prefer to do work. Rearranging personal workstations is often much easier to do in an administrative or service area than in a manufacturing environment. Often little to no consideration is given to the impact the rearranging of these personal workstations will have on other processes or the resulting costs to the company. Common work styles in administrative and service areas include nest builders, professors, innovators, and loners.

The nest builder. Nest building occurs when a service provider takes ownership of a working area. A nest builder stakes a claim by filling his/her workspace with numerous personal items — family pictures, a radio, a calendar, posters, mementos, and other personal items — to ensure a certain comfort level. Nest builders seldom leave their work areas except for breaks. They require others to come to them for assistance or information. A nest builder unilaterally decides what work to do and when to do it, often accumulating sufficient work to be batched together so it can be finished all at one time before moving on to another task. Nest builders often lay claim to a valuable resource (a copier, printer, computer terminal, binding machine, etc.), requiring others to seek their permission before gaining access to the resource.

The tenured professor. Because of tenure, longevity, or special skills, this service provider thinks he/she has paid their dues, earning the right to perform only the work they personally choose to do, leaving less desirable work to others. Some service routines may be thought of as too menial or beneath their dignity to do, so tenured professors *cherry pick* only the work they want to do. Others working in the same service area may even have to wait for the tenured professor to make his/her work selections before making their own — better to wait for the professor than to upset his/her daily routine. This posturing can, of course, delay the delivery of services to customers and cause work to pile up. In addition to being the tenured professor in the service area, he/she is frequently a nest builder in order to be left alone while completing the preferred work.

The better-idea worker. Service providers often have great ideas. Because great ideas can be empowering, some service providers implement their improvement ideas, choosing to keep their ideas to themselves (perhaps motivated by reasons related to self-esteem or to receive special recognition from management and their peers or to appear indispensable). Unilateral implementation of a great idea, however, only helps one individual. Encourage all service team members to share their ideas with others. Utilize continuous process improvement meetings or kaizen events to address improvement opportunities. New ideas and process improvements can impact an entire department. If necessary, provide incentives so great ideas can be incorporated across an entire process.

The loner. When first assigned to a job, most people are uncertain about what is expected of them and how their job is to be performed. During the usual learning curve, assistance from peers and supervisors is usually available, but once working independently, some service providers begin to develop their own personal routines for getting work done. Except for the occurrence of an occasional deficiency, little review of these routines is ever completed. Eventually these personal routines become the "official" company procedure. Over time, across all assignments in an administrative process, each service provider is likely to be working as an individual when they should be operating as a member of a team.

ADMINISTRATIVE AREAS AND NON-VALUE-ADDED WORK

How different are administrative processes and manufacturing processes? Only the output is different. Instead of producing products, service routines produce information as output. Are the people who work in service and administrative routines any different from the operators who work on the shop floor? Both are subject to the same human nature and work habit tendencies. Are administrative and service routines just as prone to performing non-value-added work and experiencing disruptions in the flow of information as operators are in the flow rate of a manufacturing line? Administrative processes follow the same operating routines that cause non-value-added work and backups on the shop floor.

The work ethic effect: busy work. Everyone wants to feel useful. Most want to be contributors to the company's mission. Most employees believe in the "a day's pay for a day's work" philosophy and work hard to live up to that philosophy. It's instinctive for these employees. Some service workers even feel guilty if they are not busy or engaged in work at all times. With a new work assignment, living up to the day's pay/day's work philosophy is usually easy to satisfy because most hours of the day are filled with learning the new assignment and ensuring that the work is completed accurately and on time. Later on, as the learning curve begins to flatten out and the service worker becomes more efficient, work that was once a major challenge now becomes routine. The assigned work load can often be completed in less time than the normal work hours in the day. When this happens, the service worker's day's pay/day's work ethic philosophy is threatened. To deal with this extra time when the job itself does not provide enough work to keep the service worker busy, he/she often invents additional work (known as *busy work*) to fill up the remaining available time in the workday. The service worker can now stay busy all day long, happily satisfying their work ethic. Although some busy work has a balancing effect by relocating work from one service worker to another, busy work is often unnecessary and almost always non-value-added. It may keep the service worker busy by filling up underutilized portions of a day, but as often as not, the busy work is not required by anyone else in the company except the service worker performing it! Even though the service worker's day is filled with work and he/she now feels they're earning their day's pay for a day's work, the busy work becomes just an additional procedure that has to be performed. After a while, the invented busy work gets built into the process and included in the standard time of the process, becoming part of the written procedure for the process. Later on, should the service worker be recognized as a good service worker and be promoted or given a new challenge in some other area of the company, or if the worker leaves the company for a better opportunity, the written procedure that includes the work invented just to stay busy will be left behind, institutionalized for posterity. With the arrival of a new employee to fill the vacant position, the cycle begins all over again. This time the invented work embedded in the departmental procedure is now performed as a part of the job. The new employee does not challenge the procedure. After working through the learning curve, the work becomes as routine and repeatable as possible. The new employee might even add or change the procedure to suit an individual work ethic or to satisfy a personal preference. Eventually, even this employee will leave the position, starting the cycle all over again. Similar to the "telephone game" in which a whispered message is passed from one person to another until it returns to the originator in a form that does not resemble the original whispered message. After a few cycles of service workers performing and expanding the task, the original work required will not resemble the current description of the procedure. If the efficiency of procedures is not frequently challenged, bloated procedures will be passed from one employee to the next in a never-ending cycle.

The Lean operating model and busy work. The Lean operating model simply tries to determine if work actually changes the *form, fit, or function* of the service being provided. Do certain work elements add value for a customer or end user? Are any non-value-added work elements adding cost and time to the service being provided? If a work task can be eliminated, the time required to perform that task can also be eliminated, which results in a faster response time.

The mistrust effect: evolved procedures. In the business world, some companies and individuals have a long-held perception that others are out to sabotage, subvert, or even steal from them. These *others* could be customers, component suppliers, transportation services, MRO (maintenance, repair, and overhaul) suppliers, consultants, service providers, and even employees and co-workers. How valid is this perception? Perhaps there was a time when deceptive practices were common in the industry and some suppliers and employees could not be trusted. It's possible that at one time or another, some companies and individuals were actually intentionally or unintentionally unscrupulous. No company or individual wants to become the victim of deceptive practices! So as a safeguard against deception and dishonesty, policies and procedures are developed to ensure that certain faulty or dishonest activities cannot have a harmful effect on the company. These safeguards subsequently became tasks built into existing policies and procedures. Because of a few unscrupulous individuals or companies, all companies or the business associates of a particular company become "tarred with the same brush." Multiply the number of evolved procedures within a process devised to deal with mistrust by the number of processes needed to complete a service routine and it should be no surprise that the work volume exceeds the number of people assigned to do the work. Soon overtime increases and employees become overworked. To keep up with the workload, the department's headcount is permanently increased. Adding additional employees is one of the most popular solutions for overcoming the diminished capacity of a department. Adding staff rather than asking questions about the purpose of the work being done or who uses the information being provided is the quickest way for a manager to increase departmental capacity. Rarely is the actual work content itself challenged.

The Lean operating model and evolved procedures. Lean methods simply want to know if a work task is still necessary. If a task is deemed unnecessary, it should be eliminated! Is it practical to apply the same defensive strategy across the board to all business associates and work tasks? Have more progressive policies caused a shift in thinking about the honesty and trustworthiness of suppliers, contractors, and employees? Has technology improved to the point where a task has become obsolete or is no longer needed? Revisit any reasons for mistrust and the subsequent work tasks associated with them to eliminate non-value-added work tasks that were created because of mistrust.

Questionable non-value-adding work is cumulative among all processes and departments in an organization. Just as units pass through various departments in a traditional manufacturing system, service routines that require the expertise of multiple specialties or processes are routed through individual departments for the completion of their portion of the work. Like individual departments on a traditional manufacturing shop floor, service departments often have little concern about efficiency or the utilization of value-added information by upstream and downstream departments. Each department acts as an island in the flow of processes to be completed. How much of the time required for performing these service routine processes is value-added? Is the information required to take action or to make a decision actually provided? How much information is redundant or superfluous and does nothing to provide substantive information to decision makers? The further upstream a department is from the customer, the less visible the impact will be on departmental goals and performance criteria.

The imbalance effect: work grouping. As is done on a traditional manufacturing shop floor, a common practice in office environments is the grouping of like work together into departments. Organizing administrative work into departments of specialization and physically separating them into administrative areas scattered throughout the company creates the same dynamic as physically separating the manufacturing departments on the shop floor — grouping work by function causes imbalances in the process flow of service routines. Once a department makes its contribution to the service routine or administrative function, the service routine is shuttled off to the next department as soon as possible with little concern for any issues that may delay ultimate delivery of the service to the customer. If one department's process completes a service routine faster than the downstream department, the spatial separation of the departments hides the imbalance between the two departments. This out-of-sight, out-of-mind structure also desensitizes problems other departments may be having, causing disconnects between all the processes required for the completion of the functions of these departments.

The location effect: increased queue time. In many companies, individual departments in a service process stream are typically located in different offices, on different floors, in different buildings, and even in different states or countries. The physical location of these service departments contributes little to expedite the upstream and downstream processes required to speed the service routines though the facility to completion. Similar to the manufacturing facility, inventory in these service departments in the form of WIP service routines can pile up while waiting in a queue to be scheduled for completion as a batch quantity before moving on to a downstream process. Processing of administrative and service routines in batch quantities causes large amounts of queue time to accumulate between processes. Queue time is always non-value added time that increases response time to the customer. Except for small companies that have all of their administrative processes located in the same office, resolution of a service routine issue can also be difficult and time-consuming if a service process must be returned upstream for rework.

The Lean operating model and service and administrative routines. Administrative routines are a series of processes that are dependent on each other to complete an output. The dynamics of completing the work of an administrative routine to produce a specific outcome are the same in an office environment as on the manufacturing shop floor. With a little modification, the same Lean techniques used on the shop floor can be applied to service, administrative, and information routines. These routines can be studied and balanced to produce the administrative, service, or information work in the sum of their work content time only. Non-value-added work can be identified and then challenged to reduce or eliminate years of busy work that has accumulated as a result of the efforts to satisfy the work ethic of certain individuals. Just as on the shop floor, the number of resources necessary to perform value-added work can be identified and the physical alignment of resources can be rearranged so the output of one process is consumed directly into its downstream process with little or no movement. When the resources in each process are balanced and working as a cell instead of individual departments located throughout the facility, the work waiting in queues at points in the process can be greatly reduced. Figure 11.1 illustrates the routing a customer order can take once it enters an administrative queue.

Designing a Service Routine to Become Lean

When designing a Lean factory, representative products are chosen to represent *families* of the products to be made on the Lean manufacturing line. This is done to facilitate a faster and more manageable line design during the transformation phase of a Lean project. Choosing representative products ensures that sufficient

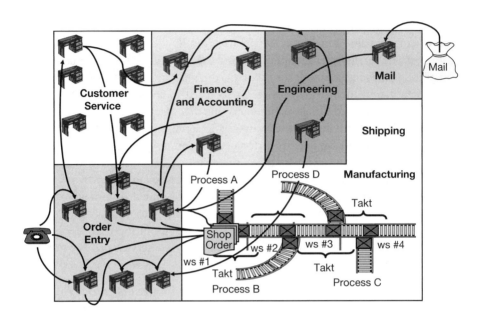

Figure 11.1. Routing flow by departments of specialization taken by a customer order after entering an administrative queue.

information is captured to accurately reflect the day-to-day activity on the factory floor and the impact of customer demand on resources when designing the Lean line. When designing a service routine to become Lean, choosing a representative service function requires thinking about the service itself. Focus on the deliverable provided to the end customer. What is the service product? Focus on the entire series of processes required to complete conversion of intellectual information into a product the customer can use. For example, instead of considering only the purchasing process in the purchasing department, think of the requesting location and the required approval processes, the receiving process, the delivery process, the stockroom receiving process, the three-way match process, and the accounts payable process as a series of processes required to deliver a service (the product). The service product is not just the purchase order or the receiving report. The product of this service routine is delivery of the ordered materials to the original requester and the subsequent payment to the supplier. The *best* Lean service routine candidate focuses on the deliverable of the service function as the last step in a series of processes to meet the customer's needs (internal and external).

Managers of traditional functional departments seldom visualize the bigger picture of an entire service routine or administrative function by considering the numerous work tasks performed throughout a series of other functional departments with each performing their specific roles in completing the service or administrative function. Although seeing much more than what occurs in one's own department can be difficult, managers of functional departments must look at the big picture of a service routine or administrative procedure. They must think of their department's contribution as a component of the entire service delivered to the end customer. For example, a purchasing manager might find it difficult to relate the work required in the purchasing department to convert a purchase request from a satellite location, complete with all the procedural and legal requirements, into an actual purchase order to the work required in the accounts payable department to issue a check as payment to the supplier. For most service deliverables, converting a service request into a service delivery will require the expertise of multiple functional experts from a series of departments throughout the company.

Now consider the movement and distance traveled from one department to another in addition to the time required in each department to complete processing of a service request. The response time to the customer begins with the time the service routine travels from the first department to the last. When received at each department, the service request must go to the end of the line to wait its turn for processing in a new batch queue. If a customer asks to expedite a service document or complete a service request as soon as possible, visualize the non-value-added move, wait, and queue times created in each department that must be circumvented to satisfy the customer's request for priority. Estimate the financial resources tied up in service routines waiting for processes that are now unavailable for more value-added activities. Criticism is often directed at the amount of tangible inventory of discrete units of production on the shop floor, but how much working capital is represented by incomplete or in-process administrative and service routines?

Using Lean Tools to Document the Flow of a Service Routine

Just like the products being manufactured on the shop floor, the output of service routines requires conversion into a final form as a result of a series of processes. Often these processes are grouped together into departments based on the expertise of the human resources completing them: engineering, customer service, finance, and accounting. If processes are to become Lean, understanding the relationship of the processes used to complete the service routine and the sequence in which they are used is necessary. Which process is done before another? Where does a document or service request go next? A simple device for visualizing the sequence of processes would be to remove the roof of the office areas in the facility and then track the movement of a service request throughout the building. Since physically removing the roof is impractical, the next best thing to do is to

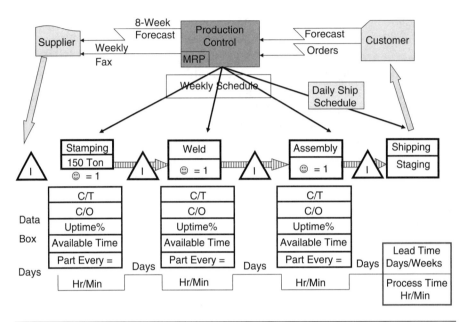

Figure 11.2. A value stream map.

document a service routine or the flow of documents using a value stream map, a spaghetti diagram, a process flow diagram, or a flowchart.

The value stream map. A VSM is a popular stand-alone tool used in a Lean transformation to document the flow of information and materials from receipt of customer demand to shipment of finished products to the customer. A VSM is also often used to track customer demand through a manufacturing facility. A VSM can be divided into two parts, with the top part documenting the loop from receipt of demand from a customer, to the planning and purchasing process from a supplier, to the manufacturing shop floor, back to the shipping of the demand to the customer. The bottom half of a VSM documents the manufacturing processes where conversion takes place and shows the location of inventories, number of days of lead time, cycle time, machine uptime, and utilization (Figure 11.2). If the same processes are used to produce products, the level of detail in a VSM is satisfactory for documenting repetitive processes, but some products use optional processes while others share processes or do not require all of the same processes as most of the product family during manufacturing. A single VSM illustrates the flow of materials, but provides little information about how work is done on the shop floor for all products. Just as a VSM does not provide the detail necessary to implement a new operating system, the documentation in the top and bottom

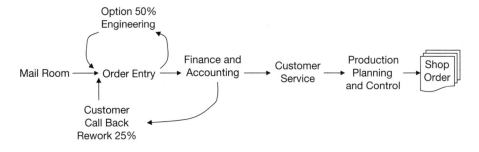

Figure 11.3. A process flow diagram: the order entry to shop order processes.

halves is too general to thoroughly analyze the work tasks of administrative or service routines and the manufacturing cycles of demand planning and customer fulfillment functions. Better tools for understanding the flow of work through a series of processes are the PFD (process flow diagram) and the SWD (standard work definition). The PFD identifies the processes used to produce a product. The SWD documents in great detail the individual work tasks, standard times, and quality criteria for each process. Instead of using Sticky Note symbols to document the processes and averages of time for identifying work content as is done with a VSM, a PFD and a SWD capture in exact detail the work required to convert intellectual knowledge (the raw material) into a finished service product.

The process flow diagram. A PFD is an excellent tool for documenting processes and their relationship to one another. A PFD ensures that all processes where work is completed are identified for each product family and shows the relationship of the processes and how they flow together to produce a product or service routine. In the case of a service routine or an administrative function, a PFD shows the flow of processes required to complete a service to a customer. Figure 11.3 shows the order entry to shop order processes. With a PFD, there is no blending of cycle times with performance measures of utilization or overall equipment effectiveness (OEE).

When completed, the differences in detail between the PFD and VSM are apparent. For the processes identified for each product by family using a PFD, the SWD requires a summary of work tasks, the standard time per task, and quality criteria per task for each process of the PFD. The determination of value-added or non-value-added must be documented for each task on the SWD. This step is particularly critical for improving a service routine. When documented, some tasks may obviously be the result of the work ethic effect or mistrust effect. Maybe no one can explain why a task is done. "It's just always been this way" is a common reason for why work is done in a process. Maybe a predecessor taught this

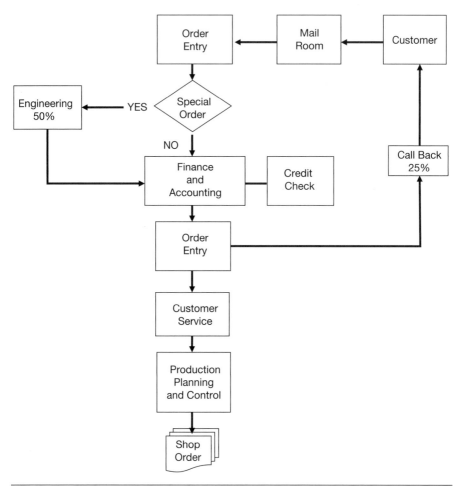

Figure 11.4. A flowchart: customer order to shop order.

method for completing a task, so it's never been questioned before. Predicting that most service routines contain significant non-value-added activities in their processes is not unreasonable. A series of non-value-added tasks can easily expand the cycle time of a service routine. As seen in the manufacturing area, the value-added work content is usually the smallest component of a service routine while the non-value-added time embedded in the processes does nothing more than increase the total lead time.

The flowchart. Some prefer to use a flowchart to document service processes instead of a PFD. Both show the processes required to complete a service activity. Figure 11.4 illustrates the same process as documented in the PFD in Figure 11.3.

In the service routine, *process* refers to a functional department of a company. A department is formed to group like work together and to concentrate the skills and knowledge required for the function.

The standard work definition. The SWD used for documenting service routine tasks can also be used to document quality criteria for a service process. The definition of quality for service routines is the same as for manufactured products. Make a decision about the *one best correct way* to complete a service routine. If the work can be completed using more than one method, but only one is the best way, document the *one correct way*. Do not leave the decision to the individuals performing the routine to interpret the one best way to complete the task. All work in a service routine must be completed according to a predetermined quality specification established by management.

The value-added analysis. A value-added analysis document, as with an SWD, documents the individual tasks for each process chronologically and in detail (Figure 11.5). Standard time is recorded in a separate column based on the work task, work type, time, value-added (VA) or non-value-added (NVA), etc. The work types can be represented by icons for the different time categories, e.g., setup ($\triangle$), queue ($\bigcirc$), value-added ($\square$), and move ($\Rightarrow$). Setup time is time spent in preparation to do other work, e.g., collecting all authorized signatures required to approve a requested activity or to complete value-added work. Queue is the time waiting at a workstation in an inbox or a computer for the purpose of batching work prior to performing the value-added work of that process. Move is the time required to relocate work to the next process or task within the process. As the times for the work tasks of the process are identified, the times are recorded in the most appropriate column on the value-added analysis worksheet. For example, if a task does not change the *form, fit, or function* of the service routine, its time is recorded in the non-value-added (NVA) column. At the same time, the corresponding icon indicating the work type is selected. When completed, the times recorded in the individual columns are summed to indicate the amount of time required for each category. Date stamping of the *time received* and the *time departing* each functional department helps to determine the total elapsed time spent in the department. The value-added analysis breaks down the individual activities that make up the total time spent in a department by separating the times into value-added and non-value-added activities. Non-value-added activities are candidates for elimination.

Kaizen activities. When designing a Lean factory, the processes used to convert raw materials into finished products are documented on the SWD *as is* or *as they are today*. Even if improvements are suggested or necessary, kaizen activity improvements of manufacturing processes must wait until the processes have

Sequence	Work Task	Type	VA	NVA	Distance	Observation
1		△ O ▢ ⇨				
2		△ O ▢ ⇨				
3		△ O ▢ ⇨				
4		△ O ▢ ⇨				
5		△ O ▢ ⇨				
6		△ O ▢ ⇨				
7		△ O ▢ ⇨				
8		△ O ▢ ⇨				
9		△ O ▢ ⇨				
10		△ O ▢ ⇨				
11		△ O ▢ ⇨				
12		△ O ▢ ⇨				
13		△ O ▢ ⇨				
14		△ O ▢ ⇨				
15		△ O ▢ ⇨				
16		△ O ▢ ⇨				
17		△ O ▢ ⇨				
18		△ O ▢ ⇨				
19		△ O ▢ ⇨				
20		△ O ▢ ⇨				
21		△ O ▢ ⇨				
22		△ O ▢ ⇨				
23		△ O ▢ ⇨				
24		△ O ▢ ⇨				
25		△ O ▢ ⇨				
26		△ O ▢ ⇨				
27		△ O ▢ ⇨				
28		△ O ▢ ⇨				
29		△ O ▢ ⇨				
30		△ O ▢ ⇨				
Total			0	0	0	

Figure 11.5. A value-added analysis template for a product process. VA, value-added; NVA, non-value-added; setup (△), queue (O), value-added (▢), and move (⇨) times.

been balanced and products are flowing at the Takt rate with the correct number of resources. Service routines and administrative processes, however, do not have to wait for balancing and product flow to occur. Kaizen activities in these functions can often begin simultaneously with the documentation of the current *as is* process. The size and scope of continuous improvement activities should not be limited to large dramatic ideas. Focus on any size of improvement — large or small. Continually identifying improvement opportunities is the most important criteria. Kaizen is based on making small changes on a regular basis that improve productivity, safety, and effectiveness while reducing waste. Kaizen philosophy is "do it better, make it better, and improve it, even if it isn't broken." Kaizen involves establishing standards while continually working to improve them. Kaizen also involves providing the training materials and supervision needed for employees to achieve higher standards and maintain their ability to meet their improvement goals on an on-going basis. If a value-added analysis form were used to document the work tasks, the non-value-added activities can be summed up in its individual column. Improvement opportunities by work type will be clearly indicated by the icons. The goal of Lean is to produce products or services in the sum of their work content time only. If setup time is chosen for kaizen improvement, then all of the times recorded as non-value-added setups are automatically candidates for elimination. The kaizen team can then review each task on the value-added analysis form to see if it can be eliminated or its elapsed time reduced. For example, how many signatures are required for approval? What dollar amount requires approval? Can this dollar amount be raised to eliminate the need for an approval signature, thus eliminating a task? Creative thinking and an energetic kaizen team can reduce or eliminate many of the mistrust effect or work ethic effect times embedded in service routines and administrative process. Eliminating non-value-added times shortens the total overall time to more closely approach the sum of the value-added time.

The 5 Why technique. When eliminating non-value-added work from a process, challenging *why* a work task is performed usually reveals if the task is really necessary for the process. The 5 *Why* technique is simple to use. Knowledge of statistical analysis is not required to complete the 5 *Why* technique. The technique is based on the theory that the answer to the first *why* will lead to another *why* question. It's effective in manufacturing and administrative functions for determining if a task is value-added or even necessary. To determine if a task is non-value-added, begin by asking *why is this task required*? Using that answer, ask *why* the work is necessary a second time, a third, and so on. By repeatedly asking *why*, the real reason for a task will be revealed. Once the real reason is revealed, deciding if the work task is still valid in the current environment or if it can be eliminated will be a simple matter for the kaizen team. Simple steps are used to perform the 5 *Why* test:

- **Step 1.** Document the specific work task (or problem) in writing to formalize and define the task completely and to achieve the consensus of the kaizen team.
- **Step 2.** Ask the first *why is this work task required* question and indent the answer below the work task.
- **Step 3.** If the resulting answer does not identify the root reason for the work task (or cause of the problem) identified during Step 2, ask *why* a second time and indent that answer under the problem statement.
- **Step 4.** Continue asking *why* as many times as necessary to identify the root reason for the work task (or cause of the problem). Record the answer each time until the kaizen team reaches agreement that the root reason for the work has been identified.

The 5 *Whys* technique is particularly effective for identifying work tasks that have been institutionalized as a result of the work ethic effect or the mistrust effect, but the technique can also help to identify other root cause issues and reveal the relationships between them. Even though the technique is known as the 5 *Whys*, needing to ask *why* more than five times to find the root requirement for a work task is rare.

Using Lean Methodology to Determine Service Routine Volume and the Required Resources

Product volume has a significant impact on the number of manufacturing resources that will be required to meet customer service expectations. When a Lean manufacturing line is being designed, identifying the products and then establishing the volume of products expected to be produced on the line in the future is usually difficult to determine. One thing is certain — the forecasted volume of products can never be precise. Predicting the volume of service routines and administrative functions is just as difficult. As was done when the Lean line was designed, the solution to predicting the volume of service routines and administrative functions is to accept the likelihood of forecasting errors and optimize the number of resources by matching them to customer demand. Whether in manufacturing processes or service routines, overutilization of resources is *waste*. Employees who are not kept busy when working on service routines or administrative functions eventually begin to invent work just to appear *busy* to management.

The Takt time. Takt time can be used to determine the output rate for service routines and administrative functions. What is the rate and frequency of the completion of work during the available time on a given day? The time that a manufacturing resource is available to do work is known as *available minutes per day* (total time minus time for breaks, lunch, training, and personal time away from a workstation). By dividing the available minutes per day by the anticipated throughput volume at full capacity, the rate at which each service routine or administrative function must be completed to satisfy customer demand can be identified. As with manufacturing volume, throughput volume for a service routine must project the anticipated volume for that process for a predetermined period into the future.

The standard work. The standard work required for every service routine and administrative function must also be known to determine how many labor resources (human and machine) are needed to complete a service routine or administrative function within the Takt time target. The processes required to produce a service routine output are identified on the PFD for each product. The standard work and individual work tasks are documented on the SWD and the value-added analysis form. Just as in the manufacturing area, a question must be answered — how many resources (humans, workstations, and machines) are necessary to produce the customer demand volume of service routines or administrative functions for the identified V_c? The number of resources required for the anticipated volume is calculated by dividing the standard work listed on the SWD by the Takt time. The dividend of this formula identifies the number of people required to perform that volume of standard work to achieve the Takt time output rate. In addition, the calculation identifies the number of workstations required to accommodate the resources performing the work. (A workstation for a service routine or administrative function is usually a desk where a person sits to complete work.) As in the manufacturing area, on the days when customer demand does not require the number of resources identified for the V_c, adjusting the number of resources downward will be necessary. Instead of having the resources remain idle, slow down their pace of standard work to match the reduced volume, or invent work to stay busy, adjust resources on a daily basis to compensate for fluctuating demand. Add or subtract resources on a daily basis to match the customer demand volume for that day. The most common resource in service routines or administrative functions is the human resource. When a human resource is not required for a particular day's standard work, assign that resource to another activity outside the process. Unfinished projects or other incomplete activities are usually waiting to have human resources assigned to their completion.

Work cells. Most service routines and administrative functions require the standard work of many processes. These processes usually involve work assigned to functional departments that are physically located throughout the facility, in an adjacent building, or even in another state or country. Because of this typical arrangement of administrative departments, the SWD often reveals that significant wait and move times are associated with completing a service routine. Even with electronic records transmitted at the speed of light on a computer monitor, wait time and move time are usually required before the standard work in the next process of a service routine can commence. Remember that designing the Lean manufacturing line required relocating manufacturing resources next to one another so products on the line could flow from one process to the next at a Takt rate until completion. The goal was to complete the standard work in only the sum of its value-added work content time. Does the logic of relocating a machine resource from a machining department to a Lean manufacturing line to eliminate move, wait, and queue time on the shop floor suggest that the same logic can be used to relocate human resources from far-flung department locations? Is the logic used any different? Is grouping intellectual property resources any different than grouping machine resources on the shop floor? Have human resources been grouped and located simply to maintain a departmental headcount? To be more effective, would it be logical to relocate human resources so they are right next to the process that consumes the information provided by their process? Would working side-by-side in the same location eliminate much of the wait, queue, and move time associated with a service routine? In a Lean facility, service routines, administrative functions, and manufacturing processes must share the same goal: to complete standard work in only the sum of its value-added work content time. The same relocation logic applied to the manufacturing area can be applied to service routines and administrative processes. Developing a work cell helps to accomplish that goal. Developing a work cell may require relocating human and workstation resources from their functional departments to a shared location where all of the processes are laid out to resemble the PFD. The work cell must accommodate the number of resources that have been determined to be required to complete the standard work at the V_c. Formation of the work cell merely means that identified resources will be located somewhere else to perform their work even though their primary reporting relationship with their current functional manager will not change. The opportunities to develop the flow of service routines and administrative functions are limited only by your imagination. Lean design tools can be used for the development of multifunction cells whenever multiple processes are required to produce a specific solution, achieve a goal, or produce an outcome. Potential service routine candidates for cell formation include:

- The purchase order request and three-way match through supplier payment cycle

- The research and development concept, engineering design, and manufacturing cycle
- The customer order receipt, manufacturing, and invoice cycle
- The receiving, quality approval, warehousing, material issues, and production cycle of raw materials
- The customer demand, manufacturing, purchasing, and supply chain cycle

Managers of functional departments may consider the relocation of their workers to satellite locations to be a diminution of their departments and challenge the relocation project. To avoid this situation, prior to the relocation of any resources, ensure functional managers that although their resources will be relocated physically, the primary reporting relationships of these resources with their current functional managers will not change. Retaining primary reporting relationships with current functional department managers ensures that core competency and continued functional expertise and training are retained.

COMMUNICATION: THE VALUE OF SHARING COMMON KNOWLEDGE ENTERPRISE-WIDE

A Lean organization recognizes each function in the company as being one component of an entire system. In a Lean organization, all functional areas must work together toward achieving the common goals of the company's total business strategy. To improve and optimize the entire system, understanding how each component of the company works individually and together to make the entire system work as efficiently as possible is required. Communicating the company's total business strategy to the manufacturing and administrative areas and sharing information and knowledge assist in making an organization as Lean as possible.

Achieving excellence requires having a commitment to share the knowledge gained from a Lean transformation. Provide a formal infrastructure to facilitate the flow of information throughout your company. Encourage an open environment for communication by including time for knowledge sharing in the Takt time calculation for each process. Any costs associated with making time available to share knowledge should be acknowledged as an investment rather than an incremental increase in overhead cost. The time built into the daily schedule to encourage knowledge sharing is a small investment compared to the cost of knowledge lost from the failure to communicate it throughout the organization.

Communicate company strategy. Lack of communication is a primary complaint in many companies. Employees often say they don't know or understand the vision of the company or its business strategy. These complaints become exponential deeper down into the organization chart. Employees at lower levels on the organization chart think they're more out of the communication loop than staff members nearer the top. The business strategy of a Lean organization focuses on reducing the total cost of processes and products, causing an increase in market share. A Lean company's business strategy must include the goals of being the highest-quality, lowest-cost, fastest-delivery manufacturer in the industry while providing customers with administrative functions that are high-quality, mistake-free, at the lowest cost, and delivered in the shortest possible time. In the Lean environment, the customer is supreme. The point behind making the transformation to a Lean operating system in the first place is to improve customer satisfaction by having improved product quality, minimum lead time, and the lowest cost — benefits that provide the differentiation required by customers to buy the company's products. To have maximum impact, the Lean operating system requires an effective communication flow. All employees must understand the company's overall strategy. Communicate it simply and thoroughly throughout the organization — from the boardroom to the shop floor to the mechanical room. Include employees at every level of the organization in the communication loop. It's not an easy task, but a necessary one if every employee is to work toward a common goal.

Document the standard work. The SWD defines the individual work tasks in a process and the correct sequence for completing the tasks in the process. Each work task identifies the required quality criteria for the task. Standard work documents the best practice *today*. Lean companies are familiar with the concept of assigning standard work to individual workstations and having employees flex to the workstations to perform the work rather than bringing work to a personal workstation. The purpose of standard work is not to turn employees into mindless robots or to allow only the completion of repetitive tasks. Standard work has several purposes: to document the current best practice by identifying the one correct way to complete each task; to provide knowledge benchmarking for others; and to encourage continuous improvement of a process. Lean business strategy requires continuously improving standard work to have a minimum of non-value-added work, causing each process to be as efficient as possible.

Analyze existing processes continuously. Knowledge is gained each time a process is improved. Gaining knowledge and making subsequent improvements in processes can only be accomplished through ongoing critical analysis of the existing processes. (Toyota continues to seek best practices 60 years after their first setup-reduction project!) If no attempts are made to improve the processes, what action or event would require a current policy or procedure to be critically examined? Rather than waiting for a failure to occur, continuously examine existing processes to identify the *best* practices and then incorporate them by sharing the knowledge gained throughout the organization. Lean thinking ultimately becomes institutionalized in a company as a result of the constant search for the best practice. Continuous improvement is vitally important in a Lean organization. It cannot be limited to the shop floor. Service routines and administrative functions must also participate in continuous improvement activities. Lean methods can be applied equally in service routines, administrative functions, and manufacturing processes. Lean tools are repeatable and consistent regardless of the process or the product type. If possible, limit the search for best practices using internal resources. If internal efforts cannot identify the best practices solution, then external resources can be benchmarked or adopted into the process.

Document improvements and communicate them. When validated, all process improvements must be documented on the SWD. The SWD therefore always reflects the current best practice. Documenting improvements to a process requires discipline and commitment. If a process is improved, but the improvement is not documented, the improvement will only remain in place as long as the employee (or the team) making the improvement remains on the process. When the employee leaves, undocumented improvement ideas will leave with the employee. As an improvement becomes the prevailing best practice in a process, recognize the improvement by embedding it in the SWD of the process. The new SWD then becomes the anchor document for all subsequent labor resources performing that process — the next benchmark. It's the existing blueprint for all future improvements. Promote changing the SWD as often as necessary to reflect the best practices. Each improvement made to the SWD creates a positive cycle of continuous improvement. Beware of interpretations of standard work by an individual or a functional group that has no vested interest in the process. Ensure that a resulting practice does not serve some personal agenda at the expense of the best practice for the process. Sharing best practices requires communication: if a process is improved or changed on the first shift, the second shift must be made aware of the change. Most processes are linked. An improvement in one process will likely cause an improvement in another. A common dilemma for many companies is defining the best mechanism for documenting and communicating these improvements. The SWD fulfills this role.

Some closing words about communication. Some companies manage to survive in spite of themselves. No matter how unaware the employees are of the company's direction, its short- and long-term goals, and its stated business strategy, these companies still succeed. Muddling through with a black-hole communication strategy seems to be acceptable. This is not the case in the Lean environment. In the Lean environment, uninformed human resources waste time, energy, and money by making errors and incorrect decisions that lead to inefficiency, poor quality, rework, and scrap, the worst-case scenario. Lean organizations recognize the power of communication. Lean organizations encourage communication between employees, teams, department managers, and other departments that make the difference between reaching an organizational goal or not. Lean organizations design and implement formal processes such as SWD documentation, kaizen activities, and continuous improvement initiatives to avoid the *waste* caused by lack of communication. In a Lean organization, the elements of cost, quality, and time are objective. Lean organizations establish annual goals and objectives to achieve percentage improvements in these three measurable areas. The improvements can be measured in actual increments. The improvements to standard work best practices required to support the company's business strategy are reflected in employees' individual performance goals. Managers have performance goals that reward them for improvements in standard work best practices that result in lower cost, better quality, and less processing time. Managers must be held accountable for achieving these goals. They must also be given a good set of tools for getting the job done.

LEAN ACROSS THE ENTERPRISE

During the 1980s, terms such as *Reengineering, JIT,* and *Lean Manufacturing* became part of manufacturing lexicon. Without doubt, these new technologies were a huge paradigm shift for factories around the globe. It took some time for manufacturers to become comfortable with the new terms and to understand the technology. The technology questioned the tenets of the old familiar, comfortable, batch manufacturing systems being used to maximize resource utilization. Pioneering scientific management techniques learned from Henry Ford and Fredrick Winslow Taylor were being challenged by post-WWII Japanese manufacturer Toyota. JIT was replacing *Scientific Management* as the preferred manufacturing paradigm.

During the 1980s and through the 1990s, the term *JIT* evolved into *Lean,* which is now the commonly used term. Companies committed to Lean manufacturing had to reconcile their current operating systems with Lean technology, but once they embraced the benefits, many moved forward with their Lean initiatives. The evolution to Lean not only encompassed the tools and techniques required to transform a manufacturing facility into the Lean operating system, but it also spread to all disciplines throughout the company and to all types of industries. Lean thinking has become a well-understood, well-tested platform for improving the results of any series of processes — whether in a manufacturing facility or in an administrative support area. Today Lean principles are considered universally applicable to any series of processes in manufacturing or back office administrative areas. For some manufacturers, the results have been spotty, but with continuous improvement initiatives and ongoing kaizen activities, they continue to make progress.

Although Lean principles are applicable to any series of processes, a company that manufactures products should always begin a Lean initiative on the shop floor because the manufacturer's shop floor is where customer differentials are created and where the greatest amount of a company's money is spent. When all is said and done, however, the long-term success of a Lean manufacturing facility will always depend on the company's support functions aligning themselves with the goals and performance of the Lean line. Improving the performance of manufacturing is only the first step. Picking up on the financial and operational benefits gained from the manufacturing shop floor in the administrative support areas just makes good business sense, but only after the shop floor is successfully transformed and operational should focus be shifted to administrative and service routines.

THE IMPORTANCE OF ENTERPRISE-WIDE LINKAGE

An optimum Lean system requires the eventual transformation of the entire enterprise into a series of processes that work in harmony with one another to achieve the goals of the Lean operating system. Without an enterprise-wide Lean perspective, even the best Lean operating system can be rendered ineffective by the constraints of processes operating with a traditional batch-production, demand-push, maximum-utilization model.

Implementing Lean in all functions enterprise-wide begins with analyzing all the processes necessary to support the Lean transformation at the organizational level. Achieving enterprise-wide Lean manufacturing support begins by establishing linkages to all functional organizational processes impacted by the manufacturing shop floor. These processes must be redesigned to support one-unit-at-a-time production, matching of resources to customer demand, and managing materials with kanban systems. Ultimately, the processes deployed in functional support and administrative areas must support alignment of Lean processes throughout the supply chain and any future cross-enterprise Lean processes (Figure 12.1). Long-term success of a Lean manufacturing facility will depend on the company's support functions aligning themselves to be compatible with the goals and performance measurements of the Lean line. The challenges can be numerous. Once alignment between support functions and manufacturing has been completed, improvements achieved by kaizen and continuous improvement teams can have the desired multiplier effect on competitiveness across the entire organization with time saved, costs reduced, and higher quality being achieved.

Attaining shared objectives between functional departments and the manufacturing area can be accomplished by aligning cross-functional Lean processes

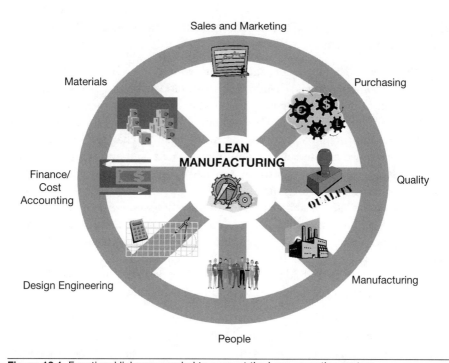

Sales and Marketing

Materials

Purchasing

LEAN MANUFACTURING

Finance/ Cost Accounting

Quality

Design Engineering

Manufacturing

People

Figure 12.1. Functional linkages needed to support the Lean operating system.

and understanding how the traditional mass production principles and the Lean operating system impact the organization differently. Enterprise-wide, new processes will have to be learned in the support functions just as was done in the manufacturing area (see Chapter 11). New conflicting objectives between support functions and the manufacturing area will challenge current performance measurements and ultimately require reconciliation among all groups. Post-mortem examinations of failed Lean transformations often reveal that a leading cause was the irreconcilable performance measures between the new Lean operating system in manufacturing and its support groups. What a shame it would be to allow an obsolete performance measurement in a single organizational silo deny the benefits of the Lean operating system to the entire enterprise!

Eliminate communication barriers. Critical to achieving shared objectives is the elimination of existing communication barriers that have been established by organizational silos over time. Open communication is required between manufacturing and administrative support organizations to expand application of the Lean tools and best practices and the Lean principle of *optimum utilization* of resources to match customer demand. Communication barriers cannot be eliminated overnight, but if a Lean operating system is to be successful enterprise-wide, eliminating them cannot be avoided.

Eliminate self-imposed organizational boundaries. Another barrier to improved communication is self-imposed organizational boundaries (e.g., departments and divisions). Self-imposed organizational boundaries are the source of power for individual managers. Organizational boundaries often create silos of expertise and informational fiefdoms that are resistant to change. Organizational silos can slow down or interrupt the flow of paper, data, and information between the processes of an administrative or service routine. Once information (electronic or paper) enters an organizational silo, the process becomes controlled by the people in the silo. Visibility is zero to other functions. Administrative turf battles, the need for authorizations, poor conformance to standards, bottlenecks, scheduling problems, and lack of feedback between processes caused by organizational silos must be eliminated. (The 5 *Whys* technique and the process design techniques for service and administrative routines described in Chapter 11 can assist in eliminating organizational communication barriers.)

Eliminate organizational isolation. Another communication barrier to eliminate is organizational isolation. Organizational silos encourage isolation from adjoining processes. Realignment of managers and staff in functional organizations may be required to eliminate communication barriers caused by the separation of administrative processes. Determine how processes can be linked together to use a set of operating policies and day-to-day procedures. Linking processes together may include the physical relocation of functional processes, the transfer of personnel and equipment, changing the information flow, and cross-training. Linking multiple functional processes together into *work cells* helps to establish linkages that can create the harmony necessary to support Lean throughout the enterprise. Also consider other linkage issues beyond the four walls of the company. Expand these linkages to include suppliers and customers. Consider suppliers and customers as extensions of the manufacturing shop floor who just happen to be located somewhere else. Determine new approaches to existing policy and procedures to develop these external relationships. Managing the supply chain upstream and downstream from the company is more than just an option. It's essential for successful, long-term, enterprise-wide Lean transformation.

Expect challenges. In most companies, the processes in their traditional operating systems are not linked to one another. The design of traditional mass production and the operating principles have always emphasized *maximum* utilization of resources, whereas Lean technology seeks the *optimization* of resources. To support the new Lean operating system, these traditional organizational structures and operating systems, the internal policies and procedures, the cross-functional linkages, and the external relationships need to be changed enterprise-wide. Humans are naturally resistant to change of any kind. Redesigning cross-functional linkages, operating systems, organization structures, and external relationships will threaten the final remnants of the traditional operating system. Loyalty to current systems may be so deeply imbedded in the manufacturing psyche at all levels that it could thwart a successful transformation to Lean. This loyalty must be redirected. Establishing policies and procedures that support the necessary linkages for transformation of the entire enterprise to Lean is no small task. As linked processes spread across multiple organizational units (divisions, departments, sections, and companies), ensure that all procedures reinforce the Lean principles and practices. Loyalty to organizational units must be secondary. In spite of company sponsorship, expect turf battles to rage on between the manufacturing and support functions during implementation of the Lean business strategy. Although administrative departments are unlikely to disappear, there is no substitute for having a shared goal of open communication between all functional areas in a Lean organization to achieve universal performance expectations of the entire company.

Forgetting why support groups exist is not uncommon. Often administrative areas are greatly removed, both physically and functionally, from the shop floor. Support groups, however, exist to support manufacturing (just as the manufacturing group exists to satisfy customer demand). If support and administrative functions are not aligned with the Lean manufacturing operating system, redundant and obsolete systems will continue to operate, creating daily conflict with the constant justification and reconciliation of the mission required among departments. How long will manufacturing and support functions be willing to operate in such a hostile environment before becoming totally frustrated and choosing to revert to the path of least resistance (*the way we used to do it*) just to make life easy again? When departments revert to the former ways of operating, other functions soon fall victim to this same game of attrition. The success of the Lean enterprise transformation cannot be jeopardized because of barriers to Lean improvements created by silo bureaucracies that are unwilling to change. Based on the definition of the word *support*, does allowing any support group to not reconcile their performance measures with the goals of manufacturing even make sense in a cohesive organization?

Monitor performance. The primary reason for a Lean transformation project in the first place is to make the company more competitive in its marketplace, thereby increasing the company's share of a finite market. If your company's products are technologically equivalent and equal in quality to competitors' products, a successful Lean operating system can provide your company with the only critical competitive differentials possible: faster delivery with shorter response time through the facility and lower cost that allows more competitive pricing. These product attributes may be the only differentials available to your company that will appeal to customers and cause them to shift more business to your company. Boasting of fast lead times, competitive pricing strategies, and the best quality is great, but what if margins in the company do not improve? In Lean, the best way to evaluate improvement is by monitoring performance measures such as market share growth, margin improvement, on-time delivery, and quality metrics rather than concentrating on 100% utilization of resources. (See Chapter 5, Table 5.1, for KPI measurements that can be used to track improvements from a Lean transformation.)

THE ORGANIZATIONAL IMPACT OF LEAN ON FUNCTIONAL DEPARTMENTS

By design, a Lean enterprise is a minimalist organization. The Lean minimalist approach to the utilization of human, workstation, machine, and inventory resources will change the way a company operates. For most companies, very few organizational groups will stay the same. Lean manufacturing will create goals and objectives in manufacturing that conflict with many of the existing goals and objectives in critical support organizations such as sales and marketing, purchasing, quality management, design engineering, finance and cost accounting, materials management, maintenance, and human resources. These conflicts must be resolved. The goals and objectives of support functions must be modified to match those of the Lean manufacturing organization.

Sales and Marketing

If a company manufactures a commodity-type product, then it's a good chance that the benefits of a Lean transformation will be invisible to the sales and marketing group. A *commodity* is a product that has value, but has little or no technological differentiation from other products in the marketplace. This lack of technological differentiation has the effect of causing the selling price of a commodity product to be close to or identical to the same product from a different manufacturer. Mass production by many manufacturers results in great quantities of products that are instantly available in the marketplace at a retail level to the customer. Because commodity-type products are perceived to be homogenous, the goal of mass producers is to never run out of their product. An out-of-stock condition means lost sales — inventory levels, delivery speed, and quality attributes are secondary attributes to product availability. There is no customer loyalty in a commodity market. If a product is unavailable, customers just purchase a competitor's product even if the price is slightly higher. In a commodity market, customers prefer instant gratification over price. They make no distinction between manufacturers.

Although many markets have numerous companies fiercely competing to increase their share of a finite market at the expense of other companies, in the truest sense of the word, most manufacturers' products are not commodities. Even in markets where numerous producers compete and differentiation takes the form of the lowest price, products approaching commodity status can still benefit from product differentiation to achieve greater levels of customer loyalty. These products can still have better quality and lower prices and be delivered faster. There's still plenty of room for product differentiation and preservation of customer loyalty with improved quality and availability.

Having lowest price as a differentiation is usually a short-lived strategy once profit margins become negatively impacted by an endless series of price reductions. Rather than engaging in damaging price wars with competitors, a better challenge for the sales and marketing group is to determine other ways to compete in the marketplace. Many opportunities for differentiating products other than price alone still exist in the virtual era of manufacturing today, e.g., providing multiple product configurations, faster delivery times, and quality that competitors cannot match. A Lean factory can provide these differentials to the sales and marketing group.

Traditionally, sales and marketing and manufacturing groups have been at opposite ends of the customer satisfaction spectrum. The main reason for this separation is the conflicting objectives of each group. The objective for the sales and marketing group is to sell as much product as possible. So when a sales representative meets with a customer, any resistance from the customer to the sale is often answered by displaying the customer catalog and promising, "You can have any feature you want, customized to your satisfaction, and have it delivered in our company's standard lead time." Back at the factory, however, promising the standard delivery lead time for a configured product can be a problem. The manufacturing group (typically materials management) is measured by the speed of inventory turnover and how well inventory investment is managed. To optimize this measurement, the manufacturing group must make critical decisions about which products are the most likely to be ordered most of the time. Component materials for those products will be kept on hand so the manufacturing group is able to produce customer demand within the customer-quoted lead time. In a sense, the manufacturing group "plays the odds" when making decisions about the products that will be ordered most of the time. Manufacturing relies on the probability that most customer demand will come in the form of these high-volume, regular-frequency-ordered products. The customer catalog, however, contains numerous product configurations requiring numerous specialized parts. If low-volume, infrequently demanded components are purchased in advance, how long will these specialized parts with a substantial inventory investment remain in inventory before being consumed in the manufacture of a product and ultimately sold? Additionally, the manufacturing group has no assurance that a customer's order quantity will match the inventory quantity. The odds of the manufacturing group correctly predicting, buying, and keeping specialized parts on hand, in the precise quantities needed, just in case the sales and marketing group sells these product configurations are too long to become a practical inventory investment policy for the company.

Because the manufacturing group is measured on management of inventory investment and speed of inventory turnover, the materials management group will opt to purchase specialized materials only when an actual customer order requiring those parts is received rather than keeping specialized parts on hand. When a customer order is received on the shop floor for a specialized or highly configured product with delivery promised in the standard lead time, conflict with the sales and marketing group is assured because additional lead time is required by suppliers for delivering the specialized component parts required to build the special configuration. Supplier lead time is incremental to the standard manufacturing lead time. Conflict arises when the manufacturing group cannot achieve the promise given by the sales and marketing group to the customer for delivery in standard lead time. Scheduling conflicts are a common cause of squabbling, mistrust, and finger pointing between the sales and marketing and manufacturing groups. The sales and marketing group complains about manufacturing's poor customer service and missed delivery dates while manufacturing is jumping through hoops to satisfy the customer's expectation of delivery in the standard lead time by expediting parts, pressuring suppliers, and paying premium transportation in hopes of meeting the promised delivery time and complaining that the sales and marketing group did not forecast the demand in time for the required specialized parts to be on hand. Sales and marketing blames manufacturing for causing them to miss their sales quotas and manufacturing blames sales and marketing for forecasts that caused a shortage of specialized parts, over- or underproduction of units, and missed delivery dates. Left unchanged, an environment of placing blame on one another will go on forever providing cover for each group when their performance measurement goals are not achieved.

The argument can be made that a Lean manufacturing transformation project should actually be sponsored by the sales and marketing organization because this group has so much to gain from a successful Lean implementation. Lean benefits can provide the sales and marketing group with the differentials they need to improve sales revenues and increase the company's market share. Who would argue that there are benefits from having the right materials on hand at the right time to meet most customer demand in the standard lead time or less? Remember that a Lean manufacturing line is designed to be capable of producing 80% of all customer demand in the sum of its work content time using designated standard parts. That means that the SKUs in this 80% revenue category can be delivered in the standard lead time with no need to wait for the delivery of specialized parts from a supplier. By design, the Lean manufacturing line can produce the other 20% of demand in the work content time plus any additional time required to purchase and receive materials from a supplier. There is no reason why the sales and marketing and manufacturing groups cannot work together to agree on which SKUs make up 80% of total sales. All remaining SKUs fall into the 20% revenue category. As their part of the bargain, the manufacturing group must commit to the delivery of all the products that make up 80% of total sales in the standard lead time. Because of this faster lead time guarantee from the manufacturing group, the sales and marketing organization now has an incentive to promote the sale of standard models that have a promised standard lead time delivery to customers (the 80% of revenue). Customers can still order special model configurations, but special orders have a different customer fulfillment policy: supplier lead time plus the company's standard lead time. To be realistic, delivery promises made to customers for special configurations must be based on lead times that allow the manufacturing group sufficient time to obtain component parts from suppliers and sufficient standard time to produce special products on the shop floor. A Lean transformation provides a perfect opportunity for the sales and marketing and manufacturing groups to work together to establish customer fulfillment policies that provide the important differentials needed by the sales and marketing group to grow market share and at the same time allow the manufacturing group to shift concentration to performance improvement rather than constantly defending production decisions and missed delivery dates.

Purchasing

Traditional purchasing organizations use a planning system (electronic or manual) to notify buyers of the components to be purchased and when the orders need to be placed to procure them. The component materials and the quantities are determined by an explosion of the indented BOM compared to the delivery dates planned by the master schedule for an end item SKU ordered by a customer. Using a *netting formula* to calculate net requirements, the planning system outputs an *order action report* recommending that a purchase order be placed for the quantity and due dates on the report. Order action reports generated by the planning system (MRP) occur on a predetermined, periodic basis. Based on company criteria, the frequency of periodic planning explosions can range from daily to every week, bi-weekly, or monthly. Once established, this routine occurs according to the predetermined schedule. Between planning system explosions, a production control group is responsible for maintaining and updating all activity that occurs on the shop floor such as closing out production orders, updating parts usage, and updating any changes to production order due dates and quantities.

The master schedule also reflects newly released orders for new customer demand and parts for new products from the engineering group. These are requirements are input with effective dates set. The purpose of all this communication with the planning system is to provide feedback to system databases to ensure the stock status report is up-to-date and that the master schedule is current with activity on the shop floor before the next planning routine is performed.

When the next explosion is performed, the timing of component deliveries and the quantities and due dates of all materials can potentially change because of the information updates from the shop floor made by the production control organization and any new demand created by the master schedule. Any changes require issuing a revised order action report. Buyers then go to work updating purchase orders to reflect the status changes. Because of quantity and date changes to existing purchase orders, the orders may require expediting. Every time the planning system is updated using the scheduled explosion cycle, this purchasing activity is repeated at the same interval. The order quantities and the due dates of existing purchase orders can change with each subsequent planning explosion. The potential for changing purchase order quantities and due dates with each scheduled iteration of the planning system also creates chaos for suppliers.

Implementation of a material kanban system to support a Lean line reverses all this activity. The kanban system makes no effort to place future purchase orders. Material resources are not committed to forecasts that might be unreliable. Replenishment is not dependent on a periodically changing mix or volume of products ordered by customers. Replenishment is not dependent on the output of a planning system to keep requirements current with the activity on the shop floor. Replenishment is never a scheduled event. The kanban system uses a series of signals that advises material handlers when material replenishment is required based on usage on the line. Materials are replenished at the same rate at which they are consumed. Once issued, a kanban signal will always generate the same replenishment quantity as calculated according to the replenishment time recorded on the label of the container. The replenishment quantity always remains the same — only the timing of replenishment changes.

For the purchasing group, the material kanban system is the complete opposite of the planning system model. No periodic planning system explosion potentially changes all purchase orders based on an order action report. Kanban signals are always a function of actual usage on the shop floor. Material kanban signals occur only when materials are depleted in the first container of the kanban system. When requirements are forwarded to a supplier according to the pull sequence, the quantity will always be the same and be based on replenishment time. A supplier may not know when a signal will be received, but the supplier will always know the quantity. It's always the same. By having a known order quantity, the supplier can use two options to smooth out demand in their factory: maintain the known quantity on hand to always be prepared to meet the delivery expectation when a replenishment signal is received or schedule the known quantity amount for the next production run in their factory. Because suppliers are assured of a certain amount of business, they can make economies of scale decisions that are best for their companies.

In a Lean operating system, buyers are expected to be actively involved in the design and ongoing operation of the kanban system. When the Lean operating system is in place, the role of a buyer shifts from maintaining purchase order quantities and due dates to optimizing the kanban system to enable it to operate as efficiently as possible, including assisting with Lean transformations at suppliers' locations, negotiating long-term blanket orders with set periods of time with suppliers, and certifying suppliers so that materials can bypass stockrooms and be delivered directly to shop floor RIP locations. These Lean activities have significant potential for reducing costs and delivery time and better using the buyer's skill, knowledge, talent, and time.

Note: If a supplier is also a Lean manufacturer, the customer-quoted lead time is the replenishment time — how long it takes to receive the signal, produce the product, and ship the product to the customer's RIP location. Until a supplier becomes Lean, the supplier may opt to manufacture the entire quantity of a blanket order and maintain a finished goods inventory that allows an immediate response to kanban signals received from the customer. For blanket orders with set periods of time, a kanban signal serves as a release against the blanket order. Blanket orders are essentially a guarantee to purchase a negotiated amount of product from the supplier over a set period of time and can be used by the supplier as collateral for a business loan. If a supplier is not a Lean manufacturer, the Lean customer company may want to assist the supplier to become Lean. Once certified, supplier replenishment times can be reduced causing smaller replenishment quantities that result in reduced inventory investment and cost for both supplier and the customer.

Quality Management

The role of quality management in a Lean operating system is the opposite of the traditional planning system model. Instead of being an organization that *reacts* to quality failures, Lean quality management is *proactive* by ensuring that the company produces products with the highest quality attribute levels (the least number of failures). Instead of *quality control* or *quality assurance*, the more commonly used terms, using the term *quality management* is more appropriate for describing the Lean goals of achieving and improving quality. *Quality* is often defined as *the meeting of standards established by specifications/tolerances at an acceptable level of conformance.* Companies define the term *acceptable level* differently. They routinely use terms such as *zero defects, six sigma,* and *defective parts per million* in company quality policies.

Most companies with Lean manufacturing systems have ingrained quality management systems that use three Lean business policies:

- Pursuit of quality is a way of life.
- The entire organization is committed to and actively involved in achieving quality goals.
- Unending, organized, company-wide efforts, including measurement and training, are directed toward continuously improving product process quality.

In Lean quality management, high quality is a central principle of a Lean organization's business strategy. Managers, staff, and operators are trained in using Lean quality management tools and practices. Operators must be certified to perform the standard work at their primary workstations. To maintain flexibility, operators must additionally be certified at one workstation upstream and downstream from their primary workstations. Certification requires operators to demonstrate that they can complete the standard work at these three workstations and perform the quality criteria assigned to each workstation in the Takt time. The quality criteria include:

- The work of the previous operator
- A self-check of the standard work assigned to the operator's primary workstation (any quality check documented on the standard work definition and the graphic work instruction)
- Another separate inspection to verify the quality criteria of the operator's standard work a second time (causes operators to become process owners)

Performing these three inspections as part of standard work increases quality awareness at workstations and maximizes workmanship quality. On a Lean manufacturing line, quality is not delegated to a downstream location or a test station. Quality is built into the product as a component of the standard work assigned to the workstation.

Remember that Lean manufacturing considers quality inspections to be non-value-added activities. Inspections are required because of lack of confidence in an upstream process. The goal of a quality management organization is to eliminate the variability in standard work tasks that requires inspection to be done. The only way to eliminate inspections is for all work tasks in a process to be fail-safe.

Eliminate internal failures. Internal failures are defects caused by workmanship errors during the manufacturing process. Eliminating workmanship errors substantially reduces internal failures. Operators on a Lean line are trained to follow in-process kanban (IPK) discipline by *never* placing a defective unit into an IPK. If a quality defect cannot be corrected at a workstation within the workstation's Takt time, the IPK for that workstation will remain empty. At the same time, the upstream IPK will remain full, prohibiting an authorization to work. Eventually, all of the upstream IPKs become filled, signaling all work to stop. In the meantime, the downstream workstations will continue to have work only until their IPKs become empty. By adhering to the IPK rule of never placing a defective unit into an IPK, no defective product should ever reach the last workstation. Final quality inspections will eventually become redundant and ultimately eliminated.

Eliminate external failures. External failures are caused by defects that result from poor-quality, supplier-provided materials or from defective manufactured products that are shipped to a customer. External failures are the most costly defects a company can experience. Correcting them at a customer's site is expensive. Not only is correcting external failures expensive, but the damage to the manufacturer's reputation can be great. In a highly competitive market, external product failures can have a devastating effect on future sales.

In a Lean supply chain, *quality* applies to the inputs, throughputs, and outputs of all processes. Defective products should never leave a Lean production line! Operators are responsible for the quality of the units they produce, but they have little to no control over the quality of supplier-provided materials. The quality management group in a Lean organization is responsible for establishing practices that prevent defective supplier-provided products from ever reaching the company's receiving dock. The quality management group must implement quality management practices across the supply chain to continually improve standards and the acceptable levels of conformance to established company quality standards so the quality of purchased materials becomes the responsibility of suppliers. Suppliers in the Lean manufacturing environment must be certified. They must certify that their incoming materials meet specification and are free of defects. Suppliers cannot rely on an inspection on the customer's receiving dock to discover workmanship defects in supplier-provided materials. Suppliers must be able to validate that their manufacturing processes are stable, repeatable, and free from defects. The quality management group must provide leadership to accomplish certification of suppliers. The goal is to achieve an operation-to-operation material receipt process. The quality management group must be certain suppliers understand the company's quality criteria and ensure that identical standards are used at both sites.

Design Engineering

The design engineering group has an important role in reducing non-value-added time. Design engineering is already involved in responding to customer demand by working with the sales and marketing group to develop new products and to improve existing products. The role of the design engineering group in designing products for functionality, however, is often a passive one based on a set of specifications. Design work is done using a CAD computer or drafting table. Often there is little to no communication with potential end users about the item being designed. When a design is completed, design engineers are often accused of just "throwing it over the wall." The perception is *let manufacturing figure out how to produce this design or incorporate it into an existing design*. Designs for products or components fresh from a drafting table are usually capable of performing the desired functions, but often serviceability occurs only after the manufacturing group invests time into modifying the item's design for ease of manufacturing. *Bend to fit, paint to match* is a common expression for the modification process performed on the shop floor.

In a Lean enterprise, to make new product designs more compatible with the Lean line design, the design engineering group should become more proactive in designing products. The design engineering group must understand the Lean operating system and the importance of balanced work stations and Takt time targets. Each new design released from engineering has a potential to impact the balance of the line. If modifications necessary to enhance the design of new products remain the responsibility of the manufacturing group, the time required for perfecting the balance of processes and engaging in continuous improvement activities in manufacturing is diminished in favor of modifying all of the new parts for the next generation of products. The design engineering group can facilitate the operation of a Lean line by ensuring that new product introductions are consistent with existing process flow diagrams, accompanying standard work definitions, and graphic work instructions and that they can be easily absorbed into the current balanced line layout.

A Lean line facilitates introducing new products. When making purchasing decisions, customers expect to see the latest and greatest in available technology. Offering products with great technology is fundamental to remaining competitive in the marketplace. Steady introduction of new products is the lifeblood of any organization. Unless a new product represents a radically new design, unlike anything else previously manufactured by the company, producing new products from the research and development group is generally not problematic for a Lean manufacturer. Most new products are frequently variations of current models with the addition of new parts. The difference between the current product and a new introduction is usually cosmetic with the only difference being appearance. Even if component parts have been added or changed to improve the functionality of the new design, the manufacturing processes required to produce a new product are likely to remain similar to the current processes. If a process flow diagram were drawn for a new product and compared to the process flow diagram of the current model, chances are good that the process flow diagrams would be nearly or even exactly identical. It's possible that a new product design might require the addition of some new manufacturing processes and the elimination of others, but a new product is usually just a change to the existing mixed-model process flow diagram. Remember that the design of the Lean shop floor layout mirrors the mixed-model process flow diagram. Processes are physically located to follow the flow of manufacturing processes for a family of products. Unless new products are a radical departure from the current design, the research and development group can facilitate the introduction of new products on an existing Lean line by ensuring that any new product introductions reflect existing process flow diagrams. The number of manufacturing resources should also be recalculated to accommodate the introduction of any new products.

Inspections are still required. Inspection work is a non-value-added activity, but unless a process is completely fail-safe, inspections are required to ensure that standard work tasks are properly completed and to eliminate defects made by operators who make independent decisions about the one correct way to perform a standard work task. Additional inspection points may even be necessary because of poor product design or modifications made by the manufacturing group to achieve functionality of a product design from the design engineering group. Many of these added inspections can be avoided if the design engineering group works proactively with manufacturing to understand the manufacturing processes used to produce products prior to releasing a new design, but if the subsequent inspections are required once the product is released to the manufacturing group, the inspections must be documented on the standard work definition. For future releases, the design engineering group should use the standard work definition as the source document and design products and components that eliminate the variability in work tasks that is causing the need for the inspections. Increasing design engineering's interface with the quality management group can also help eliminate variability in work tasks in the standard work definition by identifying the one correct way to perform a work task before the first product or component of a new release is ever produced on the Lean line. Resolving variability issues is *never* the responsibility of an operator on a Lean line. Over time, inspections can be designed out of manufacturing processes with each succeeding generation of products. As more and more inspections are eliminated, and product quality becomes even better, both lead time and working capital requirements are reduced proportionally.

Finance and Cost Accounting

Modern cost accounting systems began in the 1930s when manufacturing volumes became repetitive enough to establish standard labor times for the specific products being produced. In the early days of standard costing, labor was usually the largest component of product cost. Overhead costs were lower and raw materials were much less complex and expensive than the materials used today. As standard costing systems became the accepted accounting methodology, labor costs were naturally targeted as the most significant part of the three product costs to carefully manage. Even though the distribution of product costs has shifted since the 1930s, close management of the labor component of product cost still consumes most of manufacturing managers' time.

Even today, should labor be utilized in excess of the assigned standard time in a manufacturing department, a variance report is generated that requires an explanation by the department's manager. This never-ending emphasis on the labor component of product cost has caused most manufacturers to focus their attention almost exclusively on labor cost reduction. (One reason why many manufacturers seek to outsource their manufacturing operations is the hope that they will realize lower labor costs.) This focus, and the associated obsession with micromanagement of labor costs, soon led to the need for improved control systems for managing shop floor activity. In response to these requirements, and to satisfy the needs of cost accounting routines, routing files, production order clerks, expediters, time clocks, variance reports, and follow-up explanations to track labor costs were introduced to the manufacturing shop floor just to facilitate the comparison of actual cost to standard cost.

The cost structure of products has changed significantly over the years. Material costs are now ±60%, overhead costs are at ±30%, and for most manufacturers, labor costs have fallen to 10% of total cost. This shift has occurred because of tremendous advances in manufacturing technology. Fewer people are required to produce greater volumes of products. What has not changed is the standard cost model. The standard cost accounting model has remained essentially unchanged. How much time is spent every day in your factory collecting labor tracking information just so it can be compared to an outdated standard costing model?

Recognizing and leveraging the 80+-year restructuring of product cost distribution is the main reason why Lean manufacturers receive the benefits they claim. Lean manufacturers acknowledge the restructuring of product cost distribution and focus their efforts on the elimination of waste in the largest components of product cost in their processes, materials and overhead, rather than maximizing labor utilization. By doing so, Lean manufacturers achieve significantly lower product costs. Although Lean manufacturers have limited control over the purchase price of raw materials, using Lean methods in manufacturing can reduce the cost of materials in work-in-process and finished goods inventories. Because of the simplicity of the Lean operating system, manufacturers find they can also reduce overhead costs. By using material kanban systems and effective supplier certification efforts, Lean manufacturers usually experience improved control over the cost of their purchased material. Lean manufacturers do not ignore labor costs. To do so would be foolish. Lean manufacturers realize they must be good stewards of each of the three elements of product cost, but they also know that a 1% savings in labor costs has less return on investment than a 1% savings in material costs.

The Impact of Absorption Costing

Absorption costing (also known as the *full absorption method* or *full costing*) includes all manufacturing costs in a finished unit of inventory: the variable costs (direct materials, direct labor, and variable manufacturing overhead) and fixed manufacturing overhead. To allocate fixed overhead, the full absorption method divides fixed factory overhead costs by the number of units produced. For example, assume a company has a fixed factory overhead of $10,000. If the per-unit costs for a product are direct material, $3; direct labor, $4; variable factory overhead, $5; with a fixed factory overhead of $10,000, then the absorption costing method of computing product cost for a production run of 10,000 units would be $13 per unit: the variable cost components of $12 ($3 + $4 + $5 = $12) + $1 of allocated fixed factory overhead ($10,000 ÷ 10,000 units = $1). Conversely, the variable costing method limits product cost to only the *variable* production costs of $12. The fixed factory overhead costs of $10,000 are not absorbed into product cost using this method.

Full absorption accounting methods have conflicting objectives with the Lean operating system. The full absorption method considers inventory to be an asset on the company's balance sheet, whereas Lean considers unsold inventories as a wasted cost. Because full absorption requires all manufacturing costs to be absorbed by all units produced, the full absorption method creates an incentive to maintain high levels of inventory and to produce as much inventory as possible. As more units are produced, the fixed cost of each unit will be lower. Producing a maximum number of products is encouraged because it reduces (or *absorbs*) the fixed overhead costs by spreading these costs over more units of production. Lower unit cost, of course, translates into increased profits from the same sales revenue volume. When underutilization occurs in manufacturing, the full absorption cost accounting method generates negative variance reports. Using the full utilization model, performance reports initiated from the cost accounting group can indicate manufacturing is inefficient when, in fact, the Lean performance measurements are simultaneously reporting very good improvements in on-time delivery, improved quality, and reduced working capital — as the Lean operating system reduces inventory levels, the full costing reports show reduced profits. (A good explanation of absorption costing may be found online at the Principles of Accounting.com website, Chapter 23.)

Lean manufacturers seek to utilize only the minimum amount of resources needed to meet customer demand with little to no regard for the full absorption of all manufacturing costs. The Lean operating system can easily accommodate times when the full capacity of the factory is required. The Lean operating system can also easily accommodate the days when full capacity is not needed (intentional underutilization). A Lean manufacturer produces only the demand required each day (demand that has actually been sold): resources = demand. After the initial Lean transformation has been completed, these conflicting utilization objectives between the cost accounting group and manufacturing group can, over time, doom the long-term success of a Lean operating system.

Wherever the manufacturing and finance groups in a company struggle over conflicting utilization objectives, one or the other must eventually compromise. Either the manufacturing group abandons the Lean operating system and returns to the full-utilization production model each day to create as much sold and unsold inventory as possible or the cost accounting group alters the company's cost accounting system and agrees to accept less than full utilization of resources every day. Compromise for the cost accounting group means discontinuance of the variance reporting system of the full absorption cost accounting method and the adoption of new performance measures that are aligned with the measurements of performance used for the manufacturing group. This reconciliation of performance measures is necessary to ensure that the Lean operating system remains operational. The attributes of any new performance measurements must deemphasize 100% utilization while embracing on-time delivery, percent of first-pass quality, linearity, improved margins, and increased market share as better indicators of company success. Performance measurements based on the company's KPIs reflect the company's performance better than utilization of the labor component of product cost. Sooner or later, a decision will have to be made by management as to which compromise is best for the company.

The Challenges to Changing an Existing Cost Accounting System

Changing an existing cost accounting system is easier said than done. The cost accounting group within an individual company does not have the autonomy to act independently. The cost accounting group is subject to a series of accounting standards known as GAAP, the Generally Accepted Accounting Principles. GAAP is a collection of methods used to process, prepare, and present public accounting information. To be applicable to many types of industries, the guidelines for GAAP methods are very general. The U.S. Securities and Exchange Commission authorizes GAAP principles and FASB (the Financial Accounting Standards Board) establishes GAAP standards. The U.S. Securities and Exchange Commission requires that GAAP principles be followed for financial reporting by publicly traded companies. Although GAAP principles are not written in law, most industries in the U.S. are expected to follow them. GAAP is applicable only in the U.S. Other countries have versions that are similar. Following GAAP ensures that all companies present standard information that adheres to a few basic principles: consistency, relevance, reliability, and comparability.

Consistency. All information in public financial statements is to be gathered and reported in the same manner across all periods. For example, the way inventory is accounted for from one period to another (e.g., FIFO or LIFO) cannot be changed without noting the change in financial statements. Otherwise, the ability to make comparisons with previous periods would be lost. There must be a valid reason for making the reporting change. Before changing financial reporting to support a Lean operating system, the cost accounting group must educate all stakeholders in the company about the change. Maintaining consistency and losing the ability to compare a previous year's results with this year's results are primary reasons reported by many cost accounting professionals for their unwillingness to change the cost accounting system in a Lean enterprise.

Relevance. The information reported in public financial statements (and other public statements) must be appropriate and have significance for the reader. It must assist an individual evaluating the financial statement to make an educated decision regarding the future financial state of the company. A Lean operating system changes the cost structure in the factory. The Lean operating system must be explained to all company stakeholders so the new Lean manufacturing metrics will align with current decision making.

Reliability. The information reported in financial statements must represent a clear picture of what actually occurred in the company (and is currently occurring). The information reported must be verifiable by an independent party, e.g., if an independent auditor were to base a report on the reported information, the results would be the same.

Comparability. The information reported in financial statements and other documentation must ensure comparability with similar businesses within the industry. Without comparability, investors cannot discern differences between companies within an industry. They cannot benchmark how one company is doing compared to its peers. Changed performance measurements in the Lean operating system challenge traditional performance measurements. The Lean performance measurements may never be the same as those of traditional organizations within the same industry. Benchmarking a Lean enterprise with a traditional operating system will be difficult. In comparison, the Lean organization may actually appear to be worse in inventory and cost measurements (e.g., in the absorption of fixed overhead) than a traditional manufacturer. The importance of the comparability principle cannot be overstated. Comparability of information is a primary reason for having GAAP.

Because GAAP is beyond the local control of an individual company, reporting requirements are difficult to modify to suit the Lean performance measures. Explaining the accounting differences between the performance measurements in the Lean operating system and the traditional cost accounting system to stakeholders and the investment community is tricky, especially to those who are comfortable with an existing system. If a compromise between the two systems cannot be made, the prospects of the Lean operating system going forward will be in jeopardy. How long can the plant manager, production managers, or the VP of operations defend the benefits of reduced inventory, faster delivery, reduced cost of quality, and better shop floor utilization against traditional cost accounting reports that continually report underutilization, lack of full absorption, and inventory as an asset before being ground down by a cost accounting system that does not reflect the benefits of a Lean operating system?

Materials Management

The materials management group typically has responsibility for production planning, inventory control, purchasing, and distribution functions. Implementation of the Lean operating system will impact each of these areas.

Production planning. In a traditional operating system, a production planning function creates the master schedule that drives the planning system (i.e., MRP), performs the requirements planning explosion, develops the production schedules, issues the production orders, and inputs feedback information from shop floor activity into the planning system. When the Lean operating system is operational, output from the master schedule will be of less significance. A statement of customer demand will still be required, but is optional in the form of production orders released from the planning system. The need for firm planned orders and future planned orders is diminished as a scheduling mechanism in a Lean manufacturing facility. The Lean line only needs to know the daily sequence of the released orders to indicate manufacturing priority. Planned and firm planned orders in a master schedule will still be required to generate order action reports for suppliers and for the purchasing function to determine material requirements into the future, but the Lean line itself has no need for computer-generated released production orders. All that is needed is a listing of the customer backlog so a planner or scheduler can determine the daily sequence of production for the actual customer demand on the Lean line. As long as the planning system still launches production orders for use by manufacturing, it must receive feedback about the status of those production orders. Any released production orders sent to the shop floor and completed in manufacturing will still need to be reported to production planning because the production control function is still responsible for maintaining the feedback loop to the planning system. Pick lists, kit lists, or parts lists and all order close-out requirements, however, are no longer required when a two-bin material kanban system is in place. Diminished data maintenance requirements will cause production planning to become much more simplified. The production planning group will still be the central clearinghouse for collecting customer demand and introducing that demand into manufacturing. The production planning group will remain responsible for controlling the staffing requirements of resources used by the Lean line by sequencing daily customer demand on the line in the correct priority to satisfy customer due dates while at the same time ensuring that the V_c is not exceeded. The production planning group will still be the production control function responsible for performing the daily resource calculations to match the correct number of labor resources of the Lean line to customer demand.

Inventory control. The need for accurate inventory levels in the manufacturing area is just as important in a Lean operating system as it is in a traditional planning system. The inventory control group is still responsible for inventory accuracy. In a Lean operating system, however, inventory routines are greatly simplified because of the kanban system. Except for one-time-use kanban materials, the two-bin kanban system is self-managing. The two-bin kanban system automatically manages parts replenishment based on consumption at all of the different point-of-use locations on the Lean line. Inventory transactions are still required when material enters the manufacturing (RIP) location, but the kanban system requires fewer reporting transactions than the traditional operating system because reporting of inventory replenishment to and from the RIP and the line is no longer required. When material moves into a RIP location, inventory is increased in the RIP location and decreased in the stockroom location by an inventory transaction. The frequency of incoming transactions is dependent on the number of days of replenishment selected for storage at the RIP location. If the replenishment time for a part is 10 days, then an inventory transaction for that part will be required every 10 days. A transaction is only necessary when the RIP container is refilled and returned to the RIP location. When material from an outside supplier is delivered, an inventory transaction is required to increase the stockroom inventory by the received amount of the material. An inventory transaction is also required each time a unit of production is completed and packed off the end of the line. Many companies perform this inventory transaction using the *backflush* method. The quantities and part numbers documented on the BOM are decreased from the RIP location with the pack off of each unit. At the same time, one unit of finished goods SKU is added to the finished goods inventory. The backflush transaction is a computer routine that occurs automatically each time a finished unit leaves the last workstation of the Lean line. For the backflush method to maintain inventory accuracy in the RIP location, the BOM for each SKU must be 100% accurate. In a Lean operating system, the inventory control group must be an active participant in maintaining BOM accuracy and ensuring that all scrap reporting is recorded in the stock status report. The inventory control group also continues to perform audits, cycle counting, and discrepancy reconciliation of inventory transactions to ensure that the kanban system is working as designed.

   Distribution. In many companies, the distribution group is responsible for the management, storage, and maintenance of all incoming materials (supplier-furnished component parts, maintenance, repair and overhaul materials, and returned goods) and outgoing materials (finished goods shipments). In addition to receiving all of the materials from outside locations, the distribution group in most traditional operating systems is also required to conduct inspections of incoming components for supplier-related defects. These inspections must be coordinated with the quality management group. A hold (or quarantine) is therefore placed on inspected materials by the distribution group until they are released by a quality control group. The Lean operating system eliminates many of the non-value-added activities performed by the distribution group in the traditional operating model. Management of raw materials stored in the stockroom (or a warehouse) is also the responsibility of the distribution group. This responsibility includes the cycle counting of inventory and the movement of materials from the hold area to the stockroom and the eventual distribution of those materials to the shop floor for use in the manufacturing of products. Distribution in a Lean operating system is much like a traditional operating system. In the Lean operating system, however, the distribution group uses the two-bin kanban system to record inventory transactions for materials moving from the storeroom to the RIP locations and into the stockroom by the receipt of materials from suppliers. The distribution group in the Lean operating system participates in the certification of suppliers to help eliminate the need to recount received materials and to reduce or eliminate hold and quarantine areas. Once certified, materials from certified suppliers can bypass the stockroom and be moved directly to a RIP location, eliminating a non-value-added inventory transaction.

Equipment Maintenance

Equipment maintenance is a cost center in manufacturing companies that has a significant impact on the quality, cost, and delivery of products. Unscheduled machine downtime is a result of a machine resource failing to meet a quality criterion, having an actual failure, or experiencing some other mechanical problem that causes an operation to fail to meet its process capability. Machine resource downtime is *waste*. In a Lean operating system, downtime from an inoperable machine resource can cause the daily throughput to be missed. The key to eliminating downtime in a machine process is to be proactive: prevent downtime before it happens.

During Lean line design activity, 5S at each machine cell was completed. Each machine operator was trained to use and properly maintain equipment and machines. Keeping performance records and records of maintenance processes was required. These records are to be routinely used by the maintenance management and production management groups to ensure that machine resources are maintained on an ongoing schedule.

A total preventative maintenance (TPM) program prevents downtime. Maintenance processes in a TPM program are designed, organized, and managed to eliminate machine downtime. A TPM program enables early detection of potential problems so they can be addressed before a machine experiences a breakdown. TPM requires periodic scheduling of equipment maintenance based on the cumulative run time of a machine to detect and address problems as soon as possible. TPM empowers process operators to use diagnostic tools to continuously improve the maintenance of their assigned machine resources. Operators engage in preventative maintenance activities and work with industrial engineers, supervisors, and experts to prevent production shutdowns due to mechanical failure of a machine. Maintenance of machines becomes the responsibility of operators. Records that include Lean performance standards are maintained for machine resources, e.g., lost time; defects caused by poor maintenance, safety, and delay issues; and machine breakdowns. Maintenance requiring downtime is scheduled for routine maintenance and major equipment overhaul on a regular basis. Maintenance schedules are observed to ensure minimal unplanned, emergency, or reactive maintenance activities. Maintenance frequency and TPM routines are also considered when making new product and process design decisions and when purchasing new equipment. The goal is to eliminate maintenance issues that cause inefficient and ineffective operations during Lean production uptime. If an ineffective machine process is allowed to continuously fail and downtime is overlooked, the ability to manufacture the V_c of all downstream processes will be diminished, jeopardizing customer satisfaction.

Record all TPM procedures on a separate standard work definition and graphic work instruction. Use these tools to ensure that all preventative maintenance tasks are performed as necessary for each machine resource. Build the time necessary to perform daily maintenance routines into the Takt time formula as a reduction of the available minutes to do standard work. Providing time to perform maintenance work for machine resources eliminates the excuses for not doing it. Allow extra time at the beginning of each shift for machine operators from a previous shift to brief each other on any issues experienced with a machine and to perform their assigned 5S duties for machine maintenance.

Human Resources

Working in a Lean operating system requires the human resources to change many of their work habits. Human resources are also required to change how they've previously performed their duties. This is particularly true for operators on the shop floor in manufacturing, but it also applies to the administrative and support areas of the company. Instead of concentrating on the maximum utilization of resources, the Lean operating system requires the enterprise to refocus on eliminating waste from all processes. Every process and task will be subject to waste elimination. Eliminating waste must become the way of life.

Managing Resistance to Change

Change is never easy for most people. The good soldiers in a company might readily and even happily accept change at face value, but for others, change will always be frightening. Change for those individuals means entering the unknown. Daily routines will probably be different; the job descriptions might change; the way the jobs are done might have to be modified. Some people may have worked for years to attain a familiar, comfortable, manageable work environment. They're quite happy with the status quo. They've been able to resolve most problems on their own with procedures they've personally developed and tested over time. The first response of people who fear change is resistance (see Chapter 4). Some will defend their turf by bringing up a multitude of issues and arguments substantiating why Lean "will never work in this company." These issues and arguments are designed to sidetrack the Lean transformation. Others will be indignant. They will claim that Lean will irreparably harm the company.

A few will remain quiet. Out of sight, they will work silently to subvert any efforts to change their beloved comfort zones.

As a member of a Lean transformation team, expect resistance. Be prepared address all issues. One-on-one explanations about the training to be provided and how specific jobs will change may diminish the concerns of many, but a minority, regardless of the time given to one-on-one explanations and the training invested in gaining their acceptance, will never be completely on board with a transformation to the Lean operating system. These individuals become resisters. If resisters do not have critical roles in the Lean transformation project, and can be trusted keep negative opinions that could sabotage the success of the Lean project to themselves, they can be allowed to continue working in the Lean line environment. Maybe they will slowly get used to the new Lean ideas over time. Even better, sometimes a resister has an epiphany, suddenly coming around to accept the Lean operating system. Often this type of resister becomes a strong advocate for Lean methodology. If at some point, however, opposition from certain resisters continues, devoting additional time to converting them to accept the benefits of a Lean operating system is just a waste of time. Taking other actions is necessary. The management team may have to reassign an unrelenting resister to another area in the company, e.g., an administrative function, where the resister will have little or no direct contact with operators who have accepted the Lean operating system and are making it work successfully. If a resister is in a decision-making role, and cannot discontinue expressing disagreement with the Lean operating system, the management team may have to find work for the resister where he/she can have no direct influence over operators. If the resister continues to sabotage the Lean operating system, work will need to be found for the resister in an area of the company distant from the Lean operating system. If all areas in the company are positively affected by the Lean transformation, and opposition continues from resisters to the transformation to Lean, the best scenario for all those who have accepted the Lean operating system is for these resisters to be humanely dismissed from the company.

The Role of Operators

The primary responsibility of operators working in a Lean operating system is to complete the standard work assigned to a workstation in the Takt time target. Operators are also required to know the standard work at three workstations. Although Lean operators may know the standard work of multiple workstations, becoming certified to perform the work at three consecutive workstations is the minimum requirement for maintaining the flexibility needed by a Lean line to meet changing customer demand. To be certified, operators are required to demonstrate that they can complete the standard work in the Takt time and also perform the quality criteria assigned to each of the three workstations: their primary workstation, the upstream workstation, and the downstream workstation. Standard work at each workstation includes performing three types of work during each Takt time: checking the verified work from the upstream workstation; completing the standard work for the primary workstation; and verifying that any quality criteria identified as part of the standard work for the primary workstation have been inspected. The purpose of the three-workstation certification requirement is to provide the capability of modifying the throughput of the Lean line to match customer demand on a daily basis. Operators must also learn and follow IPK discipline.

Daily customer sales volume will determine the number of operators that must be assigned to a Lean line each day. For example, if all workstations were 100% staffed, the fully designed V_c could be produced, but if every other workstation were staffed, the throughput rate would be reduced to only 50% of the line capacity (50% V_c). At any given time during the day, every other workstation would always have one unit waiting in the IPK. The remaining operators would *flex* into the waiting workstations to complete the standard work at that workstation. This would cause the Lean line to pack one unit off the Lean line every other Takt time.

The three-workstation certification of the Lean operating system permits operators not assigned to a Lean line workstation on a given day to be assigned to another workstation or manufacturing line or where the work for which they are certified is performed. When not working on the Lean line to manufacture products, operators can also engage in kaizen and continuous improvement projects; train for additional workstation certifications; create graphic work instructions; or participate in general plant maintenance projects. This flexibility to perform various types of work is welcomed by most operators. Rather than the constant repetition of being assigned to a single workstation, operators in the Lean operating system have a variety of work to keep them challenged. The Lean system encourages maximum flexibility for all operators.

The Role of Managers

A manager in the Lean operating system should notice his or her role gradually changing from fire-fighting system breakdowns and being a disciplinarian who manages every move of every operator every day to being a coach and a team leader who enables trained, certified operators to meet the daily customer demand at the designed Takt rate of the line. Managers in the Lean operating system no longer need to constantly monitor the daily work of operators or oversee the entire line. Each operator has been certified to perform the Takt time amount of work tasks assigned to each workstation. Any operator who cannot consistently meet the Takt time target will be identified immediately by the frequent line stoppages. A struggling operator may need additional training to become proficient on the Lean line. Because IPK rules dictate that a defective unit cannot be placed into an IPK, an operator cannot advance a defective unit. Any point on the Lean line where work stops because of the inability to refill an IPK will immediately alert the line team leader to the workstation causing the line stoppage. Team members on the Lean line are also able to immediately isolate a specific problem. In most cases, resolution of short-term line stoppages can be made on a Lean line by operators who are working as a team. If the reason for the line stoppage can be resolved within a Takt time, the elapsed downtime will be limited to a single Takt time. By quickly isolating the source of problems, managers can focus their attention on ensuring that recurring problems are never duplicated. Long-term problem resolution is a much better use of management time than the perpetual fire-fighting routines common in a traditional operating system.

Operator training. Operators need training in two areas: to be certified to do the standard work of three consecutive workstations (the minimum requirement) and to ensure that they are able to manufacture all of the models that will be produced on a mixed-model line. Managers should encourage operators to learn the standard work of more than three workstations. To facilitate operator training, managers should team an operator not assigned to a workstation on a given day with an operator who is certified at other workstations to produce multiple models. The more workstations at which an operator is certified, the more flexible the Lean line is when events such as vacations, illnesses, unexpected absenteeism, etc. require reassignment of substitute operators to cover the affected workstations.

Takt time monitoring. Although managers monitor the Takt time target for a Lean line to ensure that certain daily rates of production will be met, Lean team leaders are responsible for ensuring that each daily rate of production is met. To ensure that the line's performance will complete the daily rate of sales (units) for the day, the Lean team leader must monitor the flow rate of the line several times during a shift. Any cause of flow rate deviation must be identified and resolved immediately to get the Lean line back on schedule. The team leader can follow the progress of the Lean line at any time during the day by using a flow rate measurement board located at certain points on the line. At the end of the day, the daily counts used for linearity measurements are documented, including any units that have been sidelined for quality issues. If adjustments are required, the line manager must meet every day with the production planning group to resolve any resulting customer delivery or linearity issues.

Eliminating waste. During development of the standard work definitions, significant effort was invested in identifying non-value-added work times. The standard work was then assigned to workstations in Takt time intervals. Out of necessity, the standard work included both value-added and non-value added times. The goal of the Lean operating system is to eliminate all non-value-added time from standard work. Once the Lean line is operational, *all* team members, operators, team leaders, and managers, become responsible for eliminating remaining non-value-added time from the standard work. Managers need to develop performance measurements to document the progress in reducing the non-value-added time included in the standard time. (The KPIs in Chapter 5 include performance measurements with a ratio to compare value-added time to non-value-added time.) Managers should also measure total product cycle time (TPCT) to determine how much total time has been eliminated compared to the previous year. Compared to more subjective improvement measurements such as productivity, measurement of the TPCT is objective. TPCT can be tracked mathematically using the current total product cycle time as a baseline. Managers must take the leadership role in all process improvement activities. TPCT reduction should be a component of each manager's performance review every year.

The Role of Support Staff

Office workers performing service routines and administrative functions typically do not think of themselves as being part of the manufacturing operations. Maybe it's because office workers often dress differently than workers on the shop floor. Maybe it's because they have desks in air-conditioned offices instead of workbenches or workstations in the factory. Maybe it's because office workers are indirect labor (part of overhead) for cost accounting purposes while workers on the shop floor are direct labor with a separate cost category. Maybe not having a separate cost category makes office workers feel more disconnected from customers than the operators in the factory. Office work, however, has the same effect on customer satisfaction as work done on the shop floor. Office workers are just as dependent on the company being successful as the operators on the Lean line. The success of any company is always a team effort.

The Lean methods do not make a distinction between direct and indirect labor or between processes on the shop floor and in offices. The goal of a Lean operating system is to eliminate all non-value-added time from standard work on the shop floor and in service and administrative functions. As was done on the shop floor for the manufacturing processes, the Lean operating system targets the completion of each task in service and administrative functions in the sum of its work content time only. All non-value-adding work is a candidate for elimination! The non-value-added to value-added work ratio used to measure manufacturing is also a good measurement for monitoring progress in service routines and administrative work.

Optimize is defined as *making something as perfect, as effective, or as functional as possible.* Any process can be optimized. Anything optimized will usually result in the reduction of waste. A few suggested areas for optimization include:

- Size of the supply base
- Number of transportation carriers
- Number, size, and location of distribution, retail, and dealer outlets
- Number of customers within the customer base
- Number of component parts and stock keeping units
- Number, size, and location of production facilities
- Type of information systems used and their features
- Order delivery network
- Major process, such as new product development, quality management laboratory routines, supplier rationalization, research and development, and product marketing

For most companies, being able to produce manufacturing products in the sum of their work content time only while completing service functions and administrative work in their work content time only well positions them to deliver their products to customers in less time, with better quality, and at a lower cost than their competitors.

LEAN ENTERPRISE-WIDE

For manufacturers, a Lean enterprise-wide transformation typically begins on the shop floor and is often based on the promised benefits of reduced lead time; lower inventories and correspondingly lower working capital investment; improved quality with less cost; optimized factory shop floor utilization; greater visual management; more satisfied employees; and ease of operation. The scale of benefits may vary between companies, but 3% have reported accomplishing their Lean manufacturing goals. The highly touted benefits tempted 22% of all manufacturers to initiate a Lean transformation project and caused another 34% to consider beginning a transformation.

Customer demand is rarely the same two days in a row, much less for a week or a month. By design, a Lean enterprise is a *minimalist* organization. The Lean operating system commits only the resources necessary to satisfy customer demand. Nothing more; nothing less! In the Lean operating system, resource allocation is reassigned each day based on the customer demand for that day. In the Lean operating system, the number of manufacturing and administrative/service resources rises and falls to match customer demand in proportion to the demand for the day. Unlike the standard practice of traditional systems, production schedules in a Lean manufacturing facility are *not* level. They're *not* to be maintained for a prescribed period of time (weekly or monthly). The schedule interval in a Lean factory is every day! In Lean manufacturing, fluctuation in customer demand is *not* offset by producing inventory as the result of a preset, scheduled, flat rate just because a flat rate of production is easier to manage. At the end of a scheduling period, balance in manufacturing is *not* accomplished by producing excess inventory during low periods of demand simply to maintain a steady production rate. In administrative functions, demand imbalance is *not* offset by workers slowing down the pace of their work to match decreased demand or having no work to do. In the manufacturing and administrative areas of the Lean operating system, the balancing mechanism for adjusting to customer demand swings is accomplished by the flexibility to move into or out of a process on any given day.

Lean methodology is a common-sense approach. Applying Lean techniques streamlines an organization. The organization becomes more efficient. Costs and waste are minimized. For logical reasons related to reducing costs, transformation of an enterprise to Lean should begin on the manufacturing shop floor. Once success has been realized in the manufacturing area, expanding the Lean technology to service and administrative areas of the company will be a natural progression. Similar to each step in a manufacturing process, the Lean operating system addresses the entire customer fulfillment cycle — from initial customer contact to ordering, shipping, invoicing, and final payment. All steps and substeps are candidates for tracking and analysis for waste. Expansion of Lean methodology beyond the company's four walls to the entire value chain will also be a natural progression of the Lean transformation. The same Lean techniques used internally to design the Lean manufacturing line can be used in the value chain — beginning with a customer purchasing a product at the retail level, to the distribution center, to the manufacturing process, and to the supplier. Distribution centers and retail locations can participate in two-bin, finished goods material kanban systems. Suppliers will also benefit by becoming a Lean manufacturer, offering faster delivery, higher quality, and lower cost to their customers. If extended all the way from an end-user customer to the mining of materials from the earth, Lean technology can supplant the short horizon of a planning system that is limited to only the manufacturer and suppliers.

The Lean minimalist approach to resource utilization (human resources, workstations, machines, and inventory) changes the way business is done throughout a company. In manufacturing, few organizational groups will remain unchanged. Lean creates goals and objectives for manufacturing that will conflict with many goals and objectives in support organizations. The goals and objectives of these support functions must be modified to match those of the manufacturing group. Likely, most support organizations will embrace making the necessary policy and procedural changes to support the Lean enterprise, but some may resist. Over the long term, an inability to dovetail Lean manufacturing goals, objectives, and policies and procedures with a support organization(s) can create constant friction that leads to failure of the Lean operating system.

Some closing words. During the evaluation process, invest the time necessary to determine if your company should move forward with a Lean transformation process. Do due diligence by performing a thorough analysis of the costs versus the benefits of transforming your company into a Lean operating system. Understand the cultural changes that will be required to operate the Lean system on a daily basis. Be ready to challenge long-standing paradigms that limit your company's ability to be the very best competitor in the marketplace. Establishing the techniques of Takt line balancing to produce a flow rate, resource utilization to match customer demand, IPK authorization to authorize production of another unit, and implementation of material kanban systems for material consumption and replenishment during the transformation project can become wearisome. Multiple iterations of mathematical formulas to determine the optimum solution for each process required to convert customer demand into finished products may be necessary. In addition, making the cultural changes required for these Lean benefits to become possible can be even more difficult. Many in your organization will not be comfortable with change. Often they will fight hard to maintain the comfort level of conformity. If a decision is made to move forward with your Lean implementation project, proceed with the knowledge that one challenge after another will occur during the Lean transformation of the entire enterprise. You (as well as the other sponsors) must be committed to the transformation process and be prepared to defend the benefits of Lean with gusto. You must have good arguments for those who are resistant to change. Once started, the transformation process will never end! It will outlast your career with the company. Continuous improvement will be the new way of life in the company. Although the Lean transformation will outlast your career with the company, you can take pride in having made a contribution to making your company the best it could be.

This book has free material available for download from the Web Added Value™ resource center at www.jrosspub.com

INDEX

A

ABC analysis, establishing inventory policy and, 296–297
Absorption costing, impact of, 453–454
Administrative areas
    Lean in, 414–416
    non-value-added work and, 417–421, 422
    working styles in, 416–417
AME. *See* Association for Manufacturing Excellence Study
Antibody, 143–144, 146
As-needed/one-time parts, 339–340
Association for Manufacturing Excellence (AME) Study, 4

B

Backflush transaction, 307–308
Balanced resources, 58–61
    advantages of, 59–60
    capacity utilization and, 58–59
    challenges of, 60–61
    STW and, 244
Balancing techniques, 253–260
    technique 1, 253–256
    technique 2, 256
    technique 3, 257
    technique 4, 257–258
    technique 5, 258–259
Balancing tools, four repeatable, 380–381; *See also* Balancing techniques; Lean tools; Standard work, per workstation
    add IPKs, 257, 381
    add resources, 257, 381

look for work to be eliminated, 253–256, 381
relocate work from workstation to workstation, 256, 381
Batch processing. *See* Paradigm 2: route products in batches
Batch size, determination of, 29
Benefits identification, Lean and, 89–114
    assessment of benefits (SBA), 100–104
    mechanics, challenges and, 90–92
    operational improvements, 100
    productivity, improvements in, 99
    response time improvement, 92–93
    simplified management, 97–99
    working capital requirements, 95–96
Bill of materials (BOM). *See* Indented BOM
Buffer inventory
    FGI as, 38, 45
    WIP inventory as, 93
Business case, SBA as, 105–114
    in business areas, 105
    customer satisfaction opportunities, 111–112
    floor space utilization, 110, 111
    high-volume shippers, 109, 110
    inventory costs, 107, 108
    labor costs, 106, 107
    lead time reduction, 106
    manufacturing process opportunities, 111, 112
    problematic suppliers, 110
    sales volume, 105
    supplier management opportunities, 110
    value stream mapping (VSM) in, 113

C